4/88

Beth dear
Birthday Child —
Thanks for
all the time-sharing —
Keep celebrating —
Love & luck —

Mimi Brodsky
Chenfeld

CREATIVE ACTIVITIES
for young children

CREATIVE
ACTIVITIES
for young children

Mimi Brodsky Chenfeld

HBJ

HARCOURT BRACE JOVANOVICH, PUBLISHERS

San Diego   New York   Chicago   Atlanta   Washington, D.C.
London   Sydney   Toronto

DEDICATION

To my parents, Iris and Joe Kaplan, who are still waiting for me to grow up

To my mother- and father-in-law, Rose and Charles Chenfeld, who always vote yes

To my children, Cliff, Cara, and Dan, who taught me almost everything I know

To my husband, Howard, my safest place

To my family of children, teachers, and parents who are making the journey together, "May it be beautiful before you"

PREFACE

The question has been asked: Why would a reasonably intelligent person who just completed an exhausting four years writing *Teaching Language Arts Creatively* plunge into another four years of fatigue and exhilaration writing *this* book? The answers may sound trite. The words I want to use have come to be associated with commercial products rather than our deepest feelings. Words like *love*, *joy*, and *life*. I have a commitment to those old, worn words: a special love for young children and the joy that is part of our time with them in the most life-affirming of all our activities, education.

Let me add another reason for writing this book—*worry*. I am concerned about the direction in which many of our early childhood programs are heading. I am worried because in recent years, more and more often, I have visited primary and preschool classes characterized by silence, tension, and minimal interaction. Ditto sheets and workbooks are the center of methodology. Play is a childish toy to be put away. School means "let's get down to business."

It distresses me to meet first graders who are afraid to write anything, even their names, because their letters are not perfect and they dread making mistakes. I meet more young children than ever before with minds closed to new ideas and experiences, who, instead of saying, "Yes, I'll try. It's fun!" say, "No. I won't. That's dumb!"

Graham Nash wrote a popular song urging people to "Teach Your Children Well." Children are so adaptable, so ready to learn. But what are they learning? Are we teaching our children well?

As we speed through our computerized society that worships tests and measurements, it is easy to forget about the natural and delightful ways young children learn: through play; open-ended experimentation and exploration; encouragement of curiosity and discovery; enjoyable interchanges with others; and diverse opportunities to expand concepts with imaginative activities in success-oriented environments.

This book is full of interesting information about thirteen important themes for young children, along with suggested activities that help to enrich the comprehension of those ideas as well as enrich our lives and those of our children. The activities are only a few of those possible. The Letter of Introduction explains and highlights the book.

If you have worked with young children in loving and healthful ways, you know that they teach you how they learn best. The underlying theme of this book is "All of our children are prodigies" (Yiddish proverb).

In her 1982 Academy Award acceptance speech, Maureen Stapleton thanked everyone she had ever met in her whole life. I want to express the same sentiment and thank everyone I ever met in my life, with a few specific acknowledgments. Betty Stevens typed the manuscript with devotion and care. Becky McAtee Moore, a lover of books and children, helped shape the bibliographies; Donna Crews helped Becky. Barbara Reed added her ideas. Frayda Turkel, a true friend, took time from a heavy schedule to help with permissions. Michael Joel Rosen ("Renaissance Man") contributed his wild wit and provocative ideas from beginning to end. Janis Wilson and Rosemary Anderson of the Bexley Public Library and Sally Oddi of Cover to Cover Children's

Bookstore patiently responded to my urgent calls. Two gifted and talented teachers, Dawn Heyman of the McGuffy School, Columbus, Ohio, and Marilyn Cohen of Bet Shraga Hebrew Academy of the Capital District, Albany, New York, kept the flames burning by sharing many peak teaching experiences. Barbara, Carl, Jeffrey, Douglas, and Deborah Selinger kept me informed about the joy of the learning process. Miriam Flock kept telling me the time. Aaron Leventhal, founder and director of the Days of Creation arts program, and his fantastic staff and children reaffirmed my belief in the arts as a universal language. Dr. Herb Sandberg, professor of education at University of Toledo, Toledo, Ohio, Dr. Mary Cooper, chairperson, education department, University of Michigan, Flint, and Dr. Janet Stillwell, assistant dean of the College of the Arts, Western Michigan University, Kalamazoo, inspired me in all seasons by their work and teaching. Bess "Chee Chee" Haile, my Shinnecock Indian princess friend, gave me her song. Rose Schwartz, founder and first director of the Early Childhood Program at the Leo Yassenoff Jewish Center, Columbus, invited me to "move" her teachers and students. Barbara Weinberg, director of Early Childhood Services for the Leo Yassenoff Jewish Center, Hilary Talis, head teacher, and their outstanding staff supported this endeavor with enthusiasm and practical ideas. Nancy Fromson and Alberta Levengood of the Leo Yassenoff Center offered technical assistance.

Through the Greater Columbus Art Council's Artists in the Schools program, the Ohio Arts Council's Artists in the Schools program, many conferences, conventions, in-service programs, Young Authors' Celebrations, Teachers' Centers, and workshops and educational organizations, I have been able to share ideas and experiences with thousands of children, university students, parents, and teachers across the country. Their contributions to this book are immeasurable. As many of their favorite activities as possible have been included.

A highlight of this book is the array of superb teachers and individuals devoted to the education of young children. Many people have shared their ideas but not their names. I am indebted to each and all. Some individuals gave generously of their time to respond to in-depth interviews. Special appreciation is extended to Ed Jacomo, chairperson for creative and performing arts, University Liggett School, Grosse Pointe, Michigan; Mary W. Evans, director, Early Childood Services, First Community Church, Columbus, Ohio; Moira Logan, associate professor, dance department, Ohio State University, Columbus; Marian Radke Yarrow, chief, Laboratory of Developmental Psychology, National Institute of Mental Health, Bethesda, Maryland; Mary T. Goodwin, chief nutritionist, Montgomery County Health Department, Maryland; Merle Ivers, associate professor of education, director of the Reading Center, Capital University, Bexley, Ohio; Judy Tough, director, North Broadway Childrens Day Care Program, Columbus; Diane Biswas, director, Summit United Methodist Church Preschool, Columbus; Mattie James, director of Head Start, Columbus; Greg Siegler, director, Miami Elementary Tutorial School, Miami, Florida; Jeannette Lauritsen, principal, and staff, Edison Elementary School, Grandview Heights, Ohio; Rhoda Gelles, coordinator, Extended Project Program for Academically Talented Students, Worthington, Ohio; Ronni Hochman, special education teacher, Upper Arlington Public Schools, Upper Arlington, Ohio, and Ohio State University; Ken Valimaki, art instructor, Columbus Alternative High School, Columbus; Linda Cress, district manager, Kinder Care Learning Centers, Columbus; Carol Price, teacher and coordinator of kindergarten curriculum guide, Worthington Public Schools, Worthington, Ohio; Shirley Davis, teacher, Jewish Center's Early Child Care Program, West Bloomfield, Michigan; Verna Willis, director, Christ Lutheran Preschool, Bexley, Ohio; Susan Hendrickson, teacher, First Community Church's Early Childhood Program, Columbus; Anna Grace, singer; Pouneh Alcott, director, Learning Unlimited, Columbus; Lynn Salem, teacher, Immaculate Conception School, Columbus; Nancy Roberts, teacher, Immaculate Conception School, Columbus; Betsy Distelhorst, teacher, educational and recreational programs, Columbus; Sue Coomer, teacher, Easthaven School, Columbus; Gwen Marston, folksinger and teacher, Flint, Michigan, area schools; Shirley Duncan, teacher, Dana Elementary School, Columbus; June Mock, teacher, Main Street Elementary School, Columbus; Kay Callander, teacher, Shady Lane School, Columbus; Kathy Carter, teacher, Worthington Hills School, Worthington, Ohio; Linda Meyer, teacher, Worthington Hills School, Worthington, Ohio; Barbara Kienzle, teacher, Indianola Alternative Elementary School, Columbus; Carol Minnich, Ohio Department of Mental Retardation and Developmental Disabilities; Jean Jones, nutritionist, Ohio Department of Education; and Howard Chenfeld, buyer, SCOA Industries.

The outstanding skills and energies of the staff at Harcourt Brace Jovanovich are deeply appreciated. Special thanks to Bill Wisneski and Paula Lewis Ludlow, who launched this book, and to Johanna Schmid who carried it on so competently and lovingly with the help of Albert Richards, John Holland, Mary-Ann Courtenaye, Melinda Benson, Tricia Griffith, Diane Polster, Cheryl Bower, and Eleanor Garner.

Finally, thanks to all the friends and family who never stopped encouraging this effort, especially the Berwick gang, the folks at the Bexley post office, the Kaplans, the Chenfelds, the Walchers, the Frankels, and the Cohens.

Mimi Brodsky Chenfeld

CONTENTS

PART ONE . 10

CREATIVE
ACTIVITIES
for young
children

LETTER OF INTRODUCTION

Dear Reader,

This book provides simple, accessible activities that involve all of the children and that are likely to insure success for everyone. Young children experiment with sounds, words, writing, drawing, singing, moving, and playing. The activities in this book build upon the natural ways in which children learn. Even though many of the activities were enjoyed in Central Ohio schools, children and teachers throughout the country have expanded and enriched them. Most of the activities discussed in the book have involved children from three to nine years of age—from day care, play school, and preschool classes through third grade. But teachers of older children have adapted these ideas with great success. Good ideas are not limited by age or grade.

The activities reflect my philosophy, attitudes, and values. You can tell what I believe by *what I do* and *how I do it*. Because I believe that learning is our most exciting endeavor, the activities convey a feeling of celebration as we help children make new connections, find new meanings, and achieve new levels of skill and com-

prehension. Young children need time to arrange and rearrange ideas, explore possibilities, ask questions, make mistakes, and make discoveries.

In our classrooms, children should feel safe, never humiliated and alienated. We have to protect the spirit, imagination, curiosity, and love of life and learning in young children as fiercely as we would protect an endangered species. If we pressure young children to conform, if we discourage questions and exploration, if we dim the bright lights of curiosity, then we betray our responsibilities and commitments.

I believe that our real commitment is not to curriculum, materials, methods, or measurements, but to the encouragement of children to learn about the world and themselves in healthy, life-affirming ways. I also believe that education is a shared experience. Children learn from us, and we learn from them. As Norma Canner, a movement specialist, said, "I came to teach and I stayed to learn."

My young friend Ariela helped me

learn something important, helped me to clarify values. Whenever I lovingly called her "my little bunny" or "Hi, little *sweetie*," she reminded me with great dignity: "I'm *not* a little bunny! I'm *not* a little sweetie! I'm a little *person!*" Too often, we forget that our students are little persons, wanting and needing the same respect, thoughtfulness, and consideration that we require for ourselves.

This approach requires sensitivity. For example, because we are aware of our children's situations and feelings, our language changes. Our classrooms are filled with children from broken homes, one-parent households, and sets of step-parents. Because we respect the dignity and emotions of our students, we change the traditional reference "mother" or "father" to "grownup" or "person who takes care of you." This approach requires conscious effort, but we must respond to the needs of our children if we want our other agenda, our other curriculum, to succeed.

With a book of activities, there is the

danger that it will be read in much the same way as a cookbook: Here are the ingredients and measurements; mix them together; and presto, you have the same finished product as the picture in the cookbook. It's not that way at all—which reminds me of Nana Rose's potato pancakes.

My mother-in-law, Rose Chenfeld, makes the best potato pancakes in the world. My husband urged me to get her recipe, which I did. I followed it to the letter, left nothing out. How did my potato pancakes turn out? O.K. They were not superlative, and they were definitely *not* Nana Rose's pancakes. Why not? What *secret* ingredient did she use? What extra "something" did she pour into the batter that she forgot to pass on? The secret ingredient is *herself*. She mixed her special spirit into the recipe and transformed something ordinary into something extraordinary.

The activities in this book are like recipes for potato pancakes and other lovely dishes. As you read through the pages, you will find some activities that interest you immediately, that appeal to your spirit, and reflect your personality and philosophy. After all, your own philosophy and attitudes will greatly determine *how* you use this book and *what* suggestions you adapt to your particular group of children. Remember, these are ideas to be shaped and modified. And they are good ideas only if you like them and are excited by them. Then you will mix your philosophy and personality with the suggestions, which will be further enriched as the children's energy and imagination are added.

I believe that we who work with young children are very lucky—because the world is old and children are new, because children have not yet learned to be blasé, because the whole universe is waiting to be discovered by them, and because they remind us of the daily miracle of life, whether it be in the fuzz of a caterpillar, the wing of a butterfly, or the journey of a raindrop.

Children with Special Needs

As you know, a great deal of attention has been given to children who have been loosely categorized as "exceptional children." This category has typically included children with mental retardation, learning disabilities, behavior and language disorders, physical impairments or handicaps, and abilities and

potential achievement levels defined as "gifted and talented."

In the last decade, awareness of "exceptional children" has been encouraged through the efforts of dedicated parents, educators, social scientists, and community leaders. Their achievements have resulted in programs, materials, and legislation, the most important of which is Public Law 94-142, "The Education for All Handicapped Children Act," a comprehensive law that promises free, appropriate, individualized public education and provides handicapped children with opportunities to be educated together with nonhandicapped children to the maximum extent possible. This integration is commonly known as "mainstreaming."

Because your students are very young, the chances are that most of those falling under the category of "exceptional children" have not yet been identified. The child who is a "daydreamer" may be a gifted and talented child who is pondering the question "Where does the white go when the snow melts?" And the "trouble maker" may be a child who needs special help with a learning disability.

Two highly qualified, widely respected educators talked about children with special needs. In separate discussions, they expressed how deeply they care about classroom teachers' attitudes and feelings in providing healthy, positive learning experiences for their special students.

Ronni Hochman, a special education teacher who works with children in the Upper Arlington, Ohio, school system and with university students at Ohio State University, is an articulate, enthusiastic communicator of values mixed with practical ideas. Her work is featured in William L. Heward and Michael D. Orlansky's excellent text, *Exceptional Children* (Merrill, 1980). Rhoda Gelles coordinates the Extended Project Program for Academically Talented Students in the Worthington, Ohio, school system. Rhoda's reputation for innovative program-building with children, teachers, and parents is recognized around the state. Although both educators address themselves to children on opposite ends of the learning spectrum, many of their ideas and comments merge.

Ronni emphasizes the "able" in the term "disabled" and challenges teachers with her positive philosophy. "When a child isn't succeeding, it's the teacher's problem, not the child's, because we teachers set up conditions for failure." Teachers must start where the children are and be responsive to each student's needs. Children with learning problems make progress when they have specific goals, take things one step at a time, and build on what they have already learned.

Another challenge for teachers is to create an environment in which children with learning problems can achieve success.

As Ronni explains:

In an environment where children care about each other and are encouraged to talk and work together, it isn't hard to enlist classmates in the important project of helping a child change problem behavior. Children are eager to praise, to applaud, to boast of their classmates' accomplishments *if that is the climate of the group*. Remember, we teach by example. When children see their teacher being encouraging and supportive, they learn to encourage each other. All of our kids need attention, praise, and warmth, but our kids with learning problems *especially* need that kind of reassurance from their teachers and classmates.

I want a clear conscience. I don't want to be on the list of teachers who make learning an unhappy experience for children. I want children to enjoy learning, respect each other, appreciate each other's growth and differences, and applaud each other's achievements.

Rhoda Gelles speaks of "gifted and talented" children and wonders why we have to call our bright children "gifted" when the word so often intimidates parents and worries teachers. She is concerned that labeling may result in children being treated differently. Rhoda reminds teachers that very bright children have special needs just like other children. They have to be given learning opportunities that stimulate and challenge them. Many of these children are less mature in large and small motor coordination. Some may be unable to cut, paste, and write neatly; others may be unable to color in the lines and have trouble finishing their workbooks.

Just as Ronni challenges classroom teachers to know children's special needs and interests, Rhoda asks her colleagues to consider such questions as: "What if Johnny comes into your kindergarten and can already read the newspaper? What does it do to him to go through the letters of the alphabet or beginning phonics? Does this make sense?" She suggests that the teacher find out what Johnny is interested in; use the library, make lists of questions to be answered and shared with the class, and call on families, community volunteers, and senior citizens to spend time in the classroom. The most successful classroom teachers challenge the brighter children with such open-ended experiences as research projects, computer exercises, math games, a wide variety of books and magazines, and creative writing programs.

Echoing the wishes and feelings of Ronni Hochman, Rhoda explains:

All of our kids need to share reactions, to get the benefit of others' thinking. They learn from each other. This is how we build respect and appreciation for *all* of our children. When all of our children are considered to be very important individuals, we help their self-concepts. Remember, our bright children are often labeled by others as "weird." Their unusual vocabularies can be social handicaps. When we appreciate the diversity of our children, our bright kids are included in that positive environment. They bloom in classes where there is respect and appreciation for individuality.

Don't put a fence around children who are different. Let them reach out and learn and be curious. Don't strangle them, don't squelch them in first grade. Make them love learning.

The activities in this book have been enjoyed by children all along the spectrum of learning. At the end of this Letter of Introduction is a list of sources of ideas and information about children with special needs.

The Organization of This Book

In his provocative book *What Do I Do Monday?*, John Holt discusses his theory of the Four Worlds. World One is the world of our bodies, the world under our skin. World Two is the world of our direct experiences, perceptions, and impressions. It is made up of people, places, and events that touch us directly. World Three is the world we know something about, but have not directly experienced. World Four is beyond our imagination, so it is the unknown, the impossible-to-even-talk-about World. Perhaps it is outer space, or time, or God. Through living and learning, we expand Worlds Two and Three and reduce World Four.

This book also begins with the idea that a child's first world is the world of body and feelings. Slowly the child becomes aware of family, friends, classmates, and other members of the community. Continuing to grow, the child learns about the basic need for food, clothing, and shelter, which are common to all peoples but which vary among cultures. An early fascination with colors and shapes expands to include letters, words, and numbers. Thus begins the search for keys that open doors to all worlds.

Each guide in this book contains the following sections: The Basics, Discovery Times, Suggested Vocabulary, Some Be-

ginning Activities, Talk Times, Art Times, Music Times, Movement and Play Times, Visitors and Field Trips, and Selected Bibliography. *Underpinning the activities in every section are literature and language.*

The Basics. This section provides a brief introduction to the theme of the guide. Before we share ideas with our students, we must be interested in and excited about them.

Discovery Times. This section presents important concepts to be introduced to the children through varied and enjoyable discussions and activities.

Suggested Vocabulary. Most young children already have remarkable vocabularies. This section provides words to start you off. Each word is a potential cluster of activities. The word "dog," for example, can be turned into an art project, a song, a riddle, a movement game, and a story. Think about the richness of words.

Some Beginning Activities. Teachers search for exciting ways to introduce themes and experiences. The activities suggested here include songs, stories, games, questions, and art projects. Remember, children are so eager for interesting ideas that any introduction will succeed if it is stimulating, challenging, and easily understood. The activities suggest ways to introduce a theme, but don't be surprised if the best ways are not in this book but in your classroom, brought by a child who wears an unusual T-shirt or shares an announcement or object that coincides with your plans. Be open to serendipity!

Talk Times. Children like to and want to talk. More important, they *need* to talk, not only to express themselves and form healthy relationships with others, but also to learn the language. When children learn in a relaxed environment where talking is the normal way people relate to each other as they work and play, children's language comprehension, speech, self-image, and social skills improve dramatically.

"Talk Times" provide a variety of ways to get children talking—on a one-to-one basis, in small groups, and as a class. It includes examples of stimulating discussions children have enjoyed, from problem solving to sharing feelings and ideas.

Art Times. Every guide highlights art activities that have been enjoyed by teachers and children around the country. The projects are intended to help students express their understanding of the theme, expand their imagination, and practice newly acquired skills.

Children need to experiment and enjoy the creative process. Too often they learn that there is a "right way" to do everything, and they are reluctant to experiment because they are afraid to make a mistake.

Throughout the book, puppets are featured as classroom characters and art projects. Children relate easily to puppets and often talk to or through them when they are reluctant to express their own feelings. At the end of this Letter of Introduction is a brief list of books suggesting hundreds of ways to make puppets. Discover ways that are easiest and most accessible. Don't allow

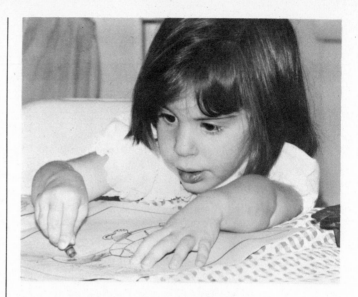

the process to become so complicated that the fun is lost.

Music Times. This section suggests musical experiences ranging from familiar lullabies to experimental exercises. Teachers are encouraged to draw upon their own knowledge and experiences and to correlate musical activities with literature, art, movement, and creative writing. At the end of this Letter is a short list of records that touch all themes and inspire activities.

Movement and Play Times. Young children express feelings, ideas, and understanding through movement and play. Just as children need to talk, so they need to move and play in a climate of encouragement and acceptance. Every guide offers natural, easy ways to move your students.

Unfortunately, some children feel self-conscious and reluctant to take part in movement exercises. These children should be encouraged rather than forced to participate. With patience, love, and tenacity, these children can be drawn into movement and play activities.

Visitors and Field Trips. Suggestions for classroom visitors and field trips are included in every guide. Such positive experiences increase understanding of a subject and provide valuable lessons in respect, appreciation, courtesy, and communication.

Selected Bibliography. Hundreds of children's books are available on the themes presented in this book. Every guide ends with a selection of outstanding books on the subject. Because the more teachers know about a subject, the more they can contribute to their students, a selected list of teacher resources is also presented in every guide. It is hoped that these books will inspire as well as inform.

At the beginning of this section I noted that literature and language are basic to the activities in this book. Because children need poetry in all their activities, a list of excellent poetry books is provided at the end of the Letter of Introduction. These books contain poems that cross all themes; the poems are for all seasons and reasons. I hope that you will always have books of poetry in your room to delight your children's minds and brighten their days.

It is important to understand that all sections of a guide are interrelated. In everyday life, words flow into songs and stories, games include movement and dance, talk spills into art and poems. The more often you connect the various experiences, the more effective each one will be.

Above all, remember that you are the heart of the activity. Your attitude, beliefs, behavior, words, and actions will determine its success. When you mix your days with love of and respect for children and when you do your best, you cannot help but succeed.

Sources of Information About "Exceptional Children"

The Council for Exceptional Children, 1920 Association Drive, Reston, Virginia 22091.

American Speech and Hearing Association, 10801 Rockville Pike, Rockville, Maryland 20852.

Association for Children with Learning Disabilities, 5255 Grace Street, Pittsburgh, Pennsylvania 15236.

National Association for Retarded Citizens, 2709 Avenue E East, Arlington, Texas 76011.

National Federation of the Blind, 218 Randolph Hotel Building, Des Moines, Iowa 50309.

Important journals published by the Council for Exceptional Children include *Behavioral Disorders, Exceptional Children, Journal for the Education of the Gifted,* and *Learning Disability Quarterly.*

Other helpful journals include *The Gifted Child Quarterly, G/T/C* (education of gifted and talented children), *Journal of Learning Disabilities, Journal of Rehabilitation,* and *Journal of Speech and Hearing Disorders.*

Books About Making Puppets

Cummings, Richard. *101 Hand Puppets.* New York: Random House, 1974.
Hopper, Grizella H. *Puppet Making Through the Grades.* Worcester, Mass.: Davis, 1966.
Krisvoy, Joel. *The Good Apple Puppet Book.* Good Apple, Inc., Box 299, Carthage, Ill. 62321.
Pels, Gertrude. *Easy Puppets.* New York: Crowell, 1951.
Ross, Laura. *Finger Puppets: Easy to Make, Fun to Use.* New York: Lothrop, Lee & Shepard, 1971.
————. *Hand Puppets: How to Make and Use Them.* New York: Lothrop, Lee & Shepard, 1969.

Records

Adventures in Rhythm. Scholastic ST 7682. Produced by Folkways Records. Distributed by Scholastic Magazine Inc.
Cliss, Henry "Buzz." *Rhythm Stick Activities.* Educational Activities, Inc.
Do You Know How You Grow? Folkways Records, FC 7082.
Finger Plays—Part of Body. Melody House Recordings, MH 87.
Guthrie, Woody. *Songs to Grow on.* Folkways Records, FC 7675.
Jenkins, Ella. *Jambo and Other Call and Response Songs and Chants.* Folkways Records, FC 7661.
————. *Play Your Instruments and Make a Pretty Sound.* Folkways Records.
————. *Rhythm and Dance.* Folkways Records, SC 7653.
————. *This is Rhythm.* Folkways Records, SR SC 7652.
————. *We Are America's Children.* Folkways Records, FC 7666.
————. *You Sing a Song and I'll Sing a Song.* Folkways Records, FC 7664.
Jervey, Arden A. *Fitness for Everyone.* Activity Records, HYP 24.
Johnson, Yvonne Cheek. *Moving Makes Me Magic.* Folkways Records, FC 7518.
Loefer, Evelyn D. *Come and See the Peppermint Tree.* Deon Records, DDT 101.
Lomax, Alan, collector. *American Folk Songs for Children.* Atlantic Recording Corp. 1350.
Louri, Dick and Jed. *Small Voice, Big Voice.* Folkways Records, FC 7547.
Marston, Gwen. *Songs for Small Fry.* Forrest Green Studios, 5004 West Francis Road, Clio, Michigan 48420.
Palmer, Hap. *The Feel of Music.* Educational Activities, AR 556.
————. *Folk Song Carnival.* Educational Activities, AR 524.
————. *Getting to Know Myself.* Educational Activities, AR 543.
————. *Learning Basic Skills Through Music,* Vols. I and II. Educational Activities, AR 514, 532.
————. *Modern Rhythm and Tunes.* Educational Activities, AR 523.
————. *Movin'.* Educational Activities, AR 546.

————. *Pretend*. Educational Activities, AR 563.

Polk, Elizabeth. *Wake Up! Calm Down Through Rhythm and Dance*. Educational Activities, AR 695.

Rey, Marcos. *Let's Play a Musical Game*. Columbia Records, HL 9522.

Reynolds, Malvina. *Malvina Reynolds Sings the Truth*. Columbia Records, CS 9414.

Schwartz, Tony. *1, 2, 3, and a Zing, Zing, Zing: Street Songs and Games of Children of New York City*. Folkways Records, FC 7003.

Seeger, Pete. *Birds, Beasts, Bugs and Bigger Fishes*. Folkways Records, FP 7011.

————. *Children's Concert at Town Hall*. Columbia Records, Mono CC 1947.

————. *Song and Play Time with Pete Seeger*. Folkways Records, FC 7525.

————. *The World of Pete Seeger*. Columbia Records, CG 31949.

Who Am I? Classroom Materials Company, Great Neck, New York 11021.

Young People's Records. *Me / Myself & I*. Children's Record Guild. 100 Sixth Ave., New York, New York.

————. *A Visit to My Little Friend*. Children's Record Guild.

Poetry Books

Adoff, Arnold. *Black Is Brown Is Tan*. Illustrated by Emily Arnold McCully, New York: Harper & Row, 1973.

————. *Eats*. Illustrated by Susan Russo. New York: Lothrop, Lee & Shepard, 1979.

————. *Friend Dog*. Illustrated by Troy Howell. Philadelphia: Lippincott, 1980.

————. *Make a Circle, Keep Us In*. Illustrated by Ronald Himler. New York: Delacorte, 1975.

————. *Tornado!* Illustrated by Ronald Himler. New York: Delacorte, 1977.

————. *Where Wild Willie*. Illustrated by Emily Arnold McCully. New York: Harper & Row, 1978.

Aldis, Dorothy. *All Together*. New York: Putnam, 1952.

Asch, Frank. *Country Pie*. New York: Morrow, Greenwillow, 1979.

Barnstone, Willis. *A Day in the Country*. Illustrated by Howard Knotts. Philadelphia: Lippincott, 1971.

Belloc, Hilaire. *The Bad Child's Book of Beasts*. Illustrated by B.T.B. New York: Knopf, 1965.

Ciardi, John. *The Man Who Sang the Sillies*. Illustrated by Edward Gorey. Philadelphia: Lippincott, 1961.

————. *You Read to Me, I'll Read to You*. Illustrated by Edward Gorey. Philadelphia: Lippincott, 1962.

Clifton, Lucille. *Everett Anderson's Nine Month Long*. Illustrated by Ann Grifalconi. New York: Holt, Rinehart & Winston, 1970.

Coatsworth, Elizabeth. *Under the Green Willow*. Illustrated by Janina Domanska. New York: Macmillan, 1971.

Cole, William, comp. *An Arkful of Animals. Poems for the Very Young*. Boston: Houghton Mifflin, 1978.

Conover, Chris. *Six Little Ducks*. New York: Crowell, 1976.

Craft, Ruth. *Pieter Brueghel's "The Fair."* Philadelphia: Lippincott, 1976.

Delaunay, Sonia. *Sonia Delaunay's Alphabet*. New York: Crowell, 1972.

De Regniers, Beatrice Schenck. *Poems Children Will Sit Still For*. New York: Citation, 1969.

Dragonwagon, Crescent. *When Light Turns into Night*. Illustrated by Robert Andrew Parker. New York: Harper & Row, 1975.

Ernest, Edward, ed. *The Kate Greenaway Treasury*. Introduction by Ruth Hill Viguers. New York: Collins, 1978.

Farjeon, Eleanor. *Then There Were Three*. Illustrated by Isobel and John Morton-Sale. Philadelphia: Lippincott, 1965.

Fisher, Aileen. *Anybody Home?* Illustrated by Susan Bonners. New York: Crowell, 1980.

————. *Do Bears Have Mothers?* Illustrated by Eric Carle. New York: Crowell, 1973.

————. *Going Barefoot*. Illustrated by Adrienne Adams. New York: Crowell, 1960.

————. *Like Nothing at All*. Illustrated by Leonard Weisgard. New York: Crowell, 1969.

————. *Out in the Dark and Daylight*. Illustrated by Gail Owens. New York: Harper & Row, 1980.

Foster, John, comp. *A First Poetry Book*. Illustrated by Chris Orr and others. New York: Oxford University Press, 1980.

Fujikawa, Gyo, comp. *A Child's Book of Poems*. New York: Grosset & Dunlap, 1969.

Greenfield, Eloise. *Honey, I Love and Other Poems*. Illustrated by Diane and Leo Dillon. New York: Crowell, 1978.

Hille-Brandts, Lena. *If I Were . . .* Illustrated by Doris Otto. Chicago: Childrens Press, 1969.

Hoberman, Mary Ann. *Hello and Good-by*. Illustrated by Norman Hoberman. Boston: Little, Brown, 1959.

————. *Yellow Butter, Purple Jelly, Red Jam, Black Bread*. Illustrated by Chaya Burstein. New York: Viking, 1981.

Hopkins, Lee Bennett, comp. *By Myself*. Illustrated by Glo Coalson. New York: Crowell, 1980.

————. *To Look at Anything*. Photos by John Earl. New York: Harcourt Brace Jovanovich, 1978.

Hurd, Edith Thacher. *Come and Have Fun*. Illustrated by Clement Hurd. New York: Harper & Row, 1962.

Jacobs, Leland B. *I Don't, I Do*. Illustrated by Frank Carlings. New Canaan, Conn.: Garrard, 1971.

————. *Playtime in the City*. Illustrated by Kelly Oechsli. New Canaan, Conn.: Garrard, 1971.

Kahn, Joan. *Hi, Jock, Run Around the Block*. Illustrated by Whitney Darrow, Jr. New York: Harper & Row, 1978.

Kherdian, David, comp. *If Dragon Flies Made Honey*. Illustrated by Jose Aruego and Ariane Dewey. New York: Morrow, Greenwillow, 1977.

Kuskin, Karla. *Any Me I Want to Be*. New York: Harper & Row, 1972.

————. *Dogs and Dragons, Trees and Dreams: A Collection of Poems*. New York: Harper & Row, 1980.

————. *James and the Rain*. New York: Harper & Row, 1957.

————. *The Rose on My Cake*. New York: Harper & Row, 1964.

Larrick, Nancy, ed. *Green Is Like a Meadow of Grass*. Illustrated by Kelly Oechsli. New Canaan, Conn.: Garrard, 1968.

Lawrence, John. *Rabbit and Pork: Rhyming Talk*. New York: Crowell, 1975.

Lear, Edward. *The Quangle-Wangle's Hat*. Illustrated by Helen Oxenbury. New York: Watts, 1969.

Lee, Dennis. *Alligator Pie*. Illustrated by Frank Newfeld. Boston: Houghton Mifflin, 1975.

————. *Garbage Delight*. Illustrated by Frank Newfeld. Boston: Houghton Mifflin, 1978.

Livingston, Myra Cohn, ed. *Listen, Children, Listen*. Illustrated by Trina Schart Hyman. New York: Atheneum, 1972.

Lobel, Arnold. *On the Day Peter Stuyvesant Sailed into Town*. New York: Harper & Row, 1971.

McCord, David. *Every Time I Climb a Tree*. Illustrated by Marc Simont. Boston: Little, Brown, 1967.

Merriam, Eve. *Catch a Little Rhyme*. Illustrated by Imero Gobbata. New York: Atheneum, 1966.

Milne, A. A. *World of Christopher Robin*. Illustrated by Ernest Shepard. New York: Dutton, 1958.

Moss, Elaine, comp. *From Morn to Midnight*. Illustrated by Salomi Ichikawa. New York: Crowell, 1977.

Opie, Iona, and Peter Opie, eds. *The Oxford Book of Children's Verse*. New York: Oxford University Press, 1973.

Plath, Sylvia. *The Bed Book*. Illustrated by Emily Arnold McCully. New York: Harper & Row, 1976.

Prelutsky, Jack. *The Sheriff of Rottenshot*. Illustrated by Victoria Chess. New York: Morrow, Greenwillow, 1982.

Saunders, Dennis. *Magic Lights and Streets of Shining Jet*. Photos by Terry Williams. New York: Morrow, Greenwillow, 1978.

Schwartz, Delmore. *''I Am Cherry Alive,'' The Little Girl Sang*. Illustrated by Barbara Cooney. New York: Harper & Row, 1979.

Smaridge, Norah. *Scary Things*. Illustrated by Ruth VanScriver. New York: Abingdon, 1969.

Stevenson, Robert Louis. *A Child's Garden of Verses*. Illustrated by Brian Wildsmith. New York: Watts, 1966.

Tripp, Wallace, comp. *A Great Big Ugly Man Came Up and Tied His Horse to Me: A Book of Nonsense Verse*. Boston: Little, Brown, 1973.

Untermeyer, Louis, ed. *Rainbow in the Sky*. Illustrated by Reginald Birch. New York: Harcourt Brace Jovanovich, 1935.

Wallace, Daisy, ed. *Fairy Poems*. Illustrated by Trina Schart Hyman. New York: Holiday, 1980.

Watson, Clyde. *Catch Me and Kiss Me and Say It Again: Rhymes*. Illustrated by Wendy Watson. Cleveland, Ohio: World, 1978.

————. *Father Fox's Pennyrhymes*. Illustrated by Wendy Watson. New York: Crowell, 1971.

I like being me.

Jesse, age 6

Matt, age 7

Jimmy, age 8

PART ONE

OUR FANTASTIC BODIES

OUR FEELINGS

OUR UNIQUENESS

1

OUR FANTASTIC BODIES

Four-year-old Kimani and 11-year-old Beth sat together watching the summer scene. Beth looked lovingly at Kimani and touched his curly black hair. "You have cute hair, Kimani," she said. "What about the rest of my body?" Kimani replied.

THE BASICS

The human body—that incredible machine, that amazing creation—is a fascinating subject for young children. Kimani and his brothers and sisters the world over are intrigued by their bodies and what they can do.

We do not need spectacular achievements to show us the wonders of the human body. Focus on a young child, such as Kimani. Follow him around and observe the countless movements and body patterns. Do not take for granted such seemingly simple activities as walking, running, hopping, skipping, sliding, clapping, leaping, and turning. To lift both feet off the floor, hold the body in air for that brief second before gravity pulls it down, and land, balanced, on both feet is a complex activity. If you know anyone who was paralyzed through illness or accident and must relearn everything from standing to walking, you can appreciate the coordination and balance necessary for the most ordinary activity.

Because their accomplishments in mastering each physical challenge are so new, most children are proud and eager to demonstrate what they can do. They have not yet learned to inhibit their feelings, to repress their joy in accomplishment. Through movement, children express responses to their inner and outer worlds. Excitement and joy tingle the muscles and lift the limbs. Disappointment or sadness lowers the head, slows the tempo. Infants move to the rhythm of human sounds. A mother's voice is the song of a baby's first dance. Your voice is the music of your classroom.

Young children never tire of "showing off" their bodies. They love repetition, familiar chants, games and challenges. Some of their earliest words are body words. Their first accomplishments are skills of body coordination. One of their greatest delights is combining two or three movements, such as clap and turn; jump and clap; and jump, clap, and turn.

Through body movement, children express their understanding of ideas and language. Ask a baby, "Where are your eyes?" and two tiny fingers point to two tiny eyes. The baby understands our words and their meaning. Babies learn about identification, location, comparison, and differentiation through activities that celebrate bodies.

cial physical or emotional problems, concentrate on the things they can do. You will be surprised at the variety of ways human beings *can* express themselves through movement. Although some children have special problems, they are whole persons who are both aware of their limitations and capable of enormous compensations. Most of these children can teach us about courage and humor.

With all your students, celebrate the wonders of the human body throughout the year. Devote a part of every day to this always exciting, relevant subject. You will keep the attention of your students when they are involved in meaningful, enjoyable discussions or activities about their bodies.

When children are given opportunities to enjoy experiences involving their bodies, they feel good about themselves and others. Along with healthy bodies, they develop healthy self-concepts. They discover and rediscover the power of mind-body harmony. "My brain is the boss of all these muscles!" a five-year-old announced after a lively session of body movement and awareness.

It is dismaying to find classrooms in preschools, day-care centers, and elementary schools that make little or no time for celebrating the human body. Many opportunities are missed to teach valuable lessons in language, social studies, social behavior, self-awareness, and number concepts.

Many years ago, before "mainstreaming," I was invited to participate in a movement session with all the children in what was then a public school for handicapped students. At the time, I was not prepared to see children who had no arms, who could not walk, and who had little muscular coordination. But there they were, eagerly awaiting the "creative movement" program in the gym. I had to toss out my usual directions, familiar vocabulary, and regular approaches that took for granted healthy bodies. We began with things everyone could do, with parts everyone could move. We raised and lowered eyebrows, shrugged shoulders, wiggled noses, and turned our mouths into O's. We laughed and sang. I learned that it was possible to celebrate the body with severely handicapped children.

If you keep your activities flexible and open-ended, every child in your group will find a meaningful and enjoyable way to participate. In the case of children with spe-

DISCOVERY TIMES

- Our bodies are made up of very interesting, specific parts.
- Each of these parts has a name and function (for example, eyes see, ears hear, tongues taste, fingers touch).
- Most people have ten toes, ten fingers, two feet, two hands, and so on.
- Some people, through accident or illness, do not have the usual number or function of body parts.
- Physically handicapped people can do extraordinary things with their bodies: blind people read through their fingers with Braille; deaf people use sign language and read lips.
- Our bodies can do so many amazing things such as walk, run, jump, dance, and climb.
- Through practice we teach our bodies to do more complicated, challenging movements.
- It is important to take good care of our bodies by exercising, eating nutritious foods, and practicing safety habits.
- Our brain is in charge. Our mind is the boss.

SUGGESTED VOCABULARY

Body Parts

head	lips	fingernails	feet
hair	chin	wrists	toes
eyebrows	face	heart	toenails
eyes	cheeks	chest	rear/bottom/
eyelashes	ears	stomach	tush/butt
nose	neck	bellybutton	bones
nostrils	shoulders	hips	blood
mouth	back	legs	muscles
tongue	arms	knees	brain
teeth	hands	ankles	skin
	fingers		

Bodies in Motion

big	loose	shake	skip
little	tight	wiggle	march
large	straight	flop	push
small	crooked	gallop	pull
tall	grow	leap	spin
short	shrink	hop	turn
heavy	curl	trot	lift
light	stretch	jump	forward

weak	fall	crawl	backward
strong	rise	walk	sideways
	reach	run	

Exercises

sit-ups	jumping jacks	squats	stretches
push-ups	leg lifts	spin arounds	arm twirls
touch toes	twists	skips	rolls
	kicks		

Naming parts of the body leads to a variety of activities. Discover eye shapes, colors, and expressions. Count teeth; discover loose and missing teeth. Discuss numbers of body parts, such as two eyes, two lips, ten fingers, and two knees. Note that hands are big, small, chubby, skinny; that they clap, carve, weave, write.

SOME BEGINNING ACTIVITIES

Start with a vocabulary word. Words for body parts, bodies in motion, and exercises are excellent openers for talk, play, art, poems, and songs.

Start with a warm-up exercise. The exercise words turned into warm-up activities help children become aware of their bodies and of the variety of shapes and movements they can master.

Start with a challenge. Children love challenges, especially if they can meet them. Be sure your challenge is accessible to everyone in the class. Here is an example: "My cousin says he can make five shapes with his body. He says that's very hard to do. Can you make five shapes with your bodies? I bet you can! That's not hard for you to do!"

Start with a photograph. Show the children a photograph of the human body in some interesting and easily assumed position. "That position looks like fun. Let's try to do what the person in the picture is doing. I know you can do it even better. Let's hold the position for five seconds."

Start with a trick. Children are proud of their physical accomplishments and are eager to show them off. "Isn't it amazing how many tricks we can do? My favorite trick is standing on one foot without falling down. Can you do that? What's your favorite trick? Show us. We'll all try it!"

Start with a loose tooth. Never let a loose or lost tooth go unnoticed. That teeth fall out to make room for new ones is fascinating to young children and can prompt them to think about the wonders of the human body.

Start with a count of body parts. Count the noses in your room. Count the fingers, hands, feet, toes, eyes. Children love to count and to look at each other. Here is a chance to talk about the universality and the uniqueness of our body parts.

Start with animal comparisons. Discuss with the children some of the amazing things that animals can do. For example, snakes coil their bodies, crocodiles open their mouths very wide, and dolphins leap high out of the water. Compare and contrast such actions with those of humans. Ask, for example, if elephants do push-ups or if fish snap their fingers.

Start with an amazing observation. Consider all the things the children did since they woke up in the morning. Here is a list that a group of kindergartners recalled in just a few minutes: woke up; stretched; sat up; got out of bed; went to the bathroom; washed; dressed; ate breakfast; played with the dog; played with toys; climbed into the school bus; and skipped into school. The list suggests ideas for pantomime, improvisation, art, story telling, and songs.

Start with a "What If . . . ?" What if you had to keep the shape you're holding now and never change it? (Demonstrate.) What if you could walk only one way or at only one speed? What if you could only crawl on your belly like a snake?

TALK TIMES

Children have important things to say about their bodies because they already have experiences and information to share. They are interested in all aspects of their bodies and show you every scratch and scraggly Band-Aid, their toenail and fingernail polish, bruises and splinters, new haircuts, and strong muscles. They make observations, ask questions, share their wonder. Leave time in your talks for appreciation and curiosity. You may not always have the answer; sometimes the answer is still unknown. But because you encourage questioning and wondering (the most important components of the learning process), your young students may grow up to find the answers.

Open-ended questions. Such questions

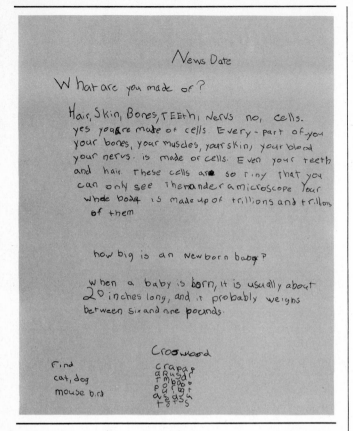

News Date

What are you made of?

Hair, Skin, Bones, Teeth, Nervs no, cells. yes you are made of cells. Every part of you your bones, your muscles, your skin, your blood your nervs. is made of cells. Even your teeth and hair These cells are so tiny that you can only see Them under a microscope Your whole body is made up of trillions and trillions of them

how big is an Newborn baby?

When a baby is born, It is usually about 20 inches long, and it probably weighs between six and nine pounds.

Crossword

Find
cat, dog
mouse bird

Ann, age 6

The above discussion provided resource material for activities in art, music, movement, pantomime, and games. The children turned the ideas into riddles, poems, and charts.

An example of how easily "Talk Time" evolves into other activities comes from a class of four-year-olds at the Jewish Center in Columbus, Ohio. For some reason, Jan Brown's students began movement sessions for about two weeks by chanting "feet, feet, feet" as they stamped into the room. Finally, I asked them what was so great about feet? They sat down and told me all the fabulous things feet do. The participation and excitement was so intense that I told them I had to record their ideas. "Read them back to us," they bubbled. When their words were read aloud, we discovered that they had actually written a wonderful chant, which they then learned and turned into a dance. Each line was expressed in a specific movement. The chant became part of their lives that year and became even more enjoyable as they taught it to other children on the playground and in the gym.

spur lively talk sessions. Examples of this kind of question are: "What do your eyes see right now?"; "What do you hear with your ears right now?"; and "What are your favorite ways to move?" One group of kindergartners responding to the question "How many ways can you move your eyes?" had some interesting observations: "Eyelashes are like little bugs' feet"; "When you sleep, your eyes are closed"; and "If I close one eye and open one other eye, it winks."

The question "What are some things *hands* can do?" triggered an outpouring of ideas from a lively group of prekindergartners. Here are some of the comments that were written on the chalkboard:

feet	feet clap	feet take little steps
feet	feet dance	feet take big steps
feet	feet kick	feet jump high
feet	feet smell	feet jump like frogs
feet jump	feet walk	feet jump like rabbits
feet hop	feet run	feet scratch
feet hop backwards	feet trip	feet dig
feet stamp	feet slip	feet draw pictures
feet wiggle	feet fall	feet gallop
feet leap	feet slide	feet feet
feet tiptoe	feet turn	feet feet
	feet jump and turn	

Observations. Observations are an excellent way to start "Talk Time." This simple observation stimulated a valuable session of experimentation and conversation in a kindergarten class: "You folks look so different when you sit up tall and straight. Your bodies seem to grow at least two inches in your seats!" We changed from slouched to straight backs and compared how our bodies felt. As we moved, we talked. Here are some excerpts from that activity: "Sometimes I stand straight and sometimes crooked"; "Sometimes I feel droopy, sometimes very tall"; "Do we *really* change size?"; "Once I felt all caved in, now I feel spread out"; and "It's fun to feel floppy-

Hands Can:

touch things	pet animals	cut, comb, brush
scratch itches	take pictures	and wash hair
pinch	shut doors	tickle
write	pick up things	clap
pick up the phone	paint	put socks on
	pick apples	

Adina added, "I know four *bad* things hands can do: Hit someone; pull somebody; push somebody; punch somebody."

floppy." You can see how easily the verbal ideas translate into movement interpretation. Without doubt, "floppy-floppy" was the favorite experiment.

Shared experiences. Armeda Starling's first-graders in Indian Run School, Dublin, Ohio, were deeply involved in a fascinating discussion about their teeth. Loose teeth, lost teeth, new teeth—the children shared experiences about how they had lost their teeth. The discussion evolved into a story-telling activity spurred by the question "Wouldn't it be fun to make up stories about missing teeth?" The children loved inventing tooth stories even more than they enjoyed telling "what really happened." The story telling led to story writing and the result was a collection of tooth stories accompanied by original illustrations. Here is one selection from the stories.

A Tooth Adventure

I was a beautiful, sparkling tooth. One day I got very loose. I wiggled and wiggled. Suddenly, I fell—down, down, down to the floor. Plop! I was picked up and pushed under a pillow. I couldn't breathe. I thought I would die. I was very sad. I was very lonely.

Then the Tooth Fairy came and rescued me. She took me to Fairy Land. There I had many friends. The Tooth Fairy made us into gorgeous jewelry. Now we can sparkle for ever and ever.

Encourage all of the children to respond. When they know you value their opinions, experiences, and questions, they develop good listening habits and respect for others.

Stopping "Talk Time" is harder than starting it. My favorite way to end a discussion is by looking at the clock and remarking, "Time flies when you're having fun! We better stop talking and start moving!" You will never end a discussion because you run out of ideas, only because you run out of time.

ART TIMES

Art projects devoted to our fantastic bodies are so plentiful and enjoyable that I offer just a sampling. These projects will inspire you to develop your own ideas.

Handprints and footprints. Children dip their hands or feet in finger paint or watercolor, then press them on a large piece of butcher paper. Write their names below their prints if they cannot write themselves. A variation of this idea is to outline each child's hand or foot on the paper and have the children color and decorate their own prints. Tape the paper to the wall to create an attractive mural.

Thumbprints, heel prints, etc. Think of the fun of discovering the variety of designs possible when thumbprints, heel prints, fingerprints, and toe prints are used. Eve Merriam's poem "Thumbprint" catches the wonder of our body parts. Surround her poem with thumbprint designs.

Thumbprint

In the heel of my thumb
are whorls, whirls, wheels
in a unique design:
mine alone.
What a treasure to own!
My own flesh, my own feelings.
No other, however grand or base,
can ever contain the same.
My signature,
thumbing the pages of my time.
My universe key,
my singularity.
Impress, implant,
I am myself,
of all my atom parts I am the sum.
And out of my blood and my brain
I make my own interior weather,
my own sun and rain.
Imprint my mark upon the world.
Whatever I shall become.[1]

Helping hands. Children trace their hands on separate papers, color them, and cut them out. Write their names on the hands. Hands can be used as indicators of daily chores or helpers of the day or just delightful decorations.

Ask the children what kinds of things hands and fingers can do. Write (or have the children write) some of those ideas on the hands.

Friendship hands. Fold a piece of construction paper in half. On one half of the paper, handprint or outline a child's hand. On the other half, print the hand of a friend. Write the names below. This activity is an excellent way to introduce the concepts of likeness and difference.

Lei of hands. I visited a kindergarten class and was welcomed with a lovely circle of friendly hands. The children had outlined and cut their hands out of brightly colored

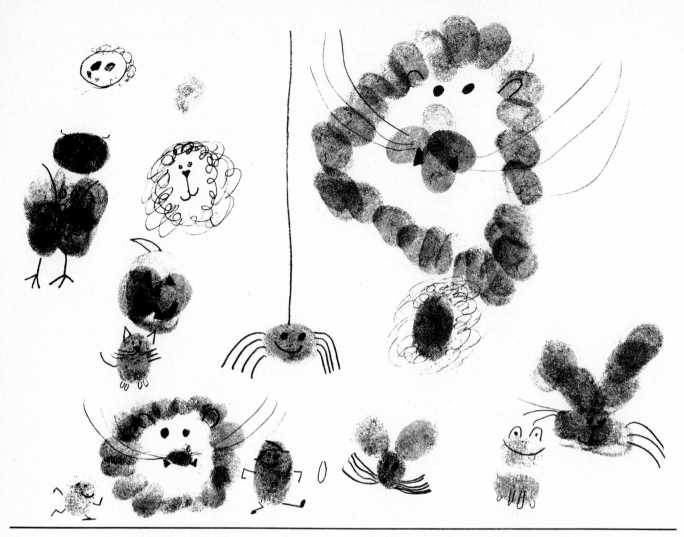

Cherie, age 7

construction paper. They decorated the hands and wrote their names on them. The hands were stapled together in a long chain. When a visitor came to the room, the children welcomed the visitor by putting the chain of hands around their shoulders.

Handouts. Children trace their hands, cut them out and use them for the cover of a hand-shaped book that they will fill with original pictures and stories. This project works with feet as well.

Left and right hands. An enjoyable way to learn right from left is to do something with the hand you want to focus attention on. Design a bracelet or ring, paint a design on that hand, or dot that hand with a chosen color to set it off. All day direct attention to the decorated hand and help the children learn that the hand is, for example, their right hand. After a few days, decorate the left hand and focus attention on it.

Finger and hand puppets. These simple, popular little puppets can be made out of a variety of "scrounge" materials—paper, cotton, flannel, or even scrounge from nature. A group of five-year-olds had the best time taping little leaves and branches to their fingers to use as hats for finger puppets. One child found a leaf that looked like a feather and created an Indian puppet named Rain Chief. An innovative teacher asked parents to send in old, torn gloves rather than throw them out. She and her students cut the fingers off the gloves and had enough fingers for each member of the class to decorate an original finger puppet. Be sure to go beyond the making of the puppets and give children plenty of time to play with their puppets. Improvisation is the most important element of the experience. De-emphasize formal performances and encourage informal interaction among children.

Lollipop face puppets. Use lollipop sticks or tongue depressors. Cut out cardboard circles and have the children draw eyes, noses, mouths, and hair to make faces. Tape or glue the puppet's face to the stick. When the face is added, a puppet is born, complete with name, voice, story, and song. **Paper-bag or sock puppets.** Of the easy-to-make puppets my favorites are paper-bag and sock puppets. Again, with plenty of scrounge material at hand, children can make distinctive puppets. Scraps of wool or material can be used for hair, buttons for eyes, cotton balls for beards and mustaches, and cardboard or felt for hats. With your children, make up names, stories, and songs for the puppets.

Eyes are probably the most distinguishing feature. Add eyes to anything and you have a creature or a character. Draw a circle, dot two eyes, and you have a face. Gather small stones, pinecones, and wood chunks. Paint eyes on them and you have little characters with their own names and personalities. Blow up balloons. Paint eyes on them and they become special characters. Add other parts, but start with eyes. **Shoe boxes of eyes, ears, noses, and mouths.** Children like to cut up magazines. From your plentiful supply of old magazines, children cut out eyes, ears, noses, and mouths and put each part in its own shoe box. After a while, you will have a shoe box full of eyes or noses. Create original faces on paper circles or paper plates using parts from each of the boxes.

Collages and montages. Body parts are the oldest, most popular artistic designs in human history. Here are two basic kinds of projects involving body parts. The children select one body part to cut out of magazines or draw. They compose an arrangement of, for example, eyes, and fill their papers with eyes of different colors, shapes, and sizes. Be sure to display all the children's work.

The other project involves a collage or montage of different body parts. The children cut out or draw body parts and arrange them in an interesting pattern on either their own paper or a large bulletin board to which all contribute.

Art appreciation. Share great works of art with your students. Libraries often lend paintings. Art books usually have excellent reproductions of masterpieces. Use the names of the artists as you show the way individual artists painted or sculpted faces and bodies. Children enjoy looking at, for example, Modigliani's faces or Renoir's hair

and faces. They marvel at how Michaelangelo carved such a perfect hand for *David* and find inspiration to model their own clay hands and feet.

Body parts through the seasons. This activity is a wonderful way to correlate understanding of changes in seasons with awareness of how the seasons affect what we do and what we wear. Here are excerpts from many preschool classes' discoveries as they discussed the seasons in relation to body parts.

Winter Hands	**Winter Feet**	**Winter Head**
wear mittens	wear boots	wears hats
make snowballs	make snow prints	wears ear muffs
build snowmen	slide on ice	wears scarves

Spring Hands
plant seeds
fly kites
steer bikes

Spring Feet
wear tennis shoes
run on the grass
peddle bikes

Spring Head
wears baseball
   caps
wears pony tails
feels the sun and
   wind in hair

Summer Hands
splash in water
throw baseballs
dig in sand and
   mud

Summer Feet
go barefoot
wear sandals
squish mud and
   sand

Summer Head
gets sunburned
wears sun hats
gets sweaty

Autumn Hands
rake leaves
throw leaves
pick apples

Autumn Feet
wear school shoes
jump in crunchy
   leaves
kick footballs

Autumn Head
sometimes wears
   scarves or hats
feels hair blowing
   in the wind

One kindergarten class created a mural divided into four sections, one for each season. Each season had its own images—snowflakes and snowdrifts for winter, green grass and tulips for spring, inviting swimming pools and lush gardens for summer, and brightly colored leaves for fall. They cut out and pasted magazine pictures of boots, scarves, hats, caps, sandals, and mittens on the different seasons, and they added their own silhouettes of hands, feet, and heads to create a fascinating work of art.

Body silhouettes. Spread butcher paper, or any other inexpensive paper, across the floor. The children lie down on the paper in any position they choose. Outline their shapes with Magic Marker. Their body shapes are cut out and ready to be decorated with features, colors, clothes, and designs, or to be colored or painted with one color to make a silhouette.

I visited a first grade where the children's silhouettes were hung across the room on a clothesline. Another kindergarten class tacked their silhouettes on the four walls of the room.

Body works collage. The children cut pictures out of magazines and newspapers that show bodies doing things such as playing, working, and resting. They create their own collages or together create a class collage. Both are exciting projects. Greg Von Stein, elementary music teacher at the Columbus Academy, Columbus, Ohio, had the most spectacular bulletin board devoted to large pictures of Baryshnikov in action.

Bodies for all seasons. Earlier in this section, I described a project that featured body parts during the seasons. Here, children cut out and draw whole bodies engaged in activities appropriate to each season of the year. Some teachers and children have created four separate murals or collages during the school year, each according to the season; others have divided the room into four parts and have completed the four designs at one time. Here are some of the images created by a kindergarten class in Kalamazoo, Michigan.

Winter Bodies
snow-ski
ice-skate
ride a sleigh
throw snowballs
build snowmen
build snow forts

Spring Bodies
plant seeds
ride bikes
fly kites
throw balls
carry umbrellas
jump in puddles

Summer Bodies
row boats
have picnics
play outside with
   with animals
go to fairs
hike
swim

Autumn Bodies
rake leaves   play football   play in school
jump in leaves   ride school buses   playgrounds

Scrounge bodies. Your supply of scrounge materials should always be ample. Give the children many opportunities to participate in the highest form of creative activity: making something out of nothing. The children use whatever materials they find; they glue, paste, tape, or clip odds-and-ends together to make body shapes.

Favorite body-works books. Here is a chance for children to gather pictures and designs of their favorite kind of body works and create their own books. (Staple the pages together; make it simple.) Among a group of four-and-a-half-year-olds, Marcie's book featured dancers, Bobby's book featured athletes, Carrie's book featured people jumping, and Jamie's book featured people eating.

Pipe cleaner bodies. Pipe cleaners bend and twist and make wonderful bodies in motion. Give the children lots of time to experiment.

Stick figures. Use Popsicle sticks, straws, toothpicks, or tongue depressors. Glue various lengths of material to shape a variety of figures.

Clay figures. Roll, push, pull, twist, pat, clap, pinch—experiment with clay and encourage the children to find ways they most enjoy working with clay. "How many different body shapes can we sculpt today?" Display and celebrate all the works.

Stuffed shirts and other classroom characters. Draw on your supply of old clothing donated by parents and friends. With your students, stuff a shirt with rags or crumpled newspapers. Pin or sew the sleeves and bottom together. Stuff a pair of slacks or jeans with the same material. Sew or pin the bottom of the trousers together. Sew, tape, or pin the stuffed shirt to the pants. Stuff a paper bag or small pillowcase and create a face with paint or scrounge materials. Add real or paper shoes, and cut out paper hands to complete the body of the "new member" of your class. Design a shape for him or her by tacking the arms and legs and head to the bulletin board.

With the children, make up a name, stories, songs, and games for your new character. Have the children, in groups of two or three, take turns giving your character a different shape every few days. I know of a stuffed character named Hermie who was an important member of his kindergarten class for the entire year. He inspired pictures, plays, and stories. Children who hardly spoke, spoke to Hermie.

Body poses. The children take turns modeling for their classmates. Encourage the children to sketch, paint, or color the model's position quickly, because it is a challenge for the model to hold a shape for more than a few minutes.

Exercise chart. Devote a special place in the room—a board or portion of a wall—to pictures and diagrams of physical exercises. Children cut out pictures of exercises from magazines and newspapers. Label the exercises so that the name is prominently displayed next to the diagram or picture.

Exercise name tags. Children write their names on a tag. Draw or cut out exercise shapes to add to their names. The tags will be used for some of the activities described later in this guide.

Exercise wheel. Paint a large cardboard circle a bright color. Divide it into sections. Have children paste an illustration of a clearly defined exercise on each section. Be sure the exercises they choose for the wheel are familiar and easy to do. Cut a pointer out of cardboard, paint it a different color, and clip it to the center of the wheel. Spin the pointer and where it stops is the exercise the children will do. Assign different children to spin the wheel each day and lead the exercises.

Exercise cards. Cut out or outline pictures of exercises and paste one on each card. Design a special pocket or place for the exercise cards. Children choose a few cards each day to start their warm-ups.

Shape-up poster. Divide the paper or portion of a wall into columns such as:

I CAN DO SIT-UPS   I CAN DO PUSH-UPS   I CAN JOG

The children write their names in each column and draw or paint a design next to their names to show "they can." Keep adding exercise sections. Children have lots of practice writing their names, creating designs, and feeling good about themselves.

MUSIC TIMES

Celebrate voices. Children do not need to be taught to sing. They naturally sing, hum, and chant, echoing the words and rhythms they hear about them, inventing their own and combining musical ideas. Sing old, new, borrowed, blue, improvised, original songs. Sing about everything. Sing as you work, walk, play, and rest. Encourage the children to make up their own songs and celebrate them. Show them how by your own example.

Celebrate songs from around the world. All people use their voices to sing. All people have songs, but their words, rhythms, and styles are often very different, reflecting the diversity of the human family. Borrow records from neighbors, family, the library, and children's families that highlight songs from different cultures. Play them (and sing along) as often as possible. Through these kinds of listening and learning opportunities, your children will learn something about the wonders of the human voice.

Songs of bodies at work. Walt Whitman's poem "I Hear America Singing" introduces the theme of songs people sing while working and playing. In his poem Whitman describes the songs of carpenters, mechanics, masons, deckhands, shoemakers, woodcutters, and mothers. So many of our most popular folk songs are based on bodies at work—railroad workers, sailors, miners, ranchers, farmers, and migrant workers. Children love to sing such work songs as "I've Been Workin' on the Railroad"; "Erie Canal"; "Jump Down, Turn Around, Pick a Bale of Cotton"; and "John Henry." Share the idea with your students that as people work, songs flow.

Tune up body parts to make music. Music is also the result of effort and practice. Musicians need nimble fingers, flexible wrists, powerful hands, and strong lungs to make music. As you listen to music and play your own, emphasize the importance of exercising special body parts and practicing for developing musical talents and skills. Invent such musical exercises as playing a piano, strumming a guitar, and blowing a wind instrument.

Body-parts rhythm band. Hearts beat, a special rhythm. Lungs exhale, inhale, their special breath rhythm. Feet jump, their special jumping rhythm. Hands clap—fast, faster, fastest; slow, slower, slowest; louder, softer—their special rhythms. Feet tap, their special tapping rhythms. Teeth click. Hands slap floor. Hands slap thighs. Hair swishes.

Experiment with body parts that make sounds and keep rhythms. Clap, tap, stamp, jump, whistle, sing, beat, and shake out rhythms. Listen to the sounds the body parts make. Work together and discover the joy of fusing energies and ideas. Play different kinds of music. Recite favorite poems and sing favorite songs accompanied by the body-parts rhythm band. Remember, musical instruments are extensions of body rhythms and sounds. We blow our breath into wind instruments. We pluck and strum string instruments. We tap, pound, and shake percussion instruments.

Shel Silverstein's poem "Orchestra" fits beautifully the body-parts rhythm band. March to it. Move to it. Play to it.

Orchestra

So you haven't got a drum, just beat your belly.
So you haven't got a horn—I'll play my nose.
So we haven't got any cymbals—
We'll just slap our hands together,
And though there may be orchestras
That sound a little better
With their fancy shiny instruments
That cost an awful lot—
Hey, we're making music twice as good
By playing what we've got![2]

Make rhythm instruments. The earliest instruments came from nature, for example, dried gourds with loose seeds, animal skins pulled tightly over shells or wood, and stones and sticks with holes in them.

Betsy Distelhorst, an outstanding creative arts teacher who works with children of all ages, has a favorite way to make drums. Cut old inner tubes into circles that will fit over the open ends of coffee cans. Punch holes around the borders of the rubber circles. Carefully place one rubber circle on each end of the hollow coffee can. Connect the two rubber skins with string, from a hole on one side to a hole on the other. If you cannot find old inner tubes, use scraps of vinyl, suede cloth, or heavy canvas.

L'Eggs eggs or small milk containers are good for making rattles or maracas. Fill the egg or the container with seeds or pebbles. Close up the egg or glue the opening on the container. They can be held in hands and shaken or attached to wooden sticks, tongue depressors, or old rulers.

Before stapling two facing paper plates together, sprinkle some pebbles, beads, or seeds on them. Paint or color the outsides of the plates in lively patterns. Attach string rings of bottle caps to the rims. Shake them up. Tambourines!

Experiment with objects that make sounds. Invent new instruments. Click two pencils together. Tap spoons on tabletops. Clap two wooden blocks together. Turn two pot covers into cymbals.

Improvised "fantastic body" songs. You have material in your knapsack of experiences to create delightful song sessions with your students that will enrich their appreciation and understanding of the fascinating ways our bodies work. The song "Ten Little Indians," for example, can be improvised to fit most body parts. Instead of Indians, count the fingers, toes, noses, eyes, and knees of your class. Leave no one out. The children will not tire of the song, even when *you* are ready to shout, "Uncle!"

With a group of first graders, we made up about fifteen different stanzas for "Ten Little Indians," using each of our bodies as the source. Here is an example:

One little, two little, three little fingers,
Four little, five little, six little fingers,
Seven little, eight little, nine little fingers,
I have ten little fingers.

My little ten little fingers are waving.
(Repeat 3 times)
Hello, hello. Goodbye, goodbye.

My little ten little fingers are tapping.
(Repeat 3 times)
Tapping, tapping, tap tap tap.

The popular song "This Is the Way We Go to School" can be adapted to verses such as "This is the way we clap our hands," "This is the way we blink our eyes," "This is the way we wiggle our nose," and "This is the way we shrug our shoulders."

Bodies respond to musical instruments. "How do violins make you want to move?" "Bongo drums?" "Flutes or trumpets?" Experiment with the sounds of different instruments and the different ways children move to each of them. The children's bodies become the shape of the sound. Stretch this exploration of music and body responses through the school year. Highlight one instrument at a time. Start with your favorite instruments and musicians. With children of all ages I have shared my favorites, from Al Hirt on the trumpet to Carlos Montoya and Andrés Segovia on flamenco guitar. If you play an instrument, share it with your students.

Music for body relaxation. In our often frenetic world, we need the feeling of inner peace and calm when the body relaxes with soothing, beautiful music. This is a time to help young children realize how much our bodies can do and still be able to rest comfortably and calmly. Encourage the children to let their minds daydream, wander, float. Later, you may want to discuss some of their images, even turn the images into pictures and poems.

Children need to find comfortable positions—sitting, leaning, or lying down. Pillows or mats on the floor are useful for those who want them.

As often as possible, tell your class the title of the music and its composer, not to test them but to give them the opportunity to hear and learn the names.

Choose lullabies, ballads, folk songs, and segments of longer pieces that are conducive to peaceful feelings. The following are some old favorites you may want to hum or sing softly during this peaceful, easy time when the body works at relaxing: "Down in the Valley," "Clementine," "Red River Valley," "The Riddle Song," "Hush Little Baby," "Puff the Magic Dragon," "500 Miles," "The Water Is Wide," "On Top of Old Smokey," "Tell Me Why?" and "Day Is Done (Taps)." Believe it or not, you can even find a few calming bands on the sound track of the popular film *Star Wars*.

If possible, sing your favorite lullabies or camp songs to the children. One of the best stories I ever heard came from a friend who substituted one day in a kindergarten class. The regular teacher always sang to the children after their snack. They asked my friend if she would sing to them. Reluctant because she felt she had a poor voice, my friend hesitated. The children urged her. Finally, she gave in, hoarsely whisper-humming a little song. When she finished, she shrugged apologetically. "That's O.K.," one child comforted her, "you did your best!" You are only being asked to do your best!

MOVEMENT AND PLAY TIMES

Movement responses. Raising hands seems to be the most accepted movement pattern in American schools. So many opportunities are missed when we limit choice of movement. Here are a few different ways children can answer questions. "Boys and girls, if you saw "Sesame Street" last night, wiggle your nose." "Children, if you have ever heard of Eskimos, tap your feet." "If you think you know the answer to two-and-two, clap it." "How many people here brought in their permission slips? Shake ten fingers if you did." Aren't these ways more interesting and fun than always raising hands?

Daily warm-ups. What better way to limber minds and muscles than exercising for a few minutes every day? Correlate exercises with curriculum, and use a variety of musical selections to accompany the exercises. Include in these warm-up sessions exercises that you and your students create as well as familiar exercises such as sit-ups, push-ups, and jumping jacks. The following are some ways that exercises can become part of your daily schedule.

Follow the leader. Children take turns leading an exercise of their choice. If the leader does something difficult to follow, encourage the others to do their best. Leaders may choose from the exercise cards or spin the exercise wheel or put their name tag next to the exercise they want to lead on the exercise chart (see descriptions of these projects in "Art Times" section above).

Exercises and numbers. "It's January 6 today. Let's do 6 exercises in honor of the number 6." Write the exercises on the board and follow them in sequence. Or "Today we're celebrating the number 8. Let's do 8 exercises. Which shall they be?"

Another aspect of numbers and exercises is to assign numbers to each warm-up. "How many jumping jacks shall we do?" Write the number on the board. "How many windmills?"

Another variation of numbers and exercises is for the birthday child to choose the exercises of the day to correspond to his or her new age. "Seven years old today? Jackie, choose seven birthday exercises!"

Animal exercises. Consider the movements of animals that can be used in exercises: hopping (grasshoppers, frogs, rabbits, kangaroos); running (dogs, foxes, squirrels, wolves); galloping (horses, donkeys, zebras); and crawling (snakes, caterpillars, lizards, salamanders). Do them. Talk about them. Extend them into art projects and games.

Exercises for seasons and special occasions. On a cold winter day, make up a few exercises based on seasonal activities such as snowball throwing, pulling on boots, and making snow angels. On Halloween, make up exercises like a rattling skeleton, a walking robot, and a cat arching its back and stretching.

Exercise change game. This is one of my favorite ways to enjoy exercises. Talk about all the exercises the children know. Encourage them to make up their own for different parts of their bodies (for example, shoulder exercise, knee exercise). Carefully explain. When the music goes on, each child may choose any exercise to do. Everyone will be different. When you give the signal (for example, shake tambourine, clap hands), everyone changes to another exercise. Minds and bodies work very fast. Children have the opportunity to choose their favorite exercises and to enjoy a unique warm-up. Use any lively, rhythmical music you like. I have used everything from Arabic belly-dance music to Appalachian round dances. The only rule is that the children must stay in their own spaces. If they jog or kick, they must stay in place.

Taking inventory. The most universally loved game of early childhood is "Show Me . . ." or "Where Is Your. . .?" For example: "Where is your nose?" "Show me your belly-button." Here is an opportunity for every child to feel success and delight. A silly variation of this game is to touch the wrong place. Pretend absent-mindedness. Young children find great delight in these "mistakes" and will correct you with glee.

"Show me" can be extended from location to movement. For example: "What can your shoulders do? Show me." "How many things can your hands do? Show me." "What can you do with your eyebrows? Show me."

Many songs and poems take inventory. As the children sing or recite, they move and touch the appropriate parts. Shel Silverstein's poem "Band-Aids" is a good example.

Band-Aids

I have a Band-Aid on my finger,
One on my knee and one on my nose,
One on my heel, and two on my shoulder,
Three on my elbow, and nine on my toes.
Two on my wrist, and one on my ankle,
One on my chin, and one on my thigh,
Four on my belly, and five on my bottom,
One on my forehead, and one on my eye.
One on my neck, and in case I might need 'em
I have a box full of thirty-five more.
But oh! I do think it's sort of a pity,
I don't have a cut or a sore![3]

Count the parts. Here is an activity that combines counting body parts and moving them. Change the movement ideas. Once in a while, for fun and laughs, mix up the counting: "Three noses. Whoops! I mean *one* nose! Sorry!"

One head (shake it)
Two eyes (blink them)
One nose (wiggle it)
Two ears (twitch them)
Two feet (stamp them)
Ten toes (tiptoe)

Two elbows (bend them)
One mouth (make an O)
Two shoulders (shrug them)
One back (stretch it)
One tummy (belly dance)

Movement machines. Our bodies are like spectacular movement machines. When we are completely still, controlling all our muscles, we are on ZERO. While we are holding at ZERO, our minds are thinking about all the parts of our body that we can move. At the signal for ONE, everyone moves one part—no matter which one. The signal for TWO starts two parts moving—any two parts. Go on to five or six parts. Then "turn on" all the parts—move *everything* that can move. By then the "machines" will be ready for OFF or STOP. After the children are tired by an activity such as this one, take a few minutes to demonstrate the amazing versatility of our bodies. Some children, for example, will be lying on their stomachs, others on their sides or on their backs, and still others will be sitting.

Changing body shapes. "Everyone keep your shape. As the tambourine shakes, find a *new shape* and hold it. Change again. Keep changing shapes and holding the new one for a few seconds." This activity is so successful and enjoyable that children often ask for it.

Dancing parts. This activity begins with the following announcement. "Ladies and Gentlemen. For the first time in (your town and state), we are pleased to present a dance of the shoulders!" Play rhythmical music and experiment with shoulder dances. Follow this activity with dances featuring noses, fingers, heads, knees, and other parts.

"Which of our parts never gets its own turn?" "Elbows," six-year-old Mike responded immediately. "Elbows never get a chance to dance!" The children sympathized with the plight of the elbows and created an elbow dance to an old Peter, Paul, and Mary folk song. Use music that you like, music that makes you want to move.

Original finger plays and hand plays. There are many books about finger plays. Teachers study the patterns and teach them to their students. But imaginative teachers and children also create their own finger plays and hand language to illustrate poems, stories, and songs.

A kindergarten class in Lansing, Michigan, showed me their original finger play to "Mary Had a Little Lamb." I jotted down their movements as they went along.

Mary (hands touch face) had a little lamb (hands pet). Repeat. Its fleece (hands tickle) was white as snow (hands reach up, fingers wiggle, hands move slowly downward to convey snow). It followed her (one hand in front of the other, fingers walking) to school one day (two hands meet, make a roof shape), which was against the rule (fingers wag scoldingly). It made the children laugh and play (tap heads, patty-cake clapping hands) to see (both hands wide with amazement) a lamb (pet) in school (roof).

Try your hand (and fingers) at improvising this kind of movement to any idea you and your children have. Be open to all their suggestions. Try to incorporate as many as possible.

Hand dances to stories and poems. There are dances thousands of years old that feature hand movements to tell stories. In keeping with that ancient tradition, children enjoy hand dances that they find in books or that they create themselves. Here is an example of an original story created by a group of four-and-a-half-year-olds and accompanied by beautiful hand movements that the children agreed on.

Once it was snowing. Everything was cold.
Everything was asleep.
Then the sun came out and warmed the ground.
It started to rain.
Seeds under the ground started to grow.
Little caterpillars crawled around.
They curled up and turned into butterflies.
The sun got hotter.
The seeds grew to flowers.
Butterflies flew around.
It was spring.

Each idea was expressed by different hand movements. The children loved the crawling caterpillars and flying butterflies so much that they insisted on doing that part over and over. John Denver's recording of "Sunshine" provided the background as the story was read aloud. After two readings the children were able to recite the story; the movements helped them to remember the sequence. In so many cases, more reluctant children participate freely if movement is confined to a specific body part, such as hands. It seems safer to them.

Movement signals. Nonverbal communication is very effective. "Wouldn't it be fun to make up some body movement signals for our class?" was the challenge to a group of first graders. With cooperation and enthusiasm, they created special body shapes and movements to convey the following messages. "Everyone please sit down"; "Attention, please"; "Time to clean up"; and "Time for a snack." The children responded to the signals immediately. They were part of the communication system for the year.

"Turn yourself into . . ." Here are a few examples guaranteed to succeed as long as they are shared with enjoyment, encouragement, acceptance, and enthusiasm.

Animals (Combine with riddles and guessing games —"Which animal am I?")
TV characters
Weather (Challenge children with more abstract ideas such as interpreting wind, rain, thunder, snow, lightning, and sunshine with their bodies.)
Something in the room (Give children the opportunity to use available shapes and designs as their inspiration.)
Seasonal characters (snowman, snow shoveler, swimmer, skiier, ice skater)
Halloween characters
Letters of the alphabet
Means of transportation
Community helpers
Story friends
Athletes
Fairy tale characters

We were playing "Turn yourself into," and it was five-year-old David's turn. He sat down, charged up a noisy engine, pressed his foot on the brake, grabbed the steering wheel, and took us for a fantastic ride, finally jerking to a stop. His classmates guessed: "A car?" No. "A bus?" No. "A taxi?" No. "An airplane?" No. They named about ten more types of transportation. I listened in wonder as these four- and five-year-olds named every item in the third-grade curriculum on transportation. Finally David lisped the answer: "Steve Authtin's vehicle!"

Of course: The children applauded. I added Steve Austin to the list of important subjects to be checked out by one checked-out teacher! Hmmmmm. Isn't "vehicle" a sixth-grade vocabulary word?

Bodies work together. If one human body is an amazing machine, imagine the possibilities when bodies work together. The challenge is: "Boys and girls, what can you make with all of your bodies working together?" Often, the teachers hide their eyes while the children meet the challenge. Joining bodies, children have created:

A train (The children formed a line, one behind the other, and held onto each other's shoulders as they choo-chooed around the room.)
A snake (The children sprawled on their stomachs, legs in a V shape, each child close to the one ahead and filling the space in the wide V. They all moved at once! Help!)
A rug (Bodies were spread out on the floor, arms and legs stretched, fingers and feet touching. "It's a rug with designs," the children explained.)
A fence (The children stood in a circle, arms joined at the elbows. Then one of the boys said, "Let's make a barbed-wire fence. A keepout fence!" It was astonishing to watch the children figure out how to convey this kind

of fence with their jagged, pointy fingers, gnarled knuckles, and sharp elbows.)

A garden (Everyone in the group started as a seed and slowly grew into a special flower or tree.)

A fire (The children sat in a circle, put their feet into the center, and moved all their feet at once. It gave the feeling and look of a kindling fire. Finally, they leaned all the way back while their legs kicked higher and higher, like the flames of a bonfire.)

A house (The children arranged themselves in a square with their arms stretched at a pointed angle above them for the roof. Two children were the door and swung open and closed.)

A pizza (The children formed a circle, lying on the floor. Some were hunched and round like tomatoes; others were flat like cheese; still others were long and straight like sausage. ''Put us in the oven,'' they instructed. The teachers pretended to push them into the oven. They made hissing sounds as they melted, oozed, and bubbled.)

Stories like *Peter Cottontail*, nursery rhymes like "Hey Diddle Diddle," song-and-dance games like "Hokey Pokey," and poems like A. A. Milne's "Hoppity" are excellent resources that inspire movement interpretation. Be flexible when you use these materials; add your own verses and movements.

VISITORS AND FIELD TRIPS

Visitors

The more you think about classroom visitors who could help your students develop a respect for our amazing bodies, the longer the list becomes. Here are just a few suggestions. (Note: Welcome classroom visitors with a lei of hands!)

Person who knows sign language. This visitor will demonstrate and explain sign language and will teach the children basic words and expressions.

Maintenance worker. A worker at the school is pleased to describe how he or she uses tools and hands to fix things and eyes to see what needs to be fixed.

Musician. If you are unable to find a professional musician to invite, a parent, junior or senior high school student, or senior citizen is an excellent choice. Ask your guest to demonstrate and teach practice exercises.

Typist. A school secretary, parent, or friend armed with typewriter and willing to demonstrate the speed and facility of trained fingers at their best, is an effective visitor.

Seamstress or tailor. This guest adds elements of delight when he or she demonstrates nimble art on dolls' clothes.

Senior citizen with magical hands. A grandparent or other senior citizen is usually expert in needle crafts such as knitting, crocheting, embroidering, creweling, or weaving. Invite such a person to be an "artist in residence" for a day and share his or her skills with your students.

Indian artisan. If you live near an Indian community, some of the artisans may be willing to visit your class and demonstrate their arts.

Traffic cop. A police officer who directs traffic with hand signals will entertain the children by demonstrating some of the signals.

Workers. The kinds of workers you will be able to invite to visit your classroom will depend largely on where you live. Miners, lumberjacks, construction workers, steel workers, fishermen and fisherwomen, and stone cutters, all demonstrate their special skills. Do they lift? Dig? Chop? Climb?

Mime. A mime is an outstanding classroom visitor. Children are fascinated by the make-up, humor, and body control. A mime demonstrates, probably more dramatically and effectively than any others, the incredible variety of body works.

Yoga teacher. In many early childhood classes around the country, children are being introduced to yoga by teachers or by visitors. The children are challenged by yoga, the interesting names of the different positions, the philosophy of a harmony of mind and body that most yoga teachers communicate.

Magician. Children who have trouble paying attention are cured instantly by a visit from a magician who dazzles the eyes with sleight-of-hand tricks.

Athlete. No matter the sport, an athlete must stay in tip-top physical shape. Children have good questions about how an athlete takes care of the body, what exercises to do, what foods to eat.

Potter, sculptor, artist. When human hands touch clay, stone, metal, or canvas, surprising shapes and designs appear. Be sure to encourage the artist to allow time for the children's participation.

Doctor, nurse. A doctor and nurse make wonderful visitors, especially if they carry their little black bags filled with instruments and demonstrate on the children.

Dancer. Whether a dancer performs jazz, ballet, folk, modern, or tap, discipline and practice are required. Ask your guest to demonstrate some of the warm-up techniques and to teach a few to your students.

Check your community resources and discover folk dancers from different backgrounds. Your children will enjoy learning how differently Scottish dancers move and look when compared to Turkish or Armenian dancers. Be sure your visitors teach you and your students a dance or two.

Make the most of the visits by following them with talks, art activities, games, songs and, of course, individual thank-you letters and pictures.

Field Trips

Gym in a high school, university, or community center. See and try the different body-building equipment. Watch teams or individuals practicing.

Dance school. Ballet, modern dance, ethnic, jazz, tap—all are interesting and valuable experiences for the children as they see how people shape their bodies with determination and discipline.

Rehearsal of a marching band at a local high school or college. Enjoy the delightful patterns and shapes unfolding before you with rhythm and sound. Watch cheerleaders, twirlers, and drum majors.

Athletic field. Watch a team practice or play. Football players move differently and do different things with their bodies than, for example, basketball players. Watch the fantastic feet of soccer players and the strong arms, hands, and legs of baseball players.

Ice-skating or roller-skating rink. Add the magnificent balance and grace of the skaters to your growing list of body works.

Band or orchestra in concert or rehearsal. Observe how disciplined and strong are the hands and fingers of musicians. Note how powerful and controlled breathing produces beautiful music.

Barber shop, beauty parlor, or animal grooming shop. Focus on skilled hands curling, combing, brushing, setting, and cutting.

Typing class or secretarial office. Speed and accuracy are the goals for skilled typists. Fingers seem to fly on the keys.

Fast-food restaurant. Workers' bodies are never still. Children watch as workers cook, wrap, count change, pour coffee, and write orders.

As you and your students enjoy field trips, correlate body awareness and movement patterns. Almost everything we do involves coordination, balance, skill, control, and practice.

Survey your community, your children's families, and your own friends and neighbors as resources. When children visit carpenters, gardeners, computer programmers, artisans, construction workers, physical therapists, and auto mechanics, for example, their appreciation of the diversity of our fantastic bodies is enhanced. Field trips also inspire activities in music, story writing, drama, movement, art, and talk time.

Remember to send thank-you letters.

NOTES

1. Eve Merriam, "Thumbprint," *It Doesn't Always Have to Rhyme* (New York: Atheneum, 1964), p. 63.
2. Shel Silverstein, "Orchestra," *Where the Sidewalk Ends* (New York: Harper & Row, 1974), p. 23.
3. Silverstein, p. 140.

SELECTED BIBLIOGRAPHY

The following books are among the best available to use with young children. Some information may be somewhat advanced, but you can use your creativity in adapting the material to your children.

Books Children Will Enjoy

Baer, Edith. *The Wonders of Hands*. Photographs by Tana Hoban. New York: Parents Magazine Press, 1970.

Brenner, Barbara. *Faces*. Photographs by George Ancona. New York: Dutton, 1970.

————. *Bodies*. Photographs by George Ancona. New York: Dutton, 1973.

Castle, Sue. *Face Talk, Hand Talk, Body Talk*. Photographs by Frances McLaughlin Gill. New York: Doubleday, 1977.

Follett, Robert, Jr. *Your Wonderful Body*. Chicago: Follett, 1961.

Gackenbach, Dick. *Pepper and All the Legs*. New York: Seabury, 1978.

Goldin, Augusta. *Straight Hair, Curly Hair*. New York: Crowell, 1966.

Grant, Sandy. *Hey, Look at Me!* Photographs by Larry Mulverhill. Scarsdale, New York: Bradbury, 1973.

Halgentholen, Jean. *My Hands Can*. New York: Dutton, 1978.

————. *My Feet Can*. New York: Dutton, 1979.

McGuire, Leslie. *You: How Your Body Works*. Illustrated by Susan Perl. New York: Platt & Munk, 1974.

Perkins, Al. *The Ear Book*. Illustrated by William O'Brien. New York: Random House, 1968.

———. *The Nose Book*. Illustrated by Roy McKie. New York: Random House, 1970.

Podendorf, Illa. *Touching and Telling*. Chicago: Childrens Press, 1971.

Purcell, Margaret Sandford. *A Look at Physical Handicaps*. Photographs by Maria S. Forrai. Minneapolis: Lerner Publications, 1976.

Richmond, M. P., B. Julius, M. A. Punds, and T. Elenore. *You and Your Health*. Glenview, Ill.: Scott, Foresman, 1977.

Rogers, Fred. *Mister Rogers Talks About Haircuts*. Illustrated by Myron Papers. New York: Platt & Munk, 1974.

Action-Packed Books

Baylor, Byrd. *Sometimes I Dance Mountains*. New York: Scribners, 1973.

Carr, Rachel. *Be a Frog, a Bird, or a Tree*. New York: Doubleday, 1973.

Eastman, P. D. *Are You My Mother?* New York: Random House, 1960.

Forte, Imogene, and Jay MacKenzie. *Try Squiggles and Squirms and Wiggly Worms*. Nashville: Incentive, 1978.

Fujikawa, Gyo. *Oh, What a Busy Day!* New York: Grosset & Dunlap, 1976.

Keats, Ezra Jack. *Snowy Day*. New York: Viking, 1962.

Kent, Jack. *Hop, Skip and Jump Book*. New York: Random House, 1974.

Le Sieg, Theo. *I Wish I Had Duck Feet*. New York: Random House, 1965.

Lippman, Peter. *Busy Wheels*. New York: Random House, 1973.

Lionni, Leo. *Swimmy*. New York: Random House, Pantheon, 1963.

Maestro, Betsy, and Giulio Maestro. *Busy Day*. New York: Crown, 1978.

McCloskey, Robert. *Make Way for Ducklings*. New York: Viking, 1941.

Mendoza, George. *Sesame Street Book of Opposites*. New York: Platt & Munk, 1974.

Merriman, Eve. *Mommies at Work*. New York: Knopf, 1955.

Sendak, Maurice. *Where the Wild Things Are*. New York: Harper & Row, 1963.

Van Gelder, Richard. *Whose Nose Is This?* New York: Walker, 1974.

Wittman, Harry H. *The Eyeglasses and the Quarter*. Minneapolis: Denison, 1968.

Yudell, Lynn Deena. *Make a Face*. Boston: Little, Brown, 1970.

Teacher Resources

Andrews, Gladys. *Creative Rhythmic Movement for Children*. Englewood Cliffs, N.J.: Prentice-Hall, 1954.

Balestrino, Philip. *The Skeleton Inside You*. New York: Crowell, 1971.

Cosgrove, Margaret. *Bone for Bone*. New York: Dodd, Mead, 1968.

Elgin, Kathleen. *The Hand*. New York: Franklin Watts, 1968.

Fichter, George S. *The Human Body*. Illustrated by Ralph E. Ricketts. New York: Golden, 1977.

Fluegelman, Andrew, ed. *The New Games Book*. New York: Doubleday, 1976.

Fryer, Judith. *How We Hear*. Illustrated by George Overlie. Minneapolis: Medical Books for Children, 1961.

Glemsa, Bernard. *The Human Body*. New York: Random House, 1968.

Gruenberg, Benjamin C., and Sidonie M. Greenberg. *The Wonderful Story of Your Body, Your Mind, Your Feelings*. New York: Garden City Books, 1960.

Hindley, Judy, and Christopher Rawson. *How Your Body Works*. Illustrated by Colin King. London: Osborne, 1975.

Joyce, Mary. *First Steps in Teaching Creative Dance to Children*, 2nd ed. Palo Alto, Calif.: Mayfield, 1980.

Kanfiner, Joe. *How We Are Born, How We Grow, How Our Bodies Work and How We Learn*. New York: Golden, 1975.

Keen, Martin L. *The Wonders of the Human Body*. Illustrated by Darrell Sweet. New York: Grosset & Dunlap, 1966.

Lauber, Patricia. *Your Body and How It Works*. New York: Random House, 1962.

McGuire, Leslie. *Susan Perl's Human Body Book*. New York: Platt & Munk, 1977.

Ravielli, Anthony. *Wonders of the Human Body*. New York: Viking, 1954.

Witkin, Kate, with Richard Philp. *To Move, To Learn*. New York: Schocken, 1978.

2

OUR FEELINGS

Four-year-old Oren was teasing his baby sister by standing in front of the TV screen and blocking the picture. Of course, she cried. Oren's father told him not to do that, but Oren continued. Finally, his father took him by the shoulders and gently pulled him away from the TV set. Oren burst into tears. His father, shocked at such an extreme reaction, reasoned with him. "C'mon, Oren, you know I didn't hurt you. I just pulled you away from the TV set so your sister could watch it." Oren's crying intensified. "Oren," his Dad repeated, "you know I didn't hurt you. I barely tapped you!" Oren wailed through his sobs, "You're talking about the body and I'm talking about feelings!"

THE BASICS

In this guide we are talking about a vitally important topic, feelings. How we feel about ourselves, about life in general at any given moment, about other people, and about the events surrounding us, all intertwine to weave the pattern of our everyday lives. In education nothing is more important than feelings, because our feelings greatly determine what and how we learn.

America is experiencing a tremendous upsurge in books and materials about feelings. It is as if we are rediscovering or, in some cases, discovering for the first time, how important feelings are in shaping and shading our life stories. Given this focus on feelings, I am shocked when intelligent people dismiss the feelings of young children. It is distressing to know that many adults still believe that children do not develop feelings until sometime before puberty, perhaps in early adolescence.

Psychologists tell us that human infants begin to express feelings shortly after birth. They respond to pleasure, to a sense of well-being, and to comforting voices differently than they do to distressing, alarming sounds and conditions. From the earliest days of life, human beings develop ways of expressing and dealing with their feelings. Sadly, most adults learn many ways to hide their feelings. Anger, jealousy, disappointment, and grief are often repressed, hidden under layers of socialized behavior which cause people to answer, "Just fine!" when asked, "How do you feel?" even when they have just been fired from a job or have filed for divorce. The new emphasis on expressing feelings, so popular in these days of "Let it all hang out!" and "I'm O.K., you're O.K.," may reverse the patterns of repression perfected by so many people who were taught: "Keep your feelings to yourself!" "Don't wear your heart on your sleeve," "Boys don't cry!" or "Don't be such a baby!" Now we realize that repression is not a healthy way to deal with our feelings.

Although some young children have already learned to hide their feelings, most of them are open in verbal and nonverbal communication. Pouty lip, quivering chin, and trusty blanket to stroke for comfort are some of the characteristics of hurt or sad feelings. Body language is usually easy to understand. You do not need four years of psychology to perceive a child who is slumped in the corner, eyes downcast, hands idle, tuned out of activity in the room. You do not need a Ph.D. in communication to conclude that Amy is happy today when she bounces into the room, flashes you a brilliant smile, hugs her playmates, and kisses a doll. Of course, children do not always express themselves so clearly. People who work with young children must be alert, sensitive, and responsive to all students, familiar with their behavior and their expressions, understanding of their problems and specific situations.

Timmy was going through a difficult time. His family was moving and his father had already left to begin the job in the new city. Timmy was angry at his father for leaving him behind, angry at his mother for being part of the plan, and resentful toward his teacher and classmates. Timmy was lucky to have Barbara Reed for his teacher. She responded to his negative behavior with understanding and compassion. She sat with

Timmy in the rocking chair in the special area of the room labeled "comfort station," and together they rocked and talked. After Timmy shared his feelings with her, Barbara suggested that they write a letter to his dad. He dictated the letter, explaining his sense of abandonment and anger, as well as fear of the unknown in a new city. Timmy put the letter in his lunch box and returned to the group activity; he appeared brighter and more interested in participating than he had before. Timmy's teacher could not change his feeling deserted by his dad, but she had confidence in her intuition and found a way to help him express his feelings and to communicate with his father.

Anyone who works with young children knows how real and valid their feelings are. Anyone who works with young children knows how important the teacher is to the child.

Mitch is in kindergarten. He is a very uptight five-year-old who has learned that

making mistakes is bad and people who make mistakes are dumb. Mitch is afraid to write his name because he is afraid to make a mistake and be dumb. He already thinks he is dumb. His self-image is low. He protects himself from falling even lower in his own sight (and that of others) by not doing anything. Where did he learn this pattern? Can his teacher introduce him to a new curriculum? If you were his teacher, how would you handle Mitch?

As teachers, we have great, even awesome power. We have the power of life and death over our students: life and death of the spirit, of curiosity, of imagination, of self-image and self-confidence, of courage. In the lives of young children, teachers are V.I.P. (Very Important People). Next to parents and grandparents, teachers are probably the most influential individuals in the world of young children.

Before we get carried away with our power, which is formidable, let us pause to acknowledge some other realities. Children have experiences outside the classroom that are not in our immediate range of influence. They have family relationships and home situations that have already taught them ways of thinking and feeling. They come to us with an emotional history. They already carry a knapsack of experiences and memories that have given them the beginnings of a view of the world and of themselves. Do they throw temper tantrums? Do they sulk? Do they shout? Do they pull hair? Do they withdraw? Do they hug? Do they share cookies?

Benjy came into preschool furious at his mother, who refused to let him bring his toy gun. He pouted for almost an hour. Finally, after consistent attempts, his teacher drew out the reason for Benjy's anger. She suggested that he draw a picture of a gun, which he did. He cut it out and played with it for the rest of the morning. When class ended, he tore it up and waved a cheerful goodbye.

Benjy's teacher freely admits that if her first suggestion had not worked, she would have tried something else. If necessary, she would have kept on trying until "something clicked." "We teachers have to be stubborn!" she grins.

The best way to send an idea is to wrap it in a person. Steve Anderson is a talented and gifted teacher who spends his time with

three-year-olds. When David first came to school, he was full of hostility; he struck other children, destroyed games, threw toys, and pulled hair. Steve, a gentle, loving, funny, reassuring person, charges the atmosphere around him with those qualities. Despite David's emotional history and home influences, in just a few weeks, he showed marked changes in behavior. He no longer hit other children or destroyed their toys. His hostility and anger visibly diminished. Today, you could not pick David out of the group as a child with emotional problems. He thawed in the warmth of Steve's influence. He *learned* another way of being and feeling. Whether David behaved differently at home is another question. We would like to think that he did, but many situations and relationships are beyond the teacher's influence.

Often, teachers successfully communicate children's feelings and ideas to parents. I like to think of teachers as *advocates*; children's interests are paramount in their hierarchy of values. Many times a child's home situation improves because of the greater understanding made possible by the teacher.

That teachers also have feelings comes

as a shock to many children. Wendy Wohlstein and her four-year-olds were talking about things that made them sad. When it was her turn, Wendy said, "When someone I really love has to go home, I feel sad." A little later, Danny came to her and said, "Mrs. Wohlstein, that was me you were talking about, wasn't it? Someone you really love has to go home!" "Yes, Danny," she said, "That's true. I'm sad when you go home, but I'm happy because I know I'll see you tomorrow." A few hours later, as the children were leaving for the day, Danny asked her, "Mrs. Wohlstein, are you feeling sad?" "Why?" She had forgotten about their earlier discussion. "Someone you love has to go. I'm going home now!" He comforted her with a hug and reassured her that she would see him the next day.

All the themes in this book are threads that run through the daily fabric of your time with young children. None is more important than feelings. Even if you plan a special emphasis on feelings for a designated time period, know that feelings will be part of your daily curriculum and cannot be relegated to a specific time slot. Life does not permit that kind of organization. Janet Stocker, Director of the School for Young Children in Columbus, Ohio, explained her approach. "We don't set aside special time to focus on feelings, because we deal with feelings every day. We are always ready with art, music, one-to-one talk, group discussion, stories, and games to respond to specific feelings as manifested by the group or by individual children. *Our teachers are always ready!*"

Jean Buker, an experienced and talented early childhood teacher, explains that teachers must not only provide support for children as they experience feelings, many of them *new* feelings, but also give children opportunities to express those feelings in healthy ways. She always has a table of pounding pegs, Playdough, and finger paints for children who need to pound, push, squeeze, and splash in order to work the anger out of their systems. She has a punching bag in the corner for children who need to actively express hostility. Jean introduced the children to these outlets by showing them that she herself felt better when she pounded a few pegs to vent her annoyance at an irritating situation. She "acted it out" by sharing her annoyance with her students, *sharing her feelings*, and then telling them that she was just going to pound some pegs very hard for a few minutes until she felt better. The children were fascinated. After she pounded in the pegs, she rolled some Playdough and slapped it against the table. "Now I feel better. Any time *you* need to pound some pegs or swish some Playdough to get rid of an angry feeling, come right over here." The children learned a few acceptable and satisfying ways to express their feelings.

Jean Buker's "pounding table" and Barbara Reed's "comfort station" are two examples of the ways teachers have designed environments that recognize the importance of feelings in the daily life of young children. Although most school budgets are limited, teachers design their space with originality and imagination. They are scroungers, scavengers, and thieves! They are geniuses!

Traveling around the country, I have seen wonderfully innovative rooms where young children live and learn and grow, rooms with room to express moods and feelings so children feel safe and accepted no matter what their mood may be. I have seen:

Cuddly corners, featuring soft pillows and blankets and huggable teddy bears, for children who need an extra snuggle to make the day.

Alone house, a large cardboard shipping box with a window cut out of it, for the one child sitting inside to be able to look out while retreating from the whirl of group activities.

Silly spot, with a box of wigs, mustaches, beards, and crazy hats, next to a mirror, where children can "mug" when they feel extra silly. A five-year-old girl explained the silly spot this way: "Sometimes you get up feeling like silly beans. Go right to our silly spot and put on a crazy face and make yourself laugh!"

Peaceful place, a small table near a special bulletin board where photos and pictures, mostly nature scenes, are displayed. "The children choose the pictures and add to them whenever they want to," the kindergarten teacher explained. On the table is a sketchbook where children draw lovely designs for others to see. "Whenever you want to get beautiful inside, you can sit at our peaceful-place table and it always

works." A member of the class led me on a tour. He showed me the arrangement of dried leaves and the papier-mâché bird on the table that the children had made for this special place.

Listening chair and *talking chair*—two chairs facing each other in a space apart from the main area of the room. One is labeled "listener"; the other, "talker." Whenever these first graders had an argument or disagreement, they sat in the special chairs and took turns talking and listening to each other until the dispute was settled. Some children nicknamed the chairs "argument chairs"; others called them "make up chairs."

How will you design your environment so that it reflects your recognition of the importance of feelings?

A word of warning: While many of the activities you plan and the experiences you share with children will be addressed to specific feelings and will be successful in encouraging healthy expression and confidence in handling emotional situations, some children have serious problems and will not be easily soothed by a "comfort station" and will not be responsive to your efforts. Tragically, there are children like five-year-old Matty, who will not participate in school activities, not even snack time. She has never smiled or talked to anyone in class. Her teachers feel frustrated and often helpless in trying to break through the gloom that fills Matty. They have talked with her parents and a counselor, but to no avail. Yet they are stubborn and will not give up on Matty.

You are not a psychiatrist, a child psychologist, or a pediatrician. In many cases, a child has been treated by such persons for severe emotional problems but has finally responded to the continuous warmth and persistence of a classroom teacher who, after shooting hundreds of arrows of love, found one to touch the heart.

Theodore Roethke wrote: "Teaching is one of the few professions that permits love."[1] With all the methods and resources available for educational purposes, it is often love that is the best resource of all, and nowhere more needed and appreciated than with young children. When Steve Anderson began working with young children at the Jewish Center in Columbus, Ohio, he said, "I've learned a lot about so many things—the creative process, curiosity, how language develops, imagination, and socialization. But, I've learned the most about the power of love."

Love is probably the most important word for teachers of young children. Examine your own feelings and strengthen your reasons for working in early education, your feelings about yourself and about children. I want to say to students who are preparing for this career: *"If you don't love kids, go into another field!"* The best teachers love children and freely express that love. They are not inhibited about touching, holding, and hugging. They not only say they love but also show their love.

Another necessary quality for teachers who work effectively with young children is *awareness.* You are alert and responsive. You don't miss a thing! You not only know but also act. Because of your influence, you have to take stands. Before modern educa-

tion coined the term "values clarification," teachers clarified values. Your very presence, your words, gestures, and responses define values.

Connie Swain, cofounder of the Community Learning Exchange in Columbus, Ohio, clearly communicated to her first graders that putdowns would never be permitted. No child would ever be allowed to humiliate or insult another child. When Derrick said cruel words to tease Betsy, the whole class froze and looked at Connie with expectant expressions. Connie responded immediately by taking Derrick out of the group for a private conference. The children quietly comforted Betsy until Connie and Derrick returned.

What can children learn from their time with you? No matter what their home environment or family history may be, in your classroom children can learn safety, trust, respect, encouragement, acceptance, fairness, joy, and love. With you, children learn that they are special, unique individuals with many talents and strengths, with interesting thoughts and important ideas.

Because you provide success-oriented experiences and are supportive and responsive, your students develop positive and healthy self-images, confidence, and the freedom and courage to *try* without worry, to *risk* without anxiety, to *explore* and *experiment* without fear of failure or humiliation. Through your guidance and encouragement, children learn to deal with their feelings in healthy ways. They are offered many outlets for emotional expression and the safety to communicate. Because you are considerate of their feelings, sensitive to their moods, and aware of and responsive to their special needs, you will help them to become stronger individuals at peace with themselves and with others.

DISCOVERY TIMES

- Everyone has feelings.
- Some feelings are good, others are bad.
- It is normal for people to have all kinds of feelings.
- It is important to be able to talk about our feelings with our families, friends, classmates, and teachers.
- We can express our feelings in many different ways.
- Our feelings are important, as are the feelings of others.
- Sometimes the way we express bad feelings hurts ourselves and others.

- We can learn healthy ways of expressing bad feelings.
- Everyone reacts differently to a situation. Each of us is unique.
- Even though we are different individuals, we share many feelings and can learn from each other.

SUGGESTED VOCABULARY

happy	eager	nice	kick
sad	impatient	stubborn	hit
glad	mischievous	ashamed	smile
mad	curious	divorced	hug
silly	brave	dead	died
serious	excited	sick	"feel good"
disappointed	nervous	hurt	"feel bad"
angry	calm	surprise	share
afraid	lonely	cry	give
shy	cuddly	laugh	love
scared	friendly	giggle	hate
jealous	unfriendly	tickle	comfort
	affectionate	break	
	mean		

You may be surprised at some of the words on the vocabulary list. Most children know many more words than we think they do. They are ardent TV viewers; they are part of many adult situations that children of earlier generations did not know; they go to drive-in movies, fast-food restaurants, bowling alleys, and miniature golf courses; and they are readers of billboards and cereal boxes.

At a recent movement session improvising various Halloween characters, three-and-a-half-year-old Richie challenged me with this question: "Mimi, do you know how the Incredible Hulk changes?" I admitted that I didn't. "Well," Richie explained, "First he gets very, very *nervous* . . ." Never underestimate the vocabulary of your students. Be ready to be surprised at the words they know how to say, even if they do not know what the words mean.

Sometimes you can help your students change the way they feel by giving them a better word to describe their feelings. One of my young friends was worried about school. "I'm so depressed!" she moaned, "I'm so depressed!" I pointed out that "depressed" is a serious word describing a clinical mental state: "How about saying that you feel 'down in the dumps,' 'blue,' or 'yuk' instead of depressed?" When she came to school the next day, she cheerfully announced: "I think I feel better. Feeling down in the dumps is a lot better than feeling depressed!"

SOME BEGINNING ACTIVITIES

Start with a feeling word. Share your feelings about the word first. "I feel so *happy* today because the sun is shining and we can go outside to play. How do *you* feel today?" This easily opens the way to an interesting, lively discussion of "What makes *you* happy?"

Start with the word "sometimes." "Sometimes" is an excellent word and concept for young children. It helps them discover that feelings change, that when they are having a bad time, it usually passes. "Sometimes" is a very reassuring word. "Sometimes I get so mad at my dog for chewing my good shoes!" was the way one teacher introduced the feeling "mad." That was all she needed to say to encourage her students to join in with their own "Sometimes . . .," which she wrote down for them and displayed on the bulletin board.

Start with a picture or photo. From your own file, choose pictures or photos showing: a close-up of a person's face expressing a specific feeling; a scene that conveys a clearly defined mood (a nature scene, a traffic jam, a playground of children); or dramatic action (two children playing together, a grownup scolding a child, a broken toy and a tearful child, animal pictures). These types of pictures are excellent ways to stimulate discussion and focus on feelings. Children are very imaginative and empathetic and are brilliant interpreters. Such questions as: "What is happening in the picture?" "Why do you think the grownup is scolding the child?" "How do you think the child feels?" and "Let's tell a story about the picture. How shall we start?" encourage children to express their ideas and feelings. It is often easier for them to talk about other people and someone else's toys and to interpret those feelings than it is to talk about their own. Remember, every response a child gives is valid, to be accepted and respected.

Start with an immediate situation (serendipity). The children planned a field trip to a pumpkin farm. On the day of the trip, it rained. Their teacher was the first to articulate disappointment. "I'm so sad that we're not going to the pumpkin farm today." This honest sharing opened the door for the children to express their own feelings of disappointment. After they planned the trip for another day, they decided to do something "very cheerful" to take their minds off the pumpkin farm. They made happy faces out of pumpkin orange paper.

Every day you will have opportunities to respond to group or individual situations that can (if you wish) lead to a focus on feelings. Whether serendipity presents itself by Alan losing his new mittens or Becky telling the class that her grandma had to go to the hospital, if you are alert and responsive, you will have many beginning ideas.

Start with a poem or story. Collect your favorite books and poems and you will find that they are excellent starters for helping children to express their feelings. I watched an outstanding discussion following the reading of parts of *Who's That in the Mirror?* (Polly Berrin Berends, Random House, 1968). The children loved the pictures and responded immediately to the text. The book *Swimmy* (Leo Lionni, Random House, Pantheon, 1963) is filled with fear, wonder, adventure, and affirmation. Florence Parry Heide's *Some Things Are Scary* (Scholastic, 1969) helps children share and even laugh at some of their fears. Poems like Shel Silverstein's "Ridiculous Rose" ("Her mama said, 'Don't eat with your fingers.' / 'OK,' said Ridiculous Rose, / So she ate with her toes!"[2]) encourage children to laugh and think of other silly things. Silverstein's Reginald Clark who is "afraid of the dark" helps children to see that they are not alone in feeling afraid, and nursery rhymes like "The Three Little Kittens" show children that losing things is sometimes "bad news" (to quote a five-year-old) and that finding things is "terrific!"

Start with something weird. Wendy Wohlstein and Rhoda Linder of the Jewish Center in Columbus, Ohio, began a discussion of "happy" and "sad" with their four-year-olds in an original and a dramatic way. This is what happened. Wendy made up her face as a happy face—turned-up lips; big, bouncy eyes; freckles; and apple-red cheeks. She wore lively overalls and a bright shirt. In contrast, Rhoda was a sad sight—lips painted downward; tears on cheeks; drab clothes. Wendy bounced; Rhoda slumped. Wendy wrote a poem that she read to the children first thing in the morning:

> I am so happy,
> I feel so good,
> I only wish that my friend could!
> She is sad. See that tear?

She hates to look in the mirror.
But me—I love it—yes siree!
A happy face is fun to see.
I look around from here to there
to see the kind of face *you* wear.
(Wendy stopped and looked at every child's face.)
Is it sad with a voice like a whine?
Or is it happy, I hope, like mine?
Happy or sad, which are you I say?
Please try to have a happy day!

The rest of the day was filled with activities and discussion about sad feelings and happy feelings.

Start with an argument. Barbara Reed and Jo Ann Hauser had tried so many ways to help their four-and-a half-year-olds at the Brookwood Presbyterian Early Childhood Program in Columbus, Ohio, learn positive ways to settle arguments, but to no avail. Hitting, slapping, pushing, and withdrawing were still the common solutions to arguments. One day Barbara and Jo Ann decided to have an argument in front of the children and, after verbalizing their differences, sit down together and work out an agreeable solution. The children were dumbfounded at the sight of their teachers arguing, and they were visibly relieved when Barbara and Jo Ann sat down together to work out their differences.

When the argument was settled, Barbara and Jo Ann turned to the students for their reactions and feelings. They found that this dramatic way of presenting the children with an alternative model to express feelings was very successful. At the end of the day, one of the more argumentative children admitted to Barbara, "I was sure glad you made up with Mrs. Hauser this morning!"

Start with a puppet or stuffed animal. Young children clap their hands to keep Tinker Bell alive because they believe in fairies, puppet friends, and stuffed-animal classmates. Keep at least one character in the classroom to communicate with the children (through you), one that has a name and feelings and ideas.

With one timid class of very young children who hung back from participation and articulation at the beginning of the school year, the teacher told them that a special new friend had come to visit with them but that the friend was very shy. This friend was hiding behind the tambourine and was afraid to meet them. "Isn't that silly, to be afraid to meet *you*?" the teacher asked. The children were very concerned. "We won't hurt you," one of the children comforted the still unseen friend. "What can we do to make our new friend feel happier?" the teacher asked. "We can wave," another child offered. The group timidly lifted their hands in tiny friendly waves. The teacher peeked behind the tambourine. "Come on," she coaxed, "The children are waving to you. Don't be such a silly willy." She looked at the children, then continued talking to the shy, hidden friend: "They don't have *mean* faces. They have very happy faces." The childrens' faces brightened into smiles. Some were still waving. "Sometimes we're shy, too, aren't we?" the teacher asked. "Oh, yes!" Immediate agreement. By the time the little five-and-dime store toy appeared—a cuddly yellow bird which the children named "Chickie"—they had forgotten their own shyness in their eagerness to reassure Chickie. Thereafter Chickie was a regular member of the class.

TALK TIMES

Children should and must talk about their feelings. They talk about them through pictures, puppets, and pantomime. They talk about them in large groups, small groups, and one-to-one conversations. Talking is valuable in itself. It gives children the chance not only to say how they feel, but also to find others who share those feelings. "Talk Time" reassures children that they are members of the human family and have common experiences. It helps them reach out to each other and develop sensitivity.

When children are eager to talk about something, they are telling you that it is a subject relevant and interesting to them. As a responsive and active listener, you can take the hint and direct their interest into other activities. "Talk Time" leads to art, music, games, stories, dance, plays, improvisations, field trips, and visitors.

In Margie Goldach and Carol Highfield's class of four-year-olds at the Jewish Center in Columbus, Ohio, talking about different feelings spilled over into creative writing and art. The children learned a lot about taking turns and being fair. No one person monopolized the conversation. Each child told about "things that scare me,"

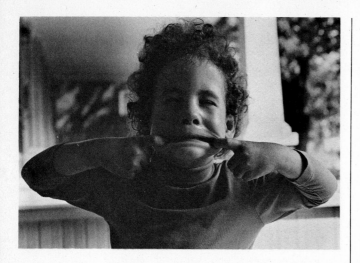

"things that make me angry," "things that make me sad," and "things that make me happy." Their teachers wrote everything they said on large construction paper in a different color for each feeling. The children chose the colors for the four sections. Here are excerpts from the charts revealing children's feelings to parents who were not always aware of them.

Things That Scare Me
Dreams about monsters that eat me (Jason)
Being locked in my room (Michelle)
My mom yelling at me (Elissa)
Godzilla picking up my bed (Nicky)
Being spanked on my tushy (Jennifer)

Things That Make Me Angry
Someone breaking my toys (Nathan)
My brother hitting me (Nicky)
My mom throwing out my barber shop toy (Jamie)
My sister treating me like a baby (Elissa)
My mommy ripping my favorite papers on the way home from school (Joy)
My mom and dad sending me to my room (Jason)

Things That Make Me Sad
My mother not taking me to the store (Monica)
My sister not letting me in her room (Elissa)
My brother not playing with me (Jennifer)
My father not taking me to his office (Jamie)
My brother taking away my toys (Bret)

Things That Make Me Happy
Being tickled (Doug)
Mom and Dad reading to me (Jodi)
Ice cream (Nicky)
Playing with my friends (Yve)
Pretending I'm a kitty (Elissa)

Magic Circle. Many teachers use this approach to talk about important topics.[3] Sitting in a circle on chairs or on the floor, children and teachers discuss thoughts and feelings. If children feel safe in your room, they feel safest in the Magic Circle, where they are encouraged to express their feelings and ideas. Some teachers set aside special times during the week for a Magic Circle session; others use it when the situation warrants.

A list of ways to make people feel happier resulted from a Magic Circle session with a group of kindergartners. Some of the suggestions that were recorded and displayed in a prominent place in the room were:

Ways to Make People Feel Happier
Share your snack (Eddie)
Sing a song together (Eric)
Look out the window together (Roosevelt)
Play with Theodore (the class teddy bear) (Julie)
Pat them (Michelle)

In this case the children not only talked about their own feelings and tried to understand the feelings of others, but also directed their thoughts and energies into compassionate responses. When you see children react this way, you can believe, with Anne Frank, that "people are really good at heart."

Children have so much to say about their experiences and feelings. Even shy children are reassured and encouraged through listening. Give your students many opportunities to talk—to you, to each other, to playthings and puppets. "There, I said it" is the kind of relief many children seem to feel after a talk session. The responses of teacher and classmates are also helpful in sorting out feelings. Through "Talk Time" you are teaching children that expression is healthy, that sharing is better than hoarding, that communicating about feelings is better than developing a sense of isolation and loneliness.

ART TIMES

There is no subject that lends itself to a greater variety of enjoyable art activities than feelings. Feelings flow into colors, shapes, and designs. Here are a few suggestions to start you thinking of your own ideas.

Paper plate faces. Paper plates are just waiting for children to turn them into faces. Children draw features or arrange already-cut out eyes, eyebrows, lips, and noses. The letters C and U are excellent models for drawing eyebrows and lips; the children discover that C's and U's facing up look happy and facing down look sad. Add wool, carpet pieces, shredded paper, or cotton puffs for hair. Add ears and hats. Display all the faces on a bulletin board.

Two-faced paper plate puppets. Turn the paper plate faces into puppets by gluing them to Popsicle sticks, tongue depressors, or cardboard toilet-paper rolls. Make a game out of the puppets by creating faces on both sides of a paper plate—a happy face on one side and a sad face on the other. Tell a story and ask the children to show the happy puppet during the happy parts of the story and the sad puppet during the sad parts. Encourage the children to make up their own stories and use their two-faced puppets to help tell their stories.

Paper plate masks. Cut out eyes, nose, and lips on the plates; punch holes in the plates where the ears should be and string wool through the holes. You have masks ready to be tied on the children's faces. Make up characters, stories, movement, and songs to go with the masks. Paper bags can also be used to make masks.

Feelings pictures. If you are talking about a particular feeling, suggest that your students draw or paint a picture conveying that feeling. Another way to encourage this valuable expression is to ask the children to "Draw a picture about the way you feel right now." (Although you may not like the way some children feel, do not be critical or judgmental.) "Tell me about your picture" or "What is in your picture?" is the kind of response that invites children to interpret their artwork.

A collage. Children cut out at home and in school pictures of happy and sad faces. Divide a board in half: one half for happy faces, the other half for sad faces. The children tack or glue their faces on the appropriate side. A variation of this idea is to cut out a gigantic happy face and a gigantic sad face and mount them side by side. The children attach their photos to the appropriate face. This dramatic display easily leads to discussion, creative writing, pantomime, and other art activities.

ABC's of happiness. Draw or cut out images from A to Z that make you and your students happy. Border the room with your happiness alphabet; bill a board; cover a wall.

Happiness board. Use images that evoke happiness. Add words (the children's words, of course) and create a display. On the display board of a first grade, words and pictures blended together. Written on a bright yellow balloon were these words: "Balloons are always happy because/they are like round pieces of sky."

Greg, age 7

a Sad clown

Flowers and raindrops. A kindergarten class had a long and intense discussion about good and bad feelings. They suggested things that made them feel good, and many children agreed that flowers fell into that category. The topic of rain came up, and one of the children said that when raindrops fell on her face, they looked like tears. The children liked the idea of teardrops and raindrops and decided that raindrops could make them feel sad.

The children then designed beautiful flowers out of colored construction paper and tissue paper, with green wool for stems. They taped their flowers to a strip of green paper on the bulletin board. The children named things that made them feel good, which their teacher wrote down. They taped their thoughts all over the beautiful garden. It looked as if the flowers were talking! Then they cut out raindrops of different colors and taped them to the blue-gray paper on the board. They dictated their sad thoughts to their teacher, and in a little while the sky was filled with teary raindrops and sad feelings.

Encourage children to design their own flowers and raindrops. It would be dull if all flowers and raindrops were the same shape and size.

What "bugs" you. Lynn Thompson and her third graders at Avalon Elementary School in Columbus, Ohio, talk about the things that "bug" them, that annoy and anger them. The children design their own bugs (with help from Lynn, if necessary), color them, and cut them out. They make the bugs large enough to include written comments about what "bugs" them.

Feelings mobiles. Each child has a hanger on which to hang pictures, shapes, and objects expressing different feelings. The most delightful one I saw belonged to 6-year-old Scott, who, with assistance from his teacher, had tied a picture of his favorite TV star (Fonzie), a picture of a black dog, a red lollipop, and a few strands of green wool to his hanger. "What does the green wool mean?" I asked. "That is for grass," he said. "I love grass to roll in when my birthday comes."

Feelings books. With pictures and drawings, children create books dedicated to all feelings or to a specific feeling. Suggest that they add words to their images. If you have extra time, help children decide on a cover

for their book and cut out the cover design as well as the pages that will form the contents. For example, Laura's book of feelings was in the shape of a house because, as she explained, "My house is my happiest thing." Brandy's book was in the shape of a baseball bat because "I'm getting a bat when I'm six and I can't wait! Ten more days!" Stephanie's book was in the shape of a circle. Every page had a circle idea on it: hula hoops, the sun, diamond rings, eyeglasses, and pizza. She smiled and said, "I love circles! See—pierced ears!"

Class book. Using a large greeting card catalogue from which the cards have been removed, begin a class project. Ask the children to cut out pictures that make them feel happy, to paste them in the book, and to write their names next to the pictures or drawings they contribute. These catalogues are large enough to allow for many illustrations from each child. The book remains on display in a prominent place so that children feel happy when they look at the pictures.

A variation of this idea is to put a happy face or sad face on the top of each page in the book. The children then paste pictures appropriate to the page.

Happy and sad tags. This is a variation of name tags. On one side of a construction paper circle, children draw a happy face; on the other side, a sad face. They may want to glue on eyes and mouth with upward curves or downward curves, rather than drawing them. Attach a string so children can wear the circles as tags, on either side, depending on how they feel.

Happy greeting cards. "You feel good when you make someone else feel good!" was one of the ideas a kindergarten teacher wanted to convey to her students. They decided to make "happiness cards," put them in a grab bag, and let everyone pick one. The children enjoyed making the cards. They drew or colored a design that made them feel good and that would also cheer someone else.

A variation of this activity is to have the children pick the name of one of their classmates out of a grab bag (keep it a secret) and then make a card for that child. In addition to the happy design or picture, the card includes the recipient's name. The cards are collected by the teacher, who then calls on one child at a time to deliver the card to the child whose name is featured.

Every child has a chance to deliver "good news." Every child receives a special card with his or her name on it. Add another delightful suggestion: "You can deliver the card any way you want to—hopping, skipping, doing any happy movement!"

Make happy cards for parents and other family members and for friends outside the class.

Happy and sad faces on stones, etc. Children love to create expressive little creatures by painting and drawing happy or sad faces on stones, buckeyes, shells, pom poms, felt scraps, walnuts, buttons, wood chips, and pinecones. Add little hats, hair, and ears. Children enjoy naming and playing with their own special character. Encourage different expressions.

Paint or draw a shape. "What kind of a shape is happiness? Draw it." "What kind of a shape is anger? Paint it." These questions stimulate good talk and expressive art. One first grader responded immediately: "Squiggly." She squiggled on her paper. "Happiness is squiggly." Another child chimed in, "My happiness is square like my room at home."

Shape feelings in clay. Children need the chance to pour their feelings into clay. Five-year-old Sandy worked very hard on his shape. When he finished, he surveyed it with great seriousness. Then, pleased with himself, he explained to his tablemates: "My clay is very sad because my daddy is in Chicago."

Andrea sculpted a small figure which she demolished as soon as it was completed. She kept sculpting it and destroying it, again and again. Finally, she said, "That's my stupid sister who took my doll and won't give it back!"

The best story about this type of art project that I ever heard concerned a preschooler who was angrily pounding a clay shape. He smashed, punched, and beat it. When it was "complete," he looked at it for a while, sighed as if relieved, and asked his teacher, "Can I press it and make a new shape?" "Sure," his teacher said, "But why?" "'Cause I'm finished being angry."

"What color do you feel today?" Young children and their teachers around the country are experimenting with colors and feelings. Talk about the different colors and the feelings they evoke. Again, *all* answers are correct. This is a time for original reac-

tions and freedom of expression. After children interpret different colors, ask them to draw, poster-paint, or finger-paint a picture using one color that expresses their feelings at the moment. Tommy colored a completely brown picture. When his teacher asked him to tell her about the picture, Tommy grinned and replied, "Today is muddy and mud is fun."

Insensitivity can kill anything. A kindergarten teacher directed her students to choose a color that matched their feeling at the moment and draw a picture with that color. One five-year-old chose black and, with thick and heavy strokes, created a grim design. The teacher's face tightened with displeasure. "Stephen, I don't think that's a very nice color. Why don't you pick a more cheerful crayon and do another picture?" Stephen tore up his paper and put his head on the table.

MUSIC TIMES

Music to paint feelings to. Music inspires art. Feelings inspire music. Find music that expresses specific moods and feelings (cowboy lullabies evoke calm; shepherds' flute songs have a lonely sound; Spanish bullfight music flashes the red cape of excitement). Give the children paper and crayons, paints, or finger paints, and instruct them to listen carefully to the music, picture it, and discover how it makes them feel. "Listen and let the music go into your brushes and paint its feelings," one teacher instructed in a poetic way. When there is no fear of failure, no worry about getting something right or wrong, children are absorbed by the musical challenge and often create wonderful works.

Leave time to ask the children afterwards, "Tell me about your pictures. Do they have a story? What were your feelings?" One first grader filled a paper with a light blue color, hardly changing the shade or texture. He told his teacher, "The music made me feel like when I fall asleep and my room turns blue."

Vary the experience. Encourage the children to paint their responses to different kinds of music. None of their pictures will look the same. "Which did you like best? Did you have a favorite?" This question followed an art-music-feelings session in which the children interpreted three kinds of music: very noisy, dissonant, urban jazz; an instrumental rendition of a sad spiritual; and lively marching band music. "I liked the last one," Kent explained. "It made me happy to think I was in a parade. It was happy like a holiday." "I liked them all," Jackie said. "Even the very sad one. I like my sad picture the best as a matter of fact."

Find a musical work that has a variety of mood changes and settle the children down for a longer listening-drawing-feeling session. One kindergarten teacher told her students that they could use larger-size paper and keep working on it for a while as the music and their feelings changed *or* use smaller sheets of paper and take new ones when different kinds of music were introduced. About half the children chose the large sheets and the result was an intriguing combination of design and color. One could really see how the moods and feelings changed. For this session the teacher used Grieg's *Peer Gynt* Suites no. 1, op. 46, and no. 2, op. 55—a dramatic and powerful work with interludes of peacefulness and sudden mystery and excitement. Let me add that this teacher considered *Peer Gynt* one of her favorite pieces of music. And so, I must repeat: Choose the music that you enjoy, whether old favorites or newly discovered treasures.

Familiar songs that evoke feelings. Most young children love songs and singing, and they learn through rhyme, rhythm, and melody. You already know many songs that express feelings as well as provide springboards for further discussion and activities about feelings. Keep track of the songs you and your children enjoy. I visited a kindergarten class where a chart of songs and feelings was prominently displayed. Here are some of the items from that chart.

Silly Songs
   I Know an Old Lady that Swallowed a Fly
   Pop Goes the Weasel
   Boom Boom, Ain't It Great to Be Crazy?

Quiet, Sleepy Songs
   Kum Ba Yah
   Michael, Row the Boat Ashore
   Rain Rain Go Away

Happy Songs
   Here Comes the Sun
   He's Got the Whole World in His Hands
   My Favorite Things
   Puff the Magic Dragon

Original songs that express feelings. Young children make up songs as naturally as they speak. They are very much like Winnie the Pooh, who is always making up hums and songs to match his feelings and moods. For example, here is a happy Pooh hum.

> Sing Ho! for the life of a Bear!
> Sing Ho! for the life of a Bear!
I don't much mind if it rains or snows,
'Cos I've got a lot of honey on my nice new nose,
I don't much mind if it snows or thaws,
'Cos I've got a lot of honey on my nice clean paws!
> Sing Ho! for a Bear!
> Sing Ho! for a Pooh!
And I'll have a little something in a hour or two![4]

This particular hum begs to be turned into a song. One day I experimented with three classes of four-year-olds. They loved the poem and said it made them "feel great!" Each class worked out a different "melody" and turned it into a special song to celebrate the life of a boy or girl. Here is the song that one class created.

> Sing Ho! for the life of a girl!
> Sing Ho! for the life of a boy!
I don't mind if I don't have toys.
I don't mind if I don't make noise.
We have lots of girls.
We have lots of boys.
> Sing Ho! for the girls.
> Sing Ho! for the boys.

For weeks "Sing Ho" was the way those preschoolers expressed happiness.

Drumbeats and heartbeats. Play a heartbeat rhythm on a tom-tom or a bongo drum, child-made or store-bought. If you do not have drums, cookie containers, coffee cans, or tabletops will do. Discuss the music of heartbeats with your students. Our hearts beat faster and louder when we are afraid, excited, angry, or full of energy. Our hearts beat slower and softer when we feel calm, safe, and loved. With your children, practice the different kinds of heartbeats.

Read or tell a story that expresses many different feelings. The children play the drums to accompany the feelings in the story—loud and fast for exciting and scary parts, soft and slow for peaceful, calm parts. Combine the drum rhythms of heartbeats with a round-robin story in which all of the children take turns adding to the action. Add other instruments to the basic drum rhythms.

Many American Indian poems are drumbeat/heartbeat songs that evoke strong feelings. The repetition in Indian poems and chants helps children to learn them easily. As you read them aloud, you cannot help chanting and feeling the pulse of the drumbeat/heartbeat.

Musical instruments play feelings. Either choose one instrument that children pass around and take turns playing, or give the children a chance to choose an instrument from the instruments box to express their feelings.

TEACHER: I feel very bouncy and merry today. Like this. (She played a bouncy rhythm on the drum and passed the drum to a child.)

FIRST CHILD: I feel like marching. (He played a steady drumbeat.)

SECOND CHILD: I feel like a silly rabbit. (She used both hands to create a hopping rhythm.)

THIRD CHILD: I feel lazy and sleepy today. I want to go to bed. (She brushed the drum with her palms.)

A group of first graders responded beautifully to a variation of this activity. The teacher introduced the idea by saying, "How do you feel today? I feel so cheery I could ring a bell." She took a bell from the instruments box and rang it. The children walked over to the box, most of them thinking about their choices, some immediately drawn to an instrument. Douglas lifted the cymbals in the air and clapped them together five or six times. "How are you feeling, Doug?" his teacher asked. "Like a noisemaker. Pow! Pow!" And he added a few more cymbal claps for emphasis.

Music for every feeling. Most of us listen to music that reflects our moods—mellow music for mellow moods, raucous music for those times when we have been sitting too long and our energy bursts forth, sad ballads for those feeling-sorry-for myself times. Sometimes we can pull ourselves out of a down mood by playing music that cheers us up. I have a friend who, whenever he is feeling out of sorts with himself and the world, plays his old favorites: the Kingston Trio and Pete Seeger. They are like old friends who never fail to reassure him and put him in touch with warm and good feelings.

Play a variety of music as background, as the center of attention, or as an important part of an activity. Help the children learn to love music and to appreciate the way it can soothe as well as energize. Share all kinds of music with children. Most young children are open to all kinds of musical experiences, from Beethoven's Ninth Symphony to Hap Palmer and Ella Jenkins.

Music tells a feelings story. This is a challenging activity to accompany a puppet show, pictures, or a story (read or improvised). With the children, decide which instruments they want to use to express the different emotions that will be part of the story or play. "Which instrument shall we play for the sad character? How shall we play the instrument so that it sounds sad?" Work out musical ideas for each character, to be played when that character appears. One kindergarten class made up a story with these characters:

Three bunnies: one shy, one happy, one glum
One mean dog that chased bunnies
Two nice children who chased the dog away

These were the instruments the class chose for each character:

Shy bunny: triangle
Happy bunny: jingle bells
Glum bunny: kazoo
Mean dog: all the percussion instruments
Nice children: all the bells

As the story was told, the children listened with the sharpest ears, ready to express the feelings of the characters the instant they heard their names.

Listen to music, tell a story. This activity involves listening, imaging, and sharing ideas. Choose music that conveys a specific feeling. Ask the children to listen to the music carefully and try to picture what is happening. Make up a story that goes with the music. Expand the idea into movement. Listen, make up a story, and turn it into a dance.

Listen to music, make a wish or tell a dream. Play mystical, dreamy music for the children as they relax and listen with imagination and feelings as well as ears. Many musical selections inspire a peaceful harmony that allows the mind to play with ideas and emotions that are rarely given time for expression. Unless you want the children to listen to words and respond to them, music without words is probably more effective for this experience.

With children of all ages, I share one of my favorite songs from *South Pacific*, "Bali Hai." We relax and stretch and let our minds go with the music. "This is dreamy music. It might make you have a beautiful little dream. This is music to make a wish to. Think of some wonderful wishes you want to make as you listen to this music." The children listen attentively, and when the piece is over, we talk about how they felt. "My dream was sunny, sunny. Nice and warm and toasty," one little girl sighed contentedly. Another child said, "My wish wanted a kite up in the sky." And yet another, "My dream was picking flowers all colors . . ." The children listened to each other attentively and shared important feelings, not always easy to express. We followed the experience with an art project and asked the children to draw pictures of their dreams or wishes.

MOVEMENT AND PLAY TIMES

Peek-a-boo faces. Peek-a-boo is probably the most popular game of very young children. Hide your face in your hands. 1-2-3 peek-a-boo. Open your hands and show your face. Show your happy face. Show another happy face. Another! How about an angry face? Grrr! Another! Invite the children: "Hide your faces. Let's see some sad faces. Now some happy faces."

Mirror, mirror on the wall. This activity is similar to the one above, but the children look in the mirror to see their own facial expressions. Then you can ask, "Which face do you like better, your happy face or your grouchy face? Why?"

Hands show feelings. Happy hands look different from mean hands. Sad hands look different from angry hands. Let hands show feelings. Give children the opportunity to try at least five variations of an idea. *They should never feel that one try at something is the total experience.*

"Turn yourself into . . ." Probably no three words in the English language can spur children into movement faster than these three words. The possibilities are limitless. Here are just a few to start your mind buzzing.

Statues. Angry statues, frightened statues, silly statues. (Remember, more than one version of each.)

Shapes. The shape of happy, the shape of sad, the shape of angry, the shape of scared.

Present Situations. A child who just lost a puppy or who just found a puppy, a child whose friend is moving away, a child whose favorite toy just broke, a child whose grandma is very sick.

The Seven Dwarfs. Bashful, Dopey, Grumpy, Sleepy, Sneezy, Doc, and Happy are excellent characters to help children express feelings. The children do shapes, walks, dances, pantomimes, and exercises for each dwarf. Bashful's dance, for example, contrasts greatly with Happy's dance. Expand the activity into art, music and creative writing. Create seven new dwarfs. Name them, describe them.

Move your shape. Ask questions to expand upon the exercise above. For example: "How does your angry shape (or statue) want to move? Want to walk? How does your angry shape run? How does your silly shape want to stand? Want to sit? How does your grouchy shape want to run? Can you do a grouchy dance? What's your grouchiest walk?" End each idea by asking the children to "shake out," "melt down," or "wiggle out" their sad, silly, or disappointed shapes. Shake a tambourine to give them transition rhythm as they prepare for the next feeling.

"What if" and other movement questions. Think of situations that involve special feelings. The best ones come from the children's own experiences. Ask such questions as:

"What if you were waiting for your friends and they didn't come? What would you do? Show me. How would you look?" (Encourage change of facial expressions as well as body responses.)

"What if your cat had kittens and they were so cute? What would you do? How would you look? Show me.

"What if you were scolded because you wouldn't let your baby sister play with your toys? How would you look? Show me.

"What if you could never change the expression on your face? What if it were always the same no matter what happened?!"

"When you're angry, jump!" and other advice to get things moving. I visited a kindergarten class and saw a handmade poster showing a child having a temper tantrum and jumping in the air. The children had discussed their feelings and had decided on appropriate movements for the different emotions. "If you're angry, jump!" was one of the children's suggestions. The teacher explained that the day a visitor was scheduled but did not appear, the children were angry. They decided to follow their own advice and jumped very hard for about two minutes. They felt much better afterwards! Other suggestions the kindergartners made and followed were: "When you're silly, do a somersault"; "When you're sad, lie down on your tummy"; "When you're happy, skip"; and "When you're afraid, do jumping jacks and shout."

Feel your way around the room. Divide the room into areas for different feelings, and use words and designs as labels. The front of the room can be labeled with a happy face and the word "happy"; the back of the room, a grouchy face and the word "grouchy." Practice by having the children go together to the happy part of the room, and experiment with happy shapes, designs, movements, and faces. Then change to the grouchy side of the room.

We tried this activity with a group of first graders and some of the phrases they used were interesting and surprising:

Grouchy Side	Happy Side
Go away	Hi
Stupid	Wanna play?
I'm not playing with *you*	Wanna dance?
I don't like you	Wanna be my friend?
Dopey	Let's go to the playground
I'm going home	Let's color
That's *mine*	Let's have our snack
	I like you
	Let's make a mobile

If the children understand the activity and show the changes for each feeling, expand the experience by letting them begin individually with the feeling place they choose or by making a grab bag of grouchy and happy faces and having the children grab a card to see which side they start on. Some children do happy things while others do grouchy things. The contrast is dramatic; it can stimulate discussion and increase awareness. After a few minutes, give a change signal. Everyone moves to another place and responds accordingly.

Add feelings. Try a sad place, a silly place, an afraid place. Add art activities to further express the feelings of the place.

Puppet shows and other improvisations. Puppets, stuffed animals, dolls, and toys all have an important place in the rooms and lives of young children. Children often express their feelings more readily through the lips of a puppet or toy animal.

If a situation that involves strong feelings occurs in your classroom, turn it into a puppet or toy animal scene. Initiate the improvisation by taking one of the puppets or toys and expressing its feelings: "Poor monkey is so sad today. What do you think is wrong with him?" The children may respond as themselves or involve other puppets and toys. "Wonder what we can do to cheer him up? Any ideas?" In one kindergarten, a downcast puppet was cheered only when the children made all the other puppets and toy animals sing a silly song to him. They applauded when the downcast puppet perked up and waved his arms gleefully.

Encourage children to play with puppets by themselves or in groups. All ways and approaches are valuable as long as the spirit is one of sharing and cooperating. Remember: encourage, accept, enjoy, guide; do not criticize, humiliate, or reject a child's ideas or expressions.

In a first grade, an ornery child who was having a bad day was encouraged to visit with one of the puppets. He handled the puppet roughly, called him names, and spanked him. "I'm gonna put you in the trash and the trashman will take you," he said. Smack. "You're naughty and you're going in the trash can." The children gathered around and watched, worried but fascinated. The teacher, thinking quickly, introduced another puppet. Her puppet had his head down and was crying. "Sniffle. Sniffle." She sniffled for the puppet until the ill-tempered puppeteer looked up from his drama. "Please don't put my friend in the trash can. I'll never see him again and I love him. Won't you change your mind, please?" The teacher's puppet begged, then whispered in the boy's ear. "If you don't put him in the trash can, we can play together."

The boy thought about it. He visibly softened and said to his puppet, "O.K. You don't have to go in the trash can." His puppet jumped up happily. The children clapped in relief as the two puppets danced together.

Masks and movement. Using masks created in art activities, combine body movement with the feeling expressed by the mask.

Pictures, feelings, movement. Have all the children respond in movement to a picture that expresses a specific feeling. "How does this picture make you feel? Show me." Or give each child a picture depicting a particular feeling and have each child move in response. Turn it into a game by asking the child to "do the feeling of the picture" without showing the picture to the other children. The rest of the children guess the

feeling and only after the guessing is the picture shown.

Music and dance. Play music with strong feeling. Ask the children to listen to the music, decide what feelings are in the music, and follow the feelings of the music with their bodies. Unless you are focusing on a specific body part, encourage the children to use the whole body.

After listening to a portion of *Scheherazade* (Rimsky-Korsakoff), a group of five-year-olds decided that the music was scary, and they did a marvelous dance showing all kinds of fright movement. After it was over, one little girl said, "I have lots of practice to dance about frightened now that my bedroom got moved upstairs."

Animals and movement. Young children truly enjoy animals, and almost any activity with an animal is guaranteed to succeed. "Let's change into cats. Are you a big cat? Little cat? What color are you? Are you sleeping? Rolling a ball of yarn? Sunning by the window? Let's see. How are you cats feeling today? Very shy? Let's see those shy cats. Very mischievous? Full of tricks? Show me what you're doing. Very sad? Why are the cats so sad? What could have happened?"

A group of six-year-olds changed into turtles. They crawled slowly. They were curious. They were frightened and hid in their shells. They slowly stuck out their heads to see if it was safe outside. They walked happily because there was no danger. "How do you feel now? Show me. Tell me." One little boy-turtle lifted his head as he walked on all fours and expressed a feeling on his face that I had not seen before. "Very proud," he glowed. "My turtle isn't afraid of dogs anymore!"

Poems, stories, and movement. Read, tell, and improvise stories and poems that express strong feelings. As the story is related, the children move and interpret it. To help this activity along, I ask the children to suppose that someone came in who did not speak our language. He or she could tell what was happening only by looking at what we were doing. So, even though the story is being told aloud, we also have to tell it with our bodies. Remember, the children do not have to move to every word or part of the story. Highlight the story with movement, unless it is that rare story with a different movement idea in *every* sentence.

Fairy tales like "The Ugly Duckling" by Hans Christian Andersen are full of feelings—loneliness, unhappiness, meanness, finally joy and surprise. Such contemporary stories as Maurice Sendak's *Where the Wild Things Are* invite children to play out feelings of fear and safety. The beloved favorite *Babar* (Laurent de Brunhoff) and all his friends and relations provide action-filled adventures with warmth, courage, disappointment, and happiness.

A. A. Milne's wonderful poem "King John's Christmas" is an example of how easily poetry can inspire movement. King John is not a kind person and he has a very sad life. All he wants for Christmas is an India rubber ball, which he gets at the end through a happy accident. A poem like this gives the children a chance to express sadness, loneliness, meanness, hope, and finally a measure of happiness. Poems and stories help children to learn compassion and sympathy.

Crazy Circle makes you feel. Draw a large circle on the floor with chalk or indicate it with your hands. Tell the children that some strange thing happened to the floor, to that circle, and gave it magical qualities. "Every time we walk into the circle, our feelings change. It's weird! Here we are just having a plain everyday day, and the minute we walk into the circle, pow!"

Most of the children will probably watch you the first time; some may follow you. Say something like, "Hope it doesn't fill with 'silly.'" Encourage the children to do the same: "It's making me do silly tricks"; "It's making me do a cartwheel"; "It's making me fall down. Plop!" The sillies have a wide range of expression! Guide by signaling, "Let's get out of this crazy circle. I'm going to jump out of it." And do so. When all the children are outside the circle, if they do not take up the game from that point, you can suggest something like, "One thing I know. I hope it doesn't turn me *grouchy*. I'm not in the mood to be grouchy today!" as you move toward the circle. Of course, the circle will make everyone act grouchy until you all get out safely.

We finished one Crazy Circle session by "abracadabraing" the circle out of existence. What was intended to be about a ten-minute activity took almost a half hour because the children had so many ideas: "It's turning us into show-offs!"; "That circle is making us into babies. Boo hoo!"; "That circle is changing us into bullies!" They never ran out of ideas, only time. Vary the activity by playing different kinds of music each time the children go into the circle.

Colors, feelings, dances. Use brightly colored pieces of material, scarves, ribbons, yarn, or tissue paper to enrich this multifaceted activity. Colors evoke feelings. Colors make us *do* things and *feel* things. *Red* makes us *stop* what we are doing. *Green* makes us *go*, keep moving. *Green* makes us *grow*. *Blue* makes us *blow* like the wind in the sky. "What else does *red* make you feel? How else does *green* make you feel?" Let the children explore one color at a time. After the children try many ways of moving to a particular color, ask them what kind of music that color wants to dance to. Fast? Slow? Loud? Soft? Choose music that fits their suggestions.

A group of first graders were working out their feelings about *orange*. "It makes me feel whirly"; "Cheerful like birthday parties and orange lollipops"; "Very bouncy"; "Sad because the leaves fall." The ideas expand into movement. Dance a rainbow of feelings!

A kindergarten class decided that *white* was very quiet, soft, sleepy, peaceful. While the class was experimenting with movement ideas, someone knocked on the door. As one of the students answered the door, she put a finger to her lips and said, "Sshhh. We're doing our *white* dance."

Songs and movement. Songs like "If You're Happy and You Know It Clap Your Hands" are popular with children and can be easily improvised. "If You're Happy and You Know It:

> stamp your feet
> blink your eyes
> tickle your nose
> touch your toes
> spin around
> run around
> hop around
> wave your arms
> tap your tummy
> wiggle your toes
> touch the sky
> point your elbows
> hug a friend

Jani Aranow of the Jewish Center in Columbus, Ohio, culminated a day of the "sillies" with an improvised song-movement game inspired by a slip of the tongue. The children were enacting a story about bears that kept climbing trees to find honey and the bees chasing them away. Of course, the bears got honey all over their bodies (make-believe) and at one point, instead of saying, "Get that honey off your face!" someone said, "Get that *funny* off your face!" which resulted in hysterics. Jani, her guitar always handy, improvised this song with the children:

> Get the funny off your face
> O my, how silly you look.
> Look in the mirror, go on, get nearer
> Your face is an awful sight.
> You say I'm wrong,
> Well so is this silly song
> So just get the funny off your face!

The children accompanied the song with crazy faces and silly movements.

VISITORS AND FIELD TRIPS

When planning programs that involve visitors and field trips, remember that you have an entire community as a resource. Draw on people and organizations in your community and you will be delightfully surprised at how many ideas you have to enhance your students' understanding of feelings.

Visitors

Folksinger. This visitor can be a professional artist, grandparent, parent, or other member of the community who has a knowledge of music from a particular culture and the desire to share it. If the visitor wears a costume from the country represented, the session will be even more exciting. Ask your visitor to perform songs that express a variety of basic human feelings that are easy to understand in any language.

Storyteller. Keep this ancient and vital art alive by inviting a storyteller from the community. Ask him or her to tell stories that evoke basic feelings, stories that encourage emotional involvement on the part of listeners, however young. Folk and fairy tales express strong feelings of disappointment, fear, love, hate, cowardice, and bravery. Our children need stories, poems, and songs to help them to *feel* a part of the human family.

Mime. Find a mime through your local arts council, theater departments of area schools, or the entertainment editor of a newspaper. Invite the mime to perform feelings for your children as well as to share exercises in mime that help children learn to articulate emotions with their bodies.

Musician. Invite someone who enjoys playing a musical instrument to share his or her talent and feelings with your children. Explain to the musician that you have been paying attention to feelings and hope that he or she will be able to increase awareness of feelings through music. Violins can evoke great sadness as well as joy; trumpets are exciting and sometimes frightening.

Actor and actress. Trained in expressing feelings clearly and articulately, an actor and actress are excellent visitors. They can demonstrate feelings with voice, facial expression, gestures, and movement. They can show the children that the same words can be said in many ways to express different feelings. Be sure to ask your guests to involve the children.

Dancer. Dance is one of the oldest means of expression and has great emotional impact. Modern, ballet, and folk dancers all have important things to say about feelings with their bodies. Remember to ask your guest to involve the children in the experience.

Baby animal. Baby animals evoke strong feelings of tenderness, protection, and love. Invite a person with a baby animal to visit your class, and be surprised at how much love even your most argumentative child will show.

Clown. Clowns have cheered people for centuries and they can share their art with your children. Every community has at least one clown who enjoys performing for young children and passing on some secrets in the process.

Poet and writer. Most writers and poets are very sensitive to their own feelings and those of others. It is a special challenge and privilege for writers to meet with young children and communicate what they feel and think as they write. Ask your local arts council or community resource program for the names of poets and writers.

Clergy, social worker, psychologist, counselor. Helping people with problems, counseling people in difficult situations, and guiding people in handling their feelings are the main concern of these members of the "helping" professions. Invite them to share with your children the part of their work that is devoted to feelings. These visitors can also reassure the children that they are not alone in their feelings, that all people have good and bad feelings, and that sometimes some people need help in expressing their feelings.

Field Trips

Senior citizens' center or home for the aged. Here is an excellent way for children to learn the happiness of giving to and sharing with others. Children take gifts, perform songs, and visit with the senior citizens. This may become a regular field trip.

Art gallery. Many paintings and sculpture express and evoke deep feelings. Talk with a guide about your special emphasis on feelings and he or she will be sure you find the works that fit your purpose.

Artist at work. Many artists and craftsmen are glad to talk with young children about their feelings and their work. Again, be sure to tell the artist about your special interest in feelings so that he or she can focus on that subject during your visit.

Play, concert, or puppet show. If you are lucky enough to have a special performance for children in your area, make every effort to have your class attend. Live performances are enriching experiences for children on many levels, especially in the way they help develop empathy.

Community center, recreation center, or "Y." This experience gives children a chance to see people of all ages doing things that make their lives happier. When we learn new skills, develop our talents, work with others, and strengthen our bodies, we are engaged in positive activities that enable us to have fuller lives. Learning, doing, and enjoying are excellent ways to ward off feelings of frustration, loneliness, and despair.

NOTES

1. Theodore Roethke, *Straw for the Fire* (New York: Doubleday, Anchor, 1974), p. 205.
2. Shel Silverstein, "Ridiculous Rose," *Where the Sidewalk Ends* (New York: Harper & Row, 1974), p. 63.
3. See the work of William Glasser for his innovative contributions to class discussions, as described in his book, *Schools Without Failure* (New York: Harper & Row, 1969).

4. A. A. Milne, "Expedition to the North Pole," *The World of Pooh* (New York: Dutton, 1957), p. 104.

SELECTED BIBLIOGRAPHY

Many books deal with feelings. This selected bibliography includes new books as well as books that have been enjoyed in classrooms for many years. Most of them should be read over and over again, discussed, and expanded upon.

Anger and Jealousy

Bigelow, Robert. *Stubborn Bear*. Illustrated by Wallace Tripp. Boston: Little, Brown, 1970.

Carle, Eric. *The Grouchy Lady Bug*. New York: Crowell, 1977.

Clymer, Ted, and Miska Miles. *Horse and the Bad Morning*. Illustrated by Leslie Morrill. New York: Dutton, 1982.

Craig, M. Jean. *The New Boy on the Sidewalk*. Illustrated by Sheila Greenwald. New York: Grosset & Dunlap, 1967.

Dickinson, Mary. *Alex and Roy*. Illustrated by Charlotte Firmin. New York: Dutton, 1982.

Kraus, Robert. *Whose Mouse Are You?* Illustrated by José Aruego. New York: Macmillan, 1970.

Lipkind, William. *Finders Keepers*. Illustrated by Nicolas Mordvinoff. New York: Harcourt Brace Jovanovich, 1951.

Malloy, Judy. *Bad Thad*. Illustrated by Martha Alexander. New York: Dutton, 1980.

Mayer, Mercer, and Marianna Mercer. *Mine!* New York: Simon & Schuster, 1970.

Ness, Evaline. *Fierce the Lion*. New York: Holiday House, 1980.

Preston, Edna Mitchell. *The Temper Tantrum Book*. Illustrated by Rainey Bennett. New York: Viking, 1969.

Sendak, Maurice. *Where the Wild Things Are*. New York: Harper & Row, 1963.

Sharmat, Marjorie Weinman. *Grumley the Grouch*. Illustrated by Kay Choaro. New York: Holiday House, 1980.

Simon, Norma. *I Was So Mad!* Illustrated by Dora Leder. Chicago: Albert Whitman, 1974.

Tester, Sylvia Root. *Feeling Angry*. Illustrated by Peg Roth Haag. Chicago: Childrens Press, 1976.

Udry, Janice May. *Let's Be Enemies*. Illustrated by Maurice Sendak. New York: Harper & Row, 1961.

Viorst, Judith. *I'll Fix Anthony*. Illustrated by Arnold Lobel. New York: Harper & Row, 1969.

Zolotow, Charlotte. *The Hating Book*. Illustrated by Ben Schecter. New York: Harper & Row, 1969.

Loneliness and Fear

Alverson, Charles E. *Bears Don't Cry*. Illustrated by Ib Ohlsson. New York: Norton, 1969.

Bograd, Larry. *Lost in the Store*. Illustrated by Victoria Chess. New York: Macmillan, 1981.

Carrick, Carol. *Lost in the Storm*. Illustrated by Donald Carrick. New York: Seabury, 1974.

Chorao, Kay. *Lester's Overnight*. New York: Dutton, 1977.

Clifton, Lucille. *Amifika*. Illustrated by Thomas Di Grazia. New York: Dutton, 1977.

Cohen, Miriam. *Jim Meets the Thing*. Illustrated by Lillian Hoban. New York: Morrow, Greenwillow Books, 1981.

Conford, Ellen. *Eugene the Brave*. Illustrated by John Larrecq. Boston: Little, Brown, 1978.

Delton, Judy. *The New Girl at School*. Illustrated by Lillian Hoban. New York: Dutton, 1979.

Gackenbach, Dick. *Harry and the Terrible Whatzit*. New York: Seabury, 1977.

————. *Little Bug*. Boston: Houghton Mifflin, Clarion Books, 1981.

Hawkesworth, Jenny. *The Lonely Skyscraper*. Illustrated by Emanuel Schongut. New York: Doubleday, 1980.

Hoff, Syd. *A Walk Past Ellen's House*. New York: McGraw-Hill, 1973.

Kuratome, Chizuko. *Helpful Mr. Bear*. Illustrated by Kozo Kakimoto. New York: Parents Magazine Press, 1966.

Lisker, Sonia O. *Lost*. New York: Harcourt Brace Jovanovich, 1975.

Montresoi, Beni. *Bedtime!* New York: Harper & Row, 1978.

Pinkwater, Manus. *Around Fred's Bed*. Illustrated by Robert Mertens. Englewood Cliffs, N.J.: Prentice-Hall, 1976.

Rivers, Kay McClanahan. *Jill Wins a Friend*. Chicago: Child's World, 1974.

Rockwell, Anne, and Harlow Rockwell. *Sick in Bed*. New York: Macmillan, 1982.

Sawer, Paul. *New Neighbors*. Illustrated by Mark Gubia. Milwaukee: Raintree, 1978.

Scott, Ann H. *Sam*. Illustrated by Symeon Shimin. New York: McGraw-Hill, 1967.

Thaler, Mike. *Moonkey*. Illustrated by Guilio Maestri. New York: Harper & Row, 1981.

Vogel, Isle-Margaret. *Don't Be Scared Book*. New York: Atheneum, 1974.

Waber, Bernard. *Ira Sleeps Over*. Boston: Houghton Mifflin, 1972.

Wells, Rosemary. *Timothy Goes to School*. New York: Dial, 1981.

Wezel, Peter. *The Good Bird*. New York: Harper & Row, 1964.

Zolotow, Charlotte. *Janey*. Illustrated by Ronald Himler. New York: Harper & Row, 1973.

Love, Acceptance, and Responsibility

Bauer, Caroline. *My Mom Travels a Lot*. Illustrated by Nancy Parker. London: Warne, 1981.

Bornstein, Ruth. *Little Gorilla*. New York: Seabury, 1976.

Chorao, Kay. *Molly's Moe*. New York: Seabury, 1976.

Dunn, Phoebe, and Iris Dunn. Words by Judy Dunn. *Feelings*. Mankato, Minn.: Creative Educational Society, 1971.

Fatio, Louise. *The Happy Lion's Treasure*. Illustrated by Roger Duvoisin. New York: McGraw-Hill, 1970.

Flack, Marjorie. *Ask Mr. Bear*. New York: Macmillan, 1932.

Hoban, Russel. *The Stone Doll of Sister Brute*. Illustrated by Lillian Hoban. New York: Macmillan, 1968.

Hughes, Shirley. *David and His Dog*. Englewood Cliffs, N. J.: Prentice-Hall, 1978.

Knotts, Howard. *The Summer Cat*. New York: Harper & Row, 1981.

Larranaga, Robert D. *Sniffles*. Illustrated by Patricia Seitz. Minneapolis: Carolrhoda Books, 1973.

Miles, Betty. *Around and Around—Love*. New York: Knopf, 1975.

Minarik, Else Homelund. *A Kiss for Little Bear*. Illustrated by Maurice Sendak. New York: Harper & Row, 1968.

Ross, David. *A Book of Hugs*. New York: Crowell, 1980.

Rylant, Cynthia. *When I was Young in the Mountains*. Illustrated by Diane Goode. New York: Dutton, 1982.

Steig, William. *Caleb and Kate*. New York: Farrar, Straus & Giroux, 1977.

————. *Sylvester and the Magic Pebble*. New York: Dutton, 1969.

————. *Tiffky Doofky*. New York: Farrar, Straus & Giroux, 1972.

Viorst, Judith. *Alexander and the Terrible, Horrible, No Good, Very Bad Day*. Illustrated by Ray Cruz. New York: Atheneum, 1972.

Williams, Margery. *The Velveteen Rabbit*. Illustrated by William Nicholson. New York: Doubleday, 1922.

Zolotow, Charlotte. *Say It!* New York: Morrow, Greenwillow Books, 1980.

————. *William's Doll*. Illustrated by William Pène du Bois. New York: Harper & Row, 1974.

Death

Borach, Barbara. *Someone Small*. Illustrated by Anita Lobel. New York: Harper & Row, 1969.

Brown, Margaret Wise. *The Dead Bird*. Illustrated by Remy Charlip. Glenview, Ill.: Scott, Foresman, 1958.

Carrick, Carol. *The Accident*. Illustrated by Donald Carrick. Boston: Houghton Mifflin, Clarion Books, 1981.

Viorst, Judith. *The Tenth Good Thing About Barney*. Illustrated by Erik Blegvad. New York: Atheneum, 1971.

White, E. B. *Charlotte's Web*. Illustrated by Garth Williams. New York: Harper & Row, 1952.

Zolotow, Charlotte. *My Grandson Lew*. Illustrated by William Pène du Bois. New York: Harper & Row, 1974.

Teacher Resources

Ashton-Warner, Sylvia. *Spearpoint*. New York: Knopf, 1972.

————. *Teacher*. New York: Simon & Schuster, 1963.

Buscaglia, Leo F. *Love*. Thorofare, N. J.: Charles B. Slack, 1972.

Conroy, Pat. *The Water Is Wide*. Boston: Houghton Mifflin, 1972.

Dennison, George. *The Lives of Children*. New York: Random House, 1969.

Herndon, James. *How to Survive in Your Native Land*. New York: Simon & Schuster, 1971.

————. *The Way It's Spozed to Be*. New York: Simon & Schuster, 1968.

Holt, John. *How Children Fail*. New York: Dell, 1970.

————. *How Children Learn*. New York: Dell, 1970.

————. *What Do I Do Monday?* New York: Dutton, 1970.

Kohl, Herbert. *36 Children*. New York: New American Library, 1973.

————. *Open Classroom*. New York: Random House, 1970.

Leonard, George B. *Education and Ecstasy?* New York: Delacorte, 1968.

Lopate, Phillip. *Being With Children*. New York: Doubleday, 1975.

Moustakos, Clark. *Teaching Is Learning*. New York: Ballantine, 1972.

Postman, Neil, and Charles Weingarten. *Teaching As a Subversive Activity*. New York: Delacorte, 1979.

Stuart, Jesse. *To Teach, To Love*. New York: World, 1970.

3

OUR UNIQUENESS

I am a nice nice boy
More than just nice,
Two million times more
The word is ADORABLE.[1]

THE BASICS

Think for a minute. Who are you? Do your features, feelings, intelligence quotient, imagination, body coordination, and personality add up? Does the sum of all your parts equal you? Despite social security number, zip code, and license plate, you are not so easy to identify. You are more than your fingerprints and dental structure. You are more elusive than your image in a photograph.

Though people may say you are "the image" of some near or distant relative, you are not that person. Sometimes you may share thought or behavior patterns with groups of people that fit a statistical study, but there are other aspects of you that will never fit a study. True, as we grow older, we give up much of our individuality to conform to society's expectations, but we still defy science to explain a single person. It is to help you help your children to cherish their individuality, even as they become more socialized, that this guide is being written.

Nowhere in human evolution has there been another person exactly like you, with your combination and arrangement of qualities, traits, and characteristics. Even identical twins are not absolutely identical. Their thoughts, their special way of looking at the world, their responses to people and situations, their dreams, fantasies, fears, and foibles are their own.

You are a special person. Because you have been born into the human family, you are gifted and talented. You have amazing strengths. You have seeds of interests waiting to be nurtured. You have abilities and skills waiting to be developed. You are bursting with potential! You have a knapsack of experiences, ideas, beliefs, and natural resources waiting to be opened. When you feel good about yourself, you glow with a special light that brightens and warms others. When you feel down in the dumps, inadequate, incompetent, untalented, your light diminishes. The world around you droops and cools.

As you are, so you teach. It is important that you reaffirm your belief in yourself: your own history, your own map of the journey of your life, your own ability to grow and learn, your own light that can warm yourself and others. It is important that you take time to remember the wonder of being human.

By the time most children come to preschool or nursery school, they have

new step, we were cheered on. Our talk turned to song; our walk, to dance. We were delighted with our drawings, our toys, our make-believe games. We were proud of our accomplishments and discoveries. We were full of courage and mighty strength. We were giants. We could see through closed doors, cause rain, and play with imaginary friends.

Because healthy children learn that they are special and wonderful, they can see beyond themselves and appreciate the special qualities of others. Because they have been encouraged and praised for their works, they can praise others. The commandment "Love your neighbor as yourself" assumes that first you learn to love and cherish yourself.

We live in a difficult and complex world. National and international tensions are constant sources of anxiety. The security

made astonishing strides in language usage and comprehension, physical coordination, and social awareness. They follow directions, initiate their own experiences, and are curious about the world around them and about the most wonderful world of all—themselves.

We are most unique and original when we are very young. In those early years, we have not yet learned what is "in," what is trite, what are the norms of our culture and the expectations of our society. When we were very young, we were honest and direct. We did not see the invisible clothes on the foolish emperor, even though the big people around us thought they did or should.

If we were lucky enough to be healthy and beloved children, our early years were years of enchantment, when we learned to love the sound of our own names and to bask in the warmth of a friendly universe. Celebrations were not limited to a few set calendar days; they were daily occurrences. When we said a new word, the people in our lives smiled and clapped. When we took a and order provided by traditional institutions are lost as mobility increases, families are disrupted, and communities grow. Individuals seek unhealthy remedies for feelings of alienation and rootlessness. Many of our young children come from broken homes and carry their own knapsacks of disappointments and sorrows.

You could conclude that trying to teach the lessons of love and wonder in such difficult times is like trying to grow flowers in cement. But rather than becoming discouraged, let us pledge greater commitment to this challenge. It is probably more important now than ever before in history that people learn to love themselves and to love one another.

What is the "wonder of me" all about? It is about celebrating ourselves, enjoying our skills and powers, sharing our ideas and works proudly and joyfully, rejoicing in our unique talents, and translating this feeling about the immense importance of each child into concrete experiences.

Mrs. A. Joseph Marsh wrote a letter to her daughter who was about to begin a teaching career. These excerpts are excellent examples of philosophy translated into behavior:

Perfume the classroom with the sweet smell of success. Be kind to your kids. Show joy at even their small achievements. Sprinkle each day with praise—sincere praise that can withstand a child's windowpane vision of the adult heart. Accent the positive—the good try; the perhaps slow but steady progress—rather than poor work on a task . . . Give your children . . . glittering souvenirs. Keep their senses awake. Take them on walks and encourage them to look . . . listen . . . touch . . . which brings up the specialness of each child. Not only does every child have unique gifts and attributes, but the same child sometimes seems to be several children—or at least several different ages in the same day. But, then, adults are like that, too. Don't you feel much more mature in some situations than others? I do. And, when I'm not feeling well, I just know I'm tiny and positively helpless . . . I'm looking forward to hearing about your first weeks of teaching. Mine, I know, were full of frazzle. And, later, when I told my kids that, like them, I had been nervous and worried about the new situation, they couldn't believe it. Well, at least I let them know I'm human. Hope I let them know, too, that I cared about them. For caring, as I'm sure you've guessed, is what this letter is all about.[2]

Because you care so deeply about each of your children, everything you do will be stamped with that commitment. What will your students learn about themselves from you? How will you teach them?

A popular bumper sticker reads: "I Lost It." Another bumper sticker boasts: "I Found It." I have always wondered what it was that we lost, and I think it has something to do with this feeling of wonder and worth, of awareness and appreciation for ourselves and others. Let us help our children glue bumper stickers to themselves that shout: "We Never Lost It!"

DISCOVERY TIMES

- Each of us is a very important person with unique personality, interests, habits, physical characteristics, talents, and wishes.
- Every day we learn something new about ourselves.
- We do things we have not done before; we learn new skills; we try different challenges.
- We are proud of our accomplishments and happy when our classmates share their interests and achievements with us.
- We are lucky to be able to enjoy our own imaginations, ideas, and questions. We have wonderful minds.
- We are capable of great learning and understanding.
- Every day we should celebrate our unique talents and appreciate and respect ourselves and others.
- We learn that through practice, difficult things become easier and obstacles can be overcome.

SUGGESTED VOCABULARY

me	birthday	different	share
myself	magic	strong	celebrate
I	special	proud	surprise
you	terrific	smart	congratulate
we	interesting	clever	thank you
us	good	curious	please
names	wonderful	learn	how nice
idea	funny	understand	I can
imagination	beautiful	grow	see
boy	handsome	question	hear
girl	pretty	wonder	touch (feel)
people	adorable	respect	smell
person	cute	laugh	taste
human being	great	appreciate	know
	important	like	think

The above list includes many words of praise because the words that children hear and see contribute to the climate of their environment. Elizabeth Hunter reported children's responses to a questionnaire by the Association for Childhood Education International on their feelings about themselves, their teachers, and their parents. Here are some answers to the question "What are some things that people in your school (teachers, principals, etc.) do to help you feel good about yourself?"

Don't yell a lot, love us, and say "Thank you!" when children
    do nice things
I feel good when you say I'm a good person
Compliment me on something I did
Put my work on the bulletin board
Treat me like I'm important
Be kind
Listen to us
Have fun with us
Respect us
Care about us
Treat us as individuals
Tell children you love them [3]

Words are not just sounds. They represent things, events, experiences. They have power and influence. They can change our mind or our mood. Remember the special words that Charlotte spun in her web to save Wilbur's life. If you want children to learn to value themselves and others, surround them with words that convey those messages, words that say: You're safe; try again; don't worry; you're doing fine; share that with us; we're glad to have you in our class; you're important; aren't we all lucky to have each other and learn from each other.

Of course, there will be unpleasant times in your classroom. Children fight with, insult, and hurt each other. Sometimes you may feel exasperated; your temper will be short. Your supply of kindness and patience may be at rock bottom. However, children survive those times if they are infrequent.

Introduce words of praise regularly and you will find that the stormy times become rare. "The wonder of me" is a lesson learned only through a living vocabulary.

SOME BEGINNING ACTIVITIES

Children learn from everything you do. Sometimes, what to you is insignificant may make all the difference in a child's day. Barbara Kienzle, who teaches a "family group" class of children ranging from kindergarten to third grade at an alternative school in Columbus, Ohio, put it beautifully when asked what activities she initiates with her students to convey "the wonder of me": "We get in the habit of sharing our appreciation all the time—for things the kids do, make, show, tell, fix, help. It's just part of everything that goes on."

As you become more conscious of how "the wonder of me" can be added, like sugar and spice and everything nice, to whatever you are doing, you will no longer need these starters.

Begin at the beginning. At the beginning of your time together, greet each child in a special way; note something special about each of them.

> Come in, Sam. I see you have a haircut today.
> Good morning, Debby. I like your Donald Duck bracelet.
> Hi, Bill. You're standing up so straight.

Start with taking attendance in a special way. While visiting the Jewish Center in Columbus, Ohio, I heard wild cheers coming from the multipurpose room. I hurried to see what was taking place. Judy West, the teacher, was taking attendance. As each name was called, the child ran, cheered on by the others, to the wall, touched it, and ran back. The children were not racing; they were showing what good runners they were as a way of saying "present." They began their day feeling good! Other classes start the day as each child responds with his or her favorite color, TV show, word, and animal.

Start with a song. Teachers like Gwen Marston, who works in area schools in Flint, Michigan, improvise everything into a song that celebrates children.[4] "Good Morning to You" evokes wide smiles as each child's name is featured: "Good morning to Bobby," "Good morning to Joey," "Good morning to Yolanda," and so on around the room.

Start with a book. Two of my favorite examples of books that start children thinking about their unique selves are Leo Lionni's *Frederick* (Pinwheel, 1973) and Robert Kraus and José Aruego's *Leo the Late Bloomer* (Simon & Schuster, Windmill, 1971). Combining outstanding illustrations and texts, these books help children develop awareness and appreciation of their abilities and their growing process. Frederick the mouse gathers bright words and warm images for cold winter days. He is a poet. Leo, who never does anything right, grows in his own time. As he blooms, he discovers that he can write, read, draw, and eat neatly.

All of our children are Frederick and enjoy the challenge of gathering words to brighten our days. And all of our children bloom in their own time. After one of our first graders wrote a delightful poem about a turtle, he said, "Just call me Frederick!" (See the bibliography at the end of this guide for further suggestions.)

Start with taking photographs. Jeanette Bosworth, who works in the Franklin County preschool program for the mentally retarded in Ohio, says that she would not teach young children without a camera. On the first day, she takes pictures of every child in the classroom and tells them, in a dramatic way, that they are important and special people. More on photographs later.

Start with a riddle. This kind of game helps children recognize and pay attention to each other in positive ways. "I'm thinking of a person in our class who just loves playing in the sandbox better than anything in the world!" Or "I'm thinking of a person in our class who just got beautiful new glasses." Or "I'm thinking of a person in our room who tells funny stories about his baby sister."

Start with a special name tag. Instead of giving the children the traditional square white name tag, let each child choose a name tag from a box of different shapes—animal, flower, circle, triangle—and decorate it. From the beginning, you are saying that we are all different; we all have our own special likes and dislikes, shapes and sizes. Even our name tags reflect our diversity and individualism.

Start with highlighting a different child each week. This year-long activity is an important component of such humanistic teaching systems as the Workshop Way, developed by Sister Grace Pilon, and of many teachers' best projects all around the country. Simply described, it is a way of giving every child special recognition and attention, over and above daily awareness and appreciation. Each week, a different child is the "Child of the Week." Many activities celebrate the special child. For example:

A bulletin board is devoted to the child, who may bring in pictures, photos, and souvenirs.

The child wears a hat, badge, name tag, shirt, or belt made especially for the occasion.

The class interviews the child and asks prepared as well as spontaneous questions. Sometimes the teacher pulls together the information from the interview and creates a pictograph about the child. Sometimes the class makes a collage about the child, based on the interview conducted earlier.

The child picks a game for the class to play, a song to sing, and a special recess activity.

The child starts as leader in a game of follow-the-leader.

The child picks the story to be read at story time.

Children make up a song, dance, game, story, or poem about or for the child.

The child teaches a song, dance, or game. The child tells a story.

The child chooses a title to headline his or her name that week. An example comes from Linda Myer and Kathy Carter's primary class at Worthington Hills elementary school in Worthington, Ohio, where one of the special children wanted to be known as *Patty Barker: Future Teacher*.

Classmates write special notes, letters and paint pictures for the child.

To culminate the week of activities, a party is given by the class to salute the child, and families and friends are invited. The child's bulletin board, collage, and crafts are featured. Songs, dances, and games are shared.

The special child can be selected in several ways. Few of the teachers I spoke with chose children in alphabetical order. As one teacher explained, "Kids with last names that start with T's and S's are always last for life when you use alphabetical order." She used a grab bag of blank papers, except for one paper that had a beautiful design on it. The child who picked the paper with the design was the next "Child of the Week."

Kathy Carter and Linda Myer, who exemplify team teaching at its best, explained that they select the child, with an exciting ceremony, by drawing the name out of a hat or finding it magically written on the board. "This way," Kathy said, "we're not confined to a choosing system that doesn't give us flexibility. Sometimes a specific child will really *need* the extra attention the week gives. We want to be able to use the project to help those kinds through difficult times. Everyone gets a turn!" Kathy and Linda send home a list of the activities for the child's special week and invite families to cooperate and contribute stories, pictures, and photographs.

Note: Save a week for yourself and join the many teachers who enjoy being the V.I.P. of the week.

TALK TIMES

When children feel secure and cared about, they are avid talkers. "The wonder of me" is a continually fascinating topic for young children as each day reveals change and growth, new accomplishments, new understandings. Remember, "Talk Time" inspires art, music, dance, games, and stories.

Imaginative questions. Felicity Boxerbaum and Connie Swain, in team teaching primary grades at Worthington Hills elementary school in Worthington, Ohio, like to begin "Talk Time" with questions like: "Which are you more like: an ice cream or a pickle?" and "Which are you more like: an ocean or a mountain?" Andrew answered the second question this way: "I'm more like an ocean 'cause an ocean changes a lot—sometimes calm, sometimes mad. That's me."

One of the most popular topics of conversation with young children is: "When I was a baby . . . Now I . . ." Most of the time, young children like to feel big: "I can do this! I can do that!" Comparing themselves to babies or remembering when they were babies and enjoying their present achievements is always exciting: "When I was a baby, I couldn't walk. Now I can walk."

This topic is an excellent movement game that will be described later in the guide.

All the things that I can do. This is another source of delightful conversation. In one kindergarten the teacher added to a list that already covered two boards. Each day a few items were added as the children talked about them. This idea, as do all the others, spills over into art, music, movement, and drama. Each day provides opportunities to help children celebrate their abilities, differences, and unique qualities through talking—one to one, in small groups, and with the whole class.

Celebrate our marvelous imaginations. Start talk sessions with observations such as these. *Tad*: "We can pretend we're a fish, but can a fish pretend he's us?" *Douglas*: "We can pretend to be a robot, but robots can't pretend anything." *Jeffrey*: "We can pretend we're monsters, but monsters can't pretend to be me."

Dreams. I visited a kindergarten in an "open" school and found the children busy with an array of activities. Three children sat in a cardboard playhouse and talked softly. I listened for a few minutes as they told each other about dreams. Dreams are an important part of "the wonder of me." Adina told about a terrible nightmare she had the night before. "What was it about?" the others asked. "I dreamed that an elephant ate my sandwich!"

When your days are full of "Talk Time," you will find much to laugh about, care about, and share if you are alert and involved. You will have many opportunities each day to help children celebrate their countless "wonders." Talking about them is an excellent way to begin.

Be sure to encourage all of the children to talk. Sometimes a few children who are more verbal than the others may dominate the conversation. *Taking turns* is an excellent way to give each child a chance to talk. So is *calling names*: "Bobby, what was *your* dream about?" (Always leave room for reluctance.) "If you can't think of a real one, make one up."

I will never forget Danielle, who had nothing to contribute when she was called on to tell what she did on the weekend. Her teacher gave her the option of making something up. "I can't think of anything that really happened," Danielle explained. Then her face lit up, "But here is a made-up story . . ." She told a wonderful story about her dog (she doesn't have a dog) having three beautiful puppies. When she finished, one of the children said: "Danielle, your made-up story was good." "What do we call that power to make up stories?" their teacher asked. "Imagination!" shouted an enthusiastic student, who tapped his forehead happily.

Word gathering. The message of this "Talk Time" is: "Oh, my! We know so many words!" Think of it. Even your youngest children know (understand) words for things in the room and outside, things in their houses, people in their families, classmates, and animals. Talking about all the words we know leads to writing them, collecting them in "word boxes" and celebrating them in posters, collages, stories, poems, and songs. Part of our wonder is language, a dynamic process.

ART TIMES

Measurement charts. One of the favorite activities of young children is growing, and nothing pleases them more than to measure

that process. Tape a long piece of white paper to the wall. Measure the height of each child and mark it with crayon or flow pen. Write or have the children write their names above their height lines. Add a design! Leave enough space between each line so that the children can decorate their heights. Be sure to put the date on the chart.

Repeat at a later date. Have the child stand next to the original line and draw a new line next to it, or start a fresh piece of paper that is attached to the first chart.

See Guide 13 for more measuring ideas.

What's in a name? Children love their names; anything that has to do with their names is a popular activity. Give each child a large piece of construction or drawing paper. Write or have the children write their names on the papers. Be sure the names stand out clearly. The children decorate their name posters by drawing pictures or designs and by cutting out and pasting pictures or words to the paper. Encourage them to draw or cut out pictures of things that mean something special to them, so the poster is a kind of personal collage. The children can also add photos of themselves to the poster. Join the activity and celebrate your name.

Silhouettes. This popular project celebrates the faces of the children in your room. Tack white paper to the wall or board. Each child sits about six inches from the board. With a flashlight, slide projector, or opaque projector, throw light on the board and cast a shadow of the child's head on the paper. Trace the outline. If the children are able, give them a turn to trace around the shadow and outline the head on the paper. Cut out the silhouette. Each child is delighted with the result.

Teachers like Betsy Distelhorst of Columbus, Ohio, encourage their students to choose any color construction paper they like as the background mat for their silhouettes. Black and dark blue are especially effective. Paste the silhouette on the paper and you have a beautiful design of each child's head to present as a gift to the family or to display in the room.

Teachers like Vickie Dove use the silhouette as the center of a collage of magazine pictures that tell about the child's favorite activities, foods, places, and relationships.

Self-portraits. Bring in an assortment of mirrors to be placed *carefully* on the ledge against the board or on shelves, or bring in a large dressing-room mirror. Invite the children to study themselves carefully and notice their own features.

Give out large pieces of paper and crayons or paint, and ask the children to color or paint pictures of themselves, self-portraits. Add names. Display all the self-portraits.

Dawn Heyman's third graders at McGuffey School in Columbus, Ohio, colored self-portraits but did not include skin color. This troubled Dawn, who cares deeply that children learn to love, respect, and accept themselves. She sat down with Audrea, with whom she has an especially close and loving relationship, and encouraged the child to find a color to match the "lovely, soft brown color of your skin." As they looked for the crayon that most closely matched Audrea's skin color, Nathan watched intently, then asked, "Miss Heyman, you wouldn't make fun of somebody's skin, would you?" Before she could answer, Nathan almost interrupted his own question by adding, "No, you would *never* make fun of us." Dawn did not need to reassure her students because they knew and loved her, but she reinforced her important message. "All of us are beautiful in our own shades, our own colors." By the time the session was over, every child had proudly added combinations of beiges, browns, and naturals to depict his or her own skin color.

"Me" mobile. Mobiles can be made many ways, but the easiest is the hanger mobile. The subject is "me" and the material is any picture, design, word, or image that reflects the uniqueness of that child. In one kindergarten class, a mischievous five-year-old, with great effort, tied a piece of chewed-up bubble gum to his mobile. When asked about it, he said "I chew so much bubble gum, my mom says I'm gonna turn into bubble gum!"

"Me" books. Young children like to watch these books grow from a few blank pages to thick, colorful collections of feelings, ideas, favorite things, memories, and wishes. Many classes work on their books all year. These books run the gamut from randomly constructed, all-inclusive collections to well-organized presentations of selected topics, such as favorite foods and games, family, and future plans.

When children are free to choose what they want to include in their books, you will be in for some surprises. Kindergartner Eric glued in the first tooth that he lost. He asked his teacher to help him write the caption: "The tooth fairy gave me twenty-five cents for this tooth." Kimmy, almost five years old, taped a tiny pebble to a page in her book. "This is one of my treasures," she wrote, with a little help from a sixth-grade friend.

Cloud pictures. Here is an imagination-celebrating activity to enjoy on a day when foamy white clouds move across a bright blue sky. After the children watch the clouds from a window or outside, talk about what they see in the shapes of the clouds. One group of first graders had many ideas; for example:

> The clouds look like ice-cream cones.
> Like a big ocean.
> Like a kitty rolling over. See, there's his head.
> Like a lot of Ping-Pong balls.

In this, as in all activities in the book, there are no right or wrong answers. Every child's view is valid and should be encouraged.

After looking at the clouds and sharing ideas, the children create cloud pictures with white paint or cotton balls and paste. Let them choose their own colored construction paper for background. Do not be dismayed if they choose a color other than blue!

Allen, age 8

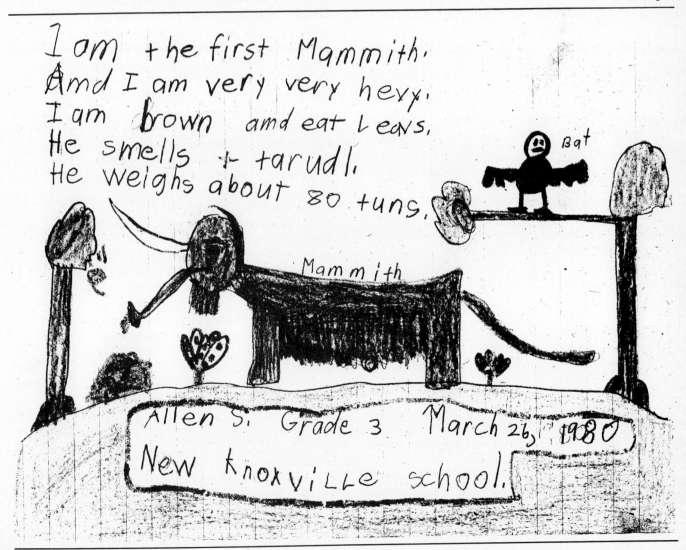

Mind pictures. An imaginative activity that Betsy Distelhorst and her young students enjoy is looking at blank paper, concentrating, and thinking about whatever comes into mind. "As soon as a few ideas pop into your heads," Betsy instructs, "pick up crayons and start drawing them."

"I can . . ." mural. Spread a large piece of paper across a chalk or bulletin board and encourage the children to think of all the things they can do. Share ideas *before* the pasting, writing, and drawing begin. Just talking about all the "I can's" gives such a boost to self-esteem that you may want to devote several sessions to this enthusiastic sharing of ideas.

Let four or five children at a time work on the mural (more, if it is larger). Each child writes his or her name and the word "can" after it. A word, drawing, or cutout picture follows the word "can." Four items spotted on an "I can" mural in a kindergarten class were:

Kevin can ice skate.

Martie can bake cookies.

Brett can teach his dog tricks.

Seth can run backwards.

Turn the mural into a follow-the-leader game with each child leading the others in performing or pantomiming the featured accomplishment.

A variation of this activity is to give the children large pieces of paper and invite them to make their own "I can" poster filled with as many of their accomplishments as there is room on the paper.

Make something out of "nothing." From your ample collection of junk, children choose odds-and-ends to create works of art. These odds-and-ends may include toothpicks, stones, macaroni, shells, twigs, cloth scraps, pieces of wire, beans, pins, beads, pieces of jewelry, and hanger wire. Use paste, glue, paper clips, tape, and wire to connect the parts.

Remember, all artists create something extraordinary out of the ordinary, and children, the best artists, need many opportunities throughout the year to exercise their imaginations and meet creative challenges.

Stars. Every child is a star! Cut out stars of different shapes and colors and have each child choose one. In the center of the star, the children write their name, paste their photograph, and paint or color an original design. On each point of the star, help them to write a word that tells about their uniqueness. Spread the stars around the room so they brighten the walls and boards and give the children lots of places to look for words and pictures celebrating themselves.

Pictures from our five sensational senses. Devote shapes, images, and pictures to what we see, hear, feel, taste, touch, and smell. Encourage children to sharpen their senses and experience more of their world. Their painting, drawing, and sculpture reflect their sharpened awareness.

Magic gardens. Michael Rosen and a group of second graders in Columbus, Ohio, talked about seeds and gardens. They went from the real to the imaginary. "What if *everything* in the world grew from a seed? What would you plant in your garden?" The children bounced ideas around with enthusiasm. They would plant tennis-shoe seeds, bike seeds, swimming-pool seeds, ice-cream-cone seeds, even puppy seeds. The talk was followed by pictures of "my magic garden." Each child's garden was unique, reflecting individual interests and wishes.

MUSIC TIMES

Name-calling songs. Once you realize how much children enjoy hearing their own names called, you will get into the habit of using their names in almost every song you sing. A well-known song such as "Michael, Row the Boat Ashore" can be used to celebrate each child in your class: "Douglas, row the boat ashore, hallelujah"; "Jeffrey, help to stem the tide . . ."

There is an old chant that goes like this:

Hello everybody and clap your hands.
Clap your hands. Clap your hands.
Hello everybody and clap your hands.
And clap your hands today.

There are many variations of its "melody," so feel free to improvise. A class of four- and five-year-olds had fun with the song when they and their teacher changed it to:

Hello, Jeannie Walcher, turn around.
Turn around, turn around.
Hello, Kira Kaplan, turn around.
Turn around today.

One kindergarten teacher reported that after a workshop in which this idea was discussed, her entire morning had been changed by using the children's names in "Rockabye Baby." "Just before our rest time," she said, "I thought I'd try the idea with one of our lullabies. We always sing a lullaby before we rest—so I thought it would take only a few minutes, but the children were so entranced and waited for their turn before they *fell* and rested that it practically became our major morning activity! And today, as I came into the room, the children asked if we could do it again!"

Rock-a-bye Stephanie, on the tree top.
When the wind blows, the cradle will rock.
When the bough breaks, the cradle will fall.
Down will come Stephanie, cradle and all.

The children sang with her, of course.

Songs like "He's Got the Whole World in His Hands" can be easily modified to celebrate each child:

He's got Brett and Neal in His hands,
He's got Jeffrey and Kira in His hands . . .

A group of four-year-olds squealed with delight with we sang a special version of "The Bear Went Over the Mountain":

The bear went over the mountain
Who do you think he saw?
He saw Bobby, Seth, and Andrew

He saw Hilary, Timmy, and Debbie
He saw Michael, Joey, and Iris
And who else did he see?
He saw . . .

Songs of sound. Children enjoy experimenting with different sounds and are quick to imitiate new sounds that they hear. Part of the wonder of human beings is that we can make so many sounds, compared with other animals such as dogs and birds. Discuss this idea with the children before you begin this activity.

Encourage each child to make up a sound and practice it for a few minutes in order to remember it. Sit in a circle and ask the children to begin making their sounds. Start with one child and continue until all the children are making their sounds at the same time. Then, one by one, each child stops until the last single sound is made.

Children may also use instruments or body claps to accompany their voices. They can hear the dramatic development from silence to crescendo.

Another variation is to talk about animal sounds. "We can imitate most animal sounds, but most animals can't imitate human sounds!" Someone may mention parrots, which are an exception. "Let's make a song of animal sounds," one teacher suggested to her class after "Talk Time." Each child contributed an animal sound as they built the rhythms in the manner described above. The result was fantastic! The children were so excited that they asked the teacher to tape it and play it for their parents at open house.

Your name is a song. All of our names have rhythm. We can chant them, clap them, and turn them into wonderful music. Sit in a circle and invite the children to make rhythms out of their names. *Charley Anderson*—slow/slow/fast-fast-fast (clap it. snap it, stamp it, chant it). Try it another way. Stress different syllables. The group, of course, joins in. Shyer children need encouragement. Watch their expressions change when they hear their names turned into music! In one class the children enjoyed their name rhythms so much that the teacher called attendance by clapping their names.

Add rhythm instruments to enrich the experience—create a symphony of names.

Add words to the name-songs (they do not have to rhyme). Here is an example composed by a group of four-year-olds:

Elizabeth Ann Washington
(E LI za beth ANN WASH ing ton)
(slow/fast-fast-fast slow slow/fast-fast)
(soft/loud/soft-soft loud loud/soft-soft)
Elizabeth Ann Washington,
Elizabeth Ann Washington.
Plays the drum. Rum. Tum. Tum.
It's such fun. Drum. Drum. Drum.
Elizabeth Ann Washington.

The wonder of me and my magical musical note. One day Jani Aranow talked with her preschool classes about how numbers are a special language for counting and letters are a special language for reading and writing. "There is a special language for writing music," she explained, and she showed them a music book filled with notes. They talked about whole notes and quarter notes, what notes look like on paper, and how people follow the notes when they play instruments and sing melodies.

Jani drew five long lines for a staff on large white paper taped to the wall. She gave each child a round "note" cut out of construction paper. The children colored and decorated their notes and wrote their names on them. One by one she called the children to put their notes somewhere in the four measures she drew on the paper. "Wherever you put your note will be a special sound. On the lines or between the lines." The children's notes filled the four measures.

Jani looked at the melody created by the children's notes and played it for them on the guitar. They were amazed at the sound. "Play it again!" She did. They realized that she was "reading" their notes and making the music from their special language. They added words to their song: "We love music. We sing all day. When the sun shines."

Gather songs. I saw a poster that read: A bird doesn't sing because he has an answer, he sings because he has a song. Sometimes we have more songs than answers. The number of songs we remember is often astonishing. Two-and-a-half-year-old Jessie received a double album of popular songs from her aunt. Three weeks later, when Jessie's aunt visited her again, Jessie knew *every* one of the *fifty-five* songs on the records!

In appreciation of the human mind, talk with your children about all the songs they know and remember. Begin a class list of songs and add to it daily. Sing as many of the songs as often as possible.

One kindergarten teacher encouraged the children to draw pictures and designs next to the song titles on the large song chart that was titled: "We Know All These Songs." Each day, a different child was appointed song leader and tacked his or her "helping-hand" name tag (see Guide 1) beside the chosen songs. The teacher was surprised to see how quickly the children not only remembered the songs but also recognized the words and pictures describing the songs.

During my visit to this kindergarten, I admired the chart and praised the children. "You people know *so many* songs. How do you remember them all?" One small spokesman pointed to his head and said, "They all fit right in here!"

Pass the instruments around. This activity is a fine conclusion to a discussion of our wonderful musical abilities. Once again, sit in a circle. Ask the children to shut their eyes and not to peek as you place rhythm instruments in their hands. Then they can open their eyes and explore their instruments. Ask a child to play a rhythm or melody on his or her instrument and have the others join in, one at a time, to accompany or play a variation until all the instruments are playing. Then signal each child to stop, one at a time, so that the music diminishes. Exchange instruments and begin again.

Part of the "wonder of me" is the discovery that we have such a range of choices and abilities. "I played a hundred instruments today," a four-and-a-half-year-old puffed proudly.

MOVEMENT AND PLAY TIMES

The wonder of growing. Nothing celebrates "the wonder of me" as delightfully and effectively as discovering how we grow and what we can accomplish now that we could not accomplish before. This activity can be presented in a variety of ways. As you read the two general approaches described

here, think about the way you would enjoy sharing the ideas and experiences with your students.

"Talk Time" introduces this activity. Talking about babies and when we were babies is probably one of the most popular topics of discussion for young children, who glow with pride as they realize their newly achieved powers.

The story of growing has been improvised and shared by thousands of young children. Every idea is expression in movement and drama as well as speech. Here is an example of part of the story told by teacher and children together as they enact it:

When we were very new babies, we were very tiny and small. How tiny and small can we make our bodies?

We could hardly do anything except sleep (soft snore), make funny noises (googly goo sounds), and cry (Waaaaaaa!).

We couldn't even turn over from our tummies to our backs or our backs to our tummies. We were stuck.

We tried and tried to turn over. Lots of times. Finally, we did it! Turned over by ourselves. Yaaaaay.

But, we couldn't turn back over and we kept trying and trying, until we finally did it! Yaaay.

When we were babies, we didn't know that our hands and feet belonged to us, belonged to our bodies. We thought they were toys or mobiles.

We couldn't even sit up by ourselves. Every time we sat up, we flopped right back over.

But, we kept trying and trying to sit up and finally, one day, we did it! We sat up all by ourselves without falling over.

The story continues with crawling, reaching, standing, and walking. Each accomplishment is the result of great effort, patience, and determination. The development of the story is exciting and dramatic. After reenacting all the steps along the way, children burst into enthusiastic demonstration:

Now we can walk, lots of ways—quietly, noisily, tip-toe, sideways, backwards, bouncy, stiff, high, low.

We can hop, skip, jump, turn, leap, slide.

We can march, run, dance, race, prance, gallop.

We can . . .

There is no end to what we can do now that we are growing more every day.

This activity may take one twenty-minute session or it may be continued for days. A group of three-and-a-half-year-olds spent twenty minutes on the turning-over part alone. They enjoyed it so much that they repeated it over and over.

Another approach to this activity takes one item at a time rather than developing the whole idea:

When we were babies, we couldn't even turn over.

Now we can turn over.

When we were babies, we could only crawl.

Now we can walk (explore).

When we were babies, we couldn't stand up without falling down.

Now we walk, run, hop, skip, and jump.

Changing shapes. If we were horses or fish, we would keep the same body shape most of the time. But because we are human, we are able to change our shapes. Children like to discover the different things

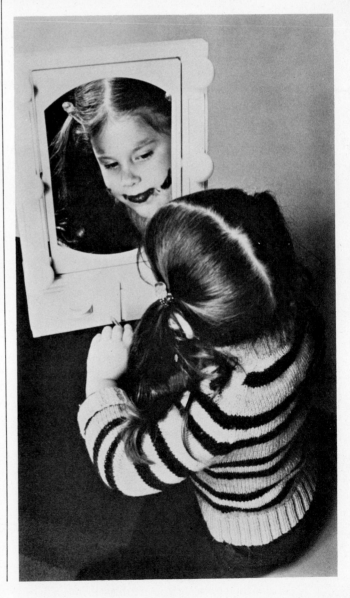

their bodies can do. Ask the children to make a shape (any shape) with their bodies. Hold the shape for the count of three or five, then change it to another shape. The children may count out loud, or you may hit a tambourine or drum to give them the signal to change. This activity can also be enjoyed with any music of regular, slow rhythm. I have used Ravi Shankar's repetitive Indian music with great success.

Magic. Only human beings create magic tricks with imagination and a sense of fun. As one kindergartner observed, "Changing to a butterfly wasn't the caterpillar's idea!" Children are fascinated by magic and their earliest "trick" is hiding their faces and playing peek-a-boo. The following magic "tricks" celebrate what only human beings can do.

Variations of peek-a-boo. Accompany these simple but wonderful "magic tricks" with the familiar "Where's . . .? There it is!" Here are examples of other kinds of peek-a-boo:

Where is your nose? Where is your nose? Where is your nose? (Cover nose, of course!) (Remove hand. Reveal nose.) There it is! Where are your eyes? Where are your ears? (And so on) (Make fists and hold them up.) Where are our fingers? Where are our fingers? Where are our fingers? (Thrust out fingers.) There they are!

Go through all the body parts. Try this idea: With your children, make grim, serious faces.

Where is your smile? Where is your smile? Where is your smile? (Smile.) There it is!

Magic show. Talk with the children about magicians. Here are some ideas about magicians and magic from a group of four-and-a half-year-olds:

Magicians do tricks.
Magicians have special wands.
Magicians make bunnies come out of hats.
Magicians make things disappear.
Magicians have tricky hands.

Scrounge around for small, colorful nylon squares to use as scarves. Find enough for all the children. Ask the children to close their eyes. Tell them you are going to put something magical in their hands. As soon as they feel it, they are to hide it somewhere in their clothing. You may have to help a few

children hide their scarves up their sleeves or in their pockets.

When all of the children have their scarves hidden, the magic story begins. Here is an example of the kind of magic show we have shared with many early childhood classes.

We have some magic scarves. But where are they? Are they in our hands? (Show fingers, front and back.) No. Are they in our mouths? (Open mouths). No. Are they in our ears? (Show ears.) No. Are they in our elbows? (Point elbows.) No. Are they in our noses? (Wiggle noses.) No. Where could they be? Are they under our arms? (Lift arms.) No. Are they under our feet? (Jump.) No. My goodness, where could the magic scarves be? (Children add ideas.)

We need some magic words. (Work them out with your class.) Let's say the magic words. (The following incantation was created by a group of first graders.)
Abracadabra peanut butter and jelly
Watch my magic tricks or I'll tickle you in the belly.

(Pull out the scarves and hold them up.) Here are the magic scarves. (Twirl them, wave them.) They can go anywhere they want to. They can make any designs in the air. They can make circles. They can make up and down lines. They can fly into the air and come down. (Throw the scarves into the air.) They can fly by themselves. (Throw the scarves up and blow them up higher.) They can fly in the air and land wherever they want to. (Throw the scarves up or blow them up and try to catch them on heads, arms, legs.)

"My scarf can land on the floor if it wants to!" said Adam. Rather than getting frustrated because his scarf kept missing his head and falling to the floor, Adam turned the situation into a trick.

Here are some more ideas for the magic scarves: Bunch them up in hands so they practically disappear and fling them suddenly into the air; turn them into butterflies and birds; turn them into flowers; spread them on the floor, turn them into horses' tails and gallop around; lay them down and blow them across the floor; put them together and turn them into a rainbow; drape them over chests or backs and turn them into queens' and kings' robes; and hold them up in front of faces, say the magic words, drop the scarves, and reveal the faces.

This activity may be accompanied by music or an improvised story.

Razzle dazzle. A junior-high cheer reached the ears of a few young siblings and became one of the "wonder of me" activities most enjoyed by all twelve classes at the Jewish Center in Columbus, Ohio.

The cheer goes like this:

Razzle dazzle (clap, clap, clap, clap)
Razzle dazzle (clap, clap, clap, clap)
My name is Caryn, I'm number one.
My razzle dazzle has just begun!
(Caryn does something, anything. The others follow. Keep a steady beat.)
Razzle dazzle (clap, clap, clap, clap)
Razzle dazzle (clap, clap, clap, clap)

Give every child a chance to be "number one" and to lead a "razzle dazzle." Some children need a little help thinking fast on their feet. Don't let them wait too long to lead a movement. Suggest something to them (jumping jack, hop, touch your toes, or tap your head). If some children do nothing during their turn, imitate their position as you cheer.

Children love cheers and are often familiar with the words and movements of junior high or high school cheers. Turn these cheers into ways of celebrating the "wonder of me."

Give me a B. (B)
Give me an O. (O)
Give me another B. (B)
Give me another B. (B)
Give me a Y. (Y)
What do we get!
BOBBY! BOBBY! YAAAAAY!

Birthdays. Of all the holidays on the calendar, the most important holiday to young children is their birthday. On that special day, the world revolves around the "birthday" child. "Six years old! Jon is six! Let's count to six. One. Two. Three. Four. Five. Six. What can we do *six times* for Jon's birthday?"

Here are just a few of the ideas suggested by young children: clap; snap fingers; stamp feet; turn around; hop; sit up; take bites of cake (imaginary); blow out candles; touch toes; wave; wiggle fingers; and do jumping jacks. Each action is performed six times in honor of the birthday.

We like to end our birthday celebration with six tricks. We play rhythmical music, from disco to dervish, and the children practice "tricks" such as balancing on one leg, waving their arms, and shrugging their shoulders.

Jokes and laughs. One of the best wonders of being human is to make jokes, to make people laugh. Children have a marvelous sense of humor. They seem to be tickled by certain things at certain ages. Humor reveals an ever-developing comprehension. We laugh because we "get it." Never underestimate humor and playfulness as excellent ways to strengthen understanding.

For instance, Steve Anderson's class of almost-three-year-olds discovered the fun of shouting "Boo" to someone who did not see them. Steve urged teachers and other adults to exaggerate their reactions when the children "scared" them. This game lasted for weeks.

Books like *Smile for Auntie* by Diane Paterson (Dial, 1976) are guaranteed to amuse children as they see page after page of an eager little person trying to make a huge, grouchy person smile. Each attempt can be improvised in movement by the children as they read.

Shadows. On a sunny day, go outside with your children and study their shadows. Depending on the hour, they will discover that:

their shadows are behind them; their shadows are in front of them; no matter how fast they run, they will always be ahead of, or behind, their shadows; and no matter what shape they make with their bodies, their shadows will do the same. Talk about shadows. Experiment with shadows. Read poems about shadows. Robert Louis Stevenson's "My Shadow" is a classic.

Take "sense walks." On clear days, take the children for walks to celebrate the five senses. Take a *sound* walk and listen to everything you see. Take a *smell* walk and focus on the smells along the way. Take a *touch* walk. Experience the different textures of tree bark, leaves, pebbles, dirt, grass, and flowers. Follow up this activity with art, music, poems and stories, talk, and creative dramatics when you return to the classroom.

Children who use only one speed. My favorite metaphor to remind children to use all their powers goes like this: "Kids, if you have ever heard of a ten-speed bike, clap your hands (or stamp feet or wiggle noses). Kids, if you have ever seen anyone ride a ten-speed bike, hold up ten fingers" (or blink ten times). After establishing that the children are familiar with a ten-speed bike, I tell this story.

Once there were kids who had ten-speed bikes (show me ten fingers). But, they used only one speed (show me one finger). When they went up hills, they could hardly pedal (pantomime effort and strain). When they went down hills, they practically fell off (wobble). We met these kids and said, "You have ten speeds, why are you using only one?" Those kids looked surprised. "We forgot about our other speeds. Thanks for reminding us!" Now they use all ten speeds, all their powers. They go up and down hills. Easy!

Then we talk about how we have even more than ten speeds. We have so many powers, but sometimes we use only one.

For the rest of the year, the children use the metaphor to remind themselves and each other to do more, not less; to expand, not shrink.

> **Ten-Speed Jumps, Ten-Speed Runs**
> We can jump only a short distance off the floor (speed one).
> We can jump a little higher (speed two).
> All the way up to *ten* and we're flying off the floor with high, high jumps!
> (Do the ten-speed runs outdoors or in an indoor area with lots of space.)
> Everyone runs in a large circle, in the same direction.
> We start with a slow-motion run (speed one).
> We run a little faster (speed two).
> All the way up to our fastest ten speed.

VISITORS AND FIELD TRIPS

Visitors

Baby. This visitor will definitely enrich the activities about growing described in this guide. If one of your students has a baby sister or brother, invite the parent and baby to your classroom. The children will see how little, helpless, and uncoordinated the baby is. Watch your students stretch with newly emerging self-image as you wonder aloud with the baby's mom or dad: "I bet your baby wishes he could do all the wonderful things these big kids can do! Don't worry. He'll be able to do them when he grows up some more."

Artist. This visitor can help children discover the creative process by starting with a blank paper or board and filling it with people, animals, shapes, and colorful designs. Cartoonists are especially delightful classroom visitors.

Magician. Invite a magician to talk about how he or she learned magic as well as to demonstrate magic tricks. Ask your guest to teach the children a simple trick.

Poet. On a blank piece of paper, the poet magically scribbles lines and curves that become letters and words and eventually poems.

Weaver. This person's work is intriguing to watch. Encourage the visitor to share a skill with the children, such as making pot-holders or lacing cardboard with material.

Inventor. Ask the inventor to tell the children the story of his or her invention in order to illustrate originality and innovation. Children should be encouraged to try inventing something themselves.

Field Trips

Sculpture or pottery class. Children discover how responsive human beings are to natural materials like clay, stone, and wood. Out of the materials nature provides, people make original shapes and designs that are both useful and beautiful.

Community or high school theater. The children will have an outstanding experience whether the set is being constructed or the stage is set for a play. Ask the manager if the children can walk carefully on the stage. Talk about the play that will be performed. What kinds of things are on the stage? What kind of scene is it? Discuss the power of imagination and the need for people to "make believe," whether they are children or adults.

Gymnastics class in a school or community center. After experimenting with so many "tricks" themselves, the children appreciate the mind-body coordination that results in spectacular gymnastic combinations. Stress practice, good health habits, and confidence as essential qualities of a gymnast. Ask the instructor to show the children an easy gymnastic exercise.

Jazz group. Improvisation should be stressed on this field trip. Children discover that jazz musicians play what they feel as they respond to the other instruments. They "make up" the music as they play it. They create new musical arrangements—the process becomes the product.

NOTES

1. Martin O'Connor, *Miracles*, ed. by Richard Lewis (New York: Bantam, 1977), p. 146.
2. Mrs. A. Joseph Marsh, "Letters to a Fledgling Teacher," *Early Years* (September 1975), pp. 36–37.
3. Elizabeth Hunter, "Tuning into Children," *Childhood Education* (October 1975), pp. 13–19.
4. Gwen Marston's extraordinary work with music and young children is widely recognized. She was featured in my book *Teaching Language Arts Creatively* (New York: Harcourt Brace Jovanovich, 1978). Her record *Songs for Small Fry* is available from Forrest Green Studios, 5004 West Francis Road, Clio, Michigan 48420.

SELECTED BIBLIOGRAPHY

Imagination and Dreams

Bornstein, Ruth Lercher. *I'll Draw a Meadow*. New York: Harper & Row, 1979.

Brown, Margery W. *Yesterday I Climbed a Mountain*. New York: Putnam, 1976.

Ellentuck, Shan. *My Brother Bernard*. New York: Abelard-Schuman, 1968.

Emberly, Ed. *Great Thumbprint Drawing Book*. Boston: Little, Brown, 1977.

Harrison, Sarah, and Mike Wilks. *In Granny's Garden*. New York: Holt, Rinehart & Winston, 1980.

Heide, Florence Parry. *My Castle*. Illustrated by Symeon Shimin. New York: McGraw-Hill, 1972.

Himler, Ronald. *Wake Up, Jeremiah*. New York: Harper & Row, 1979.

Hoban, Russell. *The Great Gum Drop Robbery*. Illustrated by Colin McNaughton. New York: Putnam, 1982.

Johnson, Crockett. *Harold's Trip to the Sky*. New York: Harper & Row, 1957.

Jossee, Barbara M. *The Thinking Place*. Illustrated by Kay Chorao. New York: Knopf, 1982.

Keats, Ezra Jack. *Dreams*. New York: Macmillan, 1974.

———. *Regards to the Man in the Moon*. New York: Scholastic, Four Winds, 1982.

———. *The Trip*. New York: Morrow, 1978.

Kent, Jack. *Mr. Meebles*. New York: Parents Magazine Press, 1970.

———. *The Scribble Monster*. New York: Harcourt Brace Jovanovich, 1981.

Krohn, Fernando. *Sleep Tight, Alex Pumpernickel*. Boston: Little, Brown, 1982.

Littledale, Freya, and Harold Littledale. *Timothy's Forest*. Illustrated by Rosalie Lehrman. New York: Lion, 1969.

Mahy, Margaret. *The Boy Who Was Followed Home*. Illustrated by Steven Kellogg. New York: Franklin Watts, 1975.

Mayers, Patrick. *Just One More Block*. Illustrated by Lucy Hawkinson. Chicago: Albert Whitman, 1970.

Ness, Evaline. *Sam, Bangs, and Moonshine*. New York: Holt, Rinehart & Winston, 1966.

Pinkwater, Honest Dan'l. *Roger's Umbrella*. New York: Dutton, 1982.

Sendak, Maurice. *In the Night Kitchen*. New York: Harper & Row, 1970.

———. *Outside Over There*. New York: Harper & Row, 1981.

Seuss, Dr. [Theodor S. Geisel]. *And to Think I Saw It on Mulberry Street*. New York: Vanguard, 1937.

Sleator, William. *That's Silly*. Illustrated by Lawrence DiFior. New York: Dutton, 1981.

Self-Image, Self-Acceptance

Bailey, Carolyn Sherwin. *The Little Rabbit Who Wanted Red Wings*. New York: Platt & Munk, 1978.

Barrett, Judi. *Animals Should Definitely Not Act Like People*. New York: Atheneum, 1980.

Barton, Byron. *Harry Is a Scaredy-Cat*. New York: Macmillan, 1974.

Berson, Harold. *A Moose Is Not a Mouse*. New York: Crown, 1975.

Bulla, Clyde Robert. *Dandelion Hill*. Illustrated by Bruce Deglen. New York: Dutton, 1982.

Carle, Eric. *The Mixed-Up Chameleon*. New York: Crowell, 1975.

Conford, Ellen. *Why Can't I Be William?* Boston: Little, Brown, 1972.

De Paoli, Tomie. *Andy (That's My Name)*. Englewood Cliffs, N. J.: Prentice-Hall, 1973.

———. *Oliver Button Is a Sissy*. New York: Harcourt Brace Jovanovich, 1979.

Ehrhardt, Reinhold. *Kikeri, or the Proud Red Rooster*. Illustrated by Bernadette. New York: World, 1969.

Ets, Marie H. *Just Me*. New York: Viking, 1965.

Fitzhugh, Louise. *I Am Three*. Illustrated by Susanna Natti. New York: Delacorte, 1982.

Freeman, Don. *Dandelion*. New York: Viking, 1964.

Johnston, Johanna. *Supposings*. Illustrated by Rudy Sayers. New York: Holiday House, 1967.

Lionni, Leo. *Alexander and the Wind-Up Mouse*. New York: Random House, Pantheon, 1969.

———. *Fish Is Fish*. New York: Random House, 1970.

———. *Pezzetino*. New York: Random House, 1975.

Oxenbury, Lelen. *Pig Tale*. New York: Morrow, 1973.

Roselli, Luciana. *The Polka Dot Child*. New York: Graphic Society, 1954.

Sargent, Robert. *A Bug of Some Importance*. New York: Scribner, 1967.

Silver, Jody. *Isadora*. New York: Doubleday, 1981.

Stanley, John. *It's Nice to Be Little*. Illustrated by Jean Tamburine. Chicago: Rand McNally, 1965.

Waber, Bernard. *"You Look Ridiculous," Said the Rhinoceros to the Hippopotamus*. Boston: Houghton Mifflin, 1966.

Growing and Becoming

Allen, Esther. *Penelope Gets Wheels*. Illustrated by Susanna Natti. New York: Crown, 1982.

Ainsworth, Judy. *When I Grow Up*. Photos by Belinda Durrie. Chicago: Childrens Press, 1969.

Aruego, José. *Look What I Can Do!* New York: Scribner, 1971.

Asch, Frank. *Turtle Tale*. New York: Dial, 1978.

Adorjan, Carol Madden. *Someone I Know*. Illustrated by Corinne Keyser. New York: Random House, 1968.

Andersen, Hans Christian. *The Ugly Duckling*. Illustrated by Adrienne Adams. New York: Atheneum, 1982.

Baylor, Byrd. *Guess Who My Favorite Person Is?* Illustrated by Robert Andrew Parker. New York: Scribners, 1977.

Behrend, June. *My Favorite Thing*. Photos by Vince Streano. Chicago: Childrens Press, 1975.

———. *Who Am I?* Chicago: Elk Grove Press, 1968.

Bright, Robert. *Gregory*. New York: Doubleday, 1969.

Brown, Marc. *Arthur Goes to Camp*. Boston: Little, Brown, 1982.

Buckley, Helen E. *Michael Is Brave*. Illustrated by Emily McCully. New York: Lothrop, Lee & Shepard, 1971.

Calloway, Northeim J. *I Been There*. Illustrated by Sammes McLean. New York: Doubleday, 1977.

Carrick, Carol. *Sleep Out*. Illustrated by Donald Carrick. Boston: Houghton Mifflin, Clarion Books, 1982.

Charlip, Remy, and Lillian Moore. *Hooray for Me!* New York: Four Winds Press, 1980.

Clifton, Lucille. *Everett Anderson's Year*. Illustrated by Ann Grifalconi. New York: Holt, Rinehart & Winston, 1974.

Coerr, Eleanor. *The Big Balloon Race*. Illustrated by Carolyn Croll. New York: Harper & Row, 1981.

Cooney, Nancy Evans. *The Blanket That Had to Go*. New York: Putnam, 1981.

Corey, Dorothy. *Tomorrow You Can*. Illustrated by Lois Axeman. Chicago: Albert Whitman, 1977.

Craig, M. Jean. *What Did You Dream?* New York: Abelard-Schuman, 1964.

De Regniers, Beatrice Schenk. *A Little House of Your Own*. Illustrated by Irene Haas. New York: Harcourt Brace Jovanovich, 1955.

Felt, Sue. *Rosa-Too-Little*. New York: Doubleday, 1950.

Fregosi, Claudia. *The Happy Horse*. New York: Morrow, 1977.

Gauch, Patricia Lee. *My Old Tree*. Illustrated by Doris Burn. New York: Coward, McCann, & Geoghegan, 1970.

Green, Mary McBurney. *When Will I Whistle?* Illustrated by Harold Berson. New York: Franklin Watts, 1967.

Hoban, Lillian. *Arthur's Funny Money*. New York: Harper & Row, 1981.

Hutchin, Pat. *Titch*. New York: Macmillan, 1971.

Isadora, Rachel. *Ben's Trumpet*. New York: Morrow, Greenwillow Books, 1979.

Iwasake, Chihiro. *Staying Home Alone on a Rainy Day*. New York: McGraw-Hill, 1968.

Jaffe, Grace, and Phyllis Goldman. *Whatever Happened to Yes?* New York: Walker, 1968.

Jewell, Nancy. *Bus Ride*. Illustrated by Ronald Himler. New York: Harper, 1978.

Keats, Ezra Jack. *Jennie's Hat*. New York: Macmillan, 1969.

———. *Whistle for Willie*. New York: Viking, 1964.

Keeping, Charles. *Willie's Fire Engine*. Illustrated by author. New York: Oxford University Press, 1980.

Lasker, Joe. *The Do-Something Day*. New York: Viking, 1982.

Moncure, Jane Belk. *All By Myself*. Chicago: Childrens Press, 1976.

Pinkwater, Manus. *Bear's Picture*. New York: Holt, Rinehart & Winston, 1972.

Piper, Watty. *The Little Engine That Could*. Illustrated by George and Doris Human. New York: Platt & Munk, 1930.

Ruck-Pauguet, Gina. *Mumble Bear*. Illustrated by Erika Dietzsch-Capelle. New York: Putnam, 1980.

Smith, Janice Lee. *The Monster in the Third Dresser Drawer and Other Stories About Adam Joshua*. Illustrated by Dick Gackenbach. New York: Harper & Row, 1981.

Smolin, Michael. *Ernie and Bert Can . . . Can You?* New York: Random House, 1982.

Stanek, Muriel. *I Can Do It*. San Diego: Benefic Press, 1967.

Yashima, Taro. *Crow Boy*. New York: Viking, 1955.

Understanding Differences

Fassler, Joan. *Howie Helps Himself*. Illustrated by Joe Lasker. Chicago: Albert Whitman, 1975.

Lasker, Joe. *He's My Brother*. Chicago: Albert Whitman, 1974.

Lionni, Leo. *Frederick*. New York: Pantheon, 1967.

Peterson, Jeanne Whitehouse. *I Have a Sister—My Sister Is Deaf*. New York: Harper & Row, 1977.

Teacher Resources

Arnstein, Flora J. *Poetry and the Child*. New York: Dover, 1962.

Bugental, J. F. T., ed. *Challenges of Humanistic Psychology*. New York: McGraw-Hill, 1967.

Buscaglia, Leo. *Living Learning and Loving*. Thorofare, N. J.: Slack, 1982.

———. *Personhood: The Art of Being Fully Human*. Thorofare, N. J.: Slack, 1978.

Dillard, Annie. *Pilgrim at Tinker Creek*. New York: Harper's Magazine Press, 1974.

Fromm, Erich. *The Art of Loving*. New York: Harper & Row, 1956.

Ghiselin, Brewster, ed. *The Creative Process*. Berkeley: University of California Press, 1952.

Hendricks, Gary. *The Centered Teacher*. Englewood Cliffs, N. J.: Prentice-Hall, 1981.

Laing, R. D. *The Politics of Experience*. New York: Random House, Pantheon, 1967.

Martin, Robert J. *Teaching Through Encouragement*. Englewood Cliffs, N. J.: Prentice-Hall, 1980.

Maslow, Abraham H. *Toward a Psychology of Being*. New York: Van Nostrand, 1968.

May, Rollo. *The Courage to Create*. New York: Norton, 1975.

Mearns, Hughes. *Creative Power*. New York: Dover, 1958.

Montessori, Maria. *The Secret of Childhood*. New York: Random House, Ballantine, 1972.

Rogers, Carl. *On Becoming a Person*. Boston: Houghton Mifflin, 1961.

PART TWO

Grand ma

Steven, age 7

OUR
FAMILIES

OUR
FRIENDS

PEOPLE
WE
MEET

4

OUR FAMILIES

Five-year-old Shane counted the sea shells he had gathered on his first trip to the beach. "Three baby shells. Six mommy shells. Ten daddy shells."

THE BASICS

Family! Our first and most universal group "game." Families are central to the lives of young children. A child's relationship with this special group of people greatly determines his or her behavior, feelings, and identity. All of the guides in Part One of this book hinge on the family situation. A hostile, negative, disruptive family life affects a child's psychological, physical, intellectual, and social development. Significant family members have a strong influence on the child. Their presence or absence causes dramatic changes of behavior. Teachers of young children can attest to the vitally important role of family members and family relationships in the daily experiences of their students.

We have all enjoyed the following scene. Children are performing a play or giving a recital. They walk onstage, peer into the darkness of the audience, and momentarily set aside their practiced lines and cues to wave and greet their family in the auditorium: "Hi, Mommy! Hi, Daddy!" First things first!

The names of family members are among the first words a young child learns, because they have the greatest, most immediate meaning. Sylvia Ashton-Warner, a teacher and writer who has influenced educators around the world with her special approach to teaching, calls this first list of words that children *want* to say, read, and write, *key vocabulary.* She builds her teaching framework around key vocabulary. She explains:

The words start often with our child's own name, but not necessarily, or Mommy and Daddy, then his brothers and sisters, even if there are nineteen of them in the family, which you find in some pill-less societies—and more than that too here and there—by which time he moves to people outside the family, things outside, animals, pets, his bike. Not all run true to this route, of course . . . man is unique and variable . . . besides, big emotional explosions can take place in the course of it, but *it's a natural guideline.*[1]

The subject of family has received a good deal of attention lately as the divorce rate, like the cost of living, continues to rise. Many American children now have two sets of families and live with one parent. Sociologists and legislators debate the legal definition of family; anthropologists prophesy the demise of the institution as we know it; and religious leaders bemoan the loss of traditional family values. At a White House Conference on families, the participants could not agree even on a definition of the word *family*.

Another important source of information about the family is the *children*. Look to your students for a working definition of family; look for the real meaning of family in their words, expressions, actions, and reactions.

June Mock, a kindergarten teacher with many years of experience, teaches inner-city, racially integrated children in public schools in Columbus, Ohio. She talked with her students about family. What is a family? Who is in your family? What does a family do? What are families for?

Debbie Comer, who teaches first graders at Worthington Estates Elementary School in Worthington, Ohio, discussed the same questions with her more privileged, more homogeneous group of children. The answers from both groups of children were amazingly similar. Here are some of their comments.

What is a family?
Mother, father, brother, and sister
People who live together in a house
Grandma, grandpa, aunts, uncles, cousins . . .
Cats, dogs, rabbits, gerbils, hamsters, fish, snails, guppies . . .
Love
People who share stuff, work hard, help each other, love each other
Group of people who are always together
(Another child added, ''Not always!'')
My babysitter is in my family 'cause she stays with me every day.
Joanie is a very, very, very good friend who comes to my house five times a week. She is like in my family.

What does a family do? What is a family for?
Takes care of us
Cooks for us
Buys food, clothes, toys
Gives us a nice room
Shares stuff
Works hard
Cares for each other, helps each other
Takes you places
Teaches us stuff
Spends holidays with us
Gives us medicine when we're sick

In answer to the question, "Does everyone have a family?" most of Debbie's first graders nodded instantly. A six-year-old said, "I don't know anyone in the world who doesn't have a family." Another child suggested, "Orphans." "They have God," a boy piped up. And a little girl calmly stated, "The whole world is God's family."

Because teaching involves caring, you will want to know some important facts about your children. The answers to questions such as the following will help guide you in your relationship with each child and will give you a direction for effective communication: Who dressed them this morning? Who put them to bed last night? Who was with them on Saturday and Sunday? Who scolds them? Who comforts them? Who prepares their supper at night? Who washes their clothes? Who buys them toys and gifts? Who celebrates with them?

These are the kind of questions that lead to an understanding of the reality of

the children's families. You may not like some of the answers. They may surprise you. You may hear children share these kinds of experiences.

WENDY (5 years old): On Saturdays Daddy and Jennifer (his girlfriend) take me to the movies. Then we go to the park.

STACY (4 years old): My big sister cooks supper. She makes spaghetti, my favorite. She gives me a bath and puts me to sleep. She's not my real sister . . .

ASHLEY (6 years old): During the week, I live with Grandma and Grandpa. On Saturday I live with my mommy.

HEIDI (5 years old): Sometimes I live with my daddy and Maxine and baby Matthew. Sometimes I live with Mommy and Stanley and the twins . . .

TINA (6 years old): I live with my mommy, my aunt, and my babysitter.

HEATHER (5 years old): I live with Mommy. Just me and Mommy. But, in the summer, I'm going to visit my daddy in Seattle.

We, as teachers, can do little to affect institutional changes—to turn back the clock to a more predictable, familiar social order. So what *can* we do? I believe the answers lie in four important words: *awareness*, *acceptance*, *respect*, and *communication*.

Without awareness, we are handicapped. We must know the facts not only with our minds but also with our hearts. When children talk to us, we must listen wisely, with all of our senses. What is this child telling me? This information is to be filed in my mind under top priority/confidential. Awareness implies sensitivity and caring. Because you are aware, your behavior changes. Because you know that five children in your room do not live with their mothers, you change the way you celebrate Mother's Day.

Because you are aware, your vocabulary changes. You no longer automatically say "mommy and daddy" as your major reference to family without watching the pain of loss sadden the face of a young child. We need to learn new ways to refer to the adults at home. We need to feel comfortable saying things like: "Ask a grownup in your family to sign this note"; "Everyone in your family is invited to our party"; and "Maybe a babysitter or friend or neighbor or someone bigger than you at home will help you cut out these pictures." If we ac-

cept and respect a child's situation, our language will reflect our attitude. Here is a painful incident, small but important.

I visited a prekindergarten class where the children were drawing family albums, one page devoted to each member of their family. Jamie drew a picture of a man on one of the pages. His teacher was writing titles for him. "Who is this?" she asked. "Mr. Andrews from next door," Jamie answered. "Well, he's not really a member of your family, dear. He's just a neighbor, isn't he? I don't think he belongs in your album." Jamie's eyes narrowed. He sucked in his breath as he went back to his seat. He never finished the family album project. Mr. Andrews was "just a neighbor," but he was the person Jamie went to after school when his door was locked. He was the person Jamie played near and talked with. He was a very special person in Jamie's life, part of Jamie's definition of family. Perhaps he was more family to Jamie than his own family members whose singular lives were too involved to make time or space for a five-and-a-half-year-old boy.

Look to the children's definitions of family; accept their reality; respect their relationships. Be aware of your language. Is it a vocabulary of inclusion or exclusion? Is it a vocabulary that touches all of your children or just some of them? Is it a vocabulary of reassurance, caring, and understanding?

Awareness also means that you hear small voices sometimes refer to you as "mommy" or "daddy." Many students consider teachers and classmates as almost a family group. Children's definitions of family also define a healthy, happy classroom: A group of people who "help each other, care for each other, share stuff, teach us stuff, give us food, take us places." Too often the classroom and teacher are the only *real* family young children can look to for comfort, safety, and trust. The following poignant incident clearly demonstrates the vital role school can play in the life of a young child.

Three-and-a-half-year-old Deena was walking with her aunt. Deena's parents have been divorced for two years. Her father lives far away, in California. Deena tugged at her aunt's arm and said, "Aunt Mary, my daddy is not a very good person!" "Why?" her aunt asked, surprised at the child's comment. "Because he lives far away and I never see him. He doesn't take care of me or play with me or help me." Her aunt explained that grownups sometimes have difficult problems that are not the fault of children and sometimes have to do things that are unpleasant and sad. Deena and her aunt walked along without saying anything. Suddenly, Deena brightened. She looked up at her aunt and said, "Aunt Mary, my preschool is a very good person!"

Deena's teacher knows how important she is to the child. She assumes this responsibility with a commitment that is sacred. She is part of Deena's family.

There are so many ways to celebrate family, ways that involve even those children whose family patterns fit no sociological survey. Because "family" is a child's most important vocabulary word and reality, it meets Ashton-Warner's definition of "native imagery." Creative teachers know that successful activities spring from relevant interests and images. No topic is more relevant to young children than family. "Whatever our child is," writes Ashton-Warner, "that's what his education is when you use his own imagery as working material . . ."[2] This guide shares delightful ways that "family" flows into "working material."

often be a "pain in the neck," but remember, we were all new babies once! It is important to share our feelings about new babies.

- We often feel as though our classmates and teachers are family.
- We are all members of a very large family—the human family.

DISCOVERY TIMES

- Family is basic to all people.
- Families have many members, including mothers, fathers, children, aunts, uncles, cousins, nieces, nephews, grandmothers, grandfathers, brothers, and sisters.
- Sometimes we have such close friends and neighbors that we think of them as family members.
- There are many kinds of family arrangements. Some children live with just one parent, an aunt, an uncle, or a grandparent. Some children have stepmothers, stepfathers, stepsisters, and stepbrothers.
- Although family groups differ, they are important because they are the special people who care for us, feed us, help us, and teach us.
- It is sad when parents divorce. Children may blame themselves for the breakup, but it is not their fault.
- Sometimes family members die. Those are very sad times. It is good that children have teachers and friends to talk to about their feelings.
- When a baby is born in the family, it is fun to be a big sister or brother and help with the new baby. Big brothers and sisters know a lot of things babies do not know and can teach them as they grow. New babies can

SUGGESTED VOCABULARY

mother	meals	church	celebrate
father	breakfast	synagogue	plant
mommy	lunch	house	buy
daddy	supper	apartment	laundry
mom	bed	car	clean
dad	bath	trips	set the table
stepmother	clothes	outings	sad
stepfather	medicine	zoo	happy
sister	presents	circus	glad
brother	toys	movies	excited
stepsister	bikes	visit	scared
stepbrother	books	parties	angry
baby	records	care	lonely
uncle	pets	help	fun
aunt	dolls	talk	argue
cousin	games	praise	hug

grandma	songs	scold	kiss
grandpa	stories	punish	tickle
nana	lullaby	teach	snuggle
papa	holidays	love	spank
relatives	birthdays	fix	play
food	picnics	show	work
eat	manners	share	travel

The above list is just a beginning. Family encompasses not only people but also events, feelings, activities, objects, and places. Once you begin jotting down words with your students that go with family themes, you will run out of room. The youngest children have lists that include objects and places: "My sister's best doll"; "Mommy's keys"; "My daddy's chair"; and "My Grandma Smith in Cleveland."

Children's initial understanding of geography is often based on the location of relatives.

Your list will reflect the uniqueness of your students. Do children in your class celebrate Japanese Boys' Day? Chanukah? Ash Wednesday? Day of Our Lady of Guadalupe? Cinco de Mayo? Passover? Easter? Dr. Martin Luther King's Birthday? From talking and sharing, doing and discovering, your children and you will learn from each other about the meaning of family. The words are clues to this deepest human relationship as well as ideas for activities.

SOME BEGINNING ACTIVITIES

Start with a new baby. The announcement by one of your students of the arrival of a baby sister or brother is a wonderful way to begin an activity on the family. "Patty is going to have a new baby brother or sister. Who in this room has a baby sister or brother at home? Who has a *big* brother or sister at home? Who is the special one-and-only child at home?"

Start with a grandparent. A grandparent is usually visiting or living with the family of at least one of your young children. "Patty's grandfather is coming to visit her tomorrow from Pittsburgh. Has anyone in this class ever had a visit from a grandpa or grandma or aunt or uncle or cousin? What are their names? Where are they from?"

Start with names and numbers. "What are the names of people in your family? How many can you name?" What a wonderful beginning for vocabulary and relationships that can develop into activities! "Can you count the number of people in your family? Try not to leave anyone out!"

Start with *The Family of Man*. This extraordinary collection of photographs celebrating the universality of family is a beautiful book to share with young children. The pictures are powerful and the children respond with questions, feelings, and shared experiences.

Start with a personal experience. Children like to be taken into the confidence of adults, especially adults they love. Laura Kaplan launched a project on family and transportation from the simplest sharing of a personal experience. She told her first graders, "I'm very excited because my cousin is coming to visit me from New York. He's coming on an airplane." This led to the question,

"Have any of your relatives come to visit you from a distant place?" The responses came quickly: "My aunt came Christmas from Atlanta"; "Daddy is coming on a plane from Jackson"; "Dee Dee and her baby, Penny, are coming on the bus from Pittsbrook" (Pittsburgh). From this reaction one can move to activities in art, drama, movement, and creative writing as discussed later in this guide.

Start with a puppet, stuffed animal, or doll. Teachers who work with very young children are lucky, because their students still believe in fantasy and a world where puppets, dolls, and stuffed animals have souls, feelings, and personalities. A puppet can introduce family themes beautifully. Kindergarten teacher Shelly Laurie, for example, slipped her hand into Elizabeth, a wide-eyed, long-lashed lady puppet, and said, "Boys and girls, Elizabeth has been invited to a family party, but she doesn't know what 'family' means! Do you?" The children shouted help to her. "Your mommy, your daddy, your cousins," they suggested. This led to a discussion of who was in *their* families, which, in turn, led to myriad activities during the next few months.

Start with a personal snapshot. Share one of your own family photos. Paste it on a solid background of construction paper and pass it around. Young children are often shocked that teachers have families. I once

Dawn Heyman of the McGuffy School in Columbus, Ohio, a lover of children and animals, has gerbils who become parents again and again. Her students name the parents, care for them, and name all the new babies. Through the gerbil families, Dawn begins her discussion and activities about human families.

TALK TIMES

What happens during "Talk Time" can blossom into your most successful activities. "Talk Time" plants ideas in your imagination.

Remember, most young children are chatterboxes. They love to talk about things that interest them, that are important to them, that affect them. Family falls under all these categories and is a prime topic for discussion. Besides providing excellent material for activities, "Talk Times" give children the opportunities to share experiences and observations. They discover that they are not alone. Others, too, have good and bad times, days when they feel loved, days when they are disappointed or angry. They begin to realize that others have people in their lives who hug them and scold them and who greatly determine the content and borders of their lives.

Open-ended questions. At all times, remember to emphasize open-ended questions rather than conversation-killing questions that yield only yes, no, or "I dunno" responses. "Talk Time" can also be cut-and-dried if you ask short-answer questions.

Teachers June Mock and Debbie Comer, whose conversations with their students about family were reported earlier in this guide, recognized that some of the students' responses led to further questions. For example, one of the answers to the question "What does a family do?" was "A family teaches us stuff." Both teachers quickly followed that response with one of their own:

brought a photo of our dogs for a classroom activity and was unprepared for the gasps that greeted me when I explained that the children in the picture were *my* children. "You can't be a mommy. You're a teacher!" was one of the more memorable pronouncements. A colleague of mine had a similar experience when she showed the children a picture of her father. "You can't have a father. You're a grownup!" was one of the comments.

This is the beginning of discovery. We are all, grownups and children, part of family groups, and those relationships are a very important part of our lives. Even grownups are somebody's children!

Start with a picture or photo display. I saw an excellent bulletin board in a kindergarten class. There were four beautiful pictures of four families: one was Oriental, one Negro, one Caucasian, and one American Indian. The people in each picture were dressed and posed differently. Each picture showed grownups and children of various ages and at least one baby in someone's arms or on someone's lap. The children were fascinated by the pictures and were spurred to excellent conversations and observations about the human family.

Start with animal families. Many teachers of early childhood education find that a wonderful way to begin activities about family is to focus on animal families, through pictures, stories, or firsthand observations.

What are some things that a family teaches us?	
To tell time	To read
To eat	To have good manners
To walk	To brush our teeth
To talk	To be nice to animals

Another of the answers that led to a new question was "A family does things together."

What does a family do together?

Goes shopping	Visits people
Takes us to the zoo	Goes to church
Takes us to the doctor	Goes to the library
Plays games	Listens to records

As you read the children's responses, think of activities that could grow naturally from them. See how many of the activities you think of are mentioned in the following pages of this guide.

Realizing how important family is to your young children, you will not be surprised if family is part of almost every "Talk Time," no matter what the topic.

Talking about wishes. Because the world of the imagination is almost as real to young children as the real world, you will hear some children contribute what sounds like "lies" to your "Talk Time." For example, four-and-a-half-year-old Lynn is an only child. She desperately wants a brother or sister. For a few weeks she did nothing but talk about the new baby her mommy was going to bring home from the hospital. But her mother was not pregnant. Because Lynn's teacher understood her strong wish, she handled Lynn's misrepresentation of the truth in an excellent manner.

One day, as the children formed their "talk circle," Lynn's teacher introduced the idea of talking about the things they wished or imagined or wanted. She began by saying, "I wish I had a horse. I love horses." The children took turns sharing their wishes. When it was Lynn's turn, she said, "I wish I had a little baby brother or sister." One of the boys said, "I thought you were getting a new baby!" The teacher came to the rescue: "Sometimes we want something so much that we think it's real. Don't you sometimes get wishes mixed up with the real stuff?" The little boy admitted he did. "You can make believe you have a baby brother or sister," another child offered. "With your doll—you can play with your doll and pretend," yet another child suggested. Without fanfare, the children continued telling their wishes.

This is another example of a sensitive, aware teacher providing safe and reassuring opportunities for children to express their deepest feelings without fear of ridicule or humiliation.

Talking about divorce or death. Feelings about family can be very painful. Many young children experience divorce of their parents or death of a family member. Their way of responding to these events may be silence, repression, and avoidance. Teachers of grieving children may also be reluctant to talk about the situation, which increases anxiety. On the other hand, spotlighting children who are mourning, can have cruel results. Many teachers find ways to encourage their students to talk as a group about these more difficult topics.

One way to help children respond is to use pictures that express more serious emotions. Watch for magazine or newspaper photos that depict a variety of feelings. Children who are reluctant to share personal experiences because they are so painful, often will express their feelings by identifying with the people in the photograph: "The girl is sad because her mommy went away"; "The boy is crying because his aunt died."

Unfortunately, few good books are available for young children that deal with these topics, but some books have helped teachers encourage children to talk freely about their experiences and problems. Books like *Where Is Daddy?* by Beth Goff (Beacon Press, 1969), *Mommy and Daddy Are Divorced* by Patricia Perry and Marietta Lynch (Dial Press, 1978), *Saturday with Daddy* by Alex Cervantes and E. DeMichael (Dandelion Press, 1982), and *Me Day* by Joan Lexau (Dial Press, 1971) deal with children learning that they are not the cause of their parents' conflicts and divorce. Read these books together and talk about the children in the story and how class members feel about the story. In this context of caring and awareness, your children will find reassurance and encouragement.

Tomie De Paola's excellent book *Nana Upstairs, Nana Downstairs* (Putnam, 1973) deals sensitively with a little boy whose mother works and who spends much of his time with his grandmother and great grandmother. The story tells about his Great Nana's death and his reactions. If you have a child in your room who has lost a family member, books such as this one will inspire important "Talk Times."

Remember, feelings, fantasies, and

fears are just as important to talk about as factual information. Talks turn into poems, stories, pictures, and songs.

ART TIMES

Most children, if given the materials and time, will happily plunge into the process of creation. Combine simple, easily accessible materials with imaginative ideas and you will have delightful, soul-satisfying activity and a room full of fascinating "works."

Elaine Crisp teaches art to elementary classes in the Wapakoneta area of Ohio. Her students are usually involved in interesting and enjoyable art projects. Family is one of her favorite themes. Michael Joel Rosen is a poet and artist who works with elementary children in the Artists-in-the-Schools program in Ohio. He is known by children and teachers for his outstandingly creative and challenging art activities. Many of Michael Rosen's and Elaine Crisp's ideas are included in this section of the guide.

Family trees. Cut out different tree shapes from construction paper or cardboard, one for each child. Freely cut leaf shapes. On each leaf, the children draw, color, paint, or paste on a picture of someone in their family. They then paste or glue their leaves to the branches. Find a wall big enough to display your forest of family trees.

Family portraits. After talking about the special groups of people who make up a person's family, introduce the idea of a picture of the family. Children decide on the size of paper they want to use for their family portraits. Elaine Crisp was surprised and delighted with the number of young children who wanted to create miniature portraits. The children fill their paper with pictures of the members of their families.

Portrait of a family member. Michael Rosen likes to focus on one family member, whichever one the children choose for a portrait. He asks questions that cause children to think about specific features: "What color is his hair?" "What color are her eyes?" "Does she wear glasses?" "What kind of shirts does he wear?" The children's minds are full of details before they begin their portraits.

When the pictures are finished, the children color in frames. A delightful aspect

of Michael's projects is the titling of the pictures in the style of great artists: "Portrait of the Artist's Mother with Umbrella"; or "Portrait of the Artist's Cousin Playing in Sandbox." All of the portraits make up a portrait gallery.

Pictures of family activities. As you can guess, this project naturally follows "Talk Time." The idea was received with great enthusiasm by Elaine Crisp's kindergartners and first graders. The pictures were titled and included the following:

My Father Driving a Tractor

My Mother Making Cookies

My Brother Playing Baseball

My Baby Brother in His Carriage

Collage of shared family activities. Children cut out or draw pictures of activities shared by their families. They paste their pictures and drawings on a large sheet of paper in any arrangement or design they choose. Their collages tell a lot about their family lives. I noted some of the pictures that five-year-old Debby included in her collage: a car; a TV set; an outdoor grill; a garden; cat food; and an original drawing of two happy faces ("That's me and Mom at the Ice Capades").

A variation of this activity is a large collage by the entire class.

Family activity sculpture. With clay, toothpicks, scrounge materials, blocks, Tinker Toys, pipe cleaners, wire, string, paste, and glue, the children create scenes of favorite family activities, such as a circus, a playground, a zoo, and Christmas.

If some children do not have a favorite activity, give them the opportunity to create a scene of an activity they would enjoy. Turn a wish into a creation.

Family scroll. Talk with the children about the idea that long ago, before people learned how to make books, they used scrolls to tell stories.

Cut butcher paper into long sheets that roll easily. Give each child a sheet (scroll). Encourage the children to write words that relate to their families (names, places, objects, events) and to draw pictures and designs that tell something about their families. They can tell a family story or just tell about their family. When the scrolls are finished, the children choose a strand of colored wool to tie it.

Be sure to take time to share the scrolls so that all of them are celebrated. Of course, they make wonderful family gifts.

Bulletin board celebrating a family member. After talking with the children about different family members, choose one to highlight, for example, grandfathers. Children bring in photos or cut pictures out of magazines that remind them of grandfathers. Add words of songs the children make up, as well as descriptions of what grandfathers do, like, say, and teach.

I saw a grandfather bulletin board on the wall of a kindergarten class. It was bright with words, photos, and illustrations. One line stays in my memory: "Grandfather is a friendly person who whispers O.K. when mommy says NO!"—Brett, five years old.

Family symbol. Scottish clans have tartans, Cub Scout dens have animal names, and Indian tribes have totems. Talk with the children about choosing a symbol for their family. It can be anything they choose—a design, a shape, a word, an initial. After they have created their family symbol, encourage them to use it as often as they want to, on as many different things.

Michael Rosen reported that a group of kindergartners drew their family symbols next to their names every time they wrote their names. One first-grade teacher wrote all the children's names on a large sheet of paper and had them draw their family symbol next to their names on the chart. After a while, the children learned all the symbols.

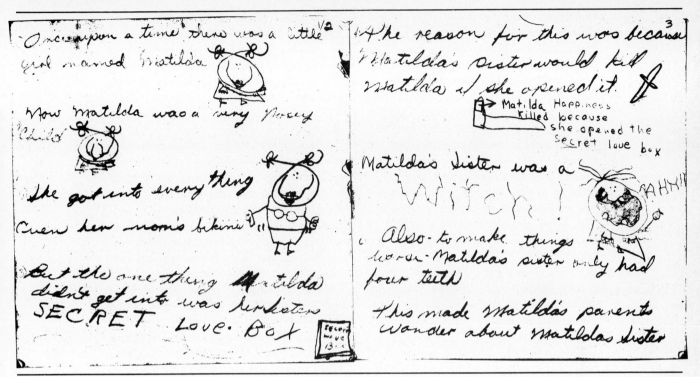

Once upon a time there was a little [1/2] girl named Matilda

Now Matilda was a very fussy child.

She got into every thing

Even her mom's bikini.

But the one thing Matilda didn't get into was her sisters SECRET Love. Box

[3] The reason for this was because Matilda's sister would kill matilda if she opened it.

Matilda Happiness killed because she opened the secret love box

Matilda's Sister was a WITCH !

Also - to make things worse - Matilda's sister only had four teeth

this made matilda's parents wonder about matilda's sister

Renee, age 8

Turn family symbols into posters. Print them on T-shirts.

Family charm bracelet. Use colored string, strands of wool, beads, pipe cleaners, or linked paper clips as the basic bracelet. The children design "charms" based on family ideas and attach them with string or thread.

Two kindergartners' bracelets stand out in my mind. Becky cut out small pictures of objects connected with her family. With her teacher's help, she mounted each one on cardboard of the same size and shape as the charm. A hole was punched at the top of the picture for string to go through, and the charm was tied to the bracelet. Some of the charms were a tricycle, a fishing pole, a crib, and a puppy.

Teddy made a bracelet for his sister's sixth birthday. It had five colorful cardboard balloon shapes with faces on them, one for each family member. Their names were written on the other side. They dangled from the bracelet on strands of brightly colored wool pulled through punched holes.

Family album. Give each child enough sheets of paper to allow a page for each family member. On each page they write the name of the person or pet highlighted, and they design the page any way they choose. The children enjoy choosing their favorite color of construction paper for the cover. Staple the pages together. Be sure to share the albums.

Family postcard. This project requires only a postage stamp, a card-size piece of heavy drawing paper, and a family address. The children draw a picture of a family member on one side of the card. The card is mailed to the family member with a brief message written by the child or dictated to the teacher or an older student. (Teachers who are scrounge experts save the blank halves of holiday greeting cards and use them for a project such as this one.)

Family place mats. On plain sheets of paper, the children design a place mat for each family member. Encourage them to create a special place mat for each person and to include the person's name. As a variation of this project, use the family symbol on the place mats. If a laminating machine is not available (and cheap), clear contact paper can be stretched over the place mats to protect them. Use them for classroom celebrations or send them home as gifts.

Family centerpiece. A wonderful family gift is a centerpiece. An easy way to create a centerpiece is to give each child a paper plate to paint or color. They may use the "scrounge box" (which should always be filled with old jewelry, seeds, scraps of material, old toys, dishes, pictures, and so on); they may collect materials from nature (leaves, pebbles, twigs, nuts, bark, sand); or they may draw, paint, and color their own patterns or pictures and paste on hunks of material to add another dimension.

Family snapshot center. Ask the children to bring in snapshots of family members. The snapshots can be pinned or taped to a large piece of paper to make a collage, or each one may be mounted on background paper. Label the snapshots, such as "Laura's Grandmother Jackson"; "Bob's cousin, Mattie"; and "Adina's sister, Ariela." You will find this Family Snapshot Center a long-lasting focus of attention and discussion.

Create a family. Children are the best collectors. Empty the pockets or lunch box of a young child and you will need no further evidence.

Invite the children to turn a group of pinecones, seashells, stones, tongue depressors, Popsicle sticks, buckeyes, nuts, seeds, marbles, spools, sticks, or buttons into a family. They decorate their "family" members, keep them in a special place, play with them, paste or glue them to a piece of cardboard if they choose, make up stories about them, and enjoy them.

Reminder: As often as possible, add words to your art projects. Titles, labels, balloon shapes with dialogue written on them, all enrich learning by expanding the visual ideas. A child draws a picture of a person. That image stands by itself. But if you want to add enjoyment and another level of learning to the experience, ask, "What is this person saying?" and write the answer in a bubble that can be attached to the picture. Now you not only see but also hear the person. Adding words also prods the imagination and helps language development.

MUSIC TIMES

Families have their favorite kinds of music and songs, both learned and improvised—songs they sing when going places, goodnight songs, songs reminding them to do chores, songs for holidays and special events. When we talk about family songs, we highlight cultural heritage.

In your knapsack of memories and experiences, you have collected songs that you can trace back to family times, camps, schools, grandparents, and holidays. This is a rich and surprising resource to be used and shared.

Remember, children can learn and enjoy most songs. Do not limit yourself to specially packaged songs for children; be open and eclectic in your selections. If you enjoy them, your children probably will too.

Lullabies. Probably the most universal songs are lullabies—peaceful, soothing, loving sounds that hush babies to sleep. Lullabies come in every language and are tributes to human heritage. Share different kinds of lullabies with your children as often as possible: during quiet times, after snacks, after strenuous activities, during quiet play times. Make room for their lullabies, original or learned. Listen as they sing to their "babies," to each other, and to themselves.

Some of the more familiar and beloved songs of this kind are: "Kum Ba Yah," "Swing Low, Sweet Chariot," "All the Pretty Little Horses," "Down in the Valley," "The Riddle Song" ("I gave my love a cherry"), "Twinkle, Twinkle, Little Star," "Greensleeves," and "Five Hundred Miles."

Songs about family places. Because "going places" is something most families do together and because families in America are scattered around the country, places and traveling are important ideas that young children easily understand. Pat Enciso, a gifted and talented teacher, adds lines and verses about her students to familiar songs. For example, she improvised "Oh Susanna": "Mary's goin' to Boston, her grandma for to see . . ."; and "Peter's goin' to Cincinnati, his cousin for to see . . ."

Barbara Weinberg, director of the Jewish Center in Columbus, Ohio, rearranged the old Thanksgiving favorite "Over the River and Through the Woods to Grandmother's House We Go" to include the childrens' relatives: "Over the river and through the woods to Cousin Jenny's house we go . . ." One child noted, "We don't go over a river to Cousin Jenny's!" When asked how his family traveled to Cousin Jenny's, he explained, "We go on the freeway and on a bridge . . ." which became a new line of the song: "Over the freeway and over the bridge to Cousin Jenny's house we go . . ."

Encourage the children to make up and share songs about going places and visiting family members.

Songs sung enroute. Many families have ritual songs they sing as they drive places. A first-grade list of "traveling songs" included such favorites as: "Found a Peanut," "Ninety-Nine Bottles of Beer on the Wall," "You Are My Sunshine," "This Old Man," "Clementine," "Twelve Days of Christmas" and "I Know an Old Lady That Swallowed a Fly!"

Songs about family members. Since children compose songs almost daily, encourage them to create songs for family members. Write down their words, and give them time to teach their songs to classmates. Gather their family songs into a special songbook that they illustrate, or devote a bulletin board to their songs and illustrate the lyrics with family photos.

A Song for Cousin Hallie
Hallie, come over, come over
   to my house.
Hallie, come over, come over
   we'll play house.

by Melissa, age 5

Favorite family music. If music is part of classroom life—not an activity relegated to a special time slot, but one that flows through everything you do—the children will bring in record albums from home. Find time to play their family music. It is important that they want to share it with you and their classmates. Bring in your family music to share with them.

Family songs. When children feel safe and cared about, they are eager to share songs they sing with their family. Many of these songs are hums or chants while doing something or going somewhere. Laura, five and a half years old, explained that when her family went on a trip, her daddy sang a special song as they drove up and down hills: "Here we go up up up the hill/and down down down the hill." The voices climbed up the scale as they went up the hill, and down the scale as they went down the hill. Laura's classmates enjoyed the little song and sang it often while they were playing and taking walks.

Patty, age six, laughed as she taught her mommy's "silly song," as she called it. Her mother sang this song when the children forgot to wash their face: "You forgot to wash your face!/It's a disgrace!/A dirty face!" Ted's aunt (he lived with his aunt) had a "scolding song" that he shared with his kindergarten classmates: "No! No! A thousand times no." The children used it often throughout the year.

Family bands or orchestras. A kindergarten class created a family of instruments. The cymbals were the fathers; the drums were the mothers; the tambourines were the brothers; the jingle bells were the sisters; and the triangles were the baby. They told stories about family characters and made up puppet shows. They used their instruments to accompany their stories and shows. For example, when father was mentioned or introduced, the cymbals were clapped. When the word "family" was said, all the instruments were played together.

A variation of this idea is the *Peter and the Wolf* approach. The children create a melody to be played by a specific instrument for each family member. A memorable highlight of a kindergarten class's "open house" was the presentation of their "family music themes." As each melody was played, the appropriate family member stood. One of the mothers was delighted by the "mothers' music," which was staccato and perky with jingle bells and tambourines. "I'm honored," she said later, "that the children think of us mothers in such happy ways!"

A common way of looking at the instruments in an orchestra is by family groupings, for example, the reed family, the string family, and the percussion family.

Songs that celebrate the human family. When we expand concern about our own families to our greater human family, we sing about the kind of world the human family should build together. Such songs not only are enjoyable to sing but also help children to appreciate that people around the world have the same kinds of yearnings.

A group of kindergartners voted Jacques Brel's "If We Only Had Love" their favorite song. Songs like "Give Peace a Chance," "He's Got the Whole World in His Hands," "I Ain't Gonna Study War No

More," "One Man's Hands," "If I Had a Hammer," and "Whose Garden Is This?" reflect a deeper sense of family.

Families from different cultures. Correlate this musical activity with photographs, pictures, or people from different cultural backgrounds. Music is both an integral part of a culture and a universal language, one that cuts across political and economic barriers and links people together. When you show a picture of a family from a particular culture, play music from that culture.

MOVEMENT AND PLAY TIMES

As discussed earlier in the guide, family is the first game children play. With or without props, children become mommies and daddies, babies and grandparents. With accessible props (hats, handbags, shopping bags, mustaches, furniture, kitchen utensils), children plunge into the game of family. Tune into their role playing. Who takes which parts? You may be needed to intervene by introducing a new character so that a child who is always relegated to a minor role in the family tries something more important.

I watched a child who always ended up being the baby, sitting in the playpen and saying "ga-ga goo-goo," receive the chance of a lifetime when the teacher picked up the toy phone and said, "Oh, Grandmother, you're coming to visit. That's wonderful. See you in a few minutes." She rushed to the "family" and told them the news. "Maybe you could be grandmother, Katie," she suggested to the child in the playpen. Katie beamed, hopped out of the playpen and hurried over to the costume rack to select a pocketbook and hat. The "parents" accepted the change very well. "We'll pretend the baby is at the baby sitter's," they decided, showing surprising flexibility. The game continued and the introduction of the new family member enriched the situations and interrelationships.

Children "left out" who "want in" can always be included by your suggesting that cousins have arrived or aunts and uncles are about to appear. Encourage the drawing of circles that "take people in."

Children blend movement, improvisation, music, dialogue, and costumes into total activity, but a teacher can often encourage further avenues of expression with

such challenges as, "Well, how does Mommy walk? How does Daddy eat? How does Baby try to stand up?" Three-and-a-half-year-old Debby, tiny feet in high heels and a flowered bonnet on her head, stood at the entrance to her playhouse waiting for her family to join her. She shifted her weight to one side, put her hand on her hip, tilted back her head, and shouted, "Come out now. I'm giving you three. One! Two! Three! Time's up!" No one had to teach her that.

Movement songs and games that feature families. Popular songs such as "The Wheels on the Bus," which already mentions family members ("The mommies on the bus go sssh sssh sssh"/"the babies on the bus go wah wah wah!") can be expanded. One group of preschoolers added these lines and appropriate movements:

> The grandpas on the bus go zzzz zzzz zzzz (snore)
> The cousins on the bus go hi hi hi (wave)
> The uncles on the bus go shake shake shake (shake hands)

"Farmer in the Dell" turned into a family affair when all kinds of relatives were "taken":

> The baby takes a brother
> The brother takes a sister
> The sister takes a grandma
> The grandma takes a cousin
> The cousin takes an uncle

The beloved French song "Frère Jacques" became a family game-dance when Marilyn Cohen and her kindergartners in Albany, New York, turned it into a family reunion. From a grab bag the children selected tags with names of relatives printed on them. To the tune "Frère Jacques," the children sang as they walked around in a circle. "Where is Grandpa? Where is Grandpa?" (The grandfathers stepped into the middle of the circle.) "There he is. There he is. "How are you this morning?" (Children waved both hands.) "Very well, I thank you" (Grandfathers waved back.) Grandfathers did any trick they wanted before rejoining the circle.

Exercise families. This activity is a variation of the game "Mother, May I" or "Giant Steps," in which children differentiate between giant steps and baby steps. Children enjoy doing "baby jumps," for example, then increasing the height of their jumps to "big sister and brother jumps" and finally to "mother, father, grandmother, and grandfather jumps."

Choose any exercise that the children enjoy. Give them a steady beat on the tambourine or drum, or play music with a steady, lively rhythm. You can increase the volume of the music as you increase the exercise.

Always begin with the "baby" category because even the most reluctant movers will show they can do "baby jumping jacks" or "baby hops."

Animal families exercises. Adapt the above activity to the theme of animals. Mom and dad kangaroos are big jumpers. Baby kangaroos take little jumps. Grandma, grandpa, mom, and dad horses have high prances. Baby horses have little prancing feet. The children enjoy the fun of showing animal families in motion, with specific movements for different family members.

Guess what the members of my family do. In this improvisation game, the children pantomime or act out something done by a member of their family. The rest of the children guess. David curled up on the floor, closed his eyes, and sucked his thumb. The class had no trouble at all guessing what David's baby brother did. Sandy went to the mirror and pretended to put on lipstick and eye makeup. She primped and admired herself while her fellow kindergartners jumped excitedly with the answer. It was Sandy's big sister's favorite thing to do.

Stories and books to move to. Three excellent books that celebrate family are examples of what is possible when movement, drama, sounds, and music are added to stories that children enjoy. In Robert McCloskey's marvelous story *Make Way for Ducklings* (Viking, 1941; Scholastic, 1972), Mr. and Mrs. Mallard look for a home for their children. As you read the story to the children, stop along the way to improvise scenes with them, or after reading the story to the children, improvise the scenes they remember most vividly. Almost every page of this beloved story suggests possibilities for movement. Let different children be the parents, Mr. and Mrs. Mallard, each time a scene changes.

Ann Nolan Clark's *In My Mother's House*, a poetic story of an Indian child's life, has many movement ideas. Take a few pages at a time; the book is too long for one session. Here is an example of the simple but evocative words that easily spur movement responses:

> When it is dark
> All of us are sleeping.   Always
> When it is day   Together.[3]
> We are working,

One group of kindergartners liked the dark and sleeping part of the story and created an elaborate ritual in which each child pantomimed undressing, going to bed, snuggling under the covers, closing eyes, and singing a lullaby. Two lines inspired about five minutes of dramatic interpretation.

P. D. Eastman's *Are You My Mother?* (Random House, 1960) is the hilarious story of a little bird who asks all the different animals and parts of nature if they are his mother. Double-up on animals to give all the children the chance to participate. (I rarely choose parts for the children, but rather encourage them to move to all the characters and action of stories, even those with many changes.)

Dear baby, here is our wisdom. Margie Goldach, a pregnant teacher at the Jewish Center in Columbus, Ohio, who also has a great sense of humor, taped her four-year-olds as they spoke to her unborn baby about the best way to get along in this world.

SCOTT: Don't eat plants.
JENNIFER: Come out and have fun!
MONICA: Don't play with matches.
NATHAN: Don't go outside by yourself.
NICKY: Don't fight.
JASON: Don't smoke.
ELLISSA: Baby, don't get into your mom's keys.
JAIMIE: I have to say, don't go under the table or you'll bump your head!

Margie realized that all these earnest and caring "don'ts" might discourage her baby from wanting to be born, so she asked the children to tell her baby what good things were waiting.

MONICA: Baby, you'll go out to dinner and you'll play with the toy turtle.
DOUG: You'll see a building and go into it.
ELLISSA: You'll have fun time playing with me!
JOEY: You'll eat good food, like orange juice.
STACY: Play on the playground.
EVE: Play with blocks.
JENNIFER: Baby, give me a kiss and a hug!

This activity gives children the chance to share their wisdom, use their imaginations, and express some of their own family experiences and feelings.

A special family for the class. Use puppets, dolls, stuffed animals, or any toy characters to create a family that will belong to all the children. With your students, name each character and decide on the family role.

Here is the lineup of a family created by a group of kindergartners, first graders, and second graders: mother: Betsy (a Barbie doll-type doll); father: Teddy (a teddy bear); daughter: Cindy (a rag doll); son: Andy (a G.I. Joe-type doll); and baby: Giggles (a baby doll). One day, the children decided to add grandparents to their classroom family and chose a Humpty Dumpty pillow doll for grandfather John and a papier-mâché puppet for grandmother Alice. Throughout the year, they told stories about their family, played with them, made up songs for and about them, drew pictures of and for them, and continually included them in their daily lives. (The toy telephone is a must for family play scenes.) This ongoing experience was especially important for the children who came from broken homes. They, even more than the others, played with and talked to their classroom family.

Family outings. "Talk Time" reveals the kinds of things families do together, such as going to zoos, circuses, fairs, and museums, and taking trips on trains and planes. Using the children's ideas, choose a family activity to re-create. With movement and improvisation, create, for example, a zoo. Discuss the various characters, animals, and action that are part of the event. Turn your room into a zoo, with special areas of the room set aside for different animals, and with imaginary animal food dispensers. Invite other classes to visit your zoo, just as the children's families visit the zoo.

One first-grade class decided to create an airport after hearing about the airplane trip one of their members took to visit grandparents. They used a large multipurpose room and turned themselves into planes waiting to take off. The teacher called each plane and directed it to take off. The "plane" flew around the room and landed back at the airport.

Family chores. With your children, list the everyday activities of families. Your list will probably include such items as:

Comb hair	Go to bed
Brush teeth	Put toys away
Dress	Feed pets
Sweep the floor	Take a bath
Set the table	

Each of these activities has special movement and rhythm. Practice them all in whatever sequence you and your children decide. Put them all together, one after the other, in a kind of "day in our family" dance. Easygoing music is fine accompaniment. A variation is to have each child be a leader for one of the activities.

The little chant "This is the way we wash our clothes, wash our clothes, wash our clothes . . . early in the morning" can be improvised for this activity. Children move as they sing.

VISITORS AND FIELD TRIPS

Visitors

Family members. Family members are a source of creative and important learning experiences. Parents, uncles, aunts, grandparents, cousins, brothers, and sisters have much to contribute to children's lives. When family members are invited, be sure they are encouraged to share something with the children, such as a skill, hobby, story, song, and something to eat.

June Mock, a teacher in Columbus, Ohio, turns "Classroom Visitors" into a gala family celebration that is a highlight of the school year.

June Mock's Family Celebration
A date is set. Invitations are sent home with every child.

If family members cannot attend, a friend or neighbor is asked to represent the child.

The children design covers for their Family Celebration books.

They design place mats and decide on what kind of food to have. Fruit is always a popular choice.

They write a "Happiness Is Having Your Family Come to School" book with different words and pictures describing "Things That Make Me Happy."

They choose songs to sing. One of their favorites is Ella Jenkins' "You'll sing a song and/I'll sing a song and/we'll sing a song together," which they teach and make into a movement game: "You'll clap your hands and/I'll clap my hands and/We'll clap our hands together."

They introduce each guest to their classmates.

They play their favorite games with their families.

The Red Balloon, the children's favorite movie, is shown, while the children sit with their family guests.

The children, dressed in their best clothes and at the peak of excitement, share refreshments and say their farewells.

Storyteller. Legends, myths, biblical tales, and ballads are often concerned with the adventures of families. Ask the storyteller to share old family stories with your children. Perhaps the storyteller could dress up like a great grandfather or great grandmother and tell stories in the old, magical way.

Folk singer. Folk music features the songs of families. Ask your guest to share songs that are common to families the world over.

Family members from other cultures. Invite family members from different cultures to share some of their foods, customs, costumes, games, songs, stories, and crafts with your children. Young children easily learn songs and words in other languages and enjoy practicing them.

Your own family members. Students are excited to meet their teacher's spouse, children, parents, and cousins. Encourage older family visitors to share stories of "when I was young."

Foster grandparents. This is a marvelous program sponsored by the federal government that brings children together with older adults in a grandparent-grandchild relationship. If you do not want to become involved in the official procedures of the federal program, enjoy the approach informally by inviting older members of your community to establish such relationships with your students. Americans are so

mobile that grandparents are often hundreds of miles away from their grandchildren. Both generations need each other.

Field Trips

Home for the aged or senior citizen center. More and more, young children are establishing relationships with senior citizens in the community and sharing enjoyable activities. This kind of program is invaluable for fostering understanding and lovingness toward people of all ages as well as filling some of the empty spaces in the lives of young children. Continue the visits throughout the year so the children know the senior citizens and enjoy art, music, games, walks, talks, and shows together. One group of children visited the senior citizen center monthly and celebrated the birthdays of that month with parties and festivities.

Places families visit. After "Talk Time" sessions in which children discuss family outings, decide which of those mentioned are feasible for you and your children to enjoy.

Family businesses. Check your community for businesses or trades that are owned and operated by families. Community people are usually flattered and eager to have children visit for a few minutes to learn about the ways families work together. Many trades are "father-son" operations, where skill and knowledge are passed from generation to generation. Children need to know about this traditional way of learning.

Folk artist. Woodcarvers, quilt makers, potters, candle makers, basket weavers and jewelry makers are among the folk artists children enjoy watching and listening to. Most folk arts were nurtured in families; when folk artists share their experiences, they invariably return to memories of their early lives.

Places where family members work. You will be surprised how responsive many of your children's relatives are to a visit by the class. One year a group of preschoolers visited Drew's daddy's dentist office, Pam's uncle's bakery, Kira's aunt's flower shop (her aunt was an employee), and Tim's cousin who worked at McDonald's.

NOTES

1. Sylvia Ashton-Warner, *Spearpoint* (New York: Random House, Vintage, 1974), p. 33.
2. Ashton-Warner, p. 39.
3. Ann Nolan Clark, *In My Mother's House*, illustrated by Velino Herrara (New York: Viking, Seafarer, 1972), p. 14.

SELECTED BIBLIOGRAPHY

A New Baby

Alexander, Martha. *Nobody Asked Me if I Wanted a Baby Sister*. New York: Dial, 1971.
———. *When the New Baby Comes, I'm Moving Out*. New York: Dial, 1979.
Berger, Terry. *A New Baby*. Milwaukee: Raintree, 1974.
Byars, Betsy. *Go and Hush the Baby*. Illustrated by Emily McCully. New York: Viking, 1971.
Greenfield, Eloise. *She Came Bringing Me That Little Baby Girl*. Illustrated by John Steptoe. Philadelphia: Lippincott, 1974.
Iwasaki, Chihiro. *A New Baby Is Coming to My House*. New York: McGraw-Hill, 1970.
Jarrell, Mary. *The Knee-Baby*. Illustrated by Symeon Shimin. New York: Farrar, Straus & Giroux, 1973.
Scott, Ann Herbert. *On Mother's Lap*. Illustrated by Glo Coalson. New York: McGraw-Hill, 1972.
Vigna, Judith. *Couldn't We Have a Turtle Instead?* Chicago: Whitman, 1975.
Zolotow, Charlotte. *Do You Know What I'll Do?* Illustrated by Garth Williams. New York: Harper & Row, 1958.

Brothers and Sisters

Berger, Terry. *Big Sister, Little Brother*. Milwaukee: Raintree, 1974.
Fujikawa, Gyo. *Me Too!* New York: Grosset and Dunlap, 1982.
Hazen, Barbara Shook. *Why Couldn't I Be an Only Kid Like You, Wigger*. New York: Atheneum, 1975.
Hill, Elizabeth Starr. *Evan's Corner*. Illustrated by Nancy Grossman. New York: Holt, Rinehart & Winston, 1967.
Prather, Ray. *Anthony and Sabrina*. New York: Macmillan, 1973.
Seuling, Barbara. *The Triplets*. Boston: Houghton Mifflin, 1980.
Spier, Peter. *Rain*. New York: Doubleday, 1982.
Wells, Rosemary. *A Lion for Lewis*. New York: Dial, 1982.
Williams, Barbara. *If He's My Brother*. Illustrated by Tomie de Paola. New York: Harvey, 1976.
Zolotow, Charlotte. *Big Sister and Little Sister*. Illustrated by Martha Alexander. New York: Harper & Row, 1966.
———. *Someone New*. Illustrated by Erik Blegvad. New York: Harper & Row, 1978.

An Only Child

Shimin, Symeon. *I Wish There Were Two of Me*. New York: Warne, 1976.

Zolotow, Charlotte. *If It Weren't for You*. Illustrated by Ben Shecter. New York: Harper & Row, 1966.

———. *When I Have a Son*. Illustrated by Hilary Knight. New York: Harper & Row, 1967.

An Adopted Child

Caines, Jeanette. *Abby*. New York: Harper & Row, 1973.

Lapsley, Susan. *I Am Adopted*. Illustrated by Michael Charlton. Scarsdale, N.Y.: Bradbury, 1974.

Milgram, Mary. *Brothers Are All the Same*. Illustrated by Rosemarie Hausherr. New York: Dutton, 1978.

Parents

Aliki. *Hush Little Baby*. Englewood Cliffs, N.J.: Prentice-Hall, 1968.

Bauer, Caroline. *My Mom Travels a Lot*. Illustrated by Nancy Parker. London: Warne, 1981.

Blaine, Margo. *The Terrible Thing That Happened at Our House*. New York: Four Winds, 1975.

Cleary, Beverly. *Ramona and Her Father*. New York: Morrow, 1977.

———. *Ramona and Her Mother*. New York: Morrow, 1979.

———. *Ramona Quimby, Age 8*. Illustrated by Alan Tiegreen. New York: Morrow, 1981.

Delton, Judy. *My Mom Hates Me in January*. Illustrated by John Faulkner. Chicago: Whitman, 1977.

Eastman, P. D. *Are You My Mother?* New York: Random House, 1960.

Kumin, Maxine W. *The Beach Before Breakfast*. Illustrated by Leonard Weisgard. New York: Putnam, 1968.

Lasker, Joe. *Mothers Can Do Anything*. Chicago: Whitman, 1972.

MacLachlan, Patricia. *Mama One, Mama Two*. Illustrated by Ruth Lercher Bornstein. New York: Harper & Row, 1982.

Maley, Anne. *Have You Seen My Mother?* Illustrated by Yutaka Sugita. Minneapolis: Carolrhoda, 1969.

McCloskey, Robert. *Blueberries for Sal*. New York: Viking, 1948.

Penn, Ruth Bonn. *Mommies Are for Loving*. Illustrated by Ed Eaberly. New York: Putnam, 1962.

Tholer, Mike. *Owly*. Illustrated by David Weisner. New York: Harper & Row, 1982.

Zolotow, Charlotte. *The Summer Night*. Illustrated by Ben Shecter. New York: Harper & Row, 1974.

Grandparents

Allen, Robert Thomas. *The Violin*. Photos by George Pastic. New York: McGraw-Hill, 1978.

Brandenberg, Franz. *A Secret for Grandmother's Birthday*. Illustrated by Aliki Brandenberg. New York: Morrow, Greenwillow, 1975.

de Paola, Tomie. *Nana Upstairs, Nana Downstairs*. New York: Viking, Penguin, 1973.

———. *Watch Out for Chicken Feet in Your Soup*. Englewood Cliffs, N. J.: Prentice-Hall, 1974.

Greenfield, Eloise. *Grandma's Joy*. Illustrated by Carole Byard. New York: Putnam, 1980.

Hutchins, Pat. *Happy Birthday, Sam*. New York: Morrow, Greenwillow, 1978.

Lasky, Kathryn. *I Have Four Names for My Grandfather*. Photographs by Christopher G. Knight. Boston: Little, Brown, 1976.

———. *My Island Grandmother*. Illustrated by Emily McCully. London: Warne, 1979.

Sobol, Harriet Langsam. *Grandpa: A Young Man Grown Old*. Photos by Patricia Agre. New York: Putnam, 1980.

Viorst, Judith. *Alexander, Who Used to be Rich Last Sunday*. New York: Atheneum, 1978.

Williams, Barbara. *Kevin's Grandma*. New York: Dutton, 1975.

Yarborough, Camille. *Cornrows*. Illustrated by Carole Byard. New York: Coward, McCann & Geoghegan, 1979.

Zolotow, Charlotte. *My Grandson Lew*. Illustrated by William Pène du Bois. New York: Harper & Row, 1974.

Family Activities

Ahlberg, James, and Allan Ahlberg. *Peek-A-Boo!* New York: Viking, 1981.

Allard, Harry. *The Stupids Step Out*. Boston: Houghton Mifflin, 1974.

Brown, Myra B. *Benjie's Blanket*. New York: Watts, 1962.

Carrick, Carol. *Out*. Illustrated by Donald Carrick. Boston: Houghton Mifflin, 1982.

Drescher, Joan E. *I'm in Charge*. Boston: Little, Brown, 1981.

Erskine, Jim. *Bedtime Story*. Illustrated by Ann Schweninger. New York: Crown, 1982.

Hall, Donald. *Ox-Cart Man*. Illustrated by Barbara Cooney. New York: Viking, 1979.

Hurd, Thacher. *The Quiet Evening*. New York: Morrow, 1978.

Merrill, Susan. *Wash Day*. Boston: Houghton Mifflin, 1978.

Ormerod, Jan. *Sunshine*. New York: Lothrop, Lee & Shepard, 1981.

Peterson, Esther Allen. *Penelope Gets Wheels*. Illustrated by Susanna Natti. New York: Crown, 1982.

Schlein, Miriam. *My House*. Illustrated by Joe Lasker. Chicago: Whitman, 1971.

Children and Divorce

Caines, Jeannette Franklin. *Daddy*. Illustrated by Donald Himler. New York: Harper & Row, 1977.

Cervante, Alex. *Saturday with Daddy*. New York: Dandelion, 1982.

Goff, Beth. *Where Is Daddy? The Story of a Divorce*. Boston: Beacon, 1969.

Lexau, Joan. *Me Day*. Illustrated by Robert Weaver. New York: Dial, 1971.

Perry, Patricia, and Marietta Lynch. *Mommy and Daddy Are Divorced*. New York: Dial, 1978.

Roy, Ron. *Breakfast with My Father*. Boston: Houghton Mifflin, Clarion, 1980.

Thomas, Ianthe. *Eliza's Daddy*. Illustrated by Moneta Barnette. New York: Harcourt Brace Jovanovich, 1976.

Zolotow, Charlotte. *A Father Like That*. Illustrated by Ben Shecter. New York: Harper & Row, 1971.

Animal Families

Balian, Lorna. *Humbug Rabbit*. Nashville: Abingdon, 1974.

Brown, Margaret Wise. *The Runaway Bunny*. New York: Harper & Row, 1972.

Cartlidge, Michelle. *The Bear's Bazaar, a Story Craft Book*. New York: Lothrop, Lee & Shepard, 1979.

Chorao, Kay. *Oink and Pearl*. New York: Harper & Row, 1981.

Ginsburg, Mirra. *Good Morning Chick*. Illustrated by Byron Barton. New York: Morrow, Greenwillow, 1980.

Hoban, Russell. *A Baby Sister for Frances*. New York: Harper & Row, 1964.

Kerr, Judith. *Mog, the Forgetful Cat*. New York: Parents Magazine Press, 1970.

Marino, Dorothy. *Buzzy Bear's Busy Day*. New York: Watts, 1965.

McCloskey, Robert. *Make Way for Ducklings*. New York: Viking, 1941.

McPhail, Donald. *Pig Grows Up*. New York: Dutton, Unicorn, 1980.

Myller, Lois. *No! No!* Illustrated by Cyndy Szekeres. New York: Simon & Schuster, 1971.

Orback, Ruth. *Hannah the Helper*. Illustrated by Judith Shuman Roth. Chicago: Whitman, 1961.

Peppe, Rodney. *The Mice Who Lived in a Shoe*. New York: Lothrop, Lee & Shepherd, 1982.

Schlein, Miriam. *The Way Mothers Are*. Illustrated by Joe Lasker. Chicago: Whitman, 1963.

Steig, William. *Farmer Palmer's Ride*. New York: Farrar, Straus & Giroux, 1977.

Zweifel, Frances. *Animal Baby-Sitters*. Illustrated by Irene Brady. New York: Morrow, 1981.

Teacher Resources

Dinkmeyer, Don, and Gary D. McKay. *The Parent's Handbook: Systematic Training for Effective Parenting*. Circle Pines, Minn.: American Guidance Service, 1982.

Faber, Adele, and Elaine Mazlish. *How to Talk So Kids Will Listen and How to Listen So Kids Will Talk*. New York: Rawson, Wade, 1980.

Ginott, Haim G. *Between Parent and Child*. New York: Macmillan, 1956.

Gordon, Thomas. *P.E.T. Parent Effectiveness Training*. New York: New American Library, 1975.

Ilg, Frances L., and Louise Bates Ames. *Child Behavior*. New York: Harper & Row, 1951.

Mason, Jerry, ed. *The Family of Children*. New York: Grosset & Dunlap, Ridge Press, 1977.

Sinberg, Janet. *Divorce is a Grown-Up Problem*. New York: Avon, 1978.

Two books that could be shared with children

Bradley, Buff. *Where Do I Belong? A Kids' Guide to Stepfamilies*. Illustrated by Maryann Cocca. Reading, Mass.: Addison-Wesley, 1982.

Harris, Robie H., and Elizabeth Levy. *Before You Were Three*. New York: Delacorte, 1977.

This guide is devoted to helping children become friendly people.

In basic terms, humans are not sea turtles left to hatch themselves and run for their lives to the water. They are not insects, left in cocoons to wing it on their own. At birth human infants are the most helpless of all mammals. They need to be held, fed, placed, cleaned, wiped, and turned for a long time before they start helping themselves. And unlike most animal babies, human infants need nurture and love to become healthy human beings. Those who lack the closeness, warmth, and safety of another person usually withdraw, develop slowly, and sometimes even become ill and die. Given that human beings have a basic need for nurturing and caring, when and how do people begin to express such qualities of friendliness as sensitivity, helpfulness, and sharing?

Fascinating research is being done to help us understand more clearly how human beings learn to be friendly people. Maya Pines, in an outstanding article called "Good Samaritans at Age Two," summarizes some important studies on this question.[1] The work of Marian Radke Yarrow, chief of the Laboratory of Developmental Psychology at the National Institute of Mental Health, is one of the research projects featured. With fellow psychologist Carolyn Zahn-Waxler and psychiatrist Robert A. King, Yarrow found that infants show empathy for the feelings of others, and many children display altruism at a surprisingly early age.

Babies are not consistent in their expressions of altruism. Some babies are much more developed than others in qualities of friendliness. What makes the difference? Are parts of the brain set aside for such learning? Are some ways of child-rearing superior to others in teaching children how to be caring people? Yarrow and her colleagues found that the children who showed the most altruism had mothers who cared very much that their children not hurt others and who conveyed that message with consistent intensity. Neutral admonitions and physical punishments or restraints without strong explanation of why children should not hurt each other were ineffective. The parents' message had to have cognitive content as well as emotional force.

5

OUR FRIENDS

Jeanie's mother was planning a party for her sixth birthday. "How many friends from your class shall we invite, Jeanie?" she asked. Jeanie looked puzzled. "How many friends from your class do you want to come to your party?" her mother clarified the question. Jeanie's puzzlement turned to unhappiness. "What's the matter, honey?" "All the children in my class are my friends," Jeanie explained.

Jeanie had her birthday party in her kindergarten class so that all of her friends could be invited.

The other major factor found by these researchers in studying how children develop altruistic feelings was the mothers' behavior toward their children. Their warmth, affection, and caring, expressed through hugs and kisses, comforting words, lullabies, cookies, and Band-Aids when needed, had a tremendous effect on the way children learned to relate to others.

Another of Yarrow's findings is significant for teachers of young children. In her study, many infants and toddlers showed distress when their parents did not react to the suffering or troubles of others on the television news. Yarrow has suggested that if parents show no concern, children may learn that caring for others is unimportant. Without realizing it, many parents may be teaching their children apathy rather than empathy.

Marian Radke Yarrow took time from her busy schedule to talk with me about her findings and ideas. She shared her enthusiasm for the work of other researchers who have shown that very young children are sensitive to the feelings of others. An example is Lois Murphy's *Roots of Sympathy* (Columbia University Press, 1937). Yarrow reminds us that children learn through pictures, stories, and activities. Because each child is unique and responds to his or her environment in a special way, there is no one way to teach children to be friendly people. However, teachers can nurture, be models, inspire, define situations, and challenge children's imaginations and feelings. Teachers must remember that most children in preschool or day care already have experience with friendliness. Teachers must continue teaching by example so that children grow in their capacity for altruism. This is a tremendous responsibility and challenge.

Another important source of information is children themselves. Linda Cress, director of Kinder Care Learning Centers in Columbus, Ohio, and I enjoyed discussions with different groups of young children, from three to seven years of age, about friendliness. The following are excerpts from talks with Jo Jo (3 years), Brien (7 years), Chris (5 years), Conrad (7 years), Bobby (3 years), Taylor (4 years), Deana (4 years), Matt (4 years), Timmy (4 years), Terrelle (7 years), Tina (7 years), and Toski (7 years).

What kind of person is a friendly person?
A buddy
Someone you trust
Someone you love
A caring, sharing person who helps you
Someone who plays with you, rides bikes with you
People who greet you, ask you nice questions like "Do you want to play?"
Someone who still likes you after you break their doll
Someone who makes you laugh when you're sad

Are babies born knowing how to be friendly, or do you think they have to learn? Who should teach them? How?
Babies are born with the brains to be friendly.
You can teach a person to be a friend if they're not dumb.
Everyone in the world could learn to be a friendly person if they wanted to.
You have to learn. Every time I go to a new school, I learn about friends.
Jo Jo learned that when he was in his mother's stomach, he was learning to be friendly. He can hear her in her stomach when she talks to people on the phone and how she talks nicely to them.
Everyone has to teach kids how to be friendly—mothers and fathers, big sisters and brothers, babysitters, teachers.
Of course, what else should teachers teach but to show kids how to be friendly.
Teachers have to teach by reading about it, studying about it, talking about it, and doing it.

Who can be your friends?
Everyone in the world
Everyone in my family and on my street and in my school
Even old people
Even little babies one day old
Even little mice and dogs are my friends

How can you be a good friend to other people?
Share snacks
Say "I'm sorry, do you forgive me?"
Try to smile when you see them
In order to be a friend, you can't yell.
If you want to be a friend, you have to give someone flowers first.

How can you help an unfriendly person learn to be friendly?
Try to be nice to them
Talk to them even if they don't want to
Tell them if they're fighting they should stop or you won't be their friend
Ask them to calm down and stop being so rough and mean or they won't have fun
Don't leave them out
Ask them how they feel today

Mary W. Evans, director of early childhood education at the First Community

Church in Columbus, Ohio, is an inspiration to teachers of young children. Thirty years of working with young children have provided plenty of data to support her views. "It gives us hope," she said, "to know that, for most children, compassion—altruistic concern for others—is learned. Some children learn more easily, but all children are capable of learning. Most children start with 'Gimmeee!' 'It's mine!' 'Me first.' We know that and acknowledge the aggressive, the angry, the jealous, the ego-centered facts of human life."

Mary Evans is convinced that we cannot teach children to be friendly people if any of their feelings are denied.

It seems as natural for children to be in conflict as in cooperation, and for us to be surprised by the conflict is to block its resolution to free people for caring. Accept the conflicts with compassion, honesty, and the ability to be as non-judgmental as possible. For instance, last week two children were fighting. I said what I saw: "You two look mad at each other." They agreed. "You two have rocks in your hands. Looks like you would like to hurt each other. You look like you want to call each other bad names."

I acknowledged their feelings without putting them down. I said what I saw. But, in this case, I had to stop them physically from hurting each other. I held their hands and said, "The reason for stopping the hurting is *because* it hurts. You two are too valuable, too precious to us to be hurt. We can't let you hurt each other. We need you!"

I took the rocks away, but I had to be sure the fight went to completion. The kids were still tense. "You still look angry? Do you want to say anything else?" It took a while, but they each told the other why they were angry. One had been building something and the other broke it down when he ran through. When they finished talking, they seemed relieved that the conflict was over. They went back to playing, showing no grudges.

You see, *the important thing is to be aware.* Good feelings are given more light when all feelings are accepted and dealt with. We have to constantly remind children of the pleasantness of good relationships. We try not to punish but to help children solve their problems. We don't say, "Who's at fault? Who's the bad guy? Who's the good guy?" Children can't learn to care for others and be warm and friendly unless that is the way they are treated. Be free of the platitudes of friendship, the stereotyped expressions, the external words. Kids can learn any words. They need behavior. They need action.

In her excellent *Guide for Teachers of Young Children,* which she shares with her staff, Mary reminds teachers that they must start with themselves, with their own experiences, attitudes, and beliefs, their own self-acceptance, their own positive self-images. She also urges teachers not to use the familiar but questionable approach that

says: "You can have my love when your behavior pleases me. I will take away my love when your behavior is inappropriate." Instead of this conditional love, she suggests that inappropriate behavior must be stopped, but love can exist in the process. Instead of saying to children: "I have to tell you how bad you are as a basis for your changing for the better," Mary believes other, more fruitful, more healthy approaches are available, such as "I accept and support you as you are. Out of this affirmation I know you will grow and learn." Please, she cajoles teachers, do not think that forceful methods like shame, bribery, threat, judgment, embarrassment, harsh scolding, and spanking make a child better. Children need clear, logical, realistic limits based on mutual respect. Unless children are treated with respect, they will not become respectful people.

Barbara Weinberg, director of early childhood services at the Jewish Center in Columbus, Ohio, devotes one day of orientation week to a discussion of how to help children socialize. "We have a word for the kind of people we're talking about," Barbara said. "*Menschen*—it's a Yiddish word meaning 'human beings'."

"Actually," Barbara continues, "everything we do in orientation and throughout the school year is devoted to this topic. The reason we have activities and a structure is to provide a framework on *how to be people*. Yes, the children are learning colors and shapes, numbers and letters, and how to eat with good manners, but are they becoming *people*? And what kind of people are they becoming? They can always learn the letter B or the number 6, but they can't always learn how to be helpful, how to care about others, how to respect themselves and others. Isn't that the most important purpose of education?"

Susan Hendrickson gives an example of how she and her colleagues at the First Community Church Early Education Program in Columbus, Ohio, met the challenge of Jason, a child who desperately needed to begin learning how to be a friendly person. Jason, a hostile four-and-a-half-year-old, who was expelled from a regimented preschool, came to Susan's class with a cluster of unfriendly behaviors that included kicking, hitting, biting, throwing things, and bullying. She tried many ways to reach Ja-

son, but he offered a solid wall of resistance. Finally, she and other staff members decided to keep him safe, keep other children and the teachers safe, keep equipment safe, and otherwise let Jason be.

"Jason adored dinosaurs and played very well by himself," Susan recalled. "Because we have the kind of class where we talk with each other about everything that's happening, the other kids knew about the problem and how we were trying to help Jason. We encouraged the other kids to tell Jason how they felt, and they did. His space was respected and rarely interrupted. When he reached out to others, especially two boys whom he seemed to want to play with the most, his hostile behavior was greeted by statements like these: 'I don't like it when you call me names, Jason'; and 'If you want to play with me, you have to stop pushing.' We let the other children teach him. We always included him, even when we knew he would say no, which he often did. But we were persistent."

Susan's face beamed as she finished the story of Jason. "Through evolution and trust, that child came around by the end of the school year. He was so happy, so relieved to be able to be friends with the other children, and they were just as happy and celebrated each sign of Jason's emerging warmth!"

Jason was lucky that Susan Hendrickson was his teacher and that his classmates were friendly and outgoing. I visited a kindergarten where the climate was very different. Children worked silently. A child like Jason sat in the "naughty chair" and did not play. Another child sat at a table by himself with his head bowed, while the other children ate their snacks. "Why are you sitting here?" I whispered to him. "Because I broke my cookie," he answered tearfully. His teacher explained to me: "This is kindergarten. These children are not babies. We don't allow playing with our cookies. Now he knows that if he wants a snack, he can't play with his food."

I sat at the table with the boy and looked around the room. Commercial bulletin-board materials were on the walls. There was little evidence of works in progress. A pile of workbooks lay on the table next to the teacher's desk. The children's voices could barely be heard. One child leaned toward another with some com-

to make friends with every child in that room? Do flowers grow in cement?

Thankfully, I had just visited another kindergarten class that was bubbling over with supplies, projects, conversation, laughter, activities, songs, and games. Children worked alone, in twos, and in small groups. Occasionally, they came together as a class for a story or puppet show. Many of their artworks were on the walls, were hanging from the ceiling, and were draped across the windows. What a mess! What a delightful mess! A chart of the class rules caught my eye.

Our Rules

1. Please try to take turns.
2. Please try to talk in friendly voices.
3. Please try not to fight.
4. Please try not to break toys.
5. Please try to be friends with everyone in the class.

"The rules," the teacher explained, "came out of a long class discussion that followed a noisy, unpleasant argument. We tried to figure out a few rules that would improve our classroom life. These are the ones that everyone voted for!"

DISCOVERY TIMES

- Friends come in all ages, shapes, colors, nationalities, and religions.
- It is fun and easy to make new friends.
- Friends share experiences and knowledge with each other.
- Sometimes friends may disagree or argue, but they can resolve their differences in many healthy ways.
- When people respect the feelings and ideas of others, a climate of trust and safety grows.
- Decision making requires cooperation and mutual respect.
- People have many ways to show that they are caring and friendly.
- When we feel good about ourselves, it is easier to feel good about others.
- Life is pleasant when people are friendly to each other.

munication that I missed, and the teacher caught it and scolded, "Michael, mind your business. I'm tired of telling you the same thing." She glanced back at me with an expression that asked for sympathy with her for the impossible task of shaping up these children for life in the Real World!

I waited in that class until school was dismissed. The cookie-breaker's mother came to pick him up and was very upset about his punishment. She explained to the teacher that in their family, when children had a slice of toast or sandwich or large cookie, they were to break it in half. Apparently, that was what the little boy was trying to do with his large chocolate chip cookie before it was taken from him.

Could Jason have turned around in that setting? Could Jeanie have been able

SUGGESTED VOCABULARY

friend	hug	hurt	take turns
buddy	argue	sleep over	cooperate
pal	disappoint	read	agree
playmate	trust	sing	disagree
partner	listen	dance	welcome

neighbor	tell	games	invite
friendly	play	birthday	"give me five"
peaceful	like	birthday party	thank you
happy	bike	blocks	you're welcome
nice	toys	puppets	please
smiling	snacks	playground	I like you
cheerful	sandbox	tricks	would you like
together	fun	TV	to play?
good	color	walk	I love you
angry	paint	talk	you're nice
share	build	wave	you're funny
help	show	shake hands	I'm sorry
	make up	discuss	

Your vocabulary list will be unique to your group of children. "Amigo," "shalom," and "bruddah" may be words your children know and use to communicate friendliness. The qualities of friendliness are manifested in various ways. We need to give children the words of warmth and communication as well as the substance. Teach them the vocabulary of friendliness in everything you do together.

SOME BEGINNING ACTIVITIES

Start with "welcome" door displays. Imaginative teachers communicate warmth and friendliness with their door displays. I walked through an early childhood center and recorded some of the displays: a school bus outline with a smiling face for every child in the class and a name on every face; a tree with falling autumn leaves and a child's name on every leaf; a wheelbarrow full of toys, with a child's name on each toy; and a burst of balloons, each balloon carrying a name.

As children approach the room, they are drawn to the lively design on the door. Finding their names and discovering their place in the group makes them realize that they are being welcomed to a friendly place.

Start with a talk and a song. Shirley Duncan, a kindergarten teacher at Dana School in Columbus, Ohio, begins the school year with the feeling of friendliness.

In the beginning, on the very first day of school, we talk about feelings. We share the fact that we came to school excited but a little worried because we were going to meet new

people and that's always scary. We wondered as we came to school whether the people in our class would become our friends. Then I tell them that I have a song that I love that talks about these kinds of feelings and I want to teach it to them. I sing "Getting to Know You" (from *The King and I*). After I sing the song through, I ask the children to sing as much as they can remember with me. Sometimes I leave out a word or two to see if they come back to me with it, and, surprisingly enough, they do! Then we sing "Getting to Know You" and shake hands with each other or just hold hands with each other as we sing.

That very first day, the first thing that happens is we establish that we're going to live with each other and try to make each other feel good, feel right at home! Not a day goes past all year that we don't talk about this. This is so important that it underlies everything we do!

Start with a special way of greeting. Shaking hands is the most familiar greeting we know, but is that the only way we can greet? Fun-loving teachers find new ways to say, "I like you. Hi! Glad we're in this class together!" These include rubbing noses, slapping five or ten fingers (this has become almost as common as shaking hands), linking thumbs or fingers, and touching foreheads or shoulders.

Start with a smile and pass it along. Pat Enciso begins the school year by helping children discover that their year together will be marked by daily experiences in friendliness.

Sometimes we pass a smile. "Passing a squeeze" is fun to see going around a circle. Squeeze a hand and pass it along. Gently, not too hard! Passing a hug definitely breaks the ice. A real challenge for the children is a "mind hug." We sit together and imagine giving everyone in the class a hug. The children's faces really reflect the idea and it's safe—the shy kids don't have to do it, they can practice in their minds! We pass winks, wiggly noses—but mostly smiles!

Start with special name tags. Children feel good when they are greeted immediately with their very own names (which most of them can recognize or read) on a delightful design that they wear around their neck on a colorful woolen strand. Popular name-tag designs include animals, happy faces, clown faces, flowers, ice-cream cones (different flavors), and kites.

Start with friendly attendance taking. Taking attendance is a good way to introduce the children to each other. It is also an excellent way to start the day with a climate of brightness and warmth. As each child's name is called, something special can be noted: "Robbie Johnson. What an interesting Bat Boy shirt"; "Melissa Laurie. I like your red ponytail ribbon"; and "Billy Walker. Did you have a haircut?" You are not only taking attendance but also helping the children look at each other with interest and respect. You are teaching them how easy it is to be kind to others.

Start with buddies. Children easily fall into cliques. Unless you plan other, more positive ways for the children to learn to know each other, play with each other, and spend time together, they may become friends with only a few other children. This guide offers a few suggestions on how to encourage the children to find a *special buddy for the day.* Obviously, this kind of activity, or cluster of activities, will be repeated so that the children will have a chance to "buddy up" with all of their classmates before the year is over. If you have an odd number of children, three of them may be buddies. Be sure you keep "buddy lists" so all children have a chance to be paired with all of their classmates.

Here is one way to help the children mix and match. Give each child a card with a special color, number, letter, design, picture, animal, or so on. Tell them that someone in the room has the exact card that they do and that they should find that special person, their buddy. After a few minutes of looking and comparing, children discover their buddies. The buddies may walk together, sit together for snacks, play together, draw or build together, do puzzles together, read together, or create puppet shows together. After a day or two, new cards are given out and new buddies are discovered and enjoyed.

As you read through this guide, note the buddy activities suggested.

TALK TIMES

It cannot be emphasized enough how important it is for children to have many opportunities to talk with each other one-to-one in small groups, or with the class as a whole. They not only learn the language when they participate in talking and listening, but also gain insight into the feelings and lives of other people as well as themselves.

Involve children in planning. When children are involved in planning their own learning activities, they discover that their opinions and the opinions of others are valuable. It is important to talk about what

kinds of things to include in a mural, or where to go for a walk. Exchanging ideas, listening to others, making choices, and cooperating to carry out a class decision are excellent experiences through which children learn how to be friendly people.

In helping children work out their good and bad feelings so that they can live happily with others, teachers encourage positive ways to solve problems that are obstacles to friendly relationships. In many classes of young children, teachers find ways such as the following.

Listening chair and talking chair (*not* naughty chair and good chair). Two children who are fighting or arguing take turns telling the other what the problems are. The person in the talking chair talks while the other listens. Then they change places. This exchange of views usually results in reconciliation.

Magic Circle (sometimes called the Glasser Circle for Dr. William Glasser, author of *Schools Without Failure*). Invite the children to sit in a special circle, where important feelings and ideas are to be honestly shared. Children must feel an involvement in and a responsibility for classroom life. They are important shapers of what happens there. For this reason, Magic Circle sessions are suggested by the children as well as the teacher. A child will ask the teacher if the class can meet in the Magic Circle to work out a problem. Such issues as taking turns, using other people's toys, and choosing participants in games are discussed in the Magic Circle.

Promises, promises. When the first graders in Tom King's class in Franklin County, Ohio, find solutions to problems, they sometimes translate them into promises of improved behavior. Tom writes their resolutions on a large chart and leaves room underneath for each child's signature. For example:

WE PROMISE TO TRY TO TAKE TURNS WITH OUR TOYS AND MATERIALS AND NOT TO FIGHT OVER THEM.

Name _____

_____

_____

Happy talk. This kind of talk includes the daily, small doses of positive reinforcement for cooperation, helpfulness, and affection demonstrated by the children. So often, teachers respond only to the negative: "Jeffrey, don't interfere with Cara's book!" or "Cliff, it's not your turn! Can't you wait?" We fail to realize that by responding only to negative situations and relationships, we are making the negative more important. Be aware when children do good things, and offer an encouraging comment, whisper, or love-pat.

I have seen teachers walk over to a group of children playing together beautifully, sit with them for a few minutes, and comment, "It's so nice when everyone plays together. That makes our whole class feel good." The children beam. When Roger helped Neal pick up the puzzle pieces Neal had dropped, his teacher noted his friendly act: "Roger, thank you for helping Neal. It's good to see people helping each other."

Happy talk is not a major event. It is like the seasoning you sprinkle over your meal. It blends with everything and adds nicely to every day.

Good deed jar. Make happy talk a visual activity. Teachers like Dawn Heyman show children an empty jar and explain, "Every time something very nice or helpful happens in our room, I'm going to put a pebble [or a jelly bean, seed, or bean] into this jar. When it's half-filled, we'll have a party to celebrate all the friendliness in our room!"

Snuggle talk. Teachers working with very young children have special equipment that need not be budgeted or allocated. Laps! Small children fit perfectly into their teachers' laps and usually consider laps their favorite places for hugging, talking, and being soothed and comforted. When a child misbehaves, a few minutes of snuggle talk is usually much more effective than a reprimand or punishment.

Heart-to-heart talk. Shirley Duncan describes such talk as dealing with her own and her children's most important experiences and questions. This kind of talk differs from problem-solving or ideas-for-activities sessions. She remembers heart-to-heart talks such as the following: "Even though our size, shape, and color may be different from each other, we all share the same kind of hopes and feelings"; and "Let's try to understand how our new child feels because we can remember when we felt strange and scared, too." Shirley is ex-

cited because this year she has a little girl named Sunshine Grey. She anticipates that "We're going to have a real heart-to-heart talk about our names!" Lucky Sunshine Grey and her kindergarten classmates to have Shirley for a teacher.

ART TIMES

Art time is the best time to encourage cooperative, friendly relationships. Through success-oriented, enjoyable art activities, children learn to rejoice in the works of others as well as themselves. Because you respect and appreciate their works and continually encourage them, they learn to respect and appreciate their own works and those of others. Once again, the words to remember in sharing art projects with young children are "open-ended" and "safe." Absolute rights and wrongs have no place in the encouraging, supportive, safe environment you want to create for your children.

Group projects. Every guide in this book features murals, collages, sculptures, and other class projects. These art activities should be part of your program, along with individual and small-group activities, because their success requires cooperation and the celebration of each contribution as it enriches the whole.

Zoo wall. One wall of a classroom of first graders was devoted to zoo animals. The children drew, cut out, and pasted about fifty kinds of animals to the wall, including bumblebees. A wonderful variation of the zoo wall was Noah's Ark. The children worked in teams of two, each team devoted to a pair of animals. The children were very proud of their parade of animals, displayed around the room (it took more than one wall), heading toward the large ark that the teacher had designed.

Garden. "We talked about gardens," the kindergarten teacher explained. "We talked about vegetables, flowers, birds, butterflies, caterpillars, and the other little animals that nibble around. We talked about how gardens need sun and rain and care. Then we spent the next few weeks slowly growing our class garden in our room. We used a lot of green felt and green tissue paper for the basic grass feeling. Some children wanted to make their flowers out of material, cotton, and scrounge net, and they did. Some children wanted to cut out pictures of vegetables and paste them on, and they did. Some children brought in wild flowers and ferns, and we set them in front of our garden scene and it really looked three-dimensional. We're not finished with it. Whenever anyone has another idea, we just add it on.

The children proudly identified the objects they contributed. "That red flower is Jackie's," one of the boys explained. "No," another boy interrupted. "It's *ours*. It's *our* garden!" Lots of important things grow in gardens.

Friendship tree. Bring a small tree into the classroom, or cut a basic tree shape out of heavy construction paper or cardboard. With your class, decide what should be added to the tree. Cut out the shapes they suggest, such as leaves, nests, birds, squirrels, fruit, and blossoms. The children may choose the shapes to color in, decorate, and add to the tree; or they may create their own. I saw one such tree that featured a kite stuck in the branches! Be sure that in addition to any other item, *every* child is represented by a leaf.

An excellent variation is the *happy face tree* that grew happy faces with children's names printed on them instead of leaves.

How about an *ice-cream cone tree*? Create a new flavor for *every* child's name from their own favorite flavors, for example, Mary Mint Chip, Peter Peanut Sparkle, and Jenny Fudge Berry.

Wall paper. The children decide what design and colors they want in their wall paper, which is, of course different from a mural. Encourage the children to decorate the wall in whatever way they choose. I have seen walls of footprints, handprints, circles, quilt designs, and stars. One class worked in small groups on specific sections of the wall paper and celebrated the colors blue and green. They had decided that each child would create original designs as long as the colors used were blue and green. The result looked like the ocean, with all its changes in movement and rhythm. The only problem, the teacher confessed, was that she had to borrow blue and green crayons and paint from about three other classes.

"Charlotte's Web." One kindergarten class enjoyed *Charlotte's Web* so much that they decided to turn their room into a web. They connected string from corner to corner and place to place by taping and gluing it. The project challenged their cooperation because the process of deciding where and how to connect the string was complicated. Finally, the whole room was a web of string. The children chose their favorite words for the teacher to write on colored construction paper, cut out the words and taped them to the web, and invited other classes to see their web.

Friends mural. The children spent a long time collecting pictures of friends that they cut out or drew or painted. Their pictures included people of all ages, colors, and cultural backgrounds. The teacher took photos of each child to be included in the mural. Each child also added the names of friends to the spaces between the pictures.

Panel partners. This activity provides another opportunity for buddies to work together on part of a group project. One class spent time talking about caterpillars and butterflies. They studied the miraculous process in their favorite book, *The Hungry Caterpillar* (Eric Carle, Putnam, 1969). Because of their fascination, they decided to illustrate scenes from that process. Each pair of buddies shared a large square of paper (a panel) and was responsible for drawing or painting a feature of the caterpillar-butterfly drama. When all of the panels were mounted on the wall in proper order, the work celebrated the story of larva, caterpillar, cocoon, and butterfly. The children were proud of their accomplishment and saw how important each panel was to the whole.

These are only a few examples of class projects. Ideas such as transportation, cir-

cus, heroes and heroines, Disney characters, undersea adventures, parades, holidays, and planetaria lend themselves well to group works.

Judy West of the Jewish Center in Columbus, Ohio, working with a group of three-and-a half-year-olds who were drawing strips of red flames for a campfire scene, waited for one child to finish. The fire was almost complete. "Hurry, Benjy," she urged. "We need your spark!"

Rock friends. The children glue smaller rocks to larger rocks to make bodies. Add pipe cleaners for arms and legs, yarn for hair. Use scraps of felt and material for clothing. Name the rock friends and use them for stories, plays, songs, and games.

Buddy pictures. Once in a while, it is fun for children to paint a picture together. Give each pair of buddies a large sheet of paper and invite them to paint or draw a picture together.

Betsy Distelhorst has shared her favorite ideas for art activities throughout this book. The following are Betsy's most enjoyable suggestions for teaching friendliness through art.

Friendship T-shirts. Ask the children to bring in an old white T-shirt. With acrylic paints, or ball-point embroidery pens, the children write their first names on *all* the T-shirts. Be sure the ink or paint does not soak through by putting a folded newspaper in the shirt as the names are written. Each child has a T-shirt featuring classmates' names.

Friendship posters, cards, and pictures. In addition to the more traditional images of friendship such as children playing together, Betsy introduces her young students to such symbols of friendship as two hands with their index fingers hooked (international deaf sign language) and the broken arrow (Indian), which means "peace." The children use these symbols, in addition to their original interpretations of friendship, for posters, cards, and pictures that are displayed or exchanged as gifts.

Buddy prints. Two buddies dip their hands into pans of paint. Each buddy has a different color. Each has a sheet of paper. Both children press their handprints on their papers and make designs. They write their names underneath their hands. They also write any messages or thoughts they want to share. Older children or teachers write the words for very young children. Each child has a buddy print to take home after it is shared or displayed. Try buddy thumbprints, footprints and fingerprints.

Draw a buddy. Two buddies look at each other carefully. With crayon, paint, chalk, or Magic Marker, they draw each other. Then they exchange pictures as gifts.

Birthday pictures. When a child celebrates a birthday, Barbara Reed asks the other children to draw pictures of gifts that they would like to give the birthday person. At the end of the day, the pictures are collected and given to the birthday child as a "birthday book."

A variation of this is to celebrate the birthdays of the month and distribute the pictures to each of the birthday children.

Giving Tree. Marlene Hartz and her primary-school students in Kalamazoo, Michigan, created a Giving Tree, based on the story by Shel Silverstein (*The Giving Tree*), Harper & Row, 1964). Apple shapes were cut out and given to each child. On their apples, the children wrote or had written for them a wish or goal that would help them to be friendlier and more generous. For example: "I'd like to give everyone I meet a smile"; or "I will take turns swinging." Each month they talk about how well they are living up to their wishes and goals. Then they write new goals on new apples.

Pass the color. This art activity encourages cooperation and sharing as part of the artistic process. Give each child a large sheet of paper and a crayon or Magic Marker. Discuss with the children the idea that every color has its own special qualities, and encourage them to experiment with a particular color. After they have done so, ask them to pass their color to someone else. Each child should then have another color crayon or Magic Marker. Ask them to think about their new color and the kinds of shapes and designs they want to create. Give them a few minutes to experiment before changing colors again.

Warm fuzzies box. Children love the story of warm fuzzies (*The Original Warm Fuzzy Tale* by Claude Steiner, Jalmar Press, 1977). Warm fuzzies are things people give to each other that make them feel good and happy. A kindergarten class, after reading the story and talking about what kinds of things warm fuzzies are, decided to collect them in a shoe box to be used as often as possible. First their teacher suggested that they cut out pictures of warm fuzzies from magazines and catalogues. Then she asked them for their own ideas, which she printed on cards. They also drew pictures of other warm fuzzies, which she helped them to label. The children decorated the box in bright, cheerful colors. Every day they chose at least one warm fuzzy idea to put into practice with their buddies or all of their classmates. Some of the warm fuzzies were: Do a fingerplay together; hold hands; make funny faces; look out the window together; sing a silly song; and take a walk together.

A classroom of friends. Shirley Duncan describes an art project that shows awareness, appreciation, friendliness, and caring. It begins on the first day of school and continues through the school year.

On the first day of school, I ask the children to draw a picture of themselves. We put them all on the board, the whole gang. "This is Me. My name. My picture."

The next day, I ask them to draw a picture of a classroom friend. We put them all up, with the children's names.

A few weeks later, I ask them to draw a picture of our classroom *friends* and not to forget their names on the pictures. They draw more children.

After just a few months, when I ask them again to draw pictures of classroom friends, invariably they draw pictures of *every kid in the class!* After the pictures are displayed on all the walls and we admire them and recognize them, we have an important talk. I remind them that only a few months before, they didn't know anyone in the class and started with a picture of themselves. Now they know and can draw every person in the class! Look how many new friends we have made!

MUSIC TIMES

Throughout this book, "Music Time" is highlighted as a time to celebrate ourselves, each other, and the creativity that stamps us as part of the human family. Any "Music Time" activity in this book fosters feelings of friendliness if it is shared with warmth and fun. Go through the book and find the music activities that fit your idea of teaching children how to be friends with each other. Add them on to the following offerings.

Original group songs. Songs that depend on the contributions of children are always growing and changing. An example is the following song improvised by a group of children who had just seen a wasp's nest. Four-year-old Crissa began by singing to the tune of "Have You Ever Seen a Lassie Go This Way or That Way?"

Have you ever seen a wasp's nest go bzzzz bzzzzzzzz?
Have you ever seen a wasp's nest go bzzz bzzz bzzz bzzz?

My Best Friend.
My best friend is Kimberly Litte.
I like to play with her.
She is fun to be with.
She ask if I would come to her birthday party. And I said yes
By Quentin

Quentin, age 6

This led to a thirty-stanza song punctuated by laughter. Here are a few excerpts from that song:

Have you ever seen a robin's nest go tweet tweet tweet tweet tweet?
Have you ever seen a robin's nest go tweet tweet tweet tweet?
Have you ever seen a mouse hole go squeak squeak squeak squeak squeak?
Have you ever seen a mouse hole go squeak squeak squeak squeak?
Have you ever seen a frog swamp go ribbett ribbett ribbett ribbett?
Have you ever seen a frog swamp go ribbett ribbett ribbett ribbett?
Have you ever seen a cowfield go moo moo moo moo moo?
Have you ever seen a cowfield go moo moo moo moo?

Welcome and greeting songs. Instead of saying "Good morning," sing it!

Good morning to you.
Good morning to you.
Good morning, dear children.
Good morning to you.

Instead of saying "Hello, everybody," sing it!

Hello, everybody, and clap your hands.
Clap your hands. Clap your hands.
Hello, everybody, and clap your hands
And clap your hands today.

Whether you sing your own original offering or join Shirley Duncan in "Getting to Know You" or choose a favorite greeting song from your knapsack of musical memories, welcoming and greeting children in song is a wonderful way to start a day of warmth and friendliness.

Songs as gifts. Because, as Thoreau believed, children begin the world anew, they understand the tradition of giving song, dance, poem, or art—as part of oneself—to others.

I have a song that I love.
I want to share it with you.
I want to give it to you as my gift to you.

Encourage the children to share their songs with classmates. One of the most popular warm fuzzies for buddies and classmates is "Share a song."

Rhythm bands, orchestras, ensembles. These words signal cooperation and combined talent and energy. Activities involving rhythm bands and orchestras, found throughout this book, suggest enjoyable experiences where children learn that together they can make harmony and beautiful music.

Friendly and unfriendly orchestras. The children were given their homemade and machine-made instruments. They practiced with them for a few minutes. Then they were told the following story. "Once upon a time, there was a wonderful orchestra. Every musician in the orchestra was the best! The musicians liked each other and enjoyed playing together. Here is how they sounded." The teacher "conducted" the orchestra, and the children puffed proudly as they played their instruments.

The story continued. "One day, a very bad thing happened. Two musicians had an argument. They would not talk to or sit near each other. The bad feeling spread to other members of the orchestra. All the musicians sat with their backs to each other. (The children enacted the story as it developed.) They did not listen to the other instruments;

they played their instruments loudly and tried to overwhelm the others. It was the worst music anyone ever heard. Here's what it sounded like."

All the hostile, negative feelings poured out as the children pounded on their drums, rang their bells, and blew their horns without direction. The cacophony was disturbing. Many children stopped playing and held their ears.

The story concluded with the angry musicians making up with each other. (The children were relieved to enact the conclusion.) When the orchestra members returned to their seats to play the concert, they felt friendly toward each other. Except for a five-year-old boy who claimed to "like the second part best," the children were pleased to play their music in harmony.

Pass the instruments, please. This is a variation of the art activity discussed earlier, in which crayons or Magic Markers are passed around to give children opportunities to use different colors, one at a time.

Discuss the idea that each instrument is special; if it could talk to us, it would tell us the way it wanted to be played. Give each child a different instrument. Encourage the children to imagine that they understand the language and wishes of their instruments. Give them a few minutes to experiment with their instruments before asking them to pass them to the people next to them. Afterward, discuss with the children their favorite instruments—the ones they most enjoyed playing and listening to.

Share your rhythm. The oldest instruments in the world are the parts of the body that make slapping, snapping, clapping, brushing, clicking, tapping sounds. Encourage the children to discover how to make rhythms with their own bodies as instruments. Give each child the chance to be "leader," to show a rhythmic body pattern and have the other children follow it. When children take turns leading and following, they learn respect and cooperation—essential qualities of friendship.

Rounds, call and response chants. When children sing rounds, such as "Row, Row, Row Your Boat," they must listen attentively and sing closely with their group. They also hear how much richer a song sounds when everyone sings different parts at the same time. Many songs that children know and enjoy lend themselves to round singing. Experiment and enjoy.

Call and response chants are extensions of conversations.

Come out and play.
O.K.
Come out and play.
O.K.

This is an example of a simple call and response song improvised by two children as they climbed a jungle gym. Many of Ella Jenkins' songs are call and response songs and can be improvised by you and your students.

A camp unit of five-year-olds sang a call and response song as they hiked along a creek.

If you come with us.
You'll have fun.
If you walk with us.
You'll have fun.
If you swim with us.
You'll have fun.

When children sing this way, friendliness and goodwill prevail. Because music is the deepest and most universal human language, we feel close to those with whom we share musical experiences. Sharing feelings through music is a special way to help children learn friendship.

MOVEMENT AND PLAY TIMES

Children do best in an environment that gives them opportunities to play with each other in enjoyable, cooperative ways. Because you are primarily responsible for the environment in your classroom, be aware of the ways that arrangements and materials encourage friendliness. As Mary Evans of the First Community Church, Columbus, Ohio, remarked, "So many of our kids' favorite games need other kids to share and play. They're seldom fun when done alone!"

Such childhood favorites as blocks, puzzles, cars and trucks, dolls, stuffed animals, sandbox, scrounge corner, puppet stage, and playhouse provide opportunities for interacting, experimenting, and discovering that individual contributions make the whole experience more enjoyable.

Ideas for organizing free play time. Look around your room and find places and objects that need more than one child at a time to play with or in them. Watch how the children play together. Free play time is popular with young children, but if they do not take turns, fight over toys, and crowd into one area, no matter how marvelous the materials and play center are, the activity is a failure. Innovative teachers have devised ways to organize free play time so that children are helped to work and play cooperatively.

Tables, symbols, activity wheels. I was impressed by the way Cuba Little, Pat Hoge, and Sharon Cole organize the free play time of their kindergartners at Thompson School in Evansville, Illinois. Their structure practically guarantees cooperation.

All of the toys and play areas of the room are introduced and discussed. Symbols, drawings, and photographs are selected to represent each toy, game, and activity. The children learn the symbols and pictures. A chart in the shape of a wheel is mounted on the board. It has the same number of sections as there are tables in the room. Each section of the wheel features a cluster of toys and activities, indicated by their symbols and pictures. The children sit at tables, each of which has a sign in the center that corresponds to a sign on a section of the wheel. The signs can be numbers, colors, shapes, or letters.

At free play time, the children go to the chart, find the sign that corresponds to that on their table, and discover what toys, games, and activities they may enjoy during free play time. Over the course of the year, the children change tables often so that they have different tablemates. Table signs on the wheel are rotated daily.

Buddies and grab bags. Once in a while, change the pace and organization of free play time by asking each team of buddies-for-the-day to pick an activity card from a grab bag. Whatever card they select is their activity for the session.

Find your name. It is fun to print the children's names on colorful cards and distribute them around the room. Children find their cards and play in that area. Teachers arrange the name cards to give opportunities for different children to play with or near each other.

Find your color. Divide the play areas of the room into sections by taping sheets of different color construction paper on the walls or windows. Label the colors. Give each child a small color card. The children find the area of the room that matches their card and that becomes their special play area for the day. Numbers, pictures, words, and shapes can also be used.

Classmate riddles. Children cannot become friends unless they know each other's names, unless they know each other. Every day should be a time of celebrating classmates through songs, greetings, and games.

Children enjoy guessing games. Look around the room. Tell the children to put on their magical *eyes*, which *see* so much more than do their everyday eyes. Use physical characteristics, clothes, jewelry, possessions, and personal qualities as clues. Ask the children to name, wave to, or gently touch the riddle child. For example, "I'm thinking of a boy who is wearing a blue T-shirt with the number 3 on it. If you know who he is, say his name." And "I'm thinking of a girl with lots of skinny braids, red and yellow beads in her hair, and a big smile. If you know who she is, say her name, hop over to her, and touch her hand."

Twenty ways to love a circle. A circle is a perfect shape for encouraging friendship. It has no beginning and no end; no front and no back of the line. In a circle everyone faces each other and no one is left out. A circle provides a feeling of belonging and safety.

I Am Making a Circle for My Self

I am making a circle for my self
    and
I am placing into that
   circle: all who are for me,
   and
   all that is inside.[2]

Of the thousands of circle activities, twenty are offered to start you thinking about your own circle of young friends.

1. Sit in a circle and shake hands with each other.

2. Sit in a circle and wave to everyone else in the cirlce.

3. Sit in a circle. Blink your eyes, wiggle your nose, and make a funny face for everyone around you in the circle.

4. Sing songs, clap hands, slap thighs, and stamp feet while sitting in a circle.

5. Tell round-robin stories while sitting in a circle. Each person has a turn to continue the story.

6. The teacher rolls or bounces a ball to each child in the circle and asks a question like: "What's your favorite color?" "What's your favorite food?" and "Can you make a silly sound?" Each child has a turn to receive the ball, respond to the challenge or question, and return the ball to the teacher.

7. Sit in a circle and pass around an imaginary shape that changes as each person receives it.

8. Sit in a circle and listen to a story, poem, or song. Encourage the children to improvise hand movements to accompany the action.

9. Sit in a circle, talk about sign language, and invent movements and gestures for such expressions as "Hello," "I like you," "Come play with me," and "This is fun."

10. Sit in a circle. Pass around a word or phrase. Everyone has a turn to repeat the word or phrase in a different way. The children will discover that a wonderful phrase such as "I love you" can be said with anger. They are astonished that a silly, playful phrase like "You cucumber!" can be hurtful when spoken in a certain way. A neutral word or phrase becomes soothing, loving, or hateful when said with different emotional expressions.

11. Sit in an unfriendly/friendly circle. Take turns making mean, unfriendly faces around the circle. How does that feel? Discuss the children's responses. Turn the circle into a friendly circle. Take turns trying different expressions and gestures of friendliness. How does that feel? Discuss responses.

12. Stand in a circle joining hands. How many ways can the circle move? Experiment. Walk into the center, back out. Hop, jump, kick, clap, turn. Face clockwise or counterclockwise. Hold hands and walk, slide, or march one way. Stop. Reverse. Work out a sequence and use music as an accompaniment.

13. Play follow the leader. Choose your favorite music and give everyone a turn to lead some kind of movement in the center of the circle. (Don't force the shy child to be leader. Skip to the next child.)

14. Turn your circle into a balloon. Stand very close together, bunched up and holding hands. Take deep, exaggerated breaths and expand into a large circle. Children enjoy pretending that the air went out of the balloon and pulled everyone into the middle. Blow up the balloon again.

15. Turn your circle into a circle of giants, Indians, monsters, animals, robots, heroes and heroines, Disney characters, cars, and Halloween characters.

16. Form a noisy circle, quiet circle, musical circle, clapping circle, laughing circle, and sneezing circle.

17. Use different kinds of music to inspire your circle. Make a circle of African jazz, or calypso dancers, a lullaby circle, and an outer space circle.

18. Make a circle of slow-moving, fast-moving, and sideways-moving people, of hands doing hand tricks and feet doing feet tricks, and of moving noses and pointing elbows.

19. Make a ten-speed circle. Everyone holds hands and walks very slowly. Begin walking a little faster, then faster and faster. Speed it up ten times until the children are practically flying around.

20. Turn your circle into a wheel, pizza, merry-go-round clock, and moon, and an ice-cream cone that is melting.

Make connections. This lively activity gives everyone the feeling of being wanted and needed. It also demonstrates how we are all linked together. Either you be leader and ask a child to stand behind you and put his or her hands on your shoulders (or on your waist), or you stand behind a child and place your hands on his or her shoulders. Wind around the room and pick up everyone in the group. Turn into a train; turn into a chain of elephants; turn into a hula line; and turn into a snake slithering around the room.

Parachutes. Many teachers of early childhood find bargains in parachutes from Army or Navy surplus stores. Parachutes are a favorite of Steve Anderson and his two-and-a-half-year-old students. "It's so easy to use the parachute," Steve explains. "We do so many things with it, like spread it on the floor and have everyone lie under it as though it were a big blanket. Everyone wakes up, stretches, shakes the parachute, and says, 'Wake up, parachute!' We lift the parachute above our heads—the children

love to run under it. So many concepts can be taught, like in and out, up and down, fast and slow. We play all kinds of circle games with the parachute. Remember, to get the parachute up in the air, everyone must work together—cooperation is essential! A beautiful group feeling develops."

When I visited, Steve and his children were celebrating Yellow Day. Steve made up a poem and the children improvised a parachute dance.

> The sun is yellow (children walk in a circle)
> Big and round (children walk in a circle)
> The sun comes up (children throw the parachute in the air)
> The sun goes down (children catch the parachute as it falls)

Friend ships. Find an old rowboat and haul it into your room. If that is impossible, use large packing boxes, baskets, or swimming or bathing tubs. Decorate them and name them Friend Ships. More than one child at a time must share them. The children play, read, rest, draw, sing, row, talk, or make music in them.

Post office. There are so many ways to play with this wonderful idea. Here are just a few suggestions to stimulate your imagination. Every child has a large mailing envelope (9 × 12 inches is a good size). The envelope is decorated with the child's photograph (if you can easily take photos), name, original design, or address and telephone number. Hang the envelopes on hooks in a special place in the room. As often as possible, distribute the "mail." Ask each child to deliver a message, letter, picture, or note to another child by finding the correct envelope and putting the message inside. This is an easy, delightful way for children to learn names and faces and to share with each other.

Puppets teach special lessons. Although American society is pluralistic, enriched by the contributions of many cultures, races, and religions, not all of our classes reflect this diversity. In classes that are culturally or racially homogeneous, it is important to help children learn to accept and respect people who are different from themselves. Books, photos, stories, songs, talks, visitors, and bulletin board displays are among the ways children can be introduced to different people in the human family. Puppets, dolls, and stuffed animals are especially effective.

Increased awareness of toy manufacturers has resulted in a variety of dolls for children of all races. Specialty shops feature dolls representing many countries and cultures. Be sure to include these dolls as regular members of your class. Give them personalities. Let them talk to the children and be part of their daily play.

The following incident is an example of how a classroom puppet contributed to the development of sensitivity of a four-and-a-half-year-old girl. Janie would not play with Luther, who was black. She would not talk to him or sit near him. She was downright mean to him. "I don't like his skin," she explained bluntly. Her parents and teachers were distressed. They tried often and in various ways to talk with her, but to no avail.

Janie's teacher became aware of how few images in the room reflected an integrated society. She went to the library and chose attractive picture books featuring black and white children playing together happily. She found magazine pictures of black and white children and posted them on her walls. She asked Janie's parents to buy her a black doll. These items may have begun to affect Janie's attitude, but only after the teacher introduced a little puppet named Rascal did her behavior toward Luther begin to change.

Rascal was rude and mean. He disliked girls with pony tails; Janie wore pony tails. He disliked children who wore tennis shoes; Janie wore tennis shoes. He said hello only to children who wore neither pony tails nor tennis shoes. Janie pouted and her eyes filled with tears the first time Rascal pushed her away.

The teacher told Rascal the same kinds of things she had been telling Janie for weeks. Now Janie began to listen attentively. Rascal seemed recalcitrant, but after a few days of rejecting Janie and others like her, Rascal hung his head and said, "I'm sorry. I don't want to hurt your feelings. Will you be my friend?" The children applauded joyfully. Thereafter Janie's teacher had something concrete to refer to when urging her to be a nicer person to Luther. "Wasn't that awful when Rascal wouldn't play with you and was mean to you?" she reminded the child. "We musn't do that to other people. It hurts their feelings too much." By the end of the sec-ond month of school, Janie and Luther played together as if they had never had a minute of tension between them.

Puppets also help children accept and know people with physical or emotional handicaps. "Kids on the Block" is a group of puppets created by Barbara Aiello, a teacher in special education (Suite 510, Washington Building, Washington, D.C. 20005). Barbara's puppets are almost life-size and are about the age of children in the third grade. They have major handicaps such as deafness, blindness, cerebral palsy, and learning disabilities.

Carol Minnich of the Ohio Department of Mental Retardation and Developmental Disabilities explained how she encouraged the introduction of "Kids on the Block" to groups of children in Ohio schools. Eighteen volunteers, most of whom were educators in special education, learned Barbara Aiello's scripts. The puppets and puppeteers visited the schools and shared their problems with their young audiences.

"We want children to have opportunities to become more familiar with people with special problems," Carol explained. "When we are more familiar with something that is different, we make the leap of accepting more easily. The children ask questions of the puppets. They are fascinated by their courage and self-sufficiency. The deaf puppet teaches them sign language. The blind puppet talks about Braille, body coordination, and the gift of listening carefully to sounds and voices. Each puppet shares some wisdom that enriches the children's awareness. How do we begin sharing and caring if we don't have a lot of experiences that deepen our ability to understand and feel for others?"

"Kids on the Block" is mentioned only so that you are aware of the work being done in special education to help "normal" children learn to understand and accept others with special problems. You need not adopt that particular program. Introduce your students to a puppet friend who happens to be blind (put sunglasses on it and give it a Seeing Eye dog-puppet) or paralyzed or deaf. Just having such a puppet in your classroom will help children learn to care.

"Don't You Push Me Down." Woody Guthrie's delightful song conveys an important message about friendship and is an example of the kind of songs children need to learn and enrich with activities.

You can play with me,
You can hold my hand;
We can skip together
Down to the pretzel man.
You can wear my mommy's dress
Wear my daddy's hat,
You can even laugh at me.
But don't you push me down.
Don't push me, push me, push me,
Don't you push me down.
Don't push me, push me, push me,
Don't you push me down.

You can play with me,
We can build a house;
You can catch my ball
And bounce it all around.
You can take my skates,
And ride them up and down,
You can even get mad at me,
But don't you push me down.
You can play with me,
We can play all day;
You can use my dishes
If you'll put them away.
You can feed me apples,
And oranges and plums,
You can even wash my face,
But, don't you push me down.*

The words suggest ideas for movement, pantomime, pictures, skits, puppet shows, and discussion. A favorite way to enjoy this song is to ask the children to find their own space on the floor, not too near other children, draw an imaginary circle around themselves to outline their space, and then listen to the song and sing along.

After the sing-along from their own spaces, the children are asked to do two kinds of movement. One is playful, happy movement; the other is scolding, warning movement—"Don't you push me down" movement. The second kind of movement accompanies the chorus.

The children improvise the song, safe in their own circles. They learn not only to listen, follow sequences, and cooperate but also to express universal feelings. That chil-

---

*"Don't You Push Me Down," words and music by Woody Guthrie, © copyright 1954 and renewed 1982, Folkways Music Publishers, Inc., New York, New York. Used by permission.

dren remember and use the ideas in this song was demonstrated when, about three weeks after doing this activity, six-year-old Amy confided to her teacher: "I had to teach my baby brother, Jonathan, that 'Don't Push Me Down' song. He keeps breaking the toys in my toy box!"

"Us Two." One of my favorite poems about friendship is A. A. Milne's "Us Two." This poem is perfect for pairs of buddies to interpret. The first stanza will give you an idea of how easily children hold hands, link arms, sit side-by-side, sway together, or play patty-cake as they listen or chant along:

Wherever I am, there's always Pooh,
There's always Pooh and Me.
Whatever I do, he wants to do,
"Where are you going today?" says Pooh:
"Well, that's very odd 'cos I was too."
"Let's go together," says Pooh, says he.
"Let's go together," says Pooh.[3]

This poem lends itself to a "mirror" activity in which children work in two's, facing each other and creating mirror images as they take turns being the leader who initiates movements.

The materials that work best with your children are those you most enjoy. So dip into your knapsack or begin a lifelong search for favorites that you can share with your children.

Sticking together. Togetherness is a way to foster friendship. If children improvise movement to *The Three Pigs*, they will find that the wolf will have no trouble blowing down their loosely arranged bodies representing straw and sticks but that wolf will never blow down their closely arranged bodies representing a house of bricks.

Migrating birds rarely fly awry. They fly in formation and follow a leader. On a clear autumn day, take the children outside. Turn yourselves into a flock of migrating birds. Be the leader and discover how delighted the children are to turn and swoop behind you.

Ducklings usually stay together, near or behind their mother. Invite the children to waddle behind you and explore the room, hall, school, and playground.

Popcorn is a collective noun. When do you pop an individual kernel of corn? Never! Turn your children into kernels of corn, gather them into a pot (designated place), add butter and salt, and turn up the heat as they pop. Don't forget sound effects!

Parades are plural. They require groups of people. By all means, encourage the children to retain their individuality while they contribute their talents and energies to the total effort.

Take a walk. Most children find that walking with someone is a friendly activity. Start with something as ordinary as taking a walk and turn it into an extraordinary experience that strengthens camaraderie and encourages learning.

On clear days in any season, take your children outside. Find old and new places to explore. Here are only a few suggestions.

Buddy walk. Buddies take a walk and hold hands.

Follow-the-leader walk. In single formation, the children take turns being the leader and choosing movements that the others follow as they walk.

Singing walk. Buddies walk, holding hands, and sing.

Animal walk. The children walk like a certain animal. A monkey walk differs from a kangaroo walk.

Noah's Ark walk. A variation of the above is a procession of animals walking two-by-two to the ark. This activity is perfect for buddies, who can choose which pair of animals they want to be.

Storybook character walk. Choose a favorite character for everyone to interpret while walking. A group of four-year-olds liked the monsters from *Where the Wild Things Are* (Maurice Sendak) and turned their walk into a procession of monsters. Take any of the characters from *The Wizard of Oz* and change the path to the yellow brick road.

Hello walk. Greet everyone and everything you pass with a friendly word or gesture, including trees, fire hydrants, and telephone poles.

Discover-the-world walk. Ask your children to put on their imaginary magical glasses that help them to see everything more fully. One group of five- and six-year-olds spent almost a half hour on the school grounds: "Green is such a beautiful color"; "Smell the grass"; "The tree is strong to lean on."

Imagination walk. Walk and wonder: What if it really rained cats and dogs? What if grass was blue? What if the clouds covered the sun and it never came out? What if squirrels did circus tricks when they ran across telephone wires? What if trees could talk? What would they say?

Stop, look, and listen walk. Use your senses just as you use your bright lights when driving. On your walk, stop and look around—behind you, above you, below you. What do you see? Listen. What do you hear?

We walk with children of all ages and stop to listen, touch, smell, see our surroundings. Because we pay attention, we find a colony of chipmunks. Peeking out of their holes, the chipmunks decide we are not dangerous. We sit in awed silence as the perky little animals race back and forth. "How come we never saw them before?" Mary Ann asks. "'Cause we didn't have our bright lights on," Todd replies. Such experiences fill children with the joy of living and the richness of sharing such moments with others.

Class projects that encourage friendliness. Animals and plants in the classroom help children become friendlier, kinder, more cooperative people because they depend on the care and goodwill of the children for their very existence.

The two projects described below relate to most areas of the curriculum as well as many components of personality and intergroup relations. As with most memorable experiences, these activities are based on surprise, and the teacher's ability to continue responding to the children's enthusiasm. As you read about these projects, imagine the excitement, celebration, moments of intense concentration, opportunities for decision making, and need for cooperation that they provoke.

Marilyn Cohen's chicks. In early spring, Marilyn Cohen of Albany, New York, read Millicent Selsam's excellent book, *From Chick to Egg* (Harper & Row, 1970), to her kindergartners. They discussed the possibility of hatching chicks in their classroom.

Marilyn found that she could obtain fertilized eggs from an egg farm, an embryologist, or a local 4H group. She built an incubator out of a styrofoam picnic basket. The center was cut out and a glass top was fitted in its place. The 4H members helped her wire the basket for warmth, and Cooperative Extension Services helped her equip the incubator with a thermostat. Marilyn remarked how willingly community people offered assistance when asked. They made excellent classroom visitors.

The children made a chick-hatching calendar of twenty-one days and decorated it with original designs. Each child had a turn to mark off a day. Every day, the children compared the picture charts given to them by Cooperative Extension and wondered what their chick embryos looked like inside the eggs. Marilyn remembered how gently and quietly even the most rambunctious

children behaved and spoke during that time. "Ssssh," the children reminded each other, "You'll disturb our chicks!"

Another classroom visitor, a 4H student, made a window in several of the eggs so the children could observe the developing hearts, blood vessels, and body parts. They were scrupulous in taking turns, not crowding, and sharing. When the chicks hatched, the children's comments were tape-recorded and became part of a book about the chicks.

The children helped assemble a brooder, using a supermarket box, woodshavings from woodworking projects, and light from a goose-neck lamp. The directions for making the brooder came from Cooperative Extension. The children decorated the outside of the brooder with lively pictures of chicks.

As the chicks grew, the children observed, noted the changes, and reported their development. They talked about names for the chicks; made up stories, songs, fingerplays, puppet shows, games, and riddles about them; and handled them with extraordinary gentleness. Every day, groups of children were responsible for feeding, giving water, and checking the chicks. These chores were added to the daily helper's Chart.

Many books were enjoyed, such as *The Chick and the Egg* (Iela and Enzo Mari, Harper & Row, 1970); *Le Poulet, a Rooster Who Laid Eggs* (Robin Fox, Lion Press, 1967); *Big Red Hen* (Mary O'Neill, Doubleday, 1971); *Little Chicken* (Margaret Wise Brown, Harper & Row, 1943); *Chicken Ten Thousand* (Jacqueline Jackson, Little, Brown, 1968); and *Window into an Egg: Seeing Life Begin* (Geraldine Lux Flanagan, Scott, 1969).

One of the most delightful of the many activities in the chicks project was one that featured paper eggs. Each child was given an oval-shaped white paper which they "cracked open" with their scissors. Tiny cardboard chicks were pushed through the eggs.

The day came, as the children knew it would, to take the chicks to a farm. It was a beautiful field trip. The children presented their chicks to the farmer, who promised to take good care of them.

Marilyn spoke highly of the value of this

experience for her kindergartners: "They not only practiced unusual cooperation but also shared wonder, caring, and responsibility. Some children who didn't otherwise relate or play together would sit around the brooder and pet the chicks together. It was a lot of work, encompassing language, art, reading, planning, learning technical things, gathering information, drawing, counting—I don't think we missed an area!"

Carol Hoffman's plants. It all started when Carol and her kindergartners and first and second graders at the Indianola Alternative School in Columbus, Ohio, studied plants. Each child received a bean seed to plant and a book to draw and write about the plants each day. The first thing the children did every morning was to run and look at their plants. They discussed and compared. Some children's plants grew faster than others! Why? This led to reading and finding out, for example, that overwatering or underwatering can kill a plant.

The mother of one of the children sent in alfalfa sprout and bean sprout seeds with directions for growing them. The children could not believe that the sprouts would grow in a dark closet. Each morning a child rinsed the sprouts and put them back in the closet. In a few days the children jumped with amazement. All the sprouts were growing! After four days, they had "lots and lots of sprouts." Carol continues the story in a letter:

My mother had given me a delicious recipe for sprouts, and I decided to cook them up for the children. I invited Kay Callander [also of the Indianola Alternative School], whose specialty is creative dramatics, to help. I became a French chef with a chef's hat, which a child had made for me out of tissue paper, a moustache, an apron, and a terrible French accent! After the children came in from recess, I walked into the room, pretended to be a French chef, and cooked up the special sprouts recipe, which the children devoured. The incredible thing was that some of the children believed we really had a visitor from France! Children's imaginations are wonderful. After our treat, I wrote the recipe on the board so the children could copy it and try it at home. We put the chef's hat in our "drama corner," and later I noticed several children playing together, pretending to be French chefs.

Carol, Kay, and the children turned themselves into flowers and plants through original stories and pictures. "What kind of a plant or flower would you like to be?" The children made cardboard puppets of the type of plants or flowers they had written about and drawn. A few of them cut eyes and mouths and made their puppets into masks. More and more students liked that idea and made colorful plant masks. They admired and enjoyed the masks so much that they decided to do something special with them. They found just the right idea—a movie. Since Kay knew about movie making ("Pull the trigger of a home movie camera and that's it," she laughed), she was invited to help.

As Carol explained: "The children thought up the story and made the props. They also did all of the acting and did the voices on the soundtrack. We went outside the school and searched for the best location for our movie. After a few rehearsals, we filmed the whole thing on a beautiful sunny day. The film was the result of long, hard work. Everyone worked together and contributed ideas. All of us felt good about it!"

Parents and friends were invited to an open house so they could see the art displays on plants and the film. The room was turned into a movie theater. The children made posters, tickets, ticket booth, signs, and invitations. When it was time to show the movie, one student handed out tickets, another sat in the ticket booth and took tickets, and others were ushers. The parents enjoyed it very much, and the children were very proud.

Carol proclaimed the plant project a great success not only because the children learned facts and skills in many subject areas, including the arts, but also because they learned to share ideas, work together, become excited about what they learned, and feel good about themselves and others.

VISITORS AND FIELD TRIPS

Visitors

Your friends. During the year, encourage your friends and neighbors to drop by and visit your children, share a snack or a story, and participate in their activities. Children need to know that you have friends of different backgrounds and ages.

Community people. If your circle of friends is small and limited, look to your community for aware and sensitive persons who know the importance to children of meeting people from diverse backgrounds.

Churches, synagogues, social and cultural organizations, and special agencies are pleased to send representatives.

Open-door policy: School friends and neighbors. The best classroom visitors are nearby adults and children who always feel welcome and who stop by to say hello. These people include custodians, secretaries, administrators, and other teachers and aides.

Armeda Starling tries to find a teacher of an older class who is as excited as she is about forming a year-long friendship between their classes. At the beginning of the year, Armeda's first graders meet their fourth-grade friends. Each child is paired with an older child. Sometimes, class numbers dictate trios. During the year, the children have many opportunities to do things with and for each other. The classes visit back and forth; teach each other songs, games, dances, and stories; present plays for each other; take walks together; celebrate holidays together; and exchange pictures, poems, and projects as gifts.

Field Trips

Community center, recreation center, or park. Children need many opportunities to see the diverse ways people work and play together.

Athletic team, marching band, or drill team in practice. The word "team" makes us think of cooperation. Teamwork means people working together.

Festival or fair. People enjoy themselves at these events and demonstrate courtesy and appreciation in a spirit of celebration.

Scout troop. Boy and Girl Scouts pledge themselves to the highest qualities of friendship. Their meetings are usually centered around projects requiring cooperation.

Petting zoo. Most zoos have areas reserved for baby animals or very tame animals. If you want to see people exhibit qualities of tenderness and gentleness, take this trip.

On field trips, help your children become aware of how people show courtesy and consideration to each other.

NOTES

1. Maya Pines, "Good Samaritans at Age Two," *Psychology Today* (June 1979), pp. 66–77.
2. Arnold Adoff, *All the Colors of the Race* (New York: Lothrop, Lee & Shepard, 1982), p. 13.
3. A. A. Milne, "Us Two," *When We Were Very Young* (New York: Dutton, 1952), p. 140.

SELECTED BIBLIOGRAPHY

Sharing Activities

Aruego, José, and Ariane Dewey. *We Hide, You Seek*. New York: Morrow, 1979.
Battle, Edith. *One to Teeter-Totter*. Illustrated by Rosalind Fry. Chicago: Whitman, 1973.
Brown, Myra Berry. *Best Friends*. Illustrated by Don Freeman. Chicago: Golden Gate, 1967.
Di Nota, Andrea. *The Great Flower Pie*. Illustrated by Loes Ehler. New York: Bradbury, 1973.
Hoffman, Phyllis. *Steffie and Me*. New York: Harper & Row, 1970.
Sharmat, Marjorie Weinman. *Gladys Told Me to Meet Her Here*. New York: Harper & Row, 1970.
———. *I'm Not Oscar's Friend Anymore*. New York: Dutton, 1975.
Simon, Norma. *I Know What I Like*. Illustrated by Dora Leder. Chicago: Whitman, 1971.
Steptoe, John. *Stevie*. New York: Harper & Row, 1969.
Udry, Janice. *Let's Be Enemies*. New York: Harper & Row, 1969.
Zolotow, Charlotte. *Hold My Hand*. Illustrated by Thomas di Grazia. New York: Harper & Row, 1972.
———. *My Friend, John*. Illustrated by Ben Shecter. New York: Harper & Row, 1968.
———. *The Quarreling Book*. New York: Harper & Row, 1963.

Making New Friends

Aliki. *We Are Best Friends*. New York: Morrow, Greenwillow, 1982.
Bollinger, Max. *The Lonely Prince*. Illustrated by Joy Obrist. New York: Atheneum, 1982.
Cohen, Miriam. *Will I Have a Friend?* Illustrated by Lillian Hoban. New York: Macmillan, 1967.
Fujikawa, Gyo. *Welcome is a Wonderful Word*. New York: Grosset & Dunlap, 1980.
Heine, Helme. *Friends*. New York: Atheneum, 1982.
Krahn, Fernando. *The Creepy Thing*. Boston: Houghton Mifflin, 1982.
Lionni, Leo. *Little Blue, Little Yellow*. New York: Astor-Honor, 1959.
Mannheim, Grete. *The Two Friends*. New York: Knopf, 1968.
Schick, Eleanor. *Making Friends*. London: Macmillan, 1969.
Sharmat, Marjore Weinman. *Rex*. Illustrated by Emily McCully. New York: Harper & Row, 1967.

Making New Friends Who Are Different

Baylor, Byrd. *Hawk, I'm Your Brother*. Illustrated by Peter Parnall. New York: Scribners, 1976.
Bemelmans, Ludwig. *Madeline in London*. New York: Viking, 1961.
Cherinos, Lito. *Lito, the Shoeshine Boy*. Translated by David Mangurian. New York: Four Winds, 1975.
Feelings, Muriel. *Zamani Goes to Market*. Illustrated by Tom Feelings. New York: Seabury, 1970.
Fowler, Carol. *Daisy Hooer Nampeyo. The Story of an American Indian*. Minneapolis: Dillon, 1977.
Freedman, Russell. *Immigrant Kid*. New York: Dutton, 1980.
Galey, Gail E. *A Story, a Story*. New York: Atheneum, 1970.
Greenfeld, Eloise. *African Dream*. Illustrated by Carole Byard. New York: Day, 1977.
Harlow, Joan Hiatt. *Shadow Bear*. Illustrated by Jim Arnosky. New York: Doubleday, 1981.
Harrison, Ted. *Children of the Yukon*. Illustrated by the author. Plattsburg, N.Y.: Tundra Books, 1977.
Lim, Sing. *West Coast Chinese Boy*. Plattsburg, New York: Tundra Books, 1979.
Politi, Leo. *Moy Moy*. New York: Scribners, 1960.
———. *Pedro, the Angel of Olvera Street*. New York: Scribners, 1946.
Rabe, Bernice. *The Balancing Girl*. Illustrated by Lillian Hoban. New York: Dutton, 1981.
Sucksdorff, Astrid Bergman. *Tooni, the Elephant Boy*. New York: Harcourt Brace Jovanovich, 1971.
Westman, Paul. *I Am Somebody: Jesse Jackson*. Illustrated by Judith Leo. Minneapolis: Dillon, 1981.
Wolf, Bernard. *Anna's Silent World*. Philadelphia: Lippincott, 1977.
———. *Connie's New Eyes*. Philadelphia: Lippincott, 1974.

Humans and Animal Friends

Balian, Lorna. *I Love You, Mary Jane*. Nashville: Abingdon, 1976.
Bonsall, Crosby. *Mine's the Best*. New York: Harper & Row, 1973.
Burningham, John. *Mr. Gumpy's Outing*. New York: Holt, Rinehart & Winston, 1970.
Mayer, Mercer. *A Boy, a Dog and a Frog*. New York: Dial, 1967.
———. *A Boy, a Dog, a Frog and a Friend*. New York: Dial, 1971.
———. *Frog Goes to Dinner*. New York: Dial, 1974.
Turkle, Burton. *Obadiah the Bold*. New York: Viking, 1965.

Animals and Animal Friends

Delton, Judy. *Three Friends Find Spring*. Illustrated by Giulio Maestro. New York: Crown, 1977.

———. *Two Good Friends*. Illustrated by Giulio Maestro. New York: Crown, 1974.

Grahame, Kenneth. *Wind in the Willows*. Illustrated by Michael Hague. New York: Holt, Rinehart & Winston, 1980.

Hoban, Russell. *Best Friends for Frances*. Illustrated by Lillian Hoban. New York: Harper & Row, 1969.

Holl, Adelaide. *The Runaway Giant*. Illustrated by Mamoru Funai. New York: Lothrop, Lee & Shepard, 1967.

Keats, Ezra Jack. *Kitten for a Day*. New York: Watts, 1974.

———. *Pssst! Doggie*. New York: Watts, 1973.

———. *Skates*. New York: Watts, 1973.

Lionni, Leo. *In Rabbit's Garden*. New York: Random House, 1973.

Lobel, Arnold. *Frog and Toad Are Friends*. New York: Harper & Row, 1970.

———. *Uncle Elephant*. New York: Harper & Row, 1982.

Marshall, James. *George and Martha*. Boston: Houghton Mifflin, 1974.

———. *Yummers*. Boston: Houghton Mifflin, 1973.

Massie, Diane Redfield. *A Birthday for Bird*. New York: Parents Magazine Press, 1966.

Michalkon, Sergel, and Bernhard Nest. *The Naughty Little Kid*. Chicago: Childrens Press, 1969.

Peet, Bill. *The Ant and the Elephant*. Boston: Houghton Mifflin, 1972.

Steig, William. *The Amazing Bone*. New York: Farrar, Straus & Giroux, 1976.

———. *Amos and Boris*. New York: Farrar, Straus & Giroux, 1971.

Waechter, Friedrich Karl. *Three Is Company*. Translated by Harry Allard. New York: Doubleday, 1980.

Wells, Rosemary. *Timothy Goes to School*. New York: Dial, 1981.

Teacher Resources

Adoff, Arnold, ed. *I Am the Darker Brother*. New York: Macmillan, 1970.

Brown, Dee. *Bury My Heart at Wounded Knee*. New York: Holt, Rinehart & Winston, 1971.

Cole, Ann, Carolyn Haas, Elizabeth Heller, and Betty Weinberger. *Children Are Children Are Children: An Activity Approach to Exploring France, Iran, Japan, Nigeria, and the U.S.S.R.* Illustrated by Lois Axeman. Boston: Little, Brown, 1978.

Craig, Eleanor. *P.S. You're Not Listening*. New York: Barron, 1972.

Daniels, Steven. *How 2 Gerbils, 20 Goldfish, 200 Games, 2,000 Books and I Taught Them How to Read*. Philadelphia: Westminster, 1972.

Fluegelman, Andrew. *The New Games Book*. New York: Doubleday, 1976.

Glasser, William. *Schools Without Failure*. New York: Harper & Row, 1969.

Gross, Beatrice, and Ronald Gross. *Will It Grow in the Classroom?* New York: Dell, 1974.

Haley, Alex. *Roots*. New York: Doubleday, 1976.

Handlin, Oscar. *The Uprooted*. New York: Grosset & Dunlap, 1951.

Howe, Irving. *World of Our Fathers*. New York: Harcourt Brace Jovanovich, 1976.

Joseph, Stephan, ed. *The Me Nobody Knows: Children's Voices from the Ghetto*. New York: Avon, 1972.

Kingston, Maxine. *China Men*. New York: Knopf, 1980.

———. *The Woman Warrior*. New York: Knopf, 1976.

Kohl, Herbert. *On Teaching*. New York: Schocken Books, 1976.

Lewis, Oscar. *Children of Sanchez*. New York: Random House, 1961.

Liu, Sarah, and Mary Lou Vittitow. *Games Without Losers*. Nashville: Incentive, 1975.

Marshall, Kim. *Law and Order in Grade 6E. The Story of Chaos and Innovation in a Ghetto*. Boston: Little, Brown, 1972.

Purkey, William W. *Inviting School Success*. Belmont, Calif.: Wadsworth, 1978.

Satir, Virginia. *Peoplemaking*. Palo Alto, Calif.: Science and Behavior Books, 1972.

Slavin, Robert E. *Using Student Team Learning*. Baltimore: Johns Hopkins University Press, 1978.

Publications about minority groups can be obtained by writing to:

Afro-American Studies Resource Center, Circle Associates, 126 Warren Street, Roxbury, Massachusetts 02119.

Anti-Defamation League, B'nai B'rith, Publication Department, 823 United Nations Plaza, New York, New York 10017.

Association of American Indian Affairs, 432 Park Avenue, New York, New York 10016.

Journal of Creative Behavior (Creative Education Foundation), State University College, Buffalo, New York 14222.

Social Education (Journal of the National Council of Social Studies), 1515 Wilson Boulevard, Arlington, Virginia 22209.

University of Wisconsin Ethnic and Minority Studies Center, University of Wisconsin, Stevens Point, Wisconsin 54481.

6
PEOPLE WE MEET

If I am not for myself, who am I?
If I am only for myself, what am I?
Separate yourself not from the community.

Hillel

THE BASICS

In the ever-expanding world of young children, the idea of community becomes a reality as they move beyond their homes and families and recognize the important ways people depend on each other, not only for love, affection, security, and enjoyment, but also for useful everyday functions.

The idea of work, of what people do, fascinates young children. They are open to the people and ideas they encounter. They have dozens of questions for the bus driver, the trash collector, the plumber. They are curious without labeling or judging, without looking up or down at occupations they discover. They have not yet learned the prejudices and stereotypes that often accompany various job descriptions and workers in our society. Their view is horizontal, not vertical. "People who help us" is a vast panorama to young children, who do not know or care about the ladder of success. Teachers in early childhood education should strive to preserve the open, respectful, appreciative view of children toward the world of work.

A little girl ran into the office of Barbara Stovall, director of the Southside Settlement House in Columbus, Ohio. She was radiant about the guest artist whom Southside had sponsored to work with the children for a weekend: "I loved him! He was so great! Thank you for bringing him here!"

"Why did you love him so much?" Barbara asked. "He said I could do anything I want to do. He said, whatever I want to be in this world, I can be!" Barbara was curious: "What is it you want to be?" "A cashier!" the child beamed.

Teachers in early childhood education also have the opportunity to influence their children's views of roles and occupations for men and women. I visited a kindergarten class recently where one corner of the room was set aside for dolls and another corner for trucks. Girls were discouraged from playing with trucks, while the boys were discouraged from playing with dolls. What lessons were those children learning? Were they being deprived of developing a sense of freedom of opportunity for people without regard to race, creed, color, age, or sex? What will the organization of your classroom say about your values?

Although boys cannot be "mommies," they can enjoy many of the jobs that "mommies" have traditionally done, such as caring for babies, cooking, shopping, comforting, and organizing households. More and more men are performing these functions today. Likewise, girls cannot be "daddies," but they can do yardwork, wash the car, learn to manage money, and prepare for jobs and careers. Women are doing so in record numbers. Some are even driving trucks.

We are living through a social revolution in the way we look at and aspire to work. Men are nurses and dancers. Women are doctors and plumbers. Our children must be enlightened and strengthened with imagination and self-confidence as they confront the opportunities now open to them—options that were not possible even a decade ago.

Even when our purpose is noble and enlightened, our language often reflects stereotypes. Become aware of gender-specific words, especially pronouns. An easy way to avoid such language is to use the plural form. For example, instead of saying "a doctor" and then referring to the doctor as "he," say "doctors" and "they." Also, try to change traditional titles like mailman, policeman, and fireman to letter carrier, police officer, and fire fighter.

As teachers share talk and activities about what people do, they begin to introduce children to the idea of neighborhood and community. Pouneh Alcott, founder and director of a unique school, Learning Unlimited, in Columbus, Ohio, has a strong commitment to the place of her school in the surrounding community. The children know the streets around the school. They know their neighbors by name. They eat at the local hamburger restaurant, stand at the bus stops, and note the houses being built and renovated. After one of their favorite old houses was demolished, they took pieces from the demolition to make collages as a way of keeping the house. They watched as a new parking lot replaced the rubble and debris. Pouneh reported that because her students have made the neighborhood part of their daily life, neighbors drop in to share hobbies, ideas, and snacks with the children.

Across the city from Learning Unlimited, young children in Rhoda Linder and Sandi Jacobsen's class at the Columbus Jewish Center are learning about community through various experiences. Here is the letter Rhoda and Sandi sent to the children's families to explain their new theme.

Everyone!

These mild days have sure been a relief! Do you think it's a tease?

We'll be using *all* our senses this week to learn about community helpers. We'll begin by singing, "Who Are the People in our Neighborhood?" We'll discuss what our relatives do for a living and see what the children's conceptions of these jobs are. Then we'll name our restaurant and make Wednesday "Waitress and Waiter Day!" We'll have real and pretend food, dishes galore, drinks, trays, menus, pads and pencils, and we'll invite some grown-ups in for breakfast specials.

For "Restaurant Day," we'll prepare *pancakes, juice, bagels, butter* and *cream cheese,* and we'll have an array of pretend foods to choose from.

For art we'll make our own *money* and *chef hats.*

Thursday, we will look forward to "Veterinary Medicine Day." One of the dads, who is a veterinarian, will be in around 9:30 to inform us about his work. We'll discuss what we'd like to be when we grow up.

This is a good day to send in *stuffed animals* with your child. We promise only the best care for them. If you come in, we'll take care of you, too!

In art we'll be making dogs with stethoscopes on. Hopefully, Bexley Library will supply us with a good story about vets.

Friday will be "Hair Beautiful Day" as we discuss and pretend to be hairdressers. We'll work on dolls from home with washable hair, and we'll have portable sinks set up. Any appropriate materials you could send in would be of great help to the success of our hairdressing parlor (name to be announced). Thanks!

We'll try to do some finger painting on Friday, and we'll practice cutting our wallpaper with interesting designs all week.

A field trip is planned for next Wednesday or Thursday to the fire station. I'd like to have someone who hasn't been to come along!

Materials we need:
1) Beauty parlor aids (Friday)
2) Junk mail (for "Post Office Day" next week)
3) Dolls that can get wet (Friday)
4) Stuffed animals (Thursday)

Till next week,

Rhoda Linder and Sandi Jacobsen

As children experiment in their play, encourage them to respect and cooperate with each other, to do whatever they are pretending to do with a sense of pride (if they are baking pies, encourage them to bake their very best; if they are washing cars, to wash their very best), and to have confidence in themselves so that their play will be infused with regard for their own work and that of others. Aren't we really talking about extending the philosophy and practices of

Guide 5, on friends, toward those in the widening circle of friends and neighbors, who, in their own special ways, help us in our everyday lives? Because our children are learning many of these valuable lessons in the world of their classroom, we hope they will carry them beyond those walls and make positive, enriching contributions to the larger community, the world we all call home.

DISCOVERY TIMES

- The success of a community depends on everyone doing a good job, taking responsibility, and caring about and cooperating with others.
- We all live in communities or neighborhoods.
- Everyone's work is important and should be appreciated.
- People, in their work and in their lives, contribute to the well-being of others.
- People depend on each other and have responsibilities toward each other.
- We all have different talents, skills, and interests, that are important and should be valued.
- If people work hard, learn special skills, and achieve certain levels of accomplishment, they should be able to do any job to which they aspire.
- No matter what kind of work people do, they should do their very best and be proud of their accomplishments.

SUGGESTED VOCABULARY

help	worker	shopping	scout leader
work	office	center	ambulance
job	factory	beauty parlor	truck
chore	shop	shoe repair	bus
assignment	store	garage	subway
helper	gas station	truck driver	taxi
community	post office	mail carrier	airplane
neighborhood	fire house	mechanic	police car
clean	car wash	doctor	whistle
wash	laundry	dentist	badge
collect	cleaners	barber	telephone
sort	drugstore	nurse	typewriter
fix	office	social worker	machine
assemble	hospital	teacher	hat
organize	market	neighbor	uniform
cook	shoe store	volunteer	apron
	supermarket		

SOME BEGINNING ACTIVITIES

Start with clothing. Wear a police officer's cap or a fire fighter's helmet to introduce the idea of community helpers. Ask the

children: "Boys and girls, do you notice I'm wearing something unusual?" They will have no trouble meeting the challenge of your question, and you can easily start them off on a month-long or year-long study of community helpers.

Start with pantomime. Pantomime different community helpers for the children, and ask them to guess each one. For example, pantomime a police officer blowing a whistle and directing traffic; a doctor examining a patient (use the children, puppets, or dolls as patients); and a mechanic repairing a truck or car (use one of the classroom vehicles). If you want to emphasize one helper, pantomime several activities of that occupation. If you want to introduce the idea of community helpers, pantomime several different occupations.

Start with a classroom visitor. Be spontaneous and invite the mail carrier to say hello to your class and share a few minutes of time with your children. Or plan ahead and ask a community helper to visit your room. Prepare the children for the exciting event. Encourage them to ask the guest questions and to share ideas. Continue with activities that are related to the visit.

Start with a field trip. A field trip usually culminates class study, but many teachers find a field trip an exciting way to begin a study. Surprise the children with the idea of going to the firehouse, police station, and public library. Prepare for the field trip with discussion and questions. Follow the field trip with activities.

Start with a walk around the neighborhood. This delightful activity is an excellent way to stimulate response on all levels, especially if children are encouraged not just to walk but to stop, look, listen, and learn.

A class of kindergartners filled a chalkboard with their observations and discoveries, which included:

On Our Walk Around Our Neighborhood, We Found

two mailboxes	one newspaper store
one traffic light	our school
twelve houses	street signs
one doctor's office (M.D.)	''block parent'' house
streetlights	one carry-out store
sewers	fire hydrants
telephone poles and wires	

The walk provided them with more than enough material to begin their study of community and community helpers.

Start with pictures. Show children pictures of community helpers and ask them to guess who they are and what they are doing. Their answers will stimulate ideas for further activities.

Start with a poem. Poems are a wonderful way to help children think about the possibilities that await them. Examples include A. A. Milne's "Busy" and "Cherry Stones" (*The World of Christopher Robin*, Dutton, 1958, pp. 132–136, 137–139) and Walt Whitman's "I Hear America Singing."

I wrote a poem that has been used by children of all ages to begin this adventure. It is printed so that you can use it. Better still, write your own!

When We Grow Up

I

I'm going to be a football player
when I grow up.
I'm going to kick that football
when I grow up.
You'll watch me at the game.
You'll see my speed and strength.
I'm tackling right now
so I can be a football player
when I grow up.

I'm going to be an artist
when I grow up.
I'm going to paint pictures
when I grow up.
You'll see my flower prints.
You'll love my bright designs.
I'm doodling all the time
so I can be an artist
when I grow up.

I'm going to be a scientist
when I grow up.
I'm going to discover things
when I grow up.
I'll find a cure for ills.
I'll search those mysteries.
I ask questions every day
so I can be a scientist
when I grow up.

II

When we grow up, when we grow up,
we want the world to be
a place of friendly people
with room for you and me.
    doctor, lawyer, ice-cream scooper, cook, tailor,
    trash collector, governor, gardener, shoemaker,
    teacher, dancer, baker, builder, plumber, taxi driver,
    artist, scientist, football player
The world needs us all
to carry it along,
to build its bridges,
sing its song,
to feed its children,
to cheer its sad,
to paint its pictures,
to make it glad.

The world needs us each
and every one,
whatever our ages, whatever our shapes,
whatever our colors, whatever our lands,
to open our hearts
and reach out our hands,
to use our minds wisely
to live days of joy,
to help build a better life
for each girl and boy.

When we grow up, when we grow up,
we want the world to be
a place of friendly people
with room for you and me.

Start with a question. Spark discussion with questions such as "What do you want to be when you grow up?" "What kinds of work do you like to do?" and "What are important kinds of work needed by us all?"

Start with a riddle. "I'm thinking of someone who helps us. That person wears a special uniform and sometimes directs traffic. That person will help you find your way if you are lost. That person tries to keep you safe from harm. Who is it?"

Start with the Yellow Pages. Show children the local Yellow Pages and explain that it lists most of the people in the community who provide services. Read some of the types of services offered.

TALK TIMES

Many teachers restrict their ideas about community helpers to a few familiar occupations. At a recent workshop, I mentioned to the teachers that I was working on this guide. One of the teachers rolled her eyes wearily and commented sarcastically, "Oh, your basic fireman and policeman bit. Dull!" Her flame would have been rekindled if she could have participated in the fantastic discussion that Pat Stumphauzer and Cliffy Withers had with their three- and four-year-olds in the Learning Unlimited School in Columbus, Ohio.

The children discussed "people who help us." Their responses included the following persons, as well as descriptions of their occupations.

doctor	person who mows lawns	clothes cleaner
nurse		house builder
minister	person who shovels snow	truck driver
salesman		zookeeper
mailman	veterinarian	candy shop lady
policeman	street cleaner	diaper man
fireman	trash collector	TV newsman
ambulanceman	telephone man	newspaperboy
soldier	wireman	tape recorder man
teacher	toy maker	guy who fixes broken stuff in the house
dentist	car mechanic	
barber	circus man	
taxi driver	highway fixer	rug cleaner
bus driver	car washer	Girl Scout leader
gas station man	librarian	Boy Scout leader
airplane pilot	chair man (furniture repairman)	Salvation Army man

It should be noted that young children still identify most occupations by gender. Teachers have the opportunity to teach new vocabulary and a new way of thinking.

Observations. Fascinating discussions develop from shared observations. When I was a child, I was amazed that whatever needed to be done, someone did it! I shared with the children my feeling about the ingenuity and industriousness of human beings and their ability to meet whatever needs arise. "Isn't it amazing, boys and girls, that someone is always able to do a job that needs to be done? For example, if you need your car fixed, someone knows how to fix it!" The children could hardly contain their ideas.

If your lights go out, you can call and get a guy to get them on again.
If you fall down and hurt yourself, you can go to the doctor.
If your tree gets sick, a tree man can make it get better.
If your bike breaks, you go to the bike store and it gets fixed.

Later we improvised plays based on the children's comments. "My dog is sick. Who can make him better?" asked a child who held a stuffed dog close to her. "I can. I'm a 'vesternarian'!" a future vet responded immediately.

Questions, based on observations, that also spur lively discussions are: "What kinds of workers come to your house?" "What kinds of workers do you see in your neighborhood?" "What kinds of skills and qualities are needed for certain jobs?" and "I wonder how people get to be doctors, mechanics, teachers, and cooks?"

Unemployment. Because unemployment is a fact of life for millions of people in our country, it is likely to be a topic of discussion, especially if you have an open, trusting relationship with the children in your class.

"My Daddy doesn't have a job," shy, five-year-old Cindy said in the middle of a class talk about work. Her teacher replied: "Your Daddy may not have a job where he goes out to work every day right now. He may get one sometime. But doesn't he still do things for you and your family?" Cindy quickly responded: "He takes me to school. He takes my brother to Scouts. He brings in groceries for my mom. He helps me with puzzles . . ." The teacher noted, "He does a lot of important things that help you. It's hard work being a daddy." The teacher's comments changed Cindy's expression from dull to bright. "Yes, he does," she smiled.

Be as open as possible to find ways to express respect and compassion for all of the situations that may be introduced during "Talk Times." You may not be able to do anything about unemployment or welfare programs, but you can do something about attitudes and feelings—your own and those of your students. You can help them to see that people must not be defined by their jobs alone. Even though Cindy's father is unemployed, he is a good daddy, a good neighbor, a good citizen, a person who makes a contribution to society. Try not to be judgmental; look within yourself for ways to understand and accept situations and relationships that may be unfamiliar to you. Your commitment is to help strengthen your young students with feelings of confidence, courage, and self-worth, however diverse their situations. "Talk Times" help.

ART TIMES

If your room is supplied with scrounge material, you will have the resources for delightful art activities celebrating community helpers. The key word is simplicity. Children

SIMPLIFY

readily accept a button as a dial, a slip of scrap paper as a ticket, and a paper bag as a mail pouch. They easily transform a sheet of paper into an airplane, a milk carton into a skyscraper, and a shoe box into an office.

The importance of simplicity was dramatically demonstrated by a teacher of five-year-olds who finished her morning exasperated over a project that grew too complicated. The children were making fire fighters' boots. Instead of simply wrapping black construction paper around the children's legs and taping it, she was using an intricate set of directions that involved folding down the paper on top to make it look more like real boots. Some of the children folded their papers correctly, others did not. Some of the children finished the activity in a few minutes and were strutting around in their firefighters' boots, while others, clearly upset, were messing up their "folds" and waiting impatiently to be helped. They never finished the project and went home feeling disappointed and defeated.

Classroom helpers. A feeling of community begins in the classroom, where children take specific responsibilities and contribute to the welfare of others. Even if your school is lucky enough to have a crackerjack custodian, the children need to be assigned jobs in the room.

If you travel across the country, you will see as many variations of the idea of class-

room helpers as there are teachers. Basically, there are two ways to organize this activity: List the children's names with an envelope next to each name; or list the jobs with an envelope next to each job. The children check the envelope daily for either a job or their name. The job assignments in one kindergarten class included sweeping, dusting, watering plants, feeding fish, leading songs, cleaning up after snacks, leading exercises, and putting blocks away.

Helping hands is a favorite way to indicate classroom helpers. The children trace their hands on cardboard or heavy construction paper and cut them out. They write their names on the hands and decorate them. The hands fit into the envelope, pockets, or slits next to the job list.

Happy faces is another delightful way for children to discover their daily assignments. Cut out round head shapes with a bit of the necks attached. Draw headband lines across the forehead area. Write or have the children write their names on the headbands. Children decorate the rest of the face. The faces slip easily into the pockets or slits next to the job list.

Symbols are good job indicators. Discuss each job with the children, decide on an appropriate symbol, and use construction paper or cardboard for cutouts that fit easily into the slits next to the children's names.

Hopping helpers is a favorite activity of some Indiana kindergartners who were each given a cardboard kangaroo to color or paint. The children's names were written on the kangaroos with Magic Markers or dark crayons. All of the kangaroos were tacked to a bulletin board. Baby kangaroos holding signs describing various classroom jobs were slipped into the big kangaroos' pouches. The children rushed in eagerly each day to see if they had a baby kangaroo. Their motto was: "Let's do our jobs! Hop to it!"

Around the country, teachers and children change the ordinary helpers' charts into the extraordinary, such as job wheels (complete with spinners), space journeys (each child's rocket lands on a different job in the shape of a planet), and circus trains (each car designates a chore, and the children's cards are in the shape of circus animals and characters that fit into the cars).

Turn yourself into a community helper. Many community helpers have easily identifiable uniforms and equipment. Here are some suggestions for making these articles for the children to play with.

Nurses' caps. Fold a white piece of paper. Fit it on each child's head. Fasten it together with masking tape.

Doctors' surgical lights. Rhoda Linder and Wendy Wohlstein and their four-year-olds played doctor for days with their official-looking headbands. They gave each child a strip of paper for a headband and small circles to color yellow or orange (for light). The children pasted their circles in the middle of their headbands and fastened the headbands around their heads.

Stethoscopes. Rhoda and Wendy and their students also made stethoscopes. They cut the little sections out of egg cartons, punched holes on each side, and attached pipe cleaners.

Stethoscopes can also be made from spools. Wrap the spool in aluminum foil, thread a strong piece of string or wool through the spool, and fasten the two ends of the string or wool together.

Furniture. Collect small twigs and sticks, tongue depressors, and toothpicks for furniture making. Glue them together to make chairs, beds, tables, and couches for dollhouses. Other materials for young furniture makers are assorted boxes and flaps and sheets of cardboard of all sizes.

Telescopes. Ask parents to send in the cardboard cores from rolls of paper towels. The children paint them black or another dark color. When dry, they make perfect telescopes.

Barbershop clients. Blow up balloons. With Magic Markers, the children paint faces on the balloons. When dry, they are ready to be sprayed with shaving cream and shaved with dull knives or tongue depressors. "Who's next?"

Instrument panels. Give each child a sheet of shirt cardboard or a medium-sized cardboard box. Encourage the children to create their own panel by gluing on various materials from the scrounge collection, such as buttons, pins, spools, paper clips, scraps of material, jewelry, and pebbles, or drawing different shapes on the panels with Magic Markers. Old lamp frames, hanger wire, and long pipe cleaners make fine steering wheels.

TV announcers' microphones. Clothespins or cardboard toilet paper rolls make excellent microphones. Paint them an appropriate color. Give each child a chance to report the news.

TV sets. TV announcers feel better when they are surrounded by a TV set. Turn a medium-sized box into a TV set by cutting off the bottom of the box, gluing or taping the rest of the box tightly, and cutting out a screen in the front. The children paint the box and add dials (buttons, bottle caps, or cardboard circles) to the area next to or beneath the screen. The children take turns slipping up into the box so their heads fill the screen area.

Zoo keepers' animals. Draw pictures of animals that live in the zoo. Or shape zoo animals with pipe cleaners, clay, Playdough, rocks, electronic wire, driftwood, yarn, cotton, and scrounge materials. Or glue or paste animals to the bottom of a shoe box. Each child makes a small zoo and pretends to be the keeper.

Interior designers' windows. Interior designers, painters, and artists help make a community more beautiful through their creative works. Paint original designs and pictures on your windows with poster paint. Give all the children an opportunity to add their own contributions to the pattern. Poster paint looks terrific on windows and is easy to wash off when you need a change of color or mood.

Police officers' badges. Cut badge shapes out of cardboard and give one to each child, or have them cut out their own.

Wrap each badge in a piece of aluminum foil. Using double-sided masking tape, attach the badges to the children's chests.

Police officers' hats. Motorcycle police officers wear helmets; traffic police wear white hats; and patrol officers wear blue hats. Give the children strips of paper for headbands. Outline the different hats on paper. Children (or you) cut hat shapes out of construction paper. The children color or paint the hats according to the shapes. Tape the hats to the headbands.

Police officers' walkie-talkies. Use small cereal boxes and paint them any walkie-talkie color. Punch a hole in each box. Connect two boxes with a long piece of string. Now police officer buddies can communicate emergencies and other information to each other.

Fire fighters' hats. You can create a simple fire fighter's hat by following the basic directions for police officer's hats. But if you are like Sue Coomer, kindergarten teacher at Easthaven School in Columbus, Ohio, and you want a super art project that features counting, weaving, following directions, sequences, over-under, and listening, you can make a fire fighter's hat this way.

Draw an overview of a fire fighter's hat on red paper. Each child cuts out the shape. Cut eight strips of red paper, about 1½ inches wide, for each child. Number four of the strips, 1-2-3-4. Place the numbered strips next to each other vertically. Discuss the concept of over-under with the children. Weave the other four strips through the first four horizontally, one at a time, the first over-under, the second under-over, and alternate the next two. When the eight strips are interwoven, cut ovals in the middle of the hat shapes. Lift the interwoven strips and place them over the oval. Staple the connecting ends together to the hat (four staples).

The hats fit right on top of the children's heads. The only thing Sue does for her kindergartners is the stapling. The children are proud of their hats and wear them when they visit the fire house.

Draw yourself as a community helper. Children enjoy drawing or painting themselves as different characters. Here is their chance to portray themselves as police officers, telephone repair workers, bus drivers, secretaries, doctors, or any of the helpers you have discussed. Be sure to ask the children to write the title on the bottom of the picture, or have you write it for them.

Collage of community helpers. The children cut out pictures of community helpers from magazines, catalogues, and newspapers. They draw or paint their own illustrations. All the children contribute cut-out or original pictures of community helpers to a large collage. With Magic Markers, print the names of different helpers, over the pictures and in the spaces (if there are any spaces).

Make gifts for a community helper. Paint or draw cards, pictures, or posters, and present them to a favorite community helper. I had the good fortune to be in a school office when a kindergarten class knocked on the door, came in beaming with smiles, and gave the school secretary love letters, greeting cards, and pictures. She was moved to tears! (So was I!)

What's in a snack? A bulletin board of helpers! This is the story of how a simple snack of milk, cookies, and bananas led Louise Johnson and her first graders at Avery Elementary School in Ohio into stimulating and enjoyable activities.

One day, as the children were sitting down for snack, Louise thought of all the people and processes that made that taken-for-granted snack possible. She asked questions like: "Where does the milk come from?" "How did it get to us?" "Where do bananas come from?" and "What goes into an oatmeal cookie?" The questions elicited answers that produced more questions. "We get bananas from the supermarket." "Yes, but where did the supermarket get them?"

Before she realized what was happening, Louise and her children were having fascinating discussions, heads bent over globes and maps, looking for banana-producing countries and tracing railroad lines and truck routes. These are just a few of the persons who were identified as having helped to produce the snack of the day.

dairy farmers	cookie factory workers
cows	grain elevator operators
banana pickers	delivery people
sailors of banana boats	people who load milk cans
truck drivers	store clerks
freight train conductors	paper workers who make
store owners	the package for the
grain farmers	cookies
sugar cane plantation	workers in the milk
workers	container factory

Pictures of containers of milk, a banana, and an oatmeal cookie were pasted to a large bulletin board. "Then the fun began," Louise explained. "The children drew any aspect of any of the people or processes that had a part in their snack. We drew lines going out in all directions from our center snack design. The children pasted up their pictures of farmers, banana pickers, sailors, truck drivers, all of the 'helpers.' It was really an amazingly enlightening as well as thoroughly enjoyable project!"

Community helpers booklets. Encourage the children to make booklets celebrating community helpers. When children make a

I am am a policworth

Neela
I would like to doe plicewoman.
I wooditwode be fun to be plicewoman.
A plicewoman is a big job.

Neela, age 7

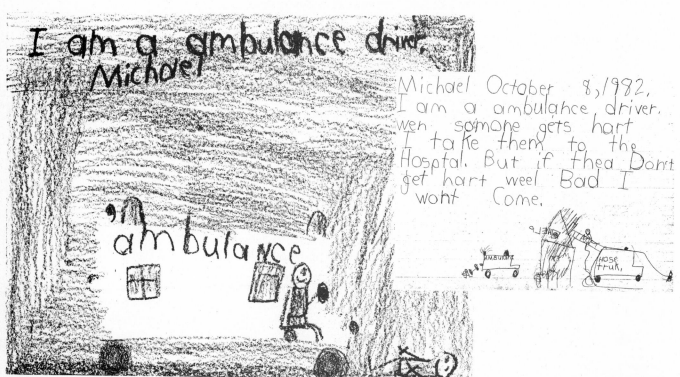

I am a ambulance driver.
Michael

Michael October 8, 1982.
I am a ambulance driver.
wen somone gets hart
I take them to the
Hosptal. But if thea Dont
get hart weel Bad I
woht Come.

ambulance

Michael, age 7

Nikki October 8, 1982

I'm a waitress

I'm a waitress who likes my job and will never be anything else and if I do I'll take my shoe and knock me black and blue.
So the only thing else to do is to do my job and do it good so I can get more mony.

Nikki, age 7

Jason October 8, 1982

I like truck drivers.
I own a truk I like to.
go on the free way and.
truck and truck. its fun to.
watch the people ride on.
it to and un load the.
truck. the end I hop you.
like it.

Jason, age 7

booklet about one kind of helper, each page is a picture, story, or symbol associated with that helper. When children make a booklet celebrating many helpers, each page is labeled; stories or words are added to the pictures to enrich the project. Staple the pages together. Ask the children to make wonderful covers.

MUSIC TIMES

Because children are thinking and talking about community helpers, they will naturally sing and make music about them. Many community helpers are honored in songs that children enjoy learning and singing. Equally enjoyable musical experiences are songs improvised and rearranged by teachers and students.

Work songs. Throughout history people sang as they worked—on canals, railroads, ships, ranches, and farms. Work songs popular with children of all ages include "Sixteen Tons," "Pick a Bale of Cotton," "Erie Canal," "Banana Boat Song," "Rock Island Railroad," and "John Henry." When you enjoy work songs with your children, be sure to include songs from other cultures.

Fill your room with the sound of singing and music!

Rearranged golden oldies. "I've Been Workin' on the Railroad" already celebrates a community helper—the railroad worker. This song turned into a community helper's song when a group of first graders and their teacher added these stanzas:

We've been working as fire fighters.
All the live-long day.
We've been working as fire fighters
just to keep the fires away.
Can't you hear the fire bell ringing?
Hurry and slide down the pole.
Can't you hear the fire bell ringing?
Hurry and put out the fire.
Fire fighters go! Fire fighters go!
Hurry and put out that f-i-r-e!
Fire fighters go! Fire fighters go!
Hurry and put out that fire!

A group of five-year-olds turned "The Bear Went Over the Mountain" into a fine community helper's song.

The bear went over the mountain.
The bear went over the mountain.
The bear went over the mountain.
And what do you think he saw?

He saw a bus driver.
He saw a bus driver.
He saw a bus driver.
Stopping at a bus stop.

Later in the year the class visited the local library and talked to the librarian. They remembered their song and easily improvised the lyrics:

And what do you think he saw?
He saw a librarian.
He saw a librarian.
He saw a librarian.
Stamping all the books.

Of course, the songs are accompanied by improvised movement.

Community helpers' bands. What kind of music would traffic officers play? Anything with whistles and horns, of course! That was the answer kindergartners gave their teacher. They distributed homemade and rhythm instruments that made whistling or honking sounds. After experimenting for a while with fast, slow, loud, soft, high, and low sounds, the children composed a police officer's fugue with two distinctive melodies.

These are the kinds of discoveries children make through discussion and translate into music.

Librarians' music would be very quiet . . .
Fire fighters' music would be first real quiet when they're sleeping in the fire house, then very loud and noisy when the siren blows, then fast as anything when the fire engine races to the fire!
Letter carriers' music is real steady, like walking!
Secretaries' music is like tapping sounds on a typewriter—rat rat rat rat rat—very fast.

Songs and music for community helper puppets. When children create community helper puppets, invite them to think of songs for their puppets to sing to the rest of the class about their work. Also encourage the children to play music appropriate to their puppet's work.

Singing telegrams and other musical mail. Discuss the kinds of mail that letter carriers deliver: happy mail, which includes invitations to parties and news of visitors coming; sad mail to say that someone is sick or that someone cannot come to visit; angry mail, such as a notice about an overdue payment; emergency mail to be answered immediately; and beautiful mail that brings greeting cards and picture postcards.

The children take turns picking a piece of mail from a mail pouch (sack or shopping bag). They decide what kind of mail it is and think of or make up a song that describes the mail. The other children guess the inspiration. Five-year-old Ruthie chose a letter and, without hesitation, burst into the song "Happy birthday to you!" The children guessed immediately—happy mail!

Community helpers' singing games. After discussing community helpers, ask the children to put on signs (you may have to write them) or special clothing or equipment turning themselves into specific community helpers. When they are ready, form a circle and enjoy a community helper's "Farmer in the Dell." This game is a favorite of Annette Shelley's kindergartners at a Franklin County School in Columbus, Ohio.

"Have You Ever Seen a Lassie?" is another popular singing game that lends itself to celebrating community helpers. Here is how one group of children sang it, as each community helper was called into the center of the circle, improvised a movement, and was imitated by the other children.

Have you ever seen a house builder go this way and that way (hammering)? Have you ever seen a house builder go this way and that?

Have you ever seen a fire fighter go this way and that way (pretending to hose a fire)? Have you ever seen a fire fighter go this way and that?

Musical gifts to community helpers. Extend the gifts of song to helpers in school and the surrounding neighborhood whom the childen have come to know. Whenever possible, find out the names of people you see and meet regularly, such as letter carriers, secretaries, custodians, delivery people, bus drivers, librarians, other teachers, and clerks.

Singing special songs for people expresses appreciation. Here is an example of such a song, presented to Mr. Benson, the letter carrier who delivered mail daily to a nursery school in Kalamazoo, Michigan.

(To the tune "You Are My Sunshine")
You are our mailman,
Our favorite mailman.
You make us happy
Every day.
You bring us letters.
You bring us postcards.
You bring us pretty stamps
Each and every day.

A group of Detroit kindergartners made up and practiced a song and walked to the office to present it to their school secretary, Mrs. Goldenberger.

(To the tune "Skip to My Lou")
Run run run to our friend,
Clap clap clap for our friend.
Mrs. Goldenberger is our very good friend.
Sing sing sing to our friend.
Make a circle around our friend.
Mrs. Goldenberger is our very good friend.

MOVEMENT AND PLAY TIMES

Young children need only time, space, and the simplest props to improvise community helpers. Your role in their play is that of a loving, supportive, and occasionally directing V.I.P. If some children are more inhibited, more cautious, more reluctant to become involved in this game, encourage them by putting a special hat on their heads, taping a badge to their chests, or asking a puppet to invite them into a playful situation. Never stop trying to help children enjoy their gifts of imagination and drama. Keep drawing circles that take them in.

Hat rack. In addition to the hats children make as art projects, keep a good collection of helpers' hats hanging in easily accessible places for children to play with. In one class, I saw these hats hanging on a hat tree: railroad worker's striped cap; police hat; construction worker's hard hat; nurse's cap; cowboy hat; sailor's cap; fire helmet; mommy's hat; and gentleman's hat. "I'm a hat snatcher," the teacher explained. "Wherever I go, and whomever I meet, I ask if they have a hat to give me for my kids."

Shoe rack. While you are scrounging, collect shoes of different types: cowboy boots, fisher's boots; lady's high heels; fire fighter's boots; men's shoes; and moccasins.

Costume box. Old white shirts make excellent uniforms for doctors, nurses, barbers, and beauticians. Bags of every size and shape, from knapsacks to mommy's pocketbooks to medicine bags, are very popular. Overalls, vests, shirts, ties, jackets, dresses, scarves, veils, and shawls are constantly used by children in their play. Be sure to include wigs, mustaches, beards, and makeup; and to have at least one mirror safely propped in an accessible place. (Children are not vain; they are curious.)

Community helpers puppet shows. Informal, spontaneous puppet shows are often a daily feature of students' lives when puppets and formal or makeshift puppet stages are always available. Occasionally, you may want to encourage specific puppet situations. Here are a few suggestions.

Interview community helper puppets. The children ask the puppets questions about their work.

Invite community helper puppets to be guests of the class and tell the children what they do.

Introduce one community helper puppet to another and start a dialogue in which they compare jobs.

Ask the puppets to sing a song about their work.

Ask the puppets to show the rest of the children what they do and have the children guess which helper they are.

Invite the community helper puppets to do their work in the classroom. For

example: "Boys and girls, this is our new mail carrier, Mrs. Envelope. She will be giving out your letters today." Or "Children, our friend Dr. Sandy Sniffles wants to check your ears and chins to see if you're all in good health!"

In all of these situations, the children are manipulating the puppets. If you think children need extra encouragement, try something like this: "Bobby, will you bring over Freddy Fire Fighter and ask him to tell us about fire safety. Thank you!"

Statues of community helpers. The children turn themselves into statues of fire fighters, police officers, doctors, trash collectors, and so on. They shake out that shape and try another.

Parades of community helpers. A parade of doctors would certainly look different from a parade of house builders. Put on some sprightly marching music and experiment with different parades. Encourage the children to think of specific actions that describe each helper so that the parades look different.

Helping hands. Think of some things helpers' hands do: cut, sew, stamp, write, type, dial, fix, hammer, paint, draw, repair, comb, press, build, polish, sort, steer, tap, mix, shake, lift, push, and pull. Talk about this first so that the children's minds are full of ideas for helping hands. Play follow-the-leader and give each child a turn to demonstrate a hand movement that the others follow.

Turn yourself into . . . Stimulate movements related to community helpers with suggestions such as these.

Turn yourself into a sleeping fire fighter. When the bell rings, jump up, get dressed, and slide down your pole.

Turn yourself into a letter carrier walking through snow, walking on ice, being chased by a dog, walking through puddles, walking up stairs, carrying a heavy bag of mail, and carrying mail full of good news.

Turn yourself into a gas station attendant putting gas in a car, cleaning the windows, and checking the oil.

Turn yourself into a mechanic fixing a car.

Turn yourself into a cashier at the supermarket.

Turn yourself into a presser ironing clothes.

Community helper movement collage. Focus on one community helper and discuss the various activities of that helper. Write them on the board as reminders of how many wonderful ideas young children can express in only a few minutes.

Here are some ideas about a police officer's actions suggested by a group of first graders.

A police officer:

walks

drives cars, motorcycles

blows whistle

writes tickets

handcuffs criminals

directs traffic

helps lost children find their moms

is very strong

talks to people

searches

helps people if they fall down

moves very fast in emergencies

chases

tells people directions

is very brave

is very smart

After the children talked about these activities, they demonstrated and practiced each one. Then they "danced" the police officers. "When the music goes on, do any of the police officer things we practiced. When the music stops, freeze. When the music goes on again, change to another one of the ideas we practiced." Because they talked, shared, and practiced, the children had no trouble expanding familiar ideas to new experiences involving changes and music.

Here is how the teacher announced this activity: "Ladies and gentlemen, for the first time in Chicago, Illinois, we are going to show you, with music and movement, the many things police officers do in their very important jobs! Here we go!" The children were wonderful in their movement patterns. They not only comprehended but also communicated. Everyone succeeded and was delighted.

Any music that has a steady rhythm works well with this activity—for example, instrumental versions of such songs as "I Feel the Earth Move Under My Feet," "The Entertainer," "Yessir, That's My Baby," and "This Land Is Your Land, This Land Is My Land." Do not feel that you must have a specific piece of music to do a creative movement activity. Children and music are flexible. Discover resources at your fingertips that you never thought of using.

Sick animals. First discuss the different animals the children know. Practice their various movements. Now, imagine the animals are sick or hurt and their movements are impaired. Give children the chance to be various animals as well as the veterinarian. Be open to the roles they want to play in this movement improvisation. If all the children want to be sick animals, you can play the veterinarian. Encourage differences in the animals' movements before and after their medical treatment.

Broken toys. Think about a mechanical toy that needs to be wound up. The children turn themselves into mechanical toys. Wind them all up at once with a winding motion above all their heads, or, if time permits, wind up each child individually. "How wonderfully these mechanical toys move! Let's do it again. Uh oh. Something went wrong. They're not moving right. They're broken. Quick, call the toy fixer!"

Some of the children become toy fixers and decide how to fix the broken toys. Sometimes they pour imaginary liquid on them, sometimes they adjust their parts, sometimes they pretend to hammer and connect. Soon the toys are fixed. Try them again; wind them up. Hooray! They're working beautifully! Listen to their sounds and watch their fantastic movements.

VISITORS AND FIELD TRIPS

Visitors

Family members. Louise Johnson starts with a discussion of what her children's family members do for a living. She writes their jobs on the board and invites family members to come in and discuss their work with the class. The children are prepared with questions, and afterward they send thank-you notes, pictures, poems, and songs.

School helpers. Every school has staff who are pleased to tell the children about their work. These people include custodians, electricians, cooks, secretaries, clerks, librarians, bus drivers, delivery people, and groundskeepers.

Neighborhood helpers. In addition to police officers, fire fighters, and letter carriers, children enjoy meeting mayors and other government officers, and workers from community service organziations such as the Red Cross, the Society for Prevention of Cruelty to Animals, the Kiwanis Club, the Society for Prevention of Blindness, and the YW or YMCA. It is important for children to know that people work at many different kinds of jobs and that people who do volunteer work are often as dedicated as professional staff. Iris Kaplan, the most honored community leader in Yonkers, New York, spends a great deal of time arranging for visitors to share with schoolchildren the many ways in which social service agencies improve the lives of people. A first-grade class had a memorable visit from a spokesperson for the city's United Way. The children were astonished at the number of agencies devoted to helping people.

Field Trips

Families' places of work. Louise Johnson's classes have visited many fascinating places because family members, informed about the children's interest in community helpers, have invited them to be special guests at such places as an orchard, a slipper factory, a freight station, a bank, an airport, and a cheese factory.

Try to make arrangements with whomever is in charge of your trip to provide a few experiences that really involve the children. For example, when a group of kindergartners visited a grocery store, the manager of the meat department took the class to the freezer and showed the children how meat was stored. At a freight transfer station a group of first graders had the opportunity to try to lift some of the smaller freight and to walk through the lot to look at license plates from all over the country.

Food pantry. Children observe the ways people help each other through the distribution of food to those in need.

Bottle, can, and newspaper recycling center. This is an excellent experience for teaching children how people cooperate to improve the community and the environment.

Voting center. Here children see how many people contribute their services to register voters, help them to vote, and keep records.

SELECTED BIBLIOGRAPHY

The Work-a-Day World

Armitage, Rhonda. *Ice Cream for Rosie.* New York: Dutton, 1982.

Behrens, Jane. *A Walk in the Neighborhood.* Illustrated by Jim Gindraux. Chicago: Childrens Press, 1968.

Berenstain, Stan. *Berenstain Bears Go to the Doctor.* New York: Random House, 1980.

————. *Berenstain Bears Visit the Dentist.* New York: Random House, 1980.

Briggs, Raymond. *Jim and the Beanstalk.* New York: Coward, McCann & Geoghan, 1970.

Brown, Margaret Wise. *Three Little Animals.* New York: Harper & Row, 1956.

Censoni, Robert. *The Shopping-Bag Lady.* New York: Holiday, 1977.

Delton, Judy. *Groundhog's Day at the Doctor.* New York: Parents Magazine Press, 1981.

de Paola, Tomie. *The Comic Adventure of Old Mother Hubbard and Her Dog.* New York: Harcourt Brace Jovanovich, 1981.

Duvoisin, Roger. *The Missing Milkman.* New York: Knopf, 1967.

Fleishman, Seymour. *Too Hot in Potzburg.* Chicago: Whitman, 1980.

Griffith, Helen V. *Mine Will, Said John.* New York: Morrow, 1980.

Kramm, Florence. *Eugene and the Policeman.* Illustrated by Charles Bracke. Chicago: Follett, 1967.

Lewis, Naomi. *The Butterfly Collector.* Illustrated by Fulivio Testa. Englewood Cliffs, N.J.: Prentice-Hall, 1978.

Miller, Alice P. *Little Store on the Corner.* New York: Scholastic, 1974.

Rockwell, Anne. *Pogo's Payday.* New York: Doubleday, 1978.

Rottman, Joel. *Night Lights.* Illustrated by Joe Lasker. Chicago: Whitman, 1972.

Sesame Street. *Who Are the People in Your Neighborhood?* New York: Random House, 1974.

People and Their Jobs

Early Career Book Series. Minneapolis: Lerner Publications. Titles include: *Careers in Agriculture*, 1974; *Careers in Animal Care*, 1974; *Careers in Banking*, 1973; *Careers in Beauty and Grooming*, 1979; and *Careers in Toy Making*, 1980.

Goldreich, Gloria, and Goldreich, Esther. *What Can She Be?* series. New York: Lothrop, Lee & Shepard. *What Can She Be?: An Architect*, 1974; *A Computer Scientist*, 1979; *A Farmer*, 1976; *A Film Producer*, 1977; *A Geologist*, 1976; *A Lawyer*, 1973; *A Legislator*, 1978; *A Musician*, 1975; *A Newscaster*, 1973; *A Police Officer*, 1975; and *A Veterinarian*, 1972.

Greene, Carla. *Policeman and Firemen, What Do They Do?* Illustrated by Leonard Kessler. New York: Harper & Row, 1978.

Gross, Ruth Belov. *If You Were a Ballet Dancer*. New York: Dial, 1979.

Hill, Mary. *My Dad's a Smoke Jumper*. Chicago: Childrens Press, 1978.

Karuss, Ronnie. *Mickey Visits the Dentist*. New York: Grosset & Dunlap, 1980.

Pitt, Valerie. *Let's Find Out About the Community*. Illustrated by June Goldsborough. New York: Watts, 1972.

Robinson, Nancy. *Firefighters*. New York: Scholastic, 1980.

Rockwell, Harlow, and Anne Rockwell. *My Barber*. New York: Macmillan, 1981.

————. *My Dentist*. New York: Morrow, Greenwillow, 1975.

————. *My Doctor*. New York: Macmillan, 1973.

Scarry, Richard. *What Do People Do All Day?* New York: Random House, 1979.

Schulz, Charles M. *Charlie Brown, Snoopy and Me*. New York: Doubleday, 1980.

White, Lawrence B., Jr. *So You Want to Be a Magician?* Illustrated by Bill Morrison. Reading, Mass.: Addison-Wesley, 1972.

Teacher Resources

Candy, Steven. *Kids' America*. New York: Workman, 1978.

Gibbons, Gail. *The Post Office Book: The Mail and How It Works*. New York: Crowell, 1982.

MATCH Program. *The City*. Boston: American Science and Engineering, 1969.

Michaels, John U. *Social Studies for Children in a Democracy*. Englewood Cliffs, N.J.: Prentice-Hall, 1972.

Perrin, Linda. *Coming to America: Immigrants from the Far East*. New York: Delacorte, 1980.

Robbins, Albert. *Coming to America: Immigrants from Northern Europe*. New York: Delacorte, 1981.

Senesh, Lawrence. *Our Working World: Cities at Work*. Chicago: Science Research Associates, 1963.

————. *Our Working World: Families at Work*. Chicago: Science Research Associates, 1963.

Spier, Peter. *People*. New York: Doubleday, 1980.

Taba, Hilda, Mary C. Durkin, Jack R. Fraenkel, and Anthony R. McNaughton. *A Teacher's Handbook to Elementary Social Studies*, 2nd ed. Reading, Mass.: Addison-Wesley, 1971.

Terkel, Studs. *Working*. New York: Avon, 1975.

Mitchell, age 7

Dinner
Stake Bensor potatos.....2$4¢
Chikin mash potatos.......1$31¢
meat appel saulse ,,,,,,,,,,,,,,,,,,,,,,,5$
pazzae large smalle meteam,,,,,$3¢
skpgihte large smalle meteam,,,,$3¢

lunch
Hambegar ,,,,,,,,,,,,,,,,,,,,,,,,,,,,,,1$35¢
saimwich Bens ,,,,,,,,,,,,,,,,,,,1$49¢
Hot dog ,,,,,,,,,,,,,,,,,,,,,,,,,,,2$40¢
tunafish salid ,,,,,,,,,,,,,,,,,,,,,,,1$43¢
egg salid ,,,,,,,,,,,,,,,,,,,,,,,,,,1$29¢

Adorvs
~~a cup of~~ fruta salid ,,,,,,,,1$
pinapple and panses ,,,,,,,,1$20¢
cottae chees frutas,,,,,,,,,,,1$22¢
eggs and tomatos ,,,,,,,,,,,1$
salid ,,,,,,,,,,,,,,,,,,,,,,,,,,,,,,,,,,,,,1$

Missy, age 7

PART THREE

THE
FOOD
WE EAT

THE
CLOTHES
WE WEAR

WHERE
WE LIVE

7

THE FOOD WE EAT

Let us sit down soon to eat
with all those who haven't eaten;
let us spread great tablecloths,
put salt in the lakes of the world,
set up planetary bakeries,
tables with strawberries in snow,
and a plate like the moon itself
from which we all can eat.[1]

THE BASICS

Food, clothing, and shelter are necessary for survival. Food means life, and there is nothing more basic than that.

When you begin thinking about food, history and geography come readily to mind. Cereal, for example, is named for Ceres, the Roman goddess of fruits and grains. Spaghetti dates from the thirteenth century, when the Venetian explorer Marco Polo brought back from the Orient his "discovery" of noodles, which the Italians turned into pasta. When you celebrate Columbus Day, remember that this courageous sailor was not searching for America but for a short route to India to collect spices.

The ancient Israelis had an abundance of goats and wild bees. When you read in the Old Testament (Numbers 13:27), "We went into the land to which you sent us. It does indeed flow with milk and honey," you are reading a description of food enjoyed by those people. As you devour your next pizza, find out about its amazing history, dating back to ancient Greece, by reading Louise Love's *The Complete Book of Pizza* (Sassafras Press, 1980).

How many cultures feature meats, cheeses, and vegetables wrapped in some kind of dough? Start the list with crêpes from France, tacos from Mexico, ravioli from Italy, blintzes from Germany, and egg rolls from China. The Earl of Sandwich would be astonished at the number and variety of sandwiches available throughout the world since the seventeenth century, when he instructed a servant to put a slice of roast meat between two pieces of bread so he could have his dinner without interrupting a card game.

The sight, smell, taste, or texture of a particular food can evoke images of people and places from earlier times. For the great French novelist Marcel Proust, the sweet smell of a pastry he enjoyed in his childhood stimulated memories that inspired the classic *Remembrance of Things Past*.

Food is part of every human celebration, from baptisms to bar mitzvahs to weddings to funerals. Blessings thanking God or the gods for food are important rituals in every religion. Food is a symbol of love, a parent's first responsibility to a baby, a nation's first responsibility to its people. Food is associated with other emotions as well. A fourth grader, describing anger, wrote: "Anger is the smell of supper burning."

The preparation of food is a basic human activity. It could even be said that the preparation of food borders on the mystical, magical, and mysterious. Michael Joel Rosen, a poet, artist, and teacher in Columbus, Ohio, who works in educational programs with children of all ages, shares his awe of the process.

The preparation of any food is an ordeal, a ritual, a procedure, a narrative event—something to do with plot, with drama! One thing happens after another. Things marinate, rise, heat—all while you are somewhere else. The plot thickens, literally! Finally, we find out what happens, we wait and see. We are as much the observer, the reader, the watcher as we are the actor, the observed, the reading. The meal, the menu, the dish all depend on a kind of mystery: Will it turn out? What will it taste like? God made this fruit; someone else made the recipe, and I followed it. There is something of discovery, of imagination.

Children are awed—I am—by the fact that dough rises and that water, sugar, butter, yeast, and flour make almost all the different cakes, cookies, noodles, and breads in the world! Bacon shrinks, concentrated orange juice expands, a drop of food coloring turns a whole cake pink, egg whites foam and become stiff. Who dreamed of beating egg whites and why? That question, that mystery, is part of cooking.

There is the whole idea of hands, the ritual of hands on—manipulation, stirring, kneading, straining, twisting, peeling, slicing. Sacred gestures, spellbinding movements . . . passing the hands over the mixing bowl three times.

There is the whole curative, healing, growing part of cooking, the whole aspect of doing a good deed, gracing the table with tastes, offering your best to those you love.

Did you know that the word *company* means "with bread"? *Companionship* means people who eat bread together. Until a few decades ago, meals were occasions for families to eat and talk together. The most important family times were mealtimes, when parents and children shared events of the day, concerns, and plans. The warm, rich smells of home-cooked meals blended with conversation in what for many people were the best times of their childhood.

Those days seem to be gone forever. More and more people skip breakfast or eat it on the run. Most families do not have lunch together. Children eat at school, parents at work. Although for some families dinner time is still a time of companionship, for many it is accompanied by loud music or television. Individual TV trays have replaced the family table. Often, children eat by themselves at a different hour than their parents.

Laurel Robertson expresses her feelings about this contemporary scene in her book *Laurel's Kitchen*.

If breakfast is the most important meal to the body, dinner may be to the spirit; not the food so much as the simple precious fact of coming together with those you love. The world we live in now is so rushed and hectic that by the end of a day, people very often find themselves feeling depleted, confused, and fragmented. This is the time of day when the warmth and conviviality of a family meal can make all the difference in the world.

She urges parents to "Be fierce as a mother lion to protect the sanctity of this hour. Fight football coaches, drama teachers, and scout leaders if you must, but keep the dinner hour intact."[2]

Another difficulty for young children is poor eating habits. Mary T. Goodwin, chief nutritionist with the Montgomery County Health Department, Rockville, Maryland, who with Gerry Pollen wrote the outstanding book *Creative Food Experiences for Children*, is eloquent in her observations. She sees children misled by advertising that glamorizes poor eating habits and encourages them to eat junk foods that may undermine their health. She says the four F's—formulated, fabricated, fake foods—are displacing wholesome foods in the diet. She notes that many children eat food which comes in boxes, packages, bags, bottles, and vending machines—food designed to be eaten on the run. She reminds us that the foods children eat affect their growth, development, ability to learn, and general behavior. We have all read newspaper reports linking diet with emotional problems, antisocial behavior, and hyperactivity.

How children eat is as important as what they eat. Mary writes, "The presentation of food in a comfortable, relaxed atmosphere, together with love, care and eye appeal, can greatly affect the way the child feels about himself and those around him. Early experiences with food may lay the

foundation for lifelong eating habits . . . *Children have to be educated to make good food selections.* Food habits which build good health are not acquired naturally; they must be learned."[3]

Mary told me a delightful story about her own children. When they were very young, they formed their own concept of her work as a nutritionist, which was revealed when Mary stayed home with the flu. Her son, then five years old, was upset that Mary was home sick: "Mom, you can't stay home!" "Why not?" Mary asked hoarsely. "Because all the junk-food pushers will get ahead of you!"

Because many homes are not places of warmth, safety, and security centered around traditional mealtimes, because the mass media bombards children with commercials about junk food, and because many foods lack nutritional value, it is important that teachers help children develop good eating habits and provide opportunities for children to share and enjoy meals with other persons (the classroom may be the only place where they learn the meaning of *company*).

If, as a teacher, you link food activities with everything you do, this guide will add to your knapsack of ideas. If you are a teacher who has not really thought about making "your daily bread" a part of the curriculum, be ready to be moved as you read. Those who believe in the importance of food as a central activity in early childhood education speak in one voice. They are powerful advocates of enlightened, nourishing, and loving education.

Jean Jones, a nutritionist with the Ohio Department of Education, echoes Mary Goodwin's feelings as she talks about helping children to be open to a variety of foods: "If you're willing to eat a large variety of foods, chances are you won't become deficient in one particular nutrient." She urges teachers to encourage children to try new foods, to be open to foods they may never have heard of or tasted.

Jeannette Lauritsen is principal of Edison Elementary School in Grandview Heights, Ohio. If you pass Edison on a school day, you are likely to notice marvelous cooking smells. Jeannette explains:

Food always connects with good conversation and warmth. It introduces a friendly atmosphere. You can feel everyone relaxing . . . Food provides success experiences for all children. It brings teachers and children closer together, minimizes the gap. Everyone participates in the project—food experiences break down sexist roles. This is one avenue where children can learn to be more grown up, responsible, to take charge. Cooking and food-related activities touch every subject, every area of the curriculum, from table manners to science and math. I see cooperation, thoughtfulness, appreciation, and courtesy developing through cooking activities. Oral language is enhanced; talk naturally comes with a process that involves children.

The teachers at Edison School share their principal's enthusiasm for food as a classroom activity. (Some of their recipes and ideas are included in this guide.) For example, here are just a few ways Julia Crabbs and her Edison first graders integrated food with other curriculum areas: *holidays*—Valentine's Day, decorated heart cookies; Halloween, pumpkin cookies with orange frosting; Easter, bunny salad (banana ears, cottage cheese tails); *food and stories*—Peter Rabbit salad, Little Red Hen bread; *creative writing and art*—silly sandwiches: *science*—grow cut-off pieces of celery, carrot, and pineapple in dishes of water (observe, take notes).

Nothing is more important for young children than the chance to "play" whatever is in their world, whatever stimulates their imaginations. Roz Ault, in her excellent book *Kids Are Natural Cooks*, points to a valuable aspect of cooking that goes beyond play. "They only pretend to drive a car, have a baby, be a doctor—but they *really* can cook and produce *real* food which *real* people will *really* eat. In light of all the other emotional, psychological connotations food has, think what a great sense of pride and accomplishment children can get by cooking something for themselves and those they love . . ."[4]

America's favorite cook, Julia Child, in her book *Julia Child and Company*, encourages the participation of children in the cooking process:

I am all for encouraging children to work productively with their hands. They learn to handle and care for equipment with respect . . . A knife is a tool, not a toy . . . Talk to children as you plan menus. Let their small, sensitive noses sniff the fish . . . Work together at the counter. Let your children arrange platters. The small rituals, like the clean hands and clean apron before setting to work; the precision of gesture, like leveling off a cupful of flour; the charm of improvisation and making something new; the pride of mastery; and the gratification of offering something one has made—these have such value to a child."[5]

Perhaps you are shaking your head and saying, "How can I encourage cooking activ-

ities when I don't have the equipment for it? I don't have appliances and supplies. I'll just have to forget it!" Wrong. You do not need large appliances and the latest gadgets to share cooking experiences with children. Schools with sinks, stoves, refrigerators, and ovens are in the minority. Think "scrounge."

Teachers around the country call on parents to send in toasters, crock pots, electric frying pans, mixing bowls, hot plates, blenders, corn poppers, whatever is needed. Parents usually come through.

In addition, the cooking experience can be a very simple activity. Diane Biswas, director of the Summit United Methodist Preschool in Columbus, Ohio, describes how three-year-olds preparing bread and butter

smiled and were genuinely tickled at having put butter on bread and then . . . eating it! The pat on the head, the encouragement from the teacher, the words "good for you" help children feel good inside. And the teacher feels good, too. It's contagious! Cooking with children does wonders for their self-concepts. The most important thing we stress to our children is that they are loved by their teachers and we care what goes into them. We care about their health. We want them to be healthy because we love them!

Children have wonderful times peeling oranges, cutting bananas, and spreading peanut butter on bread or crackers.

Not all children want to participate immediately. Some may have a "wait and see" attitude. Some may be starting careers as excellent "guests" at early ages. My friend Frayda Turkel asked her then five-year-old daughter, Ariela, if she wanted to help set the table, fold the napkins, and fill the glasses with water. Ariela replied politely, "I'll be the person who says 'Thank you.'" It is to be hoped that all children will say "Thank you." Courtesy, good manners, and thoughtfulness are integral parts of this learning-by-doing process. It is amazing how children learn to cooperate through cooking experiences.

There are as many ways to arrange food preparation and cooking activities as there are teachers. Small groups are the most popular. Many teachers give small groups of children the chance to make something or prepare something while the rest of the class works on a different activity.

"Sometimes one child at a time is involved in the process," explains Sue Coomer. When her kindergartners make butter or ice cream, one child at a time stirs. Usually Sue combines the stirring with numbers and counting. "Everyone stirs six times when we're talking about the number six!"

When Verna Willis of the Summit United Methodist Preschool in Columbus, Ohio, learned that I was writing this book, she wrote to me enthusiastically about her cooking experiences with three- and four-year-olds. Here are a few helpful excerpts from that letter.

When I cook with children, I usually arrange it during free play. The children can take part in the experience if and when they choose. It's a cooperative experience, but even those who do not participate share in the results. The experience should take place when there is plenty of time, so it's a relaxing experience.

I use two different types of cooking experiences: individual recipes, which have the ingredients broken down so each child makes his own for his own use; and group recipes, where the children take turns, coming and going during the process, then sharing the final product. I prefer the group recipes; even though they do not allow for the creativity of individual recipes, they are more social and more enjoyable.

I find that simple recipes work best. I choose ones that do not require much adult preparation or a long waiting period for the child.

When cooking in the classroom, I usually use a large recipe chart. I use pictures of the ingredients, equipment, and steps. I draw these myself on poster board and often cover them with clear contact paper. At the beginning of the activity, we look at the chart and discuss what's on it. Sometimes only two or three children are present at this stage of the activity. When we start to cook, we follow the chart and the children read the pictures. Yet, even following this chart, I still try to make sure that it's the children's experience. I encourage conversation and let the children try to solve any problems on their own first.

One day we were making a snack that called for one cup of peanut butter. They had no problem getting the peanut butter into the measuring cup, but when it came time to put the peanut butter into a big bowl, they tried to pour it out of the measuring cup. When it didn't come out, they looked puzzled. Someone tried to shake it out, but that didn't work either. They looked at me and I said something like, "I wonder how we can get that peanut butter into the bowl?" Suddenly, one of the kids remembered the knife they had used to get the peanut butter into the cup. The problem was solved and they were pleased that they had figured it out.

Most of the time we eat the finished product during snack time. We often invite a guest, like our school director. We've even sent a portion to our bus driver. The children love to share what they've prepared. Often, I send a copy of the recipe home in the school newsletter . . .

I love cooking with children and they enjoy it, too, always asking, "When are we going to do it again?"

The many benefits of cooking with children are nicely described in the following evaluation by Jeanne Jacobson, principal of the Beth Shraga Hebrew Academy in Albany, New York, of Marilyn Cohen and her kindergartners in the middle of an exciting gastronomic experience.

Evaluation of Marilyn Cohen by Jeanne Jacobson

The kindergartners had made vegetable soup with alphabet noodles, and during this period they ate the soup, cleaned up, and got ready for play. Such a lot of learning in cognitive and affective domains occurred during this happy period. In their conversation, children talked about fruits and vegetables, giving specific examples and telling or finding out how they should be classified. (Previously, children had visited an apple orchard and had made a fruit salad.) They identified the cooked pieces of vegetables and talked about which children had brought each one.

They found seeds and talked about what made the seeds grow and whether they would grow inside the person who ate them! They named alphabet letters and found those in the soup that were part of their names. Although Ms. Cohen was not, of course, present at each of the tables, she had established an atmosphere of learning and inquiry such that the children talked about intellectual concerns appropriate for their age level. The children enjoyed eating, talking, and sharing ideas. Bruno Bettelheim holds the view that we must literally feed those whom we hope to teach. Ms. Cohen feeds her children and gives them a gentle, caring environment full of exciting things to do and concepts to learn . . . She teaches them that school is a happy and safe place to learn and live. She is an exceptionally gifted teacher . . .

This guide is packed with ideas, recipes, and experiences generously shared by many teachers who never heard of the phrase "burn out" because they are too busy simmering, boiling, toasting, frying, and melting! Every activity in this guide can be used in other guides in this book. Activities involving food easily relate to numbers, letters, shapes, colors, community helpers, our fantastic bodies, family, and friends. Fit them into your scheme, your scene.

Let us end this section with a reminder that although there is hunger and poverty in America (and many of our children are victims of these tragic conditions), in other lands there is total deprivation. There is no food and children starve to death each day.

The fruits of the earth are gifts that we often take for granted, squander, and waste. There is no age young enough to begin learning compassion for those less fortunate, appreciation for the miracle of the earth, respect for the environment, and a commitment to help "spread great table-cloths,/put salt in the lakes of the world,/set up planetary bakeries,/tables with strawberries in snow,/and a plate like the moon itself/from which we all can eat."[6] Perhaps in the lifetimes of our young children, the people of the earth will truly break bread together and no one will go hungry.

DISCOVERY TIMES

- Everything that is alive must eat to live.
- Healthy bodies require nourishing food.
- We need to eat something every day from each of the four basic food groups. They are: dairy products; fruits and vegetables; poultry, meat, fish, and eggs; and grains and cereals.
- Preparing food together and eating together is an enjoyable experience.
- We can learn about cultures and traditions through food.
- Because we are thankful for our food, we should not waste it.
- We should share our food with others.

SUGGESTED VOCABULARY

food	menu	dry	follow
vegetables	teaspoon	creamy	measure
meat	tablespoon	eat	rinse
eggs	sugar	drink	slice
milk	flour	chew	digest
cereal	salt	swallow	stir
bread	pepper	sip	peel
fruit	sauce	taste	bake
food groups	batter	boil	knead
junk food	liquid	steam	roll
restaurant	delicious	simmer	pit
table	hot	scramble	seed
plates	cold	fry	grow
cups	warm	toast	leaf
bowls	sweet	dip	stem
knives	sour	add	root
forks	spicy	melt	farm
spoons	cool	pour	orchard
pots	frozen	shape	dairy
pans	lumpy	cut	recipe
mixing bowl	smooth	taste	set the table
glass	sticky	smell	clean up
napkin	crisp	squeeze	sweep
	soft	mix	clean

Each word on the list is a seed-word that yields many more. The word "fruit," for example, leads to apple, orange, pear, cherry, berry, banana, peach, and melon.

Children are amazed at how much they know. Food is a category guaranteed to astonish them. Through talking with your children, discover their favorite foods and you will have an excellent topic for class discussion and projects. Among a child's earliest words are those relating to food. A child sitting in a supermarket basket is picking up vocabulary words in every aisle.

SOME BEGINNING ACTIVITIES

Start with a taste. Nothing launches a food activity with more excitement than a taste of something wonderful. An old Yiddish joke ends with the line, "Eat first. You'll talk later!"

Start with smell. Pass around an orange, a lemon, or a grapefruit. Encourage the children to smell the citrus flavor with their eyes closed. Then, with eyes open, talk about the experience.

Start with texture. Feel the fuzziness of a peach, the smooth, hard shell of an egg, the ridges on a stalk of celery, the creaminess of peanut butter. This activity is an excellent way to begin a discussion about healthful foods.

Start with a work of art. For centuries food has been a popular subject for artists. With art books or prints from the library, introduce children to paintings such as Manet's *Still Life with Melon and Peaches*, Picasso's *Le Gourmet*, and Cezanne's *Still Life with Apples and Peaches* or his *Still Life* (bowl of oranges). Most children are amazed at how brilliantly artists capture the color, shape, and texture of the food.

Start with an announcement. A kindergarten teacher launched a unit on nutritious food this way: "Boys and girls, starting tomorrow, we are going to have healthful and delicious snacks. Do we have any suggestions on the kinds of snacks to make?" Presto: a chalkboard full of ideas and activities.

Start with a color. Questions such as the following are sure to stimulate conversation: "Isn't this banana a beautiful color? Aren't these grapes magnificent? What color are they?"

Start with a special way to take attendance. A simple direction such as this will launch conversation and activities: "Boys and girls, when I call your name today, please tell us a good food to have for breakfast."

Start with a wonder. Plato believed that there is no other beginning of learning than wonder. Children are the best wonderers, and unless they have already learned to fear being wrong, they usually have excellent responses to such questions as "I wonder where apples come from," "I wonder how bread is made," and "I wonder how peanuts turn into peanut butter."

Start with Popeye. Everyone knows that Popeye the Sailor Man has super muscles because he eats spinach! "What else can we eat if we want to grow as big and strong as Popeye?"

Start with feeding an animal. Young children are usually concerned about the welfare of animals. If you even suggest to them that you can feed gerbils fish food or fish birdseed or birds dog food, they will be horrified. This is a wonderful way to begin helping children develop an appreciation for the correct foods for animals . . . and for people!

I was kidding around with a group of five-year-olds and deliberately mixed up all the animals and food in my house. "Boys and girls, I was in such a rush today. I think I goofed everything up! I gave our bird a dog biscuit (the children laughed and screamed), I poured fish food into our dog's dish ("Fish food into the dog's dish! Oh no!"), and then—the worst thing—I poured birdseed into the fish tank!" The children showed a mixture of shock, dismay, and skeptical laughter ("Is she kidding?") Gretchen couldn't contain herself: "Mimi! You're gonna make those animals very sick!" That was the perfect response for introducing the topic of nutritious food for healthy children.

Start with an experience. Children want to know everything about their teachers. Telling them about something delicious and healthful that you enjoyed will prompt questions and activities.

TALK TIMES

Children, who like to talk about almost everything, especially enjoy talking about food. because everyone has something to say. I received a call from a teacher who needed advice on helping her unusually shy group of five-year-olds to begin expressing themselves more openly. I gave her about ten

ideas. The next day she called back, thrilled with her morning.

"This is the first day all year that every child wanted to say something. We spent a good twenty minutes at high-speed talking!" And she used only one of the suggestions! "What's your favorite food?"

Some talk starters that always work (unless the children have learned to be afraid) are

What do you like for breakfast?
What do you like for lunch?
What do you like for a snack?
What do you like for supper?
Why do we eat?
Do animals need to eat?
What are some healthy foods?
What foods are not good for us?
Did you ever help make food?
Where do vegetables come from?
What are some things we use when we eat?

ART TIMES

Favorite foods chart. This activity follows the "Talk Time" on "What is your favorite food?" The children's names are printed on one side of the chart with a colon or dash after each name. Their favorite foods are printed next to their names. Leave room for the children to draw or paste a picture of the food next to the word. Encourage the children to print their own names, if possible.

Other food chart ideas are: What I Like for Breakfast (or lunch or dinner); Healthy Food; Food That Helps Me Grow Big and Strong; and Favorite Fruits (or vegetables or grains). A variation of this idea is for the children to make their own favorite foods booklets, with each page devoted to a different category of food or meal.

Fill your plate with healthful food. Give each child a paper plate. Using magazine, newspaper, and catalogue pictures as resources, ask the children to choose nutritious food to paste on their plates. Each plate can represent a meal, feature the children's favorite foods, or be divided into four sections to represent the four food groups. Display all the plates.

Still lifes. After studying still lifes by famous painters, set up a simple still life such as a plate of fruit. Encourage the children to really look at the color, shape, and texture of the fruit and to try to convey some of those impressions on their canvases. Feature the still lifes in an art exhibit. Be sure the children have titled and signed their works.

A first-grade class was working on still lifes. After a while, the session broke into free play. Katie was bored and complained to her teacher that she had nothing to do. Her teacher suggested that she "paint the fruit." About ten minutes later, the teacher walked around to see what people were doing and there sat Katie, completely engrossed in painting designs on the bananas and oranges. Warning: Make your instructions as clear as possible.

Clay food. Even if you do not suggest it, children often roll clay into food shapes. Expand on this interest by talking about and looking at the shapes and contours of different foods—the flatness of a slice of bread, the roundness of pumpkins, the squiggliness of noodles or spaghetti, and the smooth, oval shape of eggs. Label and display the children's work.

Clay utensils. Archeologists discover cups, plates, pots, bowls, and pitchers made by ancient peoples. Modern young potters find pleasure in creating these objects to play with or display.

Fruit salad. "This fruit salad is as pretty as a rainbow!" observed five-year-old Douglas as he and his kindergarten colleagues marveled at the brightly colored fruit in a large glass bowl. Encourage the children to paint fruit on notepaper and wall paper.

Foods for seasons and holidays. The children contribute to a mural celebrating a season or holiday. Designate a section of the mural for food—in a circle for a plate or a basket, or a rectangle for a table—to celebrate the foods associated with the season or holiday. The children draw or paste pictures on the plate, basket, or table.

Please sit under the apple tree. Teachers like Sue Coomer in Easthaven School in Columbus, Ohio, cannot resist "planting" fruit trees in their rooms. Sue twists a large hunk of brown wrapping paper to make the trunk, and staples on branches. The tree is ready for the apples, which come in assorted colors of red, yellow, and green. The children choose circle shapes for apples, triangles for leaves, and long rectangles for stems. They color them and add them to the tree. Sue pastes the children's pictures on their apples and tells them, "You're the apple of my eye!"

A variation of this activity is to encour-age children to add any fruit that grows on a tree. They make shapes of apples, peaches, cherries, bananas, and so on, color them, and tape them to the branches.

Mary Goodwin describes yet another variation of the tree idea.[7] Take a walk with your children and collect some nicely shaped fallen branches. Back in the room, sink the branches in clay in a shoe box. Cover and decorate the box with green paper "grass." Hang paper, clay, Playdough, or papier-mâché fruit from the tree.

Food groups mobile. Give children a different hanger for each food group, or give them one hanger from which to hang four kinds of food, one from each group. Children cut out pictures of food, paste the pictures on construction paper and, with help if needed, cut out the shape. Now their food pictures are sturdier and better balanced, as they are stapled or taped to colored yarn that is tied to the hanger. Many teachers use smooth sticks and twigs, gathered by the children, instead of hangers.

Contrast collage. Build upon "Talk Time" sessions contrasting the value of nutritious food and the dangers of junk food. Divide a large sheet of paper in half. On one side draw a happy face at the top; on the other side, an unhappy face. Invite the children to add pictures of healthful food to the happy-face side, junk food to the other.

Food posters. Ask the children to dictate a message they would like to write on a poster about healthful food habits. Ask them where on the paper they want the message—top, bottom, or center. Write the message in pencil so they can outline the letters themselves. Older children, obviously, write their own ideas. Exhibit the posters and invite other classes as guests. Serve nutritious snacks as refreshments.

Four-year-old Patti's poster was a surrealist design of a large carrot and an eye. Her message was "Eat a Carrot for Your Eyes."

Pretzel sculpture. Annetta Dellinger's four-year-olds at Trinity Lutheran School in Marysville, Ohio, enjoy a variety of food activities, but one of their favorites is to shape bread dough into original designs, such as the letters of their names, numbers, and animals. Annetta uses the simplest of dough recipes:

2 loaves (16 ounces each) frozen bread dough, thawed
1 egg white, slightly beaten

1 teaspoon water
Coarse salt (optional)

Arrange the pretzels 1 inch apart on a well-greased baking sheet. Let them stand for 20 minutes. Brush them with a mixture of egg white and water. Sprinkle them with coarse salt, if desired. Place a shallow pan containing 1 inch of boiling water on the lower rack of the oven. Bake pretzels at 350 degrees for 20 minutes or until golden brown on a rack above the pan of water.[8]

The children enjoy shaping their pretzels, comparing designs, smelling the pretzels as they bake, and eating them.

Alphabet good enough to eat. Here is a good way to combine ABC's with nutritious foods. Print a letter of the alphabet on a sheet of white paper. With your students, decide on a delicious, nutritious food that begins with that letter. Print the name of the food. Children draw or cut out pictures to go with the letter. Use the alphabet to make a border around the room.

A variation of this activity is to invite the children to make their own alphabet books.

Tablecloths, bread covers, napkins. Use paper or scrounged white sheets for these functional yet beautiful objects. With paint, crayon, or Magic Marker, the children create designs on the material. Use their creations in the classroom during snack time or present them as gifts to families.

Spice braids. Betsy Distelhorst enriches a talk and smell session about the spices of life with this excellent project. Each child chooses strands of yarn to braid or weave together. Tie the strands at the top and the bottom. Children choose tiny squares of scrounge material. From an offering of such spices as nutmeg, cloves, cinnamon, vanilla beans, mace, and allspice, the children pick samples and put them carefully in the middle of their squares of material. Pinch the four corners together and tie with a rubber band or string. Tie each pouch of spices to the braid. Put a stick or loop through the top of the braid. Hang the braids in your room for marvelously rich and spicy smells. They make wonderful family gifts.

Kitchen witches. The Scandinavians have a delightful tradition of hanging witches in their kitchens to keep pots from boiling over and food from spoiling, and generally to protect culinary activities. Children, who love folklore, respond enthusiastically to the idea of the kitchen witch.

You can make kitchen witches in a variety of ways (just as puppets are made). One of the simplest kitchen witches I saw hung in a kindergarten class in Michigan. The children cut out their witches from construction paper and used buttons for eyes, wool or cotton for hair, and scraps of material for clothes. They glued their witches to tongue depressors and taped them (with masking tape) to the wood panel around the "cooking corner." "Since we put up our kitchen witches," one of the children explained, "all our food comes out perfect!"

Five senses sampler. Sue Coomer collects styrofoam meat trays, washes them, and uses them for projects like this one.

It is better to smell, taste, touch, see, and hear food than simply to talk about doing so. After discussing such words as bitter, sweet, sour, salty, crunchy, smooth, soft, and hard, Sue gives children styrofoam plates of food to sample, such as potato chips, pretzels, lemon, banana, peanuts, grapes, celery, apples, salt, sugar, honey, and onion.

Peanut shell art. Julia Crabbs believes in wasting nothing. First the children make peanut butter using the following recipe, which requires no cooking.

1 pound roasted peanuts
2 tablespoons salad oil
Crackers

The children shell the nuts and put them through a grinder or in a blender. Add oil until the mixture is spreadable. Spread peanut butter on crackers.

The children use the peanut shells for projects such as pasting the shells on cardboard or on boxes for mosaic designs, and combining the shells with scrounge materials such as felt, wood scraps, Popsicle sticks, and glitter to create sculptures, puppets, or "peanut people."

Eggshell mosaics. Teachers like Sherri Bishop of Summit Children's Center in Columbus, Ohio, share the wonders of eggs with their students. One of Sherri's most popular projects is to color hard-boiled eggs and display them in different color combinations for a few days. Then she and the children peel them and eat them with celery or carrots, or mash them together with mayonnaise and scoop the deviled eggs onto crackers. The children salvage the colored eggshells and arrange the pieces of shells in mosaic designs by pasting or gluing them to cardboard, wood, or boxes.

Vegetable prints. This popular activity is a by-product of making salad or vegetable soup. After talking about the different vegetables the earth yields and preparing salads and soups for the class to enjoy, instead of throwing out the ends of the vegetables, give each child a small piece. Children paint the bottom of the vegetable with watered-down tempera and stamp the design on paper. Encourage them to make their own patterns, using different vegetables or just one. When the pictures are displayed, play a game of guessing which vegetables made the prints.

Picture stories of seeds. Young children are fascinated by the magic of seeds. After discussing the amazing changes from seeds to vegetables, fruits, and flowers, give each child a seed and a sheet of drawing or construction paper. Suggest that the children glue or paste the seed to the paper and color, draw, or paint as many ideas about the seed's changes as they can think of. Many children, influenced by comic books, draw separate boxes for each stage of growth.

Centerpieces from the earth. With hand-designed tablecloths and centerpieces, an ordinary snack becomes an event. Take a walk with the children and gather pebbles, small branches, leaves, ferns, twigs, buckeyes, acorns, pinecones, and so on. Give each child a paper plate or a small aluminum pie plate on which to arrange their "treasures" into a lovely design. Use glue or paste if necessary.

Wild carrots, or Queen Anne's lace. A friend of Betsy Distelhorst told her, "There's no such thing as a useless weed. A weed is simply a plant growing in the wrong place!" Betsy takes her children for a spring walk to gather one of the most common weeds, Queen Anne's lace. The children are encouraged to pull up the plant by the roots and smell them ("They smell like carrots!"). Back at school, the children cut and wash the roots, which can be eaten raw or cooked.

After the feast, the children tie the stems together, hang them upside down, and wait for them to dry out. The design of Queen Anne's lace is beautiful. The children use it alone, mounting it on construction paper or colored cardboard and covering it with wax paper, or add it to other dry flowers for long-lasting arrangements to enjoy in class or present to family or friends as gifts.

The earth's garden. Planting a real garden is the best activity. Second best is creating a beautiful garden by using torn or cut pieces of colored construction paper, tissue paper, or painted newspaper. Encourage the children to tear long, skinny pieces for stems and short, oblong pieces for leaves. Tack a large sheet of paper to a bulletin board or wall. Children paste up stems, roots, leaves, fruits, vegetables, grains, trees, and so on.

A preschooler evaluated their garden by saying, "I think it needs to be mowed!"

Walnut zoo, boats, and Thumbelina beds. Nuts are an excellent source of protein. Walnuts are especially delicious, and their shells make delightful animals. After the children enjoy eating the meat of the walnut, ask them to turn the shells into zoo animals by gluing on bits of felt and straw, tiny buttons, and so on. Magic Markers can be used to draw on the shell. If you put a tiny ball or marble under the shell, the walnut animal will scoot down a slanted board or book.

Walnut shells also make excellent little boats. Glue, paste, or tape a toothpick or tiny stick to the bottom of the shell to make a mast. Give each child a paper sail to color or design before attaching it to the mast. Now you have a fleet of walnut ships! Turn them into "wishing boats" by standing around a tub of water and giving the children time to make a wish before gently pushing or blowing them on their journey.

Children love Thumbelina, who is no bigger than their thumbs. Make a Thumbelina out of tiny scraps of material and cotton balls. Remember, the Thumbelina must fit into the walnut-shell beds. A four-year-old kept his Thumbelina for the year. His mother said it was one of his most precious possessions.

Peanut butter play dough. Sandy Morgan's students at Edison School in Grandview Heights, Ohio, enjoy the following treat.

½ to 1 cup dry milk
1 cup peanut butter
4 tablespoons honey

Mix ingredients by hand and shape the dough into animals, letters, numbers, people, and designs. Look at everyone's wonderful works and eat them!

Be sure all hands are washed before you begin. You will probably want to wash hands after the sculpting and eating as well.

MUSIC TIMES

Songs that celebrate food. Many songs from folklore, musical shows, and TV programs have food as their main theme. Play them on records, sing them yourself, and teach them to the children. Feel free to add your own words to make them fit your themes. Some favorites of these songs are "Food, Glorious Food" (*Oliver*); "Suppertime" (*You're a Good Man, Charlie Brown!*); "The Super Supper March" (*Dr. Seuss* album); "Oats, Peas, Beans and Barley Grow" (folk song); "On Top of Spaghetti" (to the tune "On Top of Old Smokey"); "Oh, What a Beautiful Morning!" (*Oklahoma*); and "Plant a Radish" (*Fantastiks*). Enrich the songs through movement and art activities.

Improvised songs good enough to eat. Any song you and your children enjoy becomes the perfect food song when mixed with imagination and fun. Gwen Marston (listen to her marvelous record, *Songs for Small Fry*) has a good time changing the old folk song "Old John Rabbit" into a nourishing experience.

Old John Rabbit—Yes Ma'am.
Jumping in my garden—Yes Ma'am.
Eating all my vegetables—Yes Ma'am.

"What kind of vegetables?" Gwen whispers between lines of the song. The children have no trouble supplying excellent lines.

Eating all my carrots—Yes Ma'am.
Eating all my potatoes—Yes Ma'am.
Eating all my lettuce—Yes Ma'am.

They continue through the vegetables to the fruits.

The familiar children's song "Found a Peanut" was changed to a complete eating experience when a group of kindergartners made peanut butter and sang about it.

Found a peanut, found a peanut, found a peanut last night.
Last night we found a peanut, found a peanut last night.
Found another one, found another one, found another one last night.
Last night we found another one, found another one last night.

THE BUTTERFLY AND THE ROSE

The Butterfly and the Rose liked each other. They went to a hamburger shop. The Rose said, "Do you like these hamburgers?" The Butterfly said, "I hate these hamburgers." The Rose said, "Let's get our money back." Then they got their money back. Then the Butterfly and the Rose went home. When they went home the Rose said, "Those hamburgers were horrible." When they got home they went to bed. Goodnight Goodnight.

Kathy, age 7

Broke them open, broke them open, broke them open last night.
Last night we broke them open, broke them open last night.
Put them in the blender, put them in the blender, put them in the blender last night.
Last night we put them in the blender, put them in the blender last night.
Mushed them up, mushed them up, mushed them up last night.
Added oil, added salt, made peanut butter last night.
It was delicious, it was delicious, it was delicious last night.

The beloved song "If I Had a Hammer" was transformed into a food-celebrating event by the year-long musical improvisations of a group of kindergartners.

If I had an apple
I'd eat it in the morning.
I'd eat it in the evening
All over this land.
I'd eat it for breakfast.
I'd eat it for supper.
I'd eat it with all my friends and sisters and brothers
All, all over this land.

Children never tire of the things they enjoy. Use a favorite song over and over, adding new words and ideas as they are discovered and discussed.

Recipe songs. Children learn everything better by singing it. Use the steps and ingredients of easy recipes as the words for original songs, or fit the recipe words into familiar melodies. A first-grade class making applesauce with a recipe adapted from *Kids Are Natural Cooks* (Roz Ault, based on the ideas of Liz Uraneck, Houghton Mifflin, 1974, p. 5) followed brightly lettered instructions written on a large chart.

1. Cut apples into pieces
2. Add a little water
3. Cook and stir the apples
4. Mash the apples
5. Add a little honey
6. Add a little lemon juice
7. Add a bit of cinnamon
8. Stir and eat

The recipe fit perfectly the melody "Bow Bow Bow Belinda," a favorite game-dance. The children turned the recipe into a song.

Cut the apples into pieces.
Cut the apples into pieces.
Cut the apples into pieces.
Won't you make some applesauce?
Add a little water to the apples.
Add a little water to the apples.

As you write recipes for the children to follow (try to add an illustration or picture to each step), hum the rhythm of the words. There is your recipe for a new song!

Nutritious singing games. Change "Farmer in the Dell" to vegetable soup. Change "Hokey Pokey" to a salad bar. Steve Anderson and his four-year-olds made sandwich boards of vegetables. On large sheets of tagboard, the children drew or pasted pictures of specific vegetables— one vegetable for each child, the name of the vegetable on the board. Steve punched two holes at the top of each board and tied pairs of boards together with string. The children put them on and were ready for "Farmer in the Dell" vegetable soup. "The farmer needed peppers./The farmer needed peppers. Hi Ho the derry-o, the farmer needed peppers." As each vegetable was needed for the soup, a child entered the circle.

A group of five-year-olds made bib pictures that they hung around their necks. Each picture featured a different fruit and its name. They sang and danced a "Hokey Pokey" fruit salad.

You put a banana in. (banana enters circle)
You put a banana out. (banana jumps out)
You put a banana in (banana jumps in again)
and shake it all about. (banana shakes it up)
(Everyone) You do the hokey pokey and you turn around.
(Clap and jump) That's what it's all about.

Continue until all of the children have entered the circle. Then sing:

You put all the fruit in.
You put all the fruit out.
You put all the fruit in
and shake it all about.
You do the hokey pokey and you turn around.
That's what it's all about.

Music for your dining pleasure. When you dine at a fine restaurant, you usually enjoy lovely, soothing music. Sometimes one person entertains, sometimes a group of musicians plays, and sometimes the music is recorded. Discuss this with your students so they learn that music is part of the experience.

When you have food in the classroom, try to match the music with the kind of food you are eating. For example, if you are having pizza or pasta, play Italian folk music; pita bread sandwiches, Arabic, Greek, or Israeli music; corn bread or corn pudding, American Indian music. Explain the relationship between the food and the music.

A delightful variation of this idea is to give the children, one at a time or in partners, the opportunity to play music as people eat. You may want to designate one day a week for "live entertainment." The child or children who will perform eat their snack before the others so that they do not feel deprived. Emphasize the need for soft, pleasant, soothing rhythms. You will be surprised when even your champion noise-maker plays mellow tones.

Eat first, sing later. Snacks or meals become favorite times when they are followed by a few favorite songs. As soon as the children are finished with their food and before they clear the table, invite them to sing some of their favorite songs together. Choose the songs spontaneously; have the children take turns choosing songs (song leaders); or write all the songs they know on small colorful index cards, put them in a box or bag, and have the children draw a song card grab-bag style and sing it.

Cheers and chants for favorite foods. Young children are excellent cheerleaders. Improvise cheers that your children know, and celebrate nutritious foods.

A group of first graders had a marvelous session celebrating whole-grain cereals and breads with cheers such as this one.

Don't eat Twinkies.
No. No. No.
Eat whole wheat!
Yes. Yes. Yes.

The children worked out movements to accompany their cheer. On the yes, yes, yes part, they took three giant jumps, arms flung in the air. The children took turns playing instruments to add life to the cheer. **Songs of thanks for food.** Songs of thanksgiving are daily events in many schools, camps, and community centers where people break bread together. You do not have to be involved in religious dialogue to convey to children an appreciation for the gifts of the earth and for our good fortune in having enough food to eat and share with others. Many graces and songs run the gamut from "Rub a dub dub, thanks for the grub" to a jazzy, hand-clapping number such as:

God is great.
God is good.
Let us thank Him for our food.
We're gonna thank Him in the morning,
noon and night.
We're gonna thank our Lord
'cause He's out of sight.
Amen (clap clap clap clap)
Amen (same)
Amen (same)

To an original song composed and sung by four-year-olds to the tune of "Good Morning to You":

We're thankful for food.
We're thankful for food.
We're thankful for this food.
We're thankful for food.

Food instruments. Save seeds from fruit and bits of macaroni and dried beans from cooking projects. After making juice, rinse out and save the juice cans. Save pie pans as well. All of these items can be used to make instruments, such as tambourines and maracas.

Give each child two small pie pans (or paper plates). The children put a handful of macaroni or dried beans on one pan or plate. The other pan or plate is placed face down over the first. Tape the edges so the two pans are tightly closed. Decorate with paint, crepe paper, ribbons, or ruffles. Shake them and move, march, and dance to merry rhythms of tambourines.

Give each child a small orange-juice can with one end removed. (If you do not have enough cans, use cardboard toilet tissue tubes.) The children fill the cans or tubes with beans, macaroni, or peanut shells. Cover the open end with construction paper or aluminum foil and secure it with tape or rubber band. Decorate the maracas with colorful paper, streamers, or ribbons. Shake them to lively rhythms.

Special sounds for food and cooking. "Snap, crackle and pop" are not the only sounds celebrating special foods. There are sizzling, boiling, simmering, crunching, munching, pouring, sipping, melting, seasoning, cracking, sifting, scraping and a few dozen other sound effects of the cooking process. Challenge the children to use their bodies, voices, or instruments to express these actions. From simmering to boiling is an exciting musical idea. After one such experience, five-year-old Nathan remarked: "That boiling hurts your hands!" He had been playing a drum and when the boiling started, the drum beats came fast and furiously.

MOVEMENT AND PLAY TIMES

I walked through a room of young children and as I passed each cluster of children at play, I heard: "Want a cup of coffee?" (in a tiny toy cup); "We're making 'begetable' soup. You can have some" (play kitchen corner); "This cake is coming out good. Do you like carrot cake?" (sandbox cake); and "What do you want on your hamburger?" (cardboard play food).

Food and eating is one of the most popular themes of children's games. A special area of the classroom is the play kitchen, where one usually finds table and chairs; dishes and silverware; pots and pans; toy stove, sink, and refrigerator; and a closet or shelf with boxes and cans of food (homemade or scrounged). The area is usually occupied by at least one "family," eating, cooking, and talking together.

Playing store or restaurant. When children study foods, they explore the wonders of the grocery store, fruit stand, and supermarket where most of their foods are bought. Talking about food and visiting food stores introduces the delightful game of playing "store." Likewise, a trip to a restaurant or a lively discussion about restaurants leads to playing "restaurant."

These two popular games were developed to extraordinary lengths by Helen Speyer and Lori Salczer and their four-year-olds at the Jewish Center in Columbus, Ohio. Joe's Supermarket was created when the children drew, painted, and cut out pictures of food from the four food groups and pasted them on the walls. The children found a large cardboard carton in which a refrigerator had been packed. They cut out a window and door and decorated the box with pictures of food and the name Joe's Supermarket. They collected empty cereal boxes and rinsed out empty cans and jars of food that still had labels. They also made their own food out of clay, cardboard, Playdough, and miscellaneous materials. They made money out of cardboard and paper. A table and shelves were pulled to the refrigerator box. The children stocked the bottom of the refrigerator box and lined the table and shelves with "food." Toy telephones and a toy cash register were added for authenticity. Paper bags were collected for packing groceries. The children took turns buying, selling, checking out, and packing food. Joe's Supermarket was in business for well over a month.

Helen and Lori and their four-year-olds had such a good time learning about the four basic food groups and healthful food habits that the children talked about creating a restaurant where only nutritious foods would be served. They decided to name their restaurant Lamb's Restaurant.

A field trip to Seva, a health food restaurant owned and operated by Marcia Sigall, followed. The children were full of questions. Marcia gave them a grand tour and offered practical ideas for their own restaurant, including a poster of restaurant workers.

When the children returned, they set up Lamb's Restaurant. They made place mats, menus, food posters, and table decorations. Using the same play money from Joe's Supermarket, they played waitress, waiter, cook, and customer. One day, they invited another class to be the customers and

served them real banana pudding. Lamb's Restaurant was a favorite game for many weeks.

Growing dance. Children love to grow! Talk about seeds and the wonder of seeds. Then ask the children to turn into seeds, the tiniest body shapes they can create. "What kind of seeds are you? What will you grow into?" Encourage the children to think in slow motion, to change their shape and grow very slowly into fruits and vegetables. Ask them to hold their final shapes.

Accompany the growing process with silence, light taps on the tambourine, or slow, mysterious music. Three of my favorite musical pieces for this activity are John Denver's "Sunshine on My Shoulders" (*John Denver's Greatest Hits*, RCA); "Coit Tower," the theme from *The Strawberry Statement* (MGM Records); and "Tubular Bells," from *The Exorcist* (*Great Movie Themes*, Pickwick International).

Indian dances. Indians perform the Corn Dance when they want the corn to grow tall and healthy. They perform the Rain Dance when they want rain to nourish their crops. Beat a steady heartbeat rhythm on the drum or tambourine, or play Indian music. Improvise rain dances. Use fingers and hands to show the rain falling. Turn bodies in different directions to help the rain fall on all the lands. Move around the circle in steady rhythms, using arms, hands, and fingers, and turning bodies slowly.

Explore the process of planting with the children: hands on the floor, softening the earth, making furrows for the seeds, placing the seeds, and smoothing the earth over them. The children "plant" a small area, smooth down the earth, and move (walk, skip, dance) to a new area to begin again. Accompany the dance with drumbeats, tambourine shakes, or Indian music.

Indian traditions help children learn to take care of the earth and its gifts. (For catalogues of Indian music, write to Indian House, Box 472, Taos, New Mexico 87571, or Folkway Records, 43 West 61st Street, New York, New York 10023.)

Food stories and poems to improvise. Many of the children's favorite stories and poems are related to food, such as Pooh Bear's love of honey, Peter Cottontail's love of Mr. McGregor's wonderful vegetables, and Johnny Appleseed's planting apple trees throughout the land. Make this kind of literature even more special through movement and pantomime, such as the following.

Little Red Hen. In this story Little Red Hen asks everyone to help her till the soil, plant the seeds, water the ground, reap the grain, grind the flour—all the way to baking the bread. No one helps. But when the bread is baked and smells delicious, everyone wants to eat it. This story is helpful in teaching cooperation as well as the process from seed to bread.

We have played and danced this story many ways with children of all ages. One of the most popular ways is for one child to be Little Red Hen and a few children to be her chicks, who help her. The rest of the children decide who they want to be (we have had everything from horses to clowns to Superman). When the Little Red Hen approaches each character, that character does something special—horse gallops, clown does tricks, kangaroo hops—and the Little Red Hen interrupts to ask for help.

When a kindergarten class reached the end of the story, where everyone wanted to taste the bread and the Little Red Hen said, "No, you didn't help!", the children, as if rehearsed, sincerely said, "We're sorry! Can we have another chance?" The children played the story again, and this time everyone helped.

Stone Soup. This old tale has been told and retold through the ages. Marcia Brown's *Stone Soup* (Scribners, 1947) heads the list of children's favorite versions. The story involves one or two strangers (probably related to the tricky tailors who convinced the Emperor to strut down Main Street with new clothes no one could see) who come to a village. They tell the villagers that they can make stone soup. No one believes them. "We can prove it," they say. They boil a stone in a pot of water. They taste it. "Hmmmm. Very good. It might need a little carrot." Each time they taste the plain hot water, they think of another vegetable to add. The silly villagers bring the vegetables, never realizing that they are making vegetable soup. The trick works. Everyone loves the stone soup.

This is a story children truly enjoy listening to as well as improvising. We have played variations, using pictures, play food, or pantomime food to add to the pot. Each child has a turn to run home and "get a vegetable" for the soup. At the end, everyone dips an imaginary cup into the pot and murmurs how delicious stone soup tastes. The mischievous tricksters wink and giggle.

This story provides practical suggestions for vegetable soup, which many classes of young children cook and eat with gusto. They combine the story with the making of real vegetable soup.

The Little Gingerbread Boy. This old nursery story provides marvelous ideas for playing and cooking. Here is the way Verna Willis shared the story with her preschoolers in Columbia, South Carolina.

After reading the story, the children made Gingerbread Boy cookies. When Verna put the baking sheet into the oven in the school's kitchen, she planned a trick with another staff member. The partner took the cookies out and hid them in a special place. Verna made a treasure hunt trail of gingerbread pictures that led the children through the school, "chasing the Gingerbread Boy!" They followed the clues until, at last, they found their cookies. Such excitement!

Poems like "Food and Drink" by David McCord (*Take Sky*, Dell, Yearling Book, 1962, pp. 20–24) inspire imaginative movement interpretation. There are ten parts to this poem, each dedicated to a different aspect of food and drink. Children enjoy listening to each section and using their bodies to express the ideas.

A group of kindergartners listened to section 9, entitled "Salt and Pepper," and began jumping and bouncing. "We're salt and pepper shakers," they explained.

Be open and flexible in your celebration of a story or poem the children especially like. If only one part of the piece lends itself to movement and interpretation, play with that one part. The bibliography at the end of this guide contains other stories and poems to be improvised.

Cooking words are moving words. Children respond immediately to this challenge. "I'll say a word and you show me with your body that you know what this word means." Use words from recipes, cooking stories, and discussions—words such as mix, rise, chew, melt, sprinkle, taste, smell, measure, and bubble.

"Turn yourself into . . ." During discussions about various foods and their qualities, challenge the children to:

Turn yourself into a sunflower. How tall can you grow?
Turn yourself into a banana. How do you peel? (Small groups of children may work together.)
Turn yourself into an alfalfa seed. How do you sprout?
Turn yourself into a milkshake. How do you shake?
Turn yourself into peas in a pod. How does that look? (Small groups again.)
Turn yourself into a piece of toast in a toaster. How do you pop up?
Turn yourself into a whistling, steaming tea kettle.

Nutritious food vs. junk food. Remember your old football games and cheering your team and booing the rival team? Turn this idea into a fun way to emphasize the benefits of healthful food and the disadvantages of junk food by asking the children to cheer when nourishing food is named and to boo when a junk food is named: Milk—Yaaaaaay; Milky Way—Boooooo.

How food helps us. This idea is perfect for skits, pantomime, improvisations, puppet shows, and games. After the children have been introduced to various foods and their contributions to health and well-being, turn the information into games and dramas using such challenges as these: "Oh, my eyes and hair are so dull! What can I eat to help make my eyes healthy and my hair shiny? (answer: dark leafy vegetables and yellow vegetables); "What can we eat to help us grow big and strong?" (answer: high-protein food such as fish, dried peas, nuts, eggs, meat, and seeds). Ask the children to show you how big and strong they want to grow. Each area needing improvement is demonstrated by the children. Pictures and posters help the children remember specific foods.

Healthy kids, blobby kids. In the past few years, this kind of movement story has been thoroughly enjoyed by young children throughout the country. Here are excerpts that can be changed or rearranged to fit your children.

"Once upon a time, there were these terrific kids who were so healthy and strong. Let's see how these kids looked." Stop so the children can demonstrate their strengths. "These children ate healthy food like milk, eggs, cheese . . ." (pantomime drinking and eating). After a few starter words, ask what other kinds of good food the healthy children ate. You will be amazed at the long list suggested by your students as they gulp and chew imaginary food.

After you have mentioned all the foods, continue the story. "Because those kids had such strong bones and muscles, great energy and coordination, they were fabulous joggers. Here's how they jogged!" (Play music with steady beat as the children jog.) "Because they had such straight backs, good eyes, and strong legs, they were terrific skippers. Here's how they skipped!" (Have the children demonstrate their best skips.) Continue in this way; for example, "Here's how they did jumping jacks . . . touched their toes . . . hopped . . . danced."

After a while, ask the children to freeze and hold their last position. Then shake out that position and turn into a group of blobby kids. How do those kids look? "Those kids ate the worst junk. They ate things like candy bars for breakfast (boo) and whipped cream and chocolate syrup for lunch (boo). What else do you think they ate?" The children come up with the most creative junk-food combinations, such as: "Baby Ruth sandwiches with potato chips on top!"; "Bubble gum soup!"; and "Chocolate kisses in their oatmeal!" Five-year-old Mark made an awful face and declared, "That's disgusting!"

After a list of "disgusting" junk-food combinations are suggested, the real fun begins. "Well, these junk-food kids were so blobby and rusty and uncoordinated they could hardly jog. This is the way they jogged." (Students love to show this heavy-footed, fatigued-looking semijog.) "Here's how they touched their toes!" (Accompany the attempt with moans and groans.) Repeat the sequence used earlier for the healthy children.

Sometimes the story ends here, with the moral so obvious the children can recite it in their sleep: Junk food messes up your body; nutritious food gives you energy, muscles, strength to do lots of fun things. Other times, the children want a finale that gives the junk-food group a chance to change their bad habits and become physically fit.

Animals and food. A variation of the above idea focuses on animals. Tell and demonstrate a story about horses eating delicious oats. Watch how fast they gallop! Other horses eat dog and cat food and can hardly run. One group of rabbits are such good hoppers because they eat yummy vegetables, while another group eats birdseed and peanut butter and practically fall down when they hop. After a while, through the

laughter and motion, the children understand that animals also have to eat food that is nourishing for them.

Junky and Strongy and other puppets. Puppets not only entertain young children but also help them understand important concepts. Here are just a few examples of puppet activities related to nutrition.

Children make puppets representing the four major food groups. One class called them Mr. Dairy, Miss Fruity Vegetable, Miss Scrambled Egg, and Mr. Whole Grains. The puppets tell each other about the good things they do for people.

Creating puppets dedicated to their favorite foods was a popular experience for a group of first graders. Such puppet characters as Carrie Carrot, Robert Egg, Appie Apple, and Timmy Tuna Sandwich played happily for weeks.

Junky and Strongy were two puppet characters in a kindergarten class. Junky ate the worst food and was always complaining about his health. Strongy ate nutritious food and was always trying to persuade Junky to change his evil ways. Children took turns throughout the year creating dialogue for the puppets.

VISITORS AND FIELD TRIPS

Visitors

Remember that company means "with bread." Every visitor is company and should therefore be greeted by you and your students with warm hospitality, which, of course, includes refreshments. Serving refreshments to your guests provides opportunities for planning and preparing nutritious, delicious food.

There are also many wonderful classroom visitors whose lives and work are directly related to food.

Family members who love to cook and bake. This is a marvelous way for young children to discover the wealth of cultural, religious, ethnic, and regional customs and food specialties that contribute to the rich diversity of our country. Encourage family members who enjoy cooking and baking to share their feelings, customs, and expertise with your children. Stress the importance of specific holidays and the food associated with them.

Even though there is only one Chinese

child in a class of second graders, the children enjoyed an exciting Chinese New Year's celebration complete with egg rolls and almond cakes. On Martin Luther King's birthday, the grandmother of one of the black children in a kindergarten class came to school and helped the children cook a traditional meal of greens, sweet potato pudding, and fried chicken. On Chanukah, an aunt and two mothers visited a class of four-and-a-half-year-olds and spent the morning cutting up potatoes, blending them with onions, and frying them into the favorite treat of the holiday, potato "latkes." The children ate them with applesauce and sour cream. Lucy Lloyd of Columbus, Ohio, is a mom who "loves to cook with kids" and shares that feeling and activity with her children's classes. "We always talk when we cook. It's so much fun—textures, smells, following instructions, measuring out ingredients . . . The main thing is for kids to participate."

Find out who your families are, what holidays they celebrate, what family specialties they are willing to share, and roll out the welcome mat. When children enjoy "breaking bread" with others, they are likely to become understanding, appreciative, respectful adults.

Naturalists and other "wild food nuts." If you live in a smaller community, with splashes of green between roads of concrete, you will most likely be able to discover a person who knows about folk foods and edible herbs, weeds, and roots. Doris Berry of Columbus, Ohio, calls herself a "wild food nut" and enjoys sharing her knowledge and appreciation with young children. Her three favorite edible wild plants that she helps children recognize and gather are dandelions, curly dock, and wild onions. The children take them back to the classroom, wash them thoroughly, and cook them or use them in salads.

If you are lucky, someone like Doris Berry lives in your community and will be delighted to visit your children. You can also obtain information from the Park Service and local museums.

Junk Food Junky and other zany visitors. Jay Jacobs, Physical Education Director of the Jewish Center in Columbus, Ohio, turns himself into Junk Food Junky. His approach really hits the target and helps strengthen the children's resistance to junk food.

If you have an uninhibited colleague, parent, relative, friend, or neighbor who enjoys kidding around with young children, create a guest character based on a food idea. I saw a wonderful Mr. Carrot, dressed in orange with a pointy carrot hat, who told the children: "Look into my eyes. Let me look in your eyes. You need to eat more carrots!" In another school, the study of the letter P turned into a group of area teenagers dressed as Protein People. They helped children learn a lot more than that letter of the alphabet.

Athletes, cheerleaders, and dancers. Area high school athletes, cheerleaders, and dancers are held in awe by young children. Invite some of these high school friends to talk to your children, demonstrate some of their exercises and drills, and, most important, emphasize the importance of good nutrition and diet in the making of strong bodies.

Representatives from 4H, dairy council, health department. If you invite people with expertise in food and nutrition to speak with your children, be sure to ask them to bring colorful pictures, posters, and props and to dramatize their messages rather than presenting straight lectures.

Chef. You may find a family member or neighbor who is a chef by profession. By all means, invite that person to meet your children and share some experiences and techniques.

Field Trips

Each geographic area has its own resources for children and teachers to discover. The following list includes places young children around the country have visited.

> Bakeries
> Supermarkets
> Fruit and vegetable markets
> Fruit orchards
> Pumpkin patches
> Egg farms
> Dairy farms
> Cooperative food stores
> Bagel factories
> Ice cream factories
> Canning factories
> Restaurants
> Health food stores
> Community food pantries
> Grain elevators
> Dairies
> Food processing plants

Festivals. Most communities celebrate the cultural diversity of their residents. The most popular feature of these festivities, whether they are United Nations festivals, Greek festivals or St. Patrick's Day parties, is food. If possible, take your children to the party.

Historical restorations and museums. Many area museums feature historical exhibits. Food and food preparation are fascinating features of these exhibits. If you live near a restored village or house, your children will find the trip an amazing adventure into a time before fast-food drive-ins and refrigeration.

Reminder. Visitors and field trips provide inspiration and motivation for art, writing, letter writing, reading, puppetry, vocabulary building, improvisation, "Talk

Times," music, and story telling. Marilyn Cohen in Albany, New York, and Sue Coomer in Columbus, Ohio, have imaginations and energies of parallel intensity. Both teachers took their kindergartners to nearby apple orchards. The activities that followed included apple-tree art projects; counting apples; apple cores (discover the five-seed star shape); apples in fruit salad; apple pictures, stories, puppets, poems, and songs; and apples and honey for Rosh Hashanah, the Jewish New Year (for a sweet year).

NOTES

1. Pablo Neruda, "The Great Tablecloth," *Extravagaria*, tr. by Alastair Reid (New York: Farrar, Straus & Giroux, 1976), p. 47.
2. Laurel Robertson, Carol Flinder, and Bronen Godfrey, *Laurel's Kitchen* (Petaluma, Calif.: Nilgiri Press, 1976), p. 144.
3. Mary T. Goodwin and Gerry Pollen, *Creative Food Experiences for Children*, revised edition (Washington, D.C.: Center for Science in the Public Interest, 1980), pp. 13–14.
4. Roz Ault, *Kids Are Natural Cooks* (Boston: Houghton Mifflin, 1974), p. 120.
5. Julia Child, *Julia Child and Company* (New York: Knopf, 1979), p. 147.
6. Neruda, p. 47.
7. Goodwin and Pollen, p. 150.
8. Columbus *Dispatch*, February 20, 1980.

SELECTED BIBLIOGRAPHY

Cookbooks to Use with Children

Abisch, Roz, and Boche Kaplan. *The Munchy Crunchy Healthy Kid's Snack Book*. New York: Walker, 1976.

Bruno, Janet. *Cooking in the Classroom*. Belmont, Calif.: Pitman, 1974.

Cauley, Lorinda Bryan. *Pease Porridge Hot, A Mother Goose Cookbook*. New York: Putnam, 1977.

Cooper, Terry, and Marilyn Ratner. *Many Friends Cooking. An International Cookbook for Boys and Girls*. New York: Putnam, 1980.

Edge, Nellie. *Kindergarten Cooks*. Port Angeles, Wash.: Peninsula, 1975.

Ellison, Virginia. *The Pooh Cookbook*. New York: Dutton, 1969.

Dorbing, Arnold. *Peter Rabbit's Natural Foods Cookbook*. New York: Warne, 1977.

Glovach, Linda. *The Little Witch's Black Magic Cookbook*. Englewood Cliffs, N. J.: Prentice-Hall, 1972.

Johnson, Barbara, and Plemons Johnson. *Cup Cooking*. Mt. Rainier, Md.: Gryhon, 1980.

Johnson, Georgia, and Gail Pavey. *Metric Milk Shakes and Witches Cakes*. New York: Scholastic, 1976.

Moore, Eva. *The Seabury Cookbook for Boys and Girls*. New York: Seabury, 1969.

Palmer, Michele. *A Mother Goose Feast: Recipes and Rhymes*. Illustrated by Marian Federspiel. Storrs, Conn.: Rocking Horse Press, 1979.

Pinkwater, Jill. *Natural Snack Cookbook*. New York: Four Winds Press, 1975.

Zweifel, Frances. *Pickle in the Middle and Other Easy Snacks*. New York: Harper & Row, 1979.

Stories Good Enough to Eat

Aliki. *The Story of Johnny Appleseed*. Englewood Cliffs, N. J.: Prentice-Hall, 1963.

Arno, Ed. *The Gingerbread Boy*. New York: Scholastic, 1970.

Asch, Frank. *Popcorn*. New York: Parents Magazine Press, 1979.

Barrett, Judi. *Cloudy with a Chance of Meatballs*. Illustrated by Ron Barrett. New York: Atheneum, 1978.

Berenstain, Stanley, and Janice Berenstain. *The Bears' Picnic*. New York: Random House, 1966.

———. *The Big Honey Hunt*. New York: Random House, 1962.

———. *Pappa's Pizza*. New York: Random House, 1980.

Bird, Malcolm. *The Sticky Child*. New York: Harcourt Brace Jovanovich, 1981.

Brierly, Louis. *King Lion and His Cooks*. New York: Holt, Rinehart & Winston, 1982.

Brown, Marcia. *Stone Soup*. New York: Scribners, 1947.

Carle, Eric. *A Very Hungry Caterpillar*. New York: Putnam, 1969.

———. *Pancakes, Pancakes*. New York: Knopf, 1970.

Cauley, Lorinda Bryan. *The Bake-Off*. Illustrated by the author. New York: Putnam, 1978.

Charles, Donald. *Fat, Fat Calico Cat*. Chicago: Childrens Press, 1977.

Delton, Judy. *Rabbit Finds a Way*. New York: Crown, 1975.

de Paola, Tomie. *Pancakes for Breakfast*. New York: Harcourt Brace Jovanovich, 1978.

———. *Strega Nona*. Englewood Cliffs, N. J.: Prentice-Hall, 1975.

Galdone, Paul. *Jack and the Beanstalk*. New York: Scholastic, 1974.

———. *The Little Red Hen*. New York: Scholastic, 1975.

———. *The Three Bears*. New York: Scholastic, 1970.

Heller, Linda. *Lily at the Table*. New York: Macmillan, 1979.

Hoban, Russell. *Bread and Jam for Frances*. New York: Scholastic, 1969.

Hogrogian, Nonny. *Apples*. New York: Macmillan, 1972.

Hutchins, Pat. *Don't Forget the Bacon*. New York: Morrow, 1976.

Kent, Jack. *Round Robin*. Englewood Cliffs, N. J.: Prentice-Hall, 1982.

Kerr, Judith. *The Tiger Who Came to Tea*. New York: Coward-McCann, 1968.

Krauss, Ruth. *The Carrot Seed*. New York: Scholastic, 1971.

McCloskey, Robert. *Blueberries for Sal*. New York: Viking, 1976.

Potter, Beatrix. *The Tale of Peter Rabbit*. Racine, Wisc.: Western, 1970.

Rice, Eve. *Benny Bakes a Cake*. Illustrated by the author. New York: Morrow, Greenwillow, 1981.

Sendak, Maurice. *Chicken Soup with Rice*. New York: Harper & Row, 1962.

Tolstoy, Alexei. *The Big Turnip*. New York: Watts, 1968.

Watanabe, Shigeo. *What a Good Lunch!* Illustrated by Yasuo Ohtomo. New York: Collins, 1980.

Teacher Resources

Bettelheim, Bruno. *Food to Nurture the Mind*. Washington, D.C.: Children's Foundation, 1970.

Brown, Elizabeth Burton. Illustrated by Marisabina Russo. *Vegetables: An Illustrated History with Recipes*. Englewood Cliffs, N. J.: Prentice-Hall, 1981.

Goldman, Ethel. *I Like Fruit*. Illustrated by Sharon Luner. Minneapolis, Minn.: Lerner, 1969.

Goodwin, Mary F., and Gerry Pollen. *Creative Food Experiences for Children*, rev. ed. Washington, D.C.: Center for Science and the Public Interest, 1980.

Jordon, Helene J. Illustrated by Joseph Low. *How a Seed Grows*. New York: Harper & Row, 1972.

Lanski, Vicki. *Feed Me, I'm Yours*. New York: Bantam, 1978.

———. *The Taming of the C.A.N.D.Y. Monster*. Minnetonka, Minn.: Meadowbrook, 1978.

Lappe, Frances Moore. *Diet for a Small Planet*. New York: Ballantine, 1975.

Parenteau, Shirley. *Crunch It, Munch It and Other Ways to Eat Vegetables*. Illustrated by Tom Huffman. New York: Putnam, 1978.

Perl, Lila. *Junk Food, Fast Food, Health Food: What America Eats and Why*. Boston: Houghton Miffllin, 1980.

Showers, Paul. Illustrated by Anne Rockwell. *What Happens to a Hamburger*. New York: Harper & Row, 1976.

Smith, Lendon H. *Foods for Healthy Kids*. New York: McGraw-Hill, 1981.

Thomas, Linda. *Caring and Cooking for the Allergic Child*, rev. ed. New York: Sterling, 1980.

United States Department of Agriculture. *Nutritive Value of Foods*, revised edition. Washington, D.C.: Government Printing Office, 1981.

———. *What's to Eat? And Other Questions Kids Ask About Food*. Washington, D.C.: Government Printing Office, 1979.

For free material about food, write to:

Consumer Information, Pueblo, Colorado 81009.

Florida Citrus Commission, Lakeland, Florida 33802.

Food and Nutrition Information Center, National Agricultural Library, United States Department of Agriculture, Baltimore Boulevard, Beltsville, Maryland 20705.

Foods and Nutrition Service, United States Department of Agriculture, Washington, D.C. 20250.

Henry Field Seed and Nursery Company, Shenandoah, Iowa 51602. (Seed catalogue and how-to-grow-it booklet.)

Jolly Time Pop Corn Company, P.O. Box 178, Sioux City, Iowa 51102.

Kansas Wheat Commission, 1021 North Main Street, Hutchison, Kansas 67501.

National Dairy Council, 111 N. Canal Street, Chicago, Illinois 60606.

National 4-H Club Foundation, 7100 Connecticut Avenue, Washington, D.C. 20015.

United Fresh Fruit and Vegetable Association, 727 N. Washington Street, Alexandria, Virginia 22314.

8

THE CLOTHES WE WEAR

We dress

to keep dry	to disguise	for formal
to stay warm	to fantasize	occasions
to keep cool	for support	in style
to be cool	for protection	up
for work	to attract	down
for school	attention	to kill
for sleep	for self-	to look thinner
for dinner	expression	to celebrate
for sport	as a sign of	mass
just to have	class	to undress
pockets	to be one of	for battle
to please our	the guys	for partying
mothers	to mask our	for comfort
to imitate	identity	for kicks[1]

THE BASICS

Clothing, along with food and shelter, is considered one of the basic needs of human beings. Clothing (no pun intended) touches us all.

Clothing is a fascinating topic of conversation and discovery. Did you know, for example, that in ancient Egypt, people made cotton, linen, and wool; that the ancient Persians did not want to simply drape themselves in shapeless materials, so they figured out how to sew fitted sleeves into coats; and that the ancient Chinese kept the process of making silk a secret for hundreds of years?

For most of history, clothing was made by hand. In the mid-1700s, James Hargreaves invented the spinning machine and Edmund Cartwright the power loom. These inventions, followed by Singer's wonderful sewing machine, revolutionized the making of clothing. By the end of the 1800s, clothing had become a major industry in the United States and Europe. Today the United States is the leading manufacturer of clothing in the world, and New York City is on the list with Paris, London, and Rome as a world fashion center.

Ever since the snake dangled that delicious apple in front of Eve, people have devoted time, energy, and resources to thinking up clever variations of the fig leaf. The challenge of clothing has stimulated human inventiveness and creativity in countless ways. Throughout history, men and women have covered themselves with skins, furs, feathers, shells, grasses, leaves, wood, jewels, and metals. They have hidden their faces behind veils; draped themselves in capes; strapped themselves into girdles, belts and corselets; and stuffed their feet into pointy-toed, spike-heeled shoes or thigh-high boots.

Clothes reflect geography, history, religion, socioeconomic background, cultural heritage, and individual personality. They identify and describe us; they express our beliefs, allegiances, and occupations. The Amish, for example, wear no buttons because buttons are associated with the uniforms of Prussian soldiers, who oppressed them. Orthodox Jews always wear their heads covered in deference to God. Muslim women wear veils and robes as a sign of modesty. In ancient Rome, togas were worn only by free, male citizens. Indian chiefs wear special headdresses made of eagle feathers. Mennonites wear dark, somber colors because they believe bright colors are the influence of the Devil. Mussolini's Fascist soldiers were called Brown Shirts. Tough American soldiers are known as Green Berets. One of the cries of the American revolution was, "The Redcoats are coming!"

Every society has its fashion and customs, sometimes set by tradition, other times influenced by a famous person or another culture. Charles II of England liked elaborate clothes with trimmings of laces, ribbons, and ruffles. Seventeenth-century English aristocrats followed in his red-high-heeled footsteps. Amelia Bloomer, a champion of women's rights at the turn of the century, wore baggy pants and started a new style called "bloomers." The influence of other cultures is evident on modern American women wearing Indian headbands, Chinese slippers, and Arabic harem pants.

Fads are also interesting to study. The popularity of the film *Annie Hall* in the mid-1970s resulted in makeshift, no-fashion outfits.

People who work in the world of clothing and fashion have thought-provoking observations to share. One such person is Howard Chenfeld, who is considered a guru in the shoe industry because of his uncanny ability to choose styles a year in advance that American women will want to wear.

We wear clothing not only for warmth and protection, but to express who we are, our place or status in society. Our clothes often express our attitudes toward life. For example, the informal wearing of "military uniforms" parodies the military and seems to express an antiwar feeling. Sports have influenced fashion. People who don't even jog wear running shoes and jogging pants.

In our country, children's fashions reflect the most popular adult trends combined with the kids' favorite TV characters, comic strips, and movies. So you see children wearing "Fonzie" socks, "E.T." shirts, and "Annie" dresses. Kids are under more pressure than we realize to conform to the influence of the mass media. Commercials and popular characters really affect clothing consumption.

Young children are very interested in clothing: its color, texture, and style; the mechanics of putting it on and taking it off; and the technical dexterity needed for tying, zipping, buttoning, and snapping.

I went to our richest source—the children—and talked with them about clothing.

In the case of a very young child, older relatives and friends were eager to chime in, because this subject is relevant to all ages. Here are some of the findings.

Aaron is just turning three. Even though clothing is not one of his major interests (he prefers his books and records!) he has definite preferences. According to his parents, Susie and Sandy Siegel:

Aaron likes accessories: He gets a big kick out of a bow tie or belt. He loves his sandals and always has something on his head—some kind of hat. His cowboy hat is his favorite. Aaron was very excited when he went from diapers to underwear. He felt like such a big boy. He called his underwear "Superman pants." He's into fuzz! He has a pair of favorite pajamas that he loves to feel because they're fuzzy.

Melissa, who is three, enthusiastically described her favorite clothes: "My dress that my grandma who lives in Oklahoma City gave me. I like the color. It's yellow and a whole bunch of colors and has a belt and long sleeves. I wore it to the motel. I felt grown up." Melissa is most comfortable "in my blue bathing suit," and she likes "school clothes because they're warm." Her favorite pajamas "have a whole bunch of men and girls on them." Melissa can put on her shoes, "but I can't buckle them yet!"

Kyra is four and a half. She really enjoys talking about clothes:

My favorite clothes are coats. I like my light brown coat 'cause my mom bought it for me. It's special. I like shorts 'cause you don't get so hot in them. My favorite pair are these [the ones she was wearing]—they're yellow running shorts. You can race in them and I feel like I run faster. I like snow pants because I like to play in snow. I snap them myself. Snapping is better than zipping or buttoning. I learned to tie and zip from my brother's doll, Dapper Dan. I started dressing myself around three. I pick my own clothes to wear in the morning. In school, we talk about clothes a lot and the kids show each other our clothes.

Adina is just eight. Her blue dress—a summer pinafore—is her favorite: "I love it 'cause it looks pretty." She continues: "Play clothes are the best. Bathing suits are very comfortable . . . This is my best blouse 'cause I got it for my birthday from my best friend."

Adina's older sister, Ariela (10 years old), contributed her feelings about clothing: "Winter clothes are best. I feel warm and toasty . . . I love wearing my painter's hat . . . My sister and I played with lots of dolls like Ginny, Barbie, Holly Hobbie, Mandy, GI Joe, and Dressy Betsy, and we always dress them. I dress my Winnie the Pooh all the time."

We talked to Roy and Rusty, two mischievous brothers. Roy is eight and remembered that when he was five, his mom made him a Slavic suit. "It was my favorite thing to wear . . . My brother taught me how to tie my shoes. I was around six years old. Buttoning was harder than zipping."

Rusty, age 10, was eager to join the conversation. He remembered:

My favorite clothes when I was a little kid was my George Washington costume. Mom made it for me when I was four. I had a frontier hat and bib overalls, too, that I loved when I was three . . . I dressed up a boy doll in Scottish costumes—in almost all kinds of costumes—when I was five and six. My grandma made the costumes . . . I think I learned how to button when I was five. Zipping was easier! I learned that when I was four.

Recall your own childhood and try to remember the clothes you loved, what they looked like, why they meant something to you. Our clothes put us in touch with special people, places, and times of our lives. They are part of our memories and experiences. We need clothes for protection against the elements, but we seem also to have a need to decorate ourselves, to express our individuality, and to link ourselves to others through clothing.

This guide provides a wealth of learning experiences for young children. Because children feel almost as possessive of and fascinated by their clothing as they do their bodies, they are ready to respond to enjoyable activities. Don't take my word for it. See for yourself!

DISCOVERY TIMES

- Clothes protect us from cold, heat, rain, snow, wind, and hail.
- We wear different clothes in different seasons and for different reasons.
- People like to decorate their clothing with bright colors, designs, jewels, feathers, and other interesting materials.
- Clothes are made by people—sometimes by hand, other times by machines.
- Most raw material for clothing (cotton, flax, silk, wool, fur) comes from plants and animals.
- We take care of our clothing by cleaning and laundering it, hanging and folding it.
- Putting on clothes often involves buttoning, zipping, tying, and snapping. If we practice these actions, we will learn how to do them. It is fun to practice.
- Every country has special clothing. All clothes that people wear are interesting.
- We should respect the clothing of other people.

SUGGESTED VOCABULARY

clothing	jogging shorts	cap	dress-up clothes
clothes	T-shirt	denim	plaid
dress	skirt	clean	cotton
outfit	pajamas	laundry	sweatshirt
shirt	p.j.'s	scarf	dry cleaner
blouse	bathrobe	socks	put on
jacket	flannel	stockings	take off
coat	dirty	tights	iron
pants	store	leotard	zip
shorts	shoes	costume	button
sleeves	slippers	mask	unbutton
money	boots	cowboy hat	snap
shoe store	tennis shoes	zipper	wash

sweater	sneakers	wool	unsnap
slacks	sandals	price	tie
jeans	clogs	department	untie
dungarees	galoshes	store	fold
overalls	rubbers	shoelaces	put away
snowpants	gloves	play clothes	dry
gym shorts	mittens	party clothes	shop
	hat		

Young children will amaze you with their extensive vocabulary of clothing. They know not only the generic names of items, such as pants, dungarees, and socks, but also the brand names (thanks to television commercials). Their ability to add descriptive words, such as colors, types, and sizes, is impressive. In addition to the physical description and definition of their clothing, young children often tell the circumstances as well. "This shirt my Aunt Barbara brought when we saw her at the Columbus International Airport from New Jersey," five-year-old Billy explained as he showed off his new shirt. "My Nana Rose sent my blue pants with this Mickey Mouse belt and look at how many pockets for my birthday present," Seth told his fellow kindergartners.

Display words identifying pictures and parts of clothing all around your room. The children soon associate the written words with their meanings. Their sight vocabulary increases daily, painlessly and joyfully.

I visited a kindergarten room one stormy winter day and over each clothing hook was a card bearing the child's name and the clothes worn. For example:

Cara's coat	Jean's jacket	Bob's snowsuit	Dan's jacket	Neal's coat

The teacher laughingly told me that one of the children had two winter outfits and when he wore his jacket, he asked the teacher if he could change the label from "coat" to "jacket." What better way to enrich language development than the magic of creative teaching?

SOME BEGINNING ACTIVITIES

Start with weather. Rainy days mean raincoats, rubbers, and umbrellas. Snowy days mean boots, mittens, hats, scarves, snowpants, and jackets. Take advantage of special weather to introduce the main reason for clothing—protection against the elements.

Start with a class poll. Questions such as : "What is your favorite thing to wear?" and "Why do we need clothes?" start children thinking about clothes. Michele Gibson and Carol Highfield asked their four-year-olds at the Jewish Center in Columbus, Ohio, about their favorite clothes and wrote all their answers on a chart. Here are some excerpts from the chart.

SETH: Blue jeans, baseball shirts. My favorite color of clothes is red.
RICHARD: Superhero clothes are my favorites. They're fun.
JESSE: I like dresses 'cause I can wear tights with them.
ADI: My long dress to wear to parties.
PETER: My blue pants and vest. Mom says I look handsome in them.
SHANA: Skirts and T-shirts.
RACHEL: I like to play in dresses.

Class polls are terrific starters because everyone is involved and exchanging ideas immediately.

Start with a doll from another culture. Children are intrigued by costumes of other countries or ethnic origins. Lora Walters begins her discussion of clothing by introducing a Spanish doll with wide flamenco skirt, black lace mantilla and high dancing shoes. Lora explains to her students that "Maria" is from Spain and ask if they notice anything different about her. The children never fail to recognize the special clothing Maria wears, and this is Lora's starting point for weeks of clothing activities.

Start with a pantomime of dressing. Challenge the children to guess what you are doing. Give them clues such as: "We do it every day, right after we get up in the morning. You did it this morning!" When they have guessed, ask them to join you in a group pantomime. Elaborate with, "What are you putting on? How is the weather outside? Do you need help with your zipper?"

Start with a puppet who does not know what to wear. Any classroom puppet will do to involve the children in a delightful advice-giving session on clothing. If you want to evoke terrific responses, make your puppet the absent-minded type who does not realize shoes go on feet, gloves on hands, hats on heads. The children will eagerly correct their puppet friend and feel proud of their knowledge.

Start with an item of clothing. The spotlight is on sweaters or mittens or whichever item you find the most fun to discuss. Use a real article of clothing or a photograph or cutout. Tape it or tack it to a bulletin board in a central place so the children can gather round and focus their attention on it.

Start with a clothing hook. Play a game: "What is on the clothing hook?" Hang different articles of clothing on a hook and ask the children to guess each one. When the game has run its course, talk about the kinds of clothing we wear and why. This will hook the children on the topic.

Start with a celebration. Everyone enjoys celebrations, and what better idea to celebrate than everyone's clothing? Here is how one kindergarten teacher started a month-long series of experiences centered around clothing: "Let's have a cheer for Michael's Yankees T-shirt!" "Let's hear it for Joey's long sleeves!" "Everyone clap hands for Brett's brown belt!"

No one is left out. Everyone is wearing something that becomes special because a fun-loving teacher makes it so. Follow the celebration with a discussion highlighting questions, answers, and observations that will provide material for the weeks to come.

Remember: Stories, poems, pictures, songs, chants, riddles, cheers, classroom visitors—even one word—are all excellent starting activities. Most beginning activities from other guides in this book can be adapted to clothing. Better still, make up a starting activity of your own.

TALK TIMES

Steve Anderson and his young children pondered some of the following questions.

> What are clothes?
> Where do clothes come from?
> How do we get clothes?
> Why do we wear so many different clothes?
> Did people always wear clothes?
> Why do some people wear clothes that look funny to us?
> Can we tell what some people do by their special clothes?
> How do we take care of clothes?
> What are your favorite clothes to wear?
> Can babies put on their own clothes?
> How do clothes make us know we grow?

Here are a few children's comments and explanations collected through the years. Many of their follow-up questions and ideas formed the basis for activities and further discussions in the weeks following the initial group "Talk Time."

> Clothes come from moms. (Amy, age 5)
> We get clothes from our closets and house. (Randy, age 7)
> Grandmas and grandpas give us clothes. (Petie, age 4)
> We need clothes or all our skin will show. (Terry, age 5)
> Most clothes are Star Wars. (Bruce, age 5)
> Clothes are the stuff we put on after breakfast. (Nancy, age 4)
> My socks grow. They stretch bigger. (Neal, age 4)
> Babies can't put on their diapers. They'll stick theirselves. (Judy, age 4)
> Spacemen need special flying clothes. (Todd, age 5)
> I know I growed 'cause my shoes don't fit my big boy feet! (Timmy, age 4)
> I think clothes got started by the underwear. (Heather, age 8)
> Clothes are if you have to get dressed up when you don't want to. (Mikey, age 5)
> Clothes are to keep you warm when it's cold; otherwise, they're for fun! (Howie, age 6)

It is so easy to start children talking if a spirit of respect, trust, interest, and safety permeates the room. It is often necessary to stop everything else because the children have so much to say. That is when creative teachers sit everyone in a circle and encourage the children to take turns "telling." According to an African proverb, "Talking with one another is loving one another." This is a good idea to put into practice.

ART TIMES

Clothing is one of the most popular subjects in photography and illustration. Even if a children's book is not about clothing, the characters and even some of the animals in the story wear clothing.

Every day the children have a wealth of colors, textures, designs, lines, patterns, and arrangements to observe in the classroom and at home. If there is continuous emphasis on using powers of observation, the children will learn to notice how things look and how they relate to each other. So much of art enjoyment is the awareness that precedes and accompanies the activity. When "Art Times" follow "Talk Times," the pleasure is doubled.

The art activities in this guide can be rearranged and expanded upon. They are just suggestions to start you on your way.

Clothes collage. For general awareness of the variety of clothing people wear, ask the children to cut out pictures of people wearing any kind of clothing. After all the pictures are pasted on a large sheet of paper, add labels that the children suggest, such as pants, shirts, and shoes.

A variation of this idea is to focus on one kind of clothing and encourage the children to cut out pictures for a shoe collage, winter clothes collage, summer clothes collage, jeans collage, and so on. Many teachers find that small groups of children like to work together on their own special interest, so instead of one large collage, your class may want to make three or four different collages.

Make your own smock. Because yours is an active class, the children will need smocks to wear over their regular clothes while they are painting, gluing, and generally "working." Boys' old, loose-fitting cotton shirts make excellent smocks. The children enjoy designing, decorating, signing their shirts with Magic Markers, and placing them on clothes hooks or, as some classes feature, smock hooks!

Class cutouts. One of the most beloved of children's activities is to play with and dress characters, whether dolls, stuffed animals, or felt or paper cutouts. Make two large cutouts, a boy and a girl. Many teachers use the children's own life-size cutouts for this project. Using the basic body shapes, cut out simple shirts, pants, skirts, hats, mittens, coats, shoes, and other articles of clothing. The children fill in the clothing shapes with colors and designs. Encourage them to add button and zipper shapes where necessary.

Keep all the clothing shapes together in a "closet" (special box or drawer). Each day, tape up two large children's cutouts and ask the children to take turns dressing them. Masking tape makes dressing very easy.

Small cutouts. This idea is basically the same as that described above, but in this activity, the children receive their own cutout to keep, design a wardrobe for, and dress. Teachers like Lori Salczer, Helen Speyer, Hilary Talis, and Becky Blake claim that their four- and five-year-olds at the Jewish Center in Columbus, Ohio, thoroughly enjoy making the clothing, pasting it on their dolls, and showing their friends.

Family cutouts. Mary Rumm's children in Columbus had a wonderful time with the simple felt or paper figures of a family. She describes the activity.

We had various items of clothing (some cut out, some originally designed) for the children to paste or clip to the family figures. Sometimes we combined them with numbers. For example, one day we thought in three's. So Susannah found long pants for the father, medium-size pants for the mother, and small pants for the child. We encouraged the children to match the clothing to the size of the figures. In summer, we added bathing suits; in winter, mittens, boots, and hoods. This activity brought several concepts into focus (colors, numbers, shapes), and the children enjoyed making the choices, arranging and rearranging.

Portraits of myself in favorite clothing. Encourage the children to draw pictures of themselves dressed in their favorite clothes. Talk about specifics like color, length, design, and buttons before the drawing or painting begins. Awareness influences children's works. Ask the children to give their pictures titles. Accompany the pictures with stories inspired by such questions as: "Where are you going in your favorite

shapes for each child to design and color. If the child wants shoes with laces, paint or color little dots for eyelets.

After the children play with their shoes, dress their class cutouts in them, mix and match them, or display the pairs on a bulletin board or wall. I saw one such display labeled "Shoe Place." The children eagerly showed me their shoes with their names underneath.

Hats. Outline shapes of hats such as rain hats; cowboy and cowgirl hats; police officer, firefighter, and letter carrier hats; derby hats; bonnets; and clowns' hats. Each of these calls for discussion and play involving the kind of hat chosen. Hats, more than any other article of clothing, correlate with careers, weather, special occasions, and special characters.

T-shirt day. Ask the children to wear their favorite T-shirt. Have extras on hand in case a few children forget. Give the children a paper T-shirt shape and suggest that they try to reproduce the color and design of the T-shirt they are wearing. Many delightful activities develop from this project, such as: "Find John's paper T-shirt!" "Let's put all the T-shirts that have the color yellow on this side of the wall!" and "Everyone who has more than one color on his or her T-shirt, hold it up and show us." When you are finished, display all the T-shirts.

Design your own T-shirt. Send a note home asking families if they have an old white T-shirt for the children to use. Scrounge for extras in case you need them.

The easiest way to make an original shirt is to use fabric flow pens, but many teachers claim colorful Magic Markers do just as well. The children lay their shirts flat on tables or desks and choose their favorite colors. They color or draw their designs on the shirt. Encourage them to draw things or people they really enjoy. If children can write their own names, ask them to write them somewhere on their shirts. If they cannot, write the names for them.

The pleasant feature of this activity is that the children can wear the shirts immediately; they do not need drying. Play lively music and have a parade celebrating the wonderful new shirts.

Pick a pocket. Pockets amaze and delight young children. There is something magical about them. "All this stuff was in my pocket and you couldn't see it!" six-year-old Brian

clothes?" "What are you doing in your favorite clothes?" and "How do you feel while you're wearing these clothes?" Write the children's comments on paper to be displayed beside or under their pictures. Of course, if the children can write, encourage them to do their own.

Tongue depressor dolls. Use two tongue depressors for the body, two for the arms, and two for the legs. Tape them together in the middle of the body. Make a construction-paper head and tape it to the top. Name the dolls and dress them in scrounge or paper clothes. They also make great puppets.

Make your own wardrobe

Mittens. Outline children's hands on construction paper. Double the paper if you want real mittens the children can slip their hands into and wear. When the mittens are cut, put a few pieces of tape around the top and sides to hold them together. The children enjoy coloring and wearing their mittens. Turn this activity into a "find the matching mitten" game.

Shoes. Outline children's feet on construction paper or cardboard. Cut out the explained proudly as he displayed the contents of his pocket.

Cut various-sized pockets out of felt scraps or construction paper for the children to design and color. The children decide where they want to place their pockets—on pants, shirts, sleeves; on the front or back. Use masking tape to tape the pockets to their clothes for a Pocket Holiday.

Roxanne Demeter and her first graders in the Glendening School in Franklin County, Ohio, combine "Pocket Talk Time" with this art activity. They talk about such ideas as: "What will be in our pockets?" "What if we had only a tiny pocket?" "What if we were giants and had giant pockets?" "What if our pockets were magic?"

Scraps and snips, buttons and bows. This kind of scrounging is fun. Ask families to send in odds and ends of material; buttons; old, inexpensive jewelry; ribbons; snaps; feathers; laces; and so on. All sizes, colors, designs, and textures are welcome.

Each child is given a person-shape outlined on construction paper or cardboard. The children paste bits and pieces of the scrounge material to their cardboard person to complete features and clothing. The results are usually imaginative and lively. Samantha (Sammy), not quite five years old, pasted a most incredible white fur coat made of cotton puffs on her friend, "Vicki." She explained, "Vicki's all dressed up to go to the palace!"

Paint a button. Michael Rosen's youngsters have a marvelous time painting original designs and colors on plain buttons. The children use bright enamel paint. The buttons can be sewed on clothing for practical or decorative reasons.

Appliqués for special days. The calendar helps in this activity, but creative teachers are not limited to standard holidays.

Valentine's Day (wear your heart on your sleeve). The children design symbols for Valentine's Day (hearts, flowers, happy faces, whatever!); cut them out; paint, color, or paste material on them; and tape them to any part of their clothing.

Halloween. I visited a class of kindergartners who had made Halloween appliqués such as black cats, witches on broomsticks, witches' hats, and pumpkins. They wore them proudly on sleeves, pockets, and collars.

What kind of appliqués can you and your children make for such holidays as President's Day; Christmas and Chanukah; Thanksgiving; and United Nations Week? Create your own holidays, like Animal Day, Flower Day, Spring Day, Alphabet Day, Rainbow Day, Apple Day, and Friendship Day.

Clothesline. Stretch a string or rope across your room or along a wall. After the children cut out (if they can), color, paint, and paste scrounge materials on articles of clothing, they hang them on the clothesline for everyone to see!

Rainy day pictures and other weather projects. Give each child a good-sized piece of drawing paper. Decide on the kind of weather to draw, paint, and color. "Let's turn our picture into a rainy day!" The children draw their ideas of raindrops, dark clouds, wind, and lightning. When the picture is finished, encourage the children to add a person dressed in appropriate clothing.

I have seen variations of this artwork, in which cutout people are pasted on the picture and rain hats, boots, raincoats, and umbrellas are added to the figure. The effect is striking.

Enjoy creating snowy day, sunny day, and autumn day pictures, complete with seasonally dressed persons.

Dashikis. African children wear loose, comfortable, colorful shirts called dashikis. American children enjoy making and wearing these shirts. The easiest way is to cut a sheet or any large pieces of scrounge material into rectangles, folded in half. Cut a semicircle from the material along the folded edge, for the child's head to pass through. The children sew or tape the sides, or leave the sides free. Use Magic Markers and crayons (iron the shirts after the crayoning for a tie-dye effect) to create bright designs.

Indian shirts. Large brown paper bags are the best resource. Cut a hole in the bottom of the bag, for the child's head to pass through. Cut holes for arms. Fringe the bottom of the bag, the way the Indians did on their leather shirts. Be sure the bags are covered with beautiful Indian designs from nature, such as animals, trees, and water.

Note: Brown paper bags make wonderful costumes for occupations as well as clowns, animals, and storybook characters.

Greg, age 5

Encourage the children to draw, paint, or paste materials on the bags to make them lively-looking.

Jewelry. People the world over decorate themselves with beautiful and unusual jewelry. To make necklaces, bracelets, rings, and belts, the children run string, thread, or shoelaces through assorted buttons, beads and shells (with tiny holes in them), and cutout cardboard shapes (punch holes in them). Glue bits of plexiglass, wood chips, tiny stones, sand, sparkly stars, feathers, fuzz, and scraps of satin, lace, and silk to buttons and cardboard shapes (fruit shapes, animal shapes, alphabet letters, numbers, abstracts) to make pins. Glue safety pins to the back of the button or cardboard.

Clothes mobile. Wrap clothes hangers in colored yarn. The children cut articles of clothing out of cardboard or construction paper and color them. Tie pieces of string to

the hanger and attach each piece to an article of clothing. Some children enjoy making a clothes mobile of one kind of clothing. Marcie's "sweater mobile" was really outstanding.

Combine the mobile with weather and include a cutout person dressed for that weather. A group of kindergartners made sun mobiles. One of the children's hangers featured a brilliant, smiling yellow sun, a large red flower, and a cardboard girl dressed in a gorgeous blue and purple bathing suit.

Favorite clothing books. The children discuss their favorite kinds of clothing. After turning that information into a large, interesting poster, cut the shape of each child's favorite piece of clothing out of cardboard or heavy construction paper with a few pieces of plain white drawing paper underneath cut in the same shape. Staple the sheets of drawing paper to the cover. Now the children have their own shoe book, jeans book, hat book, and so on to fill with drawings, poems, and original comments about clothing.

Illustrate stories. Young children enjoy listening to stories or making up their own, then drawing and painting ideas from the stories. Laurent de Brunhoff's marvelous books about Babar the elephant feature animals in magnificently illustrated wardrobes. A kindergarten teacher told me that she discussed all aspects of clothing using Babar books.

The familiar fairy tale *Cinderella* evokes images of a girl dressed in shabby clothes contrasted with a girl dressed like a princess. Young children enjoy dividing their papers in half and drawing or painting Cinderella raggedy on one half and beautifully dressed on the other half.

The children's artistic responses to stories are always revealing and engaging. Even if their interpretations or expression differ from your own feelings about a story, accept and respect their work. Enjoy it and celebrate it.

MUSIC TIMES

Improvised songs that feature children's clothing. Nothing starts off the day more brightly than singing an easy-to-follow, familiar-sounding song naming every child in your room and a special article of clothing. We have used dozens of variations such as the following:

Good morning to Cliff's shirt,
Good morning to Bob's tennis shoes,
Good morning to Debbie's pink belt,
Good morning to Merry's hat . . .
(to the tune of "Good Morning to You")

Peter's wearing Fonzie socks,
Fonzie socks, Fonzie socks.
Peter's wearing Fonzie socks
This sunny Wednesday.
(to the tune of "Mary Had a Little Lamb")

Just look around the room at each child and lyrics will come easily.

Combine counting and clothing with a class song such as

One little, two little, three little shoes,
Four little, five little, six little shoes . . .

until every shoe on every foot is counted.

Turn "Frère Jacques" into a riddle by singing such improvised lyrics as these:

Where are Bill's blue jeans?
Where are Bill's blue jeans?
Here they are (children point to blue jeans)
Here they are.
Let's hear it for Bill's blue jeans.
Let's hear it for Bill's blue jeans.
Rah! Rah! Rah!
Rah! Rah! Rah!

Sheila Laurie of Columbus, Ohio, made up a special stanza for each of her six- and seven-year-olds to the tune of "Yankee Doodle." Here are two samples.

Melissa has a brand new jersey.
It's red, it's white and then it's blue.
She got it special for her birthday.
It really fits her nicely, too.

Chorus:
Every child in this room
Looks so very neat today.
Now we'll move to the next kid
And here is what we'll say.
Susie's got a yellow T-shirt.
It's got a turtle on the sleeve.
She wears it with her yellow tennis shorts.
The turtle's sitting on a leaf.

Old favorites like "Oh You Can't Get to Heaven" or Woody Guthrie's "Hey Lolly Lolly Lolly" are excellent for improvisation.

Oh you can't get to heaven
(repeat)
On Stevie's pocket
(repeat)
'Cause Stevie's pocket
(repeat)
Is not a rocket
(repeat)

The sillier the lyrics, the better they are. Children have zest for the ridiculous. Just be sure to include everyone.

Songs that highlight clothing and dressing. The younger the children, the more open they are to all kinds of musical experiences. Dip into your knapsack of songs and music and discover the resources ready to be tapped. There are many songs about clothing that are enjoyed by children of all ages and that can be improvised. Here are just a few suggestions.

I Got Shoes, You Got Shoes, All God's Children Got Shoes
Button Up Your Overcoat
Buttons and Bows
My Hat It Has Three Corners
Itsy Bitsy Teeny Weeny Yellow Polka Dot Bikini
Second-Hand Rose
Blue Suede Shoes
In My Easter Bonnet
In Her Hair She Wore a Yellow Ribbon
I Feel Pretty (*West Side Story*)
I've Got Something in My Pocket
Mary Wore Her Red Dress
Jenny Jenkins

My favorite versions of the last two songs are on Gwen Marston's marvelous album *Songs for Small Fry*.

Sole music for shoes. Teachers like Roxanne Demeter can spend weeks exploring the ways shoes move us and the places they take us. She tries to find music to accompany her first graders' exciting discoveries. She usually plays "whatever is around," and miraculously it fits!

Sing or play lively folk music like "This Land Is Your Land" or "I'm on My Way" for traveling shoes; music with a steady beat for marching shoes; jazzy Scott Joplin tunes for tap-dancing shoes; Appalachian round dances for running shoes; lullabies for tiptoe shoes or bedroom slippers; lively percussion arrangements for clowns' shoes; drum beats for moccasins; square-dance music for Western boots; rainy songs for boots and galoshes (see weather songs); and lyrical music for ballet slippers.

Special clothes for musicians. You would not expect a symphony orchestra to dress in cowboy and cowgirl hats and boots, and you would not expect a bluegrass band to dress in tuxedos and gowns. Talk about differences in musicians' dress with your children. Show pictures or photos (album covers often have excellent illustrations) that demonstrate the relationship between the dress and the kind of music played.

Country and western band. Make cowboy and cowgirl hats and boots out of construction paper and tissue-paper scarves for a country and western band. Use rhythm instruments to create original music, or play a country and western album and have the children accompany the recorded music with their own instruments.

Symphony orchestra. Joel Mindell shares his hobbies with his students, and one of his interests is classical music, which he often plays as background for classroom activities in Columbus, Ohio. Young children are interested to know, for example, that Mozart, one of the world's greatest composers, began his musical career at the age of five. Joel also describes the special way musicians in a symphony orchestra dress for a concert.

Doilies make excellent puffed shirtfronts for the boys. Bow ties of black construction paper, taped to the top of their "shirts," complete the outfit. The girls swish crepe-paper skirts or long skirts scrounged from the clothes box. The children seat themselves and pantomime the beautiful instruments of the orchestra as the music plays. They also enjoy playing their classroom instruments.

Rock and roll band. American children are familiar with rock groups, their sights and sounds. The children raid the scrounge box for wild shirts, pants, shoes, and skirts. When they are ready, turn on a zesty rock album and let them pretend to be the performers. Use real rhythm instruments to play along with the record, or pantomime.

Clothes and music from around the world. Just as people in different countries and regions have their own style of dress, they have their own special music. Combine the music and dress for enrichment. Wear African dashikis and play African music; Indian costumes and Indian music; Scottish kilts and Scottish music. Improvise movement.

Honor dolls from other cultures by playing music to go with their costumes. Honor classroom visitors who wear clothes reflecting their ethnic backgrounds with music from their homeland or region.

Singing and doing. Children learn everything better with a song. They practice practical skills through play songs that involve movement and sequences. Many songs lend themselves to action. Just change a few words here and there and you have perfect lyrics for helping children learn to dress themselves and take care of their clothes.

Taking care of clothes. A group of

four-year-olds enjoyed singing and moving to improvisation of "This Is the Way We Wash Our Clothes":

This is the way we wash our clothes . . .
This is the way we dry our clothes . . .
This is the way we fold our clothes . . .
This is the way we hang our clothes . . .
This is the way we wear our clothes . . .

Each sequence was repeated four or five times. The children chose clothes from their "clothes closet" to use in the song. They learned a lot about folding and hanging through singing.

Dressing. I enjoyed teaching children about dressing themselves with what seemed like hundreds of variations of "There's a Hole in the Bottom of the Sea." For example:

There's a hole in the top of the shirt.
There's a hole in the top of the shirt.
Put your head through. Put your head through.
Put your head through the hole in the top of the shirt.

There's a zipper on the front of your coat.
There's a zipper on the front of your coat.
Zip it up. Zip it down. Zip the zipper on the front of your coat.

We also used "Row Row Row Your Boat" to help the children practice zipping.

Zip, zip, zip your coat
Gently up and down.
Zippity zippity zippity zippity.
Now you can go to town.

Songs about making clothes

Cotton. Lots of clothes are made of cotton. Where do we get cotton? People pick cotton. People who pick cotton work very hard. But they also sing. Many of our folk songs come from cotton fields—for example, "Jump Down, Turn Around, Pick a Bale of Cotton." It is good for young children to know that people doing important, strenuous work sing as they work to make the time go faster, to feel closer to each other, and to find a way to enjoy the labor. The children pantomime picking cotton and sing songs with a steady beat, such as "I've Been Workin' on the Railroad" (substitute "cotton field" for "railroad"), "Here We Go 'Round the Mulberry Bush" (substitute "cotton field" for "mulberry bush"), and "Pickin' Up Paw Paws, Put Them in Your Pocket" (substitute "cotton balls" for "paw paws").

Silk comes from silkworms spinning threads for their cocoons. Imaginative teachers share this phenomenon with their children through songs. One group of first graders and their teacher changed the popular song "Glow Worm" into "Silkworm."

Spin, little silkworm, faster, better.
We need silk to make a sweater.
We need silk to make a gown
So we can wear it all 'round town.

Another class of second graders followed a "Talk Time" session about materials for clothes with an adaptation of "Inch Worm" (from the film *Hans Christian Andersen*).

Silk worm. Silk worm.
Spinning your silk cocoon.
Making scarves and blouses
For people to wear.

Weaving. The over-under pattern of weaving, common in the making of so many materials, is easier to understand when turned into a song. Here is how a group of five-year-olds practiced the weaving idea of over-under (to the tune of "Have You Ever Seen a Lassie?").

Have you ever seen wool go over,
Go under, go over, go under?
Have you ever seen wool
Get woven today?

Wool. Where did the wool come from that is in our sweaters, hats, mittens, and scarves? Lambs! Which brings us to that old favorite, "Mary Had a Little Lamb." What color was its wool? "White as snow." "Baa, Baa, Black Sheep" can be easily turned into a song. In this case, our wool is black.

A group of kindergartners sang "Mary Had a Little Lamb" and "Baa, Baa, Black Sheep" after a discussion about wool and clothing. One of the children exclaimed, "Mary's lamb and Baa Baa make us black-and-white sweaters!"

Songs about weather.

Teach your favorite songs about weather and seasons to the children. Play them on the phonograph as you pantomime dressing in appropriate clothing for the weather in the song; draw pictures showing special clothes; dress paper dolls or real dolls with special weather gear; and improvise a puppet show to go with the song. Here are just a few suggested songs.

Rain, Rain, Go Away
It's Raining, It's Pouring
Raindrops Keep Falling on My Head
You Are My Sunshine
Good Morning Merry Sunshine
Blue Skies
Here Comes the Sun
I Got the Sun in the Morning and the Moon at Night
June Is Busting Out All Over
School Days
Let It Snow
Summertime
Falling Leaves
April Showers
Winter Wonderland
Frosty the Snowman
Stormy Weather
Jingle Bells
Singin' in the Rain
Let a Smile Be Your Umbrella
On the Sunny Side of the Street
Zippity Doo Da

Weather rhythm bands. For activities celebrating different kinds of clothing, why not set the mood with original music expressing snow, rain, hail, and sunshine? Encourage the children to experiment with their instruments until they find a rhythm or melody that fits the weather. Once they hear the storm through their own music, they will create more vivid artwork and dramatic improvisations. They will even pantomime dress or practice dressing with more authenticity. Such challenging questions as "How can we reproduce the sound of thunder?" "What kind of sound can we make for snow falling?" and "Let's make the wind blow with our instruments—doesn't that sound cold and snowy?" help the children as they explore musical possibilities.

Make your own rainstorm. This is a delightful body-rhythm activity that begins with gentle rain and develops into a storm. (Of course, no one can go out in a rainstorm without raincoats, boots or galoshes, rain hat, and umbrella!)

Ask the children to hold up one hand as if they are about to clap it. Tap the palm of that hand with one finger of the other hand. Listen. After a little while of listening to the gentle tapping and a few choice comments ("Hmmm . . . what does that sound like to you? Sounds like rain to me, too. Gosh, hope it doesn't storm!"), build suspense. Now the children tap their palms with two fingers. The raindrops sound louder. Go on to three fingers. "Uh-oh, the rain is definitely coming down harder!" By the time five fingers are slapping palms, it is pouring.

Add feet stamping. "Is that thunder we hear? How can we make the sound and fury of thunder with our bodies?" Boom! Jump in air, arms outstretched. Lightning jags. Sharp elbows, arms, and legs fly out and cut the air. Wind blows. Bodies sway and turn. "What a storm! Maybe the storm will blow over." Four fingers hit palms, three fingers, two fingers, one finger. Just a tiny sprinkling. The storm is over. "Maybe the sun will come out. Maybe we'll see a rainbow."

"Sing a Rainbow" is a perfect song to play or sing. (My favorite version is on Ginni Clemmen's album *Sing a Rainbow and Other Children's Songs*, Folkways Records). Now the sun is out. "We don't need our raincoats anymore!" Pantomime taking off rain gear. "We can go play in our shorts and T-shirts. What a wonderful day!" Combine with art, movement, puppet shows, and story telling.

All-weather classics. Symphonic music lends itself to interpretations of weather, such as clear sunny mornings, howling winds, snow gently falling, storm clouds gathering, and autumn leaves blowing. What better way to convey the most basic need for clothing (protection from the elements) than to play a piece of music that suggests powerful weather conditions? With that musical experience, art, drama, movement, talk, stories, and poetry evolve.

I have used a variety of music with young children of all ages. Some of my favorite compositions are Grofé's *Grand Canyon* Suite, Stravinsky's *The Firebird* Suite, Copland's *Appalachian Spring*, Tchaikovsky's *Nutcracker* Suite, op. 71a, Grieg's *Peer Gynt* Suites no. 1 and no. 2, Sibelius's Symphony no. 5 op. 82 ("Finlandia"), Debussy's *La Mer*, Mussorgsky's *A Night on Bald Mountain*, Khachaturian's *Gayaneh* Ballet Suites, Debussy's *Clouds and Mists*, Rossini's "The Storm and the

Calm" from *William Tell* Overture, Chopin's *Raindrop* Prelude, and Vivaldi's *The Four Seasons*.

It is important for you to find the music you enjoy and listen, move, paint, write, and play to it with your students. Thomas Heck, assistant professor at the Ohio State University School of Music and head librarian of the music and dance library, highly recommends two reference books that correlate music with ideas such as rain, wind, and storm: *Recorded Bridges, Moods and Interludes*, edited by Henry Katzman (BMI, 1953); and *Music for Pictures* by Erno Rapee (Arno, 1970). Remember, most public libraries lend records.

MOVEMENT AND PLAY TIMES

Dressing up is one of the most popular kinds of dramatic play that young children *need* and enjoy. Children are the true magicians: a throw-away ribbon becomes a crown for a princess; a towel draped over a four-year-old's shoulders turns the wearer into a super-hero; a plastic cooking bowl plunked on a small head changes a little kid into a muscular construction worker.

Every room where young children learn and play (learn through play) must have an area where different kinds of clothing are accessible. Here are just a few examples seen in classrooms around the country:

Clothes Place (a special corner)
Clothes Store (specially designated shelves)
Hooked on Clothes (a wall of clothes hooks)
Clothes Trunk
Clothes Closet (portable, cardboard closet)
Clothes Basket
Hat Rack

In some rooms, separate boxes are labeled ("mittens," "shoes," "hats," and so on) and are used not only for play but also for learning-games like categorizing, finding similarities and differences, and matching. Many teachers make use of the large containers discarded by ice-cream stores. (Wash them thoroughly and dry carefully.)

Ask the families of your students as well as your own family, neighbors, and friends to scrounge in their homes for clothes of all sizes, styles, colors, and shapes to donate to your class. This should be one of the first

and most important "scrounge notes" you send.

In addition to clothing for the children, encourage families to send in cast-off baby clothes for dolls and large stuffed animals. Set aside a special box or shelf for the baby clothes. Because yours is a safe place where children and their possessions are respected and cared for, children will not hesitate to bring their beloved dolls and toy animals into the classroom.

Which comes first, the clothes or the game? It is probably fifty-fifty. Children often decide what they want to wear and who they want to be, and the story flows from the clothes. Other times, they make up a game or a story and choose clothes accordingly.

Most play activities involving clothing will proceed beautifully without you! As long as there is a fine selection of clothes and enough time to play, the children will continue until they are stopped by adult schedules.

The following suggested activities are above and beyond the children's own, very important, self-initiated games. We know that most young children are so rich in creative energies and ideas that our part in their play is that of delighted observers who enter their magic stories only to introduce a relevant theme, to encourage the inclusion of a child who is left out and who wants in, or to gently steer action away from a negative or hostile direction.

For every idea suggested, dozens are not. Your own take-offs are the best. When you are excited about an activity or an idea, the feeling is contagious. Children are susceptible to teachers' enthusiasm. Don't hesitate to dramatize a concept or introduce a character. Children want to see their teachers "hang loose" and jump into the fun!

Dress the weather person. The weather person can be a real child or a felt or paper cutout. Each day the class decides, based on the weather, how to dress the weather person. The children take turns dressing the weather person.

Find the mate. Mary Rumm made many pairs of colored mittens and shoes from plain construction paper. The children scrambled to find two of a kind, then fit their hands to a left and a right mitten or correctly set their feet on a pair of shoes. "This sounds simple," Mary reported, "but it was a fun thing that the children loved to play."

Find your name. Label different articles of scrounge clothing in the room with children's names (and/or photos) before they arrive in the morning. The game is: "Find your name and wear those clothes for the day."

Hats are tops. Teachers like Karen Wyerman of Groveport-Madison Schools in Groveport, Ohio, collect hats. At any given time, Karen has baseball caps, sailors' hats, rangers' hats, chefs' hats, hard hats, cowboy/cowgirl hats, crowns, football helmets, graduation caps, woolen ski hats, Mickey Mouse hats (with ears), ladies' straw hats, airline pilots' hats, police officers' hats, and fire fighters' helmets.

One of Karen's favorite games is to give each child a turn to sit in a special chair, close eyes, and receive a hat. When the hat is placed on the head, a mirror is held up. Karen encourages the children: "Look at yourself in the mirror. Turn yourself into the person wearing this hat. Who are you? What are you doing? How does it feel? What is your name?" After all the children have hats and have seen themselves in the mirror, they go off and play, draw, write, sing, dance, whatever their hats make them want to do.

Be sure to give children the opportunity to experience different kinds of hats. Do not designate hats on the basis of sex. Girls enjoy wearing fire-fighter helmets, and boys can wear straw gardening hats. Extend that openness to other articles of clothing.

Shoes and scarves. Leslie Zak, in her creative dramatics work with children in Columbus, Ohio, also uses hats to begin activities. But, Leslie admits, she has a grand time trying on different kinds and sizes of shoes with the children. As the children try on shoes, she asks them challenging questions such as: "How do these shoes make you feel? Show us." "Are you big or small in these shoes? Let's see." "Do these shoes make you take giant steps or tiny steps? Do they make you walk on tip-toe or skip? Show us how your shoes make you want to move."

Scarves are magical articles of clothing. They can be as dainty as handkerchiefs or as long and wide as saris. They can fit in pockets, on heads, around waists, over shoulders, across chests, into sleeves, and over faces. Scarves change children into wizards, goblins, elves, fairies, kings, queens, cowhands, pirates, clowns, trees, rainbows, wind, waterfalls, waves, circles, and snowstorms.

In a safe, warm climate of joyful exploration, you will be surprised at the many scarf ideas that pop like firecrackers and materialize like streamers in the air. Accompany scarf celebrations with a variety of music to reflect different moods and rhythms.

Pantomime dressing. Getting dressed is a popular theme of mimes and young children. Improvise a story to accompany a pantomime. "This is how these terrific boys and girls get dressed every day. First, they put on their underpants." (The children demonstrate through pantomime.) Ask them to continue the story. "What do they put on next? How do they do it?" Simple songs like Woody Guthrie's "Wake Up" are easily adapted to songs to pantomime dressing by.

We had a fantastic time with a group of first and second graders in Michigan changing "Dem Bones, Dem Bones, Dem Dry Bones" into a song to pantomime dressing. Our version went something like this:

> Oh, your hats connected to your hairy head.
> (repeat)
> Now, here's the way we dress.
> Oh, your sleeves connected to your two arms.
> (repeat)
> Now, here's the way we dress.
> Oh, your shoes connected to your ten toes.
> (repeat)
> Now, here's the way we dress.
> Oh, your shoes connected to your two feet.
> (repeat)
> Now, here's the way we dress.

I think you get the idea and can imagine what a wild session we enjoyed!

Dress class dolls and animals. This is where the collection of baby clothes comes in handy. Baby clothes are full of snaps, ties, buttons, and zippers. Young children need practice to master these skills.

If you have class animals or dolls, let the children take turns each day dressing them. If possible, encourage them to dress their "friends" according to the weather: a sweater or jacket for cold weather; shorts and a cool shirt for warm weather.

The class can decide on situations for these special friends. Are they going to a party? To the playground? Should they dress for an occasion that the class creates? Include dressing these "friends" as part of daily assignments.

"Dancing Pants" and other clothing poems to move to. Poems like Shel Silverstein's "Dancing Pants" are perfect for turning into dances. As the poem is read (children usually join in the reading), the children bounce to the rhythm of the words.

And now for the Dancing Pants,
Doing their fabulous dance.
From the seat to the pleat
They will bounce to the beat,
With no legs inside them
And no feet beneath.
They'll whirl, and twirl, and jiggle, and prance,
So just start the music
And give them a chance—
Let's have a big hand for the wonderful, marvelous,
Super sensational, utterly fabulous,
Talented Dancing Pants![2]

Play a lively jazz, disco, rock and roll, or folk album and encourage the children to "Whirl, and twirl, and jiggle and prance." Join them in the fun. You have dancing pants, too!

With hundreds of young children, we have expanded Shel Silverstein's idea of "dancing pants" to "dancing shirts," "dancing shoes," "dancing sleeves," and so on. Once children get hold of an idea, there is no limit to how far they can go with it.

A. A. Milne's "Happiness" provides a fun-filled script for a rainy-day clothing dance:

John had
Great Big
Waterproof
Boots on;
John had a
Great Big
Waterproof
Hat;
John had a
Great Big
Waterproof
Mackintosh—
And that
(Said John)
Is
That.[3]

Pantomime waterproof dressing and strutting through the rain. "How do you walk over puddles? Through puddles?" Substitute your children's names for John.

Rhoda Bacmeister's "Galoshes" captures the sloshy stomps and movement of snowy and rainy day clothing. Your children will have so much fun creating original movement interpretations of such stanzas as:

Susie's galoshes
Make splishes and sploshes
And slooshes and sloshes,
As Susie steps slowly
Along in the slush.[4]

Galoshes certainly make us move differently from sandals or bedroom slippers. Explore the differences. Again, substitute your children's names for Susie.

Stories about clothing will move you. Without your directing the activity, children naturally "act out" stories they enjoy. The characters and plot engage their imaginations and they need no prodding to make a play (improvisation) about the story. In a story they already like, you can raise awareness of clothing by asking, "What kind of clothing are you wearing?" or "Do you think Mr. Smith needs a hat?" or any other reminder. Some stories deal directly with clothing and are delightful for the children to improvise as you read the story to them or afterward.

A simple little book like *Tommy Goes Out* (Gunilla Wolde, Houghton Mifflin, 1971) practically gives directions for movement and pantomime. The story is about Tommy, who "gets up in the morning and wants to go out and play." But he has to dress himself first. What should he put on? Tommy really gets mixed up, putting on his furry hat before his sweater and his jacket before his pants, and putting his mittens on his feet. The children enjoy when people get mixed up, because they feel so smart knowing the "right way" to do things. The easiest way to enjoy this book is for all the children to act out the story as you read it. Encourage original reactions to each dilemma.

Charlie Needs a Cloak (story and pictures by Tomie de Paola, Prentice-Hall, 1973) is a brightly illustrated tale of Charlie,

a shepherd boy who needs a cloak. The story is basically the sequence of steps Charlie takes to make a cloak, beginning with the shearing of his sheep. He washes, cards, dries, dyes, and weaves the wool into cloth. He cuts, pins, and sews it and is ready with a beautiful new cloak when winter comes. The children learn a lot about clothing as they go through each activity in the making of the cloak.

I must warn you: every time I "play" *Charlie Needs a Cloak* with young children, the first scene of shearing the sheep is the longest, because all the children want to be the sheep and be chased, caught, and gently sheared.

Looking for missing things is a popular pastime of young children, who are intrigued by the interesting search described in *The Mystery of the Missing Red Mitten* (Steven Kellogg, Dial, 1974). Annie lost her red mitten and she and Oscar, the dog, search "every place I played this morning." In the course of her wanderings, Annie finds "Ralph's other boot and Herman's sweater and Ruth's sock. But, no mitten."

Discover for yourself the wonderful place the mitten is hiding. Discover for yourself how simply and naturally the children will interpret the story in movement and drama as you read it or immediately after the reading. Add life to the improvisation by cutting a red mitten out of construction paper. Do not assign parts. Encourage all the children to show all the actions in the story. For example, at one point in the story, Annie looks up at a red bird sitting on the branch of a tree, and she says, "Little bird, did you take my mitten?" If you add something like, "Let's all look up at the tree and call to the little bird," the scene will be immediately dramatized by everyone. (See the spin-off game below.)

Jack Kent has so many marvelous activities in his lively *Hop, Skip and Jump Book* (Random House PictureBack, 1974). Young children enjoy pantomiming or actually trying each of the seven funny pictures titled "Put On," "Button," "Zip," "Buckle," "Tie," "Brush," and "Comb." Turn the ideas into riddles. Have the children show any of them and ask the class to guess which one they are demonstrating. Play easy-to-move-to music and practice each of the seven movement ideas.

Lost and found game. This is a popular game that gives children experience in recognizing, naming, matching, differentiating, selecting, and comprehending. If you share *The Mystery of the Missing Red Mitten* with your children, this game is a natural follow-up.

Use a real article of clothing as the lost item. Describe it vividly. Perhaps it is the mate of a glove, sock, shoe, or mitten that can be held up as a clue. Try to hide the item in a very interesting place, such as on a doll or a stuffed animal, on the bulletin board, hanging from a mobile, or buried in the sandbox. Give hints sometimes. When the item is found, celebrate, and acknowledge everyone's cooperation in the search.

Folding, changing, rearranging. The poet Theodore Roethke wrote: "Reject nothing, but re-order all."[5] Those are excellent words about creativity, which stresses flexibility, change, experimentation, and openness to new experiences.

After a few months, why not rearrange your room? With the advice of your students, designate a new place for clothes and costumes. If the clothes and costumes are going to be moved to a new place, it will help to organize them, especially if they are "messed up," as clothes places tend to be after so much playing. Divide the class into small groups and ask each group to be responsible for gathering up particular clothing items and folding them or laying them neatly in their boxes or on shelves.

Children want so much to help and have their contributions be of value that they take this game seriously. They are conscientious about it and learn important lessons in caring for clothes. I watched a kindergarten class work on this project for almost an hour. Everyone was busy. The children on the "shoes committee" grunted and groaned as they moved the ample collection of shoes, boots, galoshes, and moccasins. "I think ours is the hardest," flushed-faced Kenny explained. "You know, shoes weigh more than socks!"

Puppets. By now you know that puppets are "friends" to most young children.

Puppets give directions and information. Puppets can give directions on how to button, hang up clothes, fold shirts, tie shoes, zip, put on shoes and gloves, and tell right from left. For some reason, when puppets play teacher, children do not become as tense or anxious about the lesson. Children need to hear instructions and information many times, in many different ways. They need plenty of practice. Let puppets teach as often as possible and give yourself a break!

Puppets get mixed up. On the flip-side of the puppet experience, children enjoy watching and correcting a puppet who "doesn't get it!" They can easily identify with the character, and there is a lot of compassion as they correct (with humor) a mixed-up "friend." Laughter is a sign that we understand. It is another way of knowing. So when children burst out laughing at the antics of a puppet who puts socks over shoes, belts around legs, or coats on backwards, they are not only finding amusement but also discovering that they know a lot about dressing.

This activity is an excellent way to help children learn to accept and respect those who may not be as fast as others. We all learn at our own pace. If a puppet can communicate that message painlessly, with warmth and humor, then a valuable lesson has been taught.

Sloppy and Neat-O: Improvised puppet show. No matter how many times Iris Bloom talked to her first graders in Westchester, New York, about picking up clothes, putting them away, folding them, and hanging them up, they went about their careless habits without batting their eyelashes. Finally, after exhausting all systems of scolding, cajoling, explaining, and warning, she presented a puppet show and named two classroom puppets Sloppy and Neat-O.

The story was that Sloppy just dropped her clothes everywhere in big piles, jumped on them, walked on them—in short, made a mess everywhere. Neat-O, on the other hand, picked up his clothes as soon as he undressed and folded them, hung them up, or put them in the hamper. Neat-O was always ready for everything—the zoo, ice cream, parties. He never had to stay home because his clothes were messy. In contrast, Sloppy kept missing out on all kinds of fun because she had to pick up her clothes.

The children laughed uproariously as Iris exaggerated Sloppy's mess (at one point the puppet was buried under the clothes). But they got the message, and from then on, the children made an effort to take better care of their clothes, often referring to the puppets in their daily play and clean-up.

Playing department store or clothing store. Just as Lamb's Restaurant did terrific business in Helen Speyer and Lori Selczer's room of four-year-olds, so clothing stores are popular enterprises in schools and centers across the country. Children sometimes clear a work table and turn it into a store. Here is where folding and hanging are practiced with a purpose. After all, who wants to buy anything from a store that just piles up clothes in a mess?

In Stevie's Shoe Store, five-year-old Stevie lined up all the play shoes in the room. He "hired" Jon as a "helper" and announced to the class that the store was open for business. When only a few children rushed to become moms and dads by putting on hats, carrying purses and briefcases, and walking like grown-ups, Stevie realized that he had not provided any money. He announced: "The store's closed. Open soon." With his helper and his teacher, he cut out strips of paper for money and gathered handfuls of bottle caps (from the scrounge jar) for change. When the store opened, customers were ready, money in hand, to buy shoes from Stevie.

Baby clothes stores are also popular. Make-believe parents, babysitters, and grandparents respond eagerly to the doll and baby clothes displayed. The advantage is that they can immediately try the clothes on their stuffed animals and dolls and pretend, with great confidence, that they know how to tie, button, snap, and zip. Practice makes perfect.

Magic pockets. Celebrate pockets! Celebrate imaginations! Ask the children to come in with a pocket or pockets on their jackets, coats, shirts, and pants. Have extras ready for children who may forget or are unable to come prepared. "How many pockets do we have?" Children love to be included in everything. Go around the room, stop at each child, and count the pockets aloud. A group of first graders was astonished to discover fifty-two pockets on the clothes they were wearing.

Start a story-telling, creative drama-movement session on "magic pockets." "What could be in your pocket that's special? Surprising? Exciting? Mysterious? Don't tell us—show us and we'll try to guess!" We had a marvelous time with a family grouping of second and third graders as they took turns giving movement hints about the contents of their pockets. When they were finished sharing their magic pockets, we made a giant dance out of all the contents. Enjoy the story and you will be able to imagine the dance: Shannon had a baby chick in her magic pocket; Richie had R2-D2 from *Star Wars*; Ali had a basketball; Ella had a new baby brother; Nate had a new pair of tennis shoes; and Joy had a bunny. We used a disco record that repeated the same beat for about ten minutes, enough time for Shannon to lead the group in baby chick movement, for Richie to lead us in R2-D2 movement, and so on. Expand "magic pockets" into art activities: "Draw a picture of what's in your pocket."

Costumes and dances. When children make or wear clown hats, of course, they want to make up a clown dance. "What about a cowboy/cowgirl hat? What kind of dance does that hat want you to make? Do you need a horse? Do you want to gallop?" Play some square-dance music and gallop away. "What about a pilot's cap? What do pilots do? Fly? Can we turn ourselves into airplanes? Arms out? Full speed ahead." Find music with a speedy, steady beat—music to fly to. Ah, white sheets for ghosts. "What kind of dance do ghosts do?" Flowing, soft, blowing movement. Sssshhh. Invisible. Every costume has movement possibilities. Ask questions that suggest ideas. Be open to all responses.

Dress and dances of children around the world. Young children are fascinated by the clothing of other cultures. Caps, aprons, and wooden shoes are worn by Dutch children; embroidered shirts and high boots by

Eastern European children from Russia, Poland, Hungary, and Rumania; wide-brimmed hats, colorful scarfs, and white shirts by Mexican children; headbands, feathers, fringed-bottom beaded shirts, and moccasins by American Indian children; and colorful shirts, flower leis, and grass skirts by Hawaiian children.

Each culture is a study in color, texture, and style. Celebrate any of the cultures with a clothing item that every child can wear, such as a sash around the waist or a scarf around the neck. Play music from that culture as you and your children form a circle and improvise a folk dance. Add food and classroom visitors to the festivities.

Clothing party. Distribute different kinds of clothing in specified places around the room. Use categories such as long-ago clothes, party clothes, work clothes, sports clothes, fairy tale clothes, and grown-up clothes. Introduce the children to the different types of clothing and encourage them to play in the clothes that most interest them.

A variation of this activity is to give each area a color or design symbol and hand out cards with the same color or symbol to the children. The children find the area that corresponds to their card and that is where they play.

This activity encourages the children to experiment and to try on clothing with which they may have little experience.

This is the way we wash our clothes. The care and cleaning of clothes is not as much fun as trying on and playing with clothes, but imaginative teachers find ways that children enjoy as they learn. After a "Talk Time" about the need for laundering clothes, play at washing clothes. Fill a tub with scrounge clothing and pantomime the steps: water, soap, rub-a-dub-dub, rinse, wring, and hang up to dry. Children also like to create movement patterns for clothes spinning in a washing machine or tumbling in a dryer.

VISITORS AND FIELD TRIPS

Visitors

Suggestions have been made throughout this book for tapping the rich resources of families, neighbors, and community members as classroom visitors.

Athletes, dancers, mimes, chefs, police officers, fire fighters, waitresses and waiters,

letter carriers, supermarket cashiers, and construction workers all bring awareness of special clothing as part of their work, hobbies, and skills. Clothing need not be the reason for a visit, but should be integrated with the experience of meeting these interesting people who are kind enough to share some of their lives with young children.

Because America is a land of immigrants (except for American Indians). its people represent a cultural diversity rich in possibilities for understanding and appreciation. In addition to their foods, crafts, music, and dance, people from other cultures offer special clothing. Be sure to include special clothing as part of visitors' agendas.

Costume designer. Most communities have a theater group associated with a high school, church, or university. If the group is small, its costume collection is probably the right size to bring into the classroom, along with a friendly member of the costume crew to show the children the different items and explain how important costumes are to the success of a play.

Doll collection. Many community people from different ethnic backgrounds treasure dolls dressed in the fashion of their culture. B'nai B'rith women, for example, have a marvelous collection called Dolls for Democracy. You may be lucky enough to live in a community where the B'nai B'rith women have such a collection and make presentations.

Scouts often study people of different cultures and, toward their badges, make dolls representing various backgrounds. The dolls and the scouts are wonderful classroom visitors.

Children of other cultures. Young children like to see other children. Check the resources in your community such as churches affiliated with a culture; for example, Russian, Armenian, Greek Orthodox, Serbian, and Macedonian churches. If you are near a university or hospital, find out if there is an international student organization. Also, children of professors, students, and doctors are likely to have a special wardrobe of clothes from their countries and are usually willing to meet your class and share their songs, games, foods, and costumes.

When a fantastic community resource person like Betsy Distelhorst teaches youngsters a craft, a dance, or a food recipe from another country, she brings a special article of clothing for the children to wear that will make them feel a part of the experience.

For example, if a class is celebrating Mexico, Betsy asks the teacher to encourage the children to wear brightly colored skirts, dark pants, and white shirts or blouses. Betsy brings colorful scarves scrounged from sewing stores, garage sales, and neighbors. The children tie the scarves around their waists or necks and are ready to learn the "Mexican Hat Dance."

Field Trips

Clothing store. Children are fascinated by the display of different styles, colors, sizes, and patterns, but they are even more interested in how people try clothes on, how clerks help them find their sizes, how clothing is wrapped and handled, and the interplay between customers and clerks (observation of manners and courtesy). As with all trips, when you return to the classroom, expand the experience into talk, art, music, drama, and movement activities, and write thank-you notes.

Dry-cleaning business. Kay Callander brings all her classes to Callander's Cleaners in Columbus, Ohio. Don Callander is familiar with young, curious, fascinated faces looking at the machines, the clothes hanging up, the trucks waiting to deliver clothes, the customers waiting their turns, the pressers, and the steam coming from the cleaning process.

Coin-operated laundry. Because clean clothing is important, children should see that people, even if they do not have their own machines at home, take time from their work or school to take care of clothes. In a coin-operated laundry, people often read or study while they wait, and many fold their clothes there.

Seasonal walk. Take a walk around the neighborhood to look at clothing, or make this interest part of a regular walk. The children are dressed for the weather, and as you walk together, notice that everyone in the street is dressed in similar outerwear. Point out the special clothing of community helpers you pass, such as delivery people, letter carriers, grocery clerks, and service station workers.

Tailor or dressmaker shop. People who make clothes show children patterns, bolts of material, sewing machines, thread, zippers, and buttons. They explain how important measuring is. When children have had a good visit, they usually return to the classroom eager to measure themselves. This is a good introduction to topics of numbers, growing, and measuring.

Shoe repair shop. If your community has a shoemaker or shoe repair shop, your children will enjoy the smell of leather; the sound of the metal; the sight of the scraps of heels, soles, and laces; and the feeling of pride in workmanship that most shoemakers still have.

Antiques shop. In addition to old furniture, books, and jewelry, clothing is a feature of many antique shops. Children, who have their own sense of time, need concrete images so they can more vividly imagine "long ago," "great, great grandmother's time," and, "how we would have dressed."

Clothing mill or factory. If you live near a clothing mill or factory, this field trip will contribute to an understanding and appreciation of the resources and skills needed to manufacture clothes.

NOTES

1. Push Pin Graphic, *Why We Dress*. 67 Irving Place, New York, New York 10003.
2. Shel Silverstein, "Dancing Pants," *Where the Sidewalk Ends* (New York: Harper & Row, 1974), p. 126.
3. A. A. Milne, "Happiness," *The World of Christopher Robin* (New York: Dutton, 1958), p. 10.
4. Rhoda Bacmeister, "Galoshes," *Arbuthnot Anthology of Children's Literature*, 4th ed., ed. by Zene Sutherland New York: Lothrop, Lee & Shepard, 1976), p. 103.
5. Theodore Roethke, *Straw for the Fire* (New York: Doubleday, 1974), p. 183.

SELECTED BIBLIOGRAPHY

A Wardrobe of Books for Children

Barrett, Judi. *Animals Should Definitely Not Wear Clothing*. Illustrated by Ron Barrett. New York: Atheneum, 1970.

Chase, Catherine. *Baby Mouse Goes Shopping*. Illustrated by Jill Elgin. New York: Elsevier-Dutton, 1980.

de Paola, Tomie. *Charlie Needs a Cloak*. Englewood Cliffs, N.J.: Prentice-Hall, 1974.

————. *Four Stories for Four Seasons*. Englewood Cliffs, N.J.: Prentice-Hall, 1977.

Freeman, Don. *Corduroy*. New York: Penguin, 1968.

————. *A Pocket for Corduroy*. New York: Viking, 1978.

Keats, Ezra Jack. *Snowy Day*. New York: Viking, 1962.

Matsuno, Masako. *A Pair of Red Clogs*. Illustrated by Kazue Mizumura. New York: Putnam, 1981.

Payne, Emily. *Katy No-Pockets*. Illustrated by H. A. Rey. Boston: Houghton-Mifflin, 1957.

Slobodkin, Esphyre. *Caps for Sale*. New York: Scholastic, 1976.

Watanabe, Shigeo. *How Do I Put It On?* Illustrated by Yasuo Ohtomo. New York: Philomel, 1977.

Watson, Paula. *The Walking Coat*. Illustrated by Tomie de Paola. Englewood Cliffs, N. J.: Prentice-Hall, 1981.

Westerberg, Christine. *The Cap That Mother Made*. Englewood Cliffs, N. J.: Prentice-Hall, 1977.

Young, Miriam. *Miss Suzy's Easter Surprise*. Illustrated by Arnold Lobel. New York: Scholastic, Four Winds, 1980.

Zion, Gene. *No Roses for Harry*. Illustrated by Margaret Bloy Graham. New York: Harper & Row, 1958.

Teacher Resources

Cavanna, Betty, and George Russell Harrison. *The First Book of Wool*. New York: Watts, 1966.

Gates, Frieda. *Easy to Make Costumes*. Englewood Cliffs, N.J.: Prentice-Hall, 1981.

Houck, Carter. *Warm as Wool, Cool as Cotton: Natural Fibers and Fabrics and How to Work with Them*. Illustrated by Nancy Winslow. Boston: Houghton-Mifflin, 1975.

Knox, Albert. *Cloth*. New York: Watts, 1976.

McCall, Edith S. *How We Get Our Clothing*. Chicago: Benefic, 1960.

Neigoff, Anne. *A Cap for Jack, A Coat for Jill*. Chicago: Whitman, 1972.

Shepherd, Walter. *Textiles*. New York: Day, 1971.

If we were robins, we would not build eagles' nests. If we were beavers, we would not need a course in dam building to construct our shelters of mud and sticks. And if we were ants, we would not call on architects to design the intricate structures of our colonies. Animals have strong instincts for survival and amazing capacities for learning to hunt food and find or build shelter. Perhaps more amazing is the ability of human beings to learn, invent, innovate, and improvise.

Our human instincts tell us to get out of the cold, rain, wind, snow, and heat. When we see wild, scary animals, our instincts tell us to run and hide. But where? Where to hide? How? How to find ways to protect ourselves from the elements?

Our earliest ancestors lived in trees, protected by leaves and branches from the heat, rain, and wind. The height of trees kept the people safe from unfriendly animals and from floods. When our ancestors found hollows in rocks, hills, and mountains, they came down from the trees and took shelter in the caves. Over the centuries, humans learned to make a variety of shelters, including tents, tepees, huts, adobes, stilt houses, houseboats, stone cottages, skyscrapers, igloos, castles, tenements, farmhouses, longhouses, yurts, mansions, trailers, log cabins, Quonset huts, and glass houses.

Wherever in the world people settled, they had to respond to three major questions as they decided how to build their houses: What is the climate? What materials can we use? How do we want to live? (Unfortunately, many people must substitute "have to live" for "want to live.") People who lived in cold places found ways to use ice, snow, and animal skins. Those in dry, desert lands built homes of clay, mud, sand, dung, straw, and animal hair. People who settled in jungles and forests had an ample supply of lumber, bark, leaves, twigs, mud, straw, and grass.

Other questions about housing arrangements include: How big shall our houses be? How many people shall live in a house? One family? One generation? Many families? Several generations? How close shall we build our houses to each other? Shall we have one large room or a house divided into smaller rooms? The solutions to these questions result in homes running the

9

WHERE WE LIVE

The walls come close around me
In a good way.
I can see them;
I can feel them;
I live with them.
This house is good to me.
It keeps me . . .[1]

gamut from isolated farmhouses to high-rise apartment houses sheltering hundreds of families.

You no doubt have your own favorite kinds of houses and daydreams about them. Here are some of my favorite fantasies. I want to spend some time with a Bedouin family on the Sinai Desert and see what is inside their sprawling tents. I would give anything to be adopted by a Rumanian gypsy family and live with them in their caravans. Let me spend a year with a Chinese family on their sampan, floating down the Yangtze River. Take me into your hogan, Navajo friend. What is inside? Let me crawl through the narrow tunnel into the warm, cozy igloo of an Eskimo neighbor. We will cover ourselves with blankets of caribou hides and tell stories around the seal-oil lamp. Finally, I want to visit my friend in her Italian villa in Venice. I want to find out how those clever Venetians built their city on water.

Chances are, for the greater part of your young childhood, you played in some kind of shelter or built some kind of structure that fit into your games, even if the walls were imaginary and the roof invisible. Making houses is an important and favorite game of young children. They build homes for toys, pets, dolls, stuffed animals, and themselves in their many roles.

Felicity Boxerbaum, a teacher and founder of the Community Learning Exchange in Columbus, Ohio, talked about her 21-month-old son, Alexander, and his favorite game.

Alexander is so busy. He works so hard at playing. He loves to build. He builds with Leggos, blocks, and cardboard boxes. Alexander's grandmother had a water heater delivered in a large cardboard box, and Alexander turned it into a house. We cut out doors and windows. Alexander loves keys and locks. I found an old chain lock that requires a key to unlock. We installed one end on the box and the other on the "door." Alexander locks and unlocks it before he goes in and out.

He takes his animals and dolls in. We put carpet scraps inside and use different textures like pictures, an egg carton, and an aluminum pie pan on the walls of his house. He carries his toys in and plays with his friends in his house. Three-, four-, and five-year-olds love it! He brings in his blanket and a pillow and pretends to go to sleep.

Pam Slayter, supervising teacher of the Head Start Program in Columbus, Ohio, remembers one of the highlights of her teaching career. A large cardboard packing box for a washing machine was given to a class of four-year-olds. After a lively group discussion, the children decided unanimously that the box would be a house. As with Alexander's house, doors and windows were cut. The children decorated their house with beautiful Magic Marker designs and pictures. One little girl taped up a towel for a curtain. They brought mats and pillows and their favorite dolls and toys into their house.

The class also made some important rules: "We all have to take good care of our house. We have to take turns playing in our house, three people at a time." The children enjoyed their house for many months.

Lisa, age five, is the lively daughter of Betty Stevens, the loyal typist of this book. Lisa has some important things to say about playing house, houses, and her feelings about shelter. Here are some excerpts from a long conversation with Lisa about houses.

We always play house. Sometimes we use Dad's canvas for his motorcycle and make it into a tent. We put toys in it. I pretend I live there. Sometimes I bring a cover and a pillow in and pretend to be sleeping . . . I use any kind of boxes and pretend they're houses for my dolls and toys. We have picnics in our houses. We use wood blocks and sticks for furniture . . . Sometimes I crawl under Dad's sheet on the porch and make believe I live in there. At night, I put my dolls to bed with their blankets and jammies.

Last year, Grandma and Grandpa Stevens built their house and Daddy helped and I watched. We went in their house and there was nothing yet—just floors and a few walls, but no rooms or closets. We slept on the floor in our sleeping bags. Now that it's all built it feels happy! It has bedrooms and food and couches and pictures and windows and stereos and record players and clothes and rooms and two bathrooms! Grandma Stevens and Grandma Schenck and Granny's house and my house make me feel good!

Alexander, Pam's Head Start class, and Lisa touch on universal aspects of playing house. Children want the protection of a house. Houses make them feel good and safe. They want to bring in their favorite playthings and friends to share in the game. Playing house gives them an opportunity to try their wings at adult roles as they put their dolls and animals in "jammies" and sing them to sleep, and arrange and rearrange the contents of their house.

In A. A. Milne's wonderful story "In Which a House Is Built at Pooh Corner for Eeyore," Eeyore's friends are concerned because poor Eeyore has nowhere to live.[2] Pooh says, "*You* have a house, Piglet, and I have a house, and they are very good houses. And Christopher Robin has a house, and even Rabbit's friends and relations have houses or somethings, but poor Eeyore has nothing. So, what I've been thinking is: Let's build him a house."

So Pooh and Piglet agree that is a "Grand Idea" and fetch sticks to build Eeyore a house at Pooh Corner. Even though there is a mix-up, the project is carried out enthusiastically, along with Pooh's song improvised for the occasion:

> "We've finished our HOUSE!" sang the gruff voice.
> "Tiddely pom!" sang the squeaky one.
> "It's a beautiful HOUSE . . ."
> "Tiddely pom . . ."
> "I wish it were MINE . . ."
> "Tiddely pom . . ."

When the usually grumpy Eeyore discovers his beautiful house, he manages a rare show of gladness. "It just shows what can be done by taking a little trouble," said Eeyore. "Do you see, Pooh? Do you see, Piglet? Brains first and then Hard Work. Look at it! *That's* the way to build a house," said Eeyore proudly.

Feelings of pride and possession play a large part in our need for shelter. No matter how humble a house, it is someone's home, which brings us to a very important point. The children who come to your room each day probably leave many different kinds of

homes. Some leave mansions with closets of clothes and luxurious toys; others leave small, tattered rooms crowded with people, secondhand playthings, and hand-me-down clothing. Some leave painfully the security and safety of their homes; others leave gladly, eager to begin a new experience in a new place. Some do not want to go home at the end of the day, because their homes fail to provide safety, protection, and warmth. Tragically, for too many children, school is the only safe, loving shelter in their lives. That responsibility is awesome.

Your attitude, your acceptance of and respect for your children's homes, no matter how different from your own, is vital in the building of trust and love in your room. Here is where stereotyped thinking and prejudiced attitudes must be fought and defeated. Openness, acceptance, respect, and understanding contribute not only to your own development as a mature, loving person, but also to your effectiveness as a mature, loving *teacher* who helps young children learn how to live with themselves and others in healthy, positive ways.

Mattie James, director of the Head Start Program in Columbus, Ohio, talks about school as an extension of home and as a very important shelter for young children. Historically, Head Start programs were located in meager, dark facilities. "But, we were always able to brighten them with teachers sensitive to childrens' needs," Mattie explained. "We brightened the drab space with love! And, with all our power, we tried to 'dress up' the dull walls. Just because people may be poor, doesn't mean they don't care about beauty, about aesthetic surroundings!"

Today, many Head Start programs are housed in more cheerful, renovated buildings. Although this aspect of shelter is important, Mattie is emphatic about priorities: "Just colors and designs, equipment and materials aren't enough if the place isn't filled with love and warmth! Teachers are the architects of the buildings. After a few days, school becomes like home. Teachers become almost like family."

As teachers of young children, as "architects" of our space, how shall we design our shelter? Mattie James and Pam Slayter talk enthusiastically about the challenges of turning school into a safe and loving home-away-from home:

We don't need the best equipment in the world. We need to be ingenious enough to use our imaginations and create special places and activities out of our beautiful junk! Our rooms have special places for the children's things: shoe boxes, cardboard liquor boxes, plastic trays, shelves with hooks. Their names are on everything! This is *their* room!

The housekeeping areas are the most popular. We have tables and chairs, dress-up clothes, stoves, refrigerators, sinks, and, believe it or not, mirrors! Most mirrors in homes are usually too high up; they're only good for "big people." We put mirrors on our walls low enough for children to clearly see themselves.

We spend a lot of time taking care of our "home." A lot of people think "poor" means "dirty." This is a tragic stereotype! We see our children learning to care for their things, keep them clean, put them away, pick up.

Because parents are involved in all aspects of the Head Start Program, family life is enriched, enhanced.

Probably no educator wrote more eloquently about the effect of environment on the development of young children than Maria Montessori. She believed that children should learn in an environment that conforms to their size, energy, and intellectual and psychic faculties. In her excellent book *The Child in the Family* she offers many recommendations about a school environment.

A school, a place built for children, must have furniture and equipment scaled to the proper size and adapted to their physical strength, so that they can move it with the same ease with which we move the furniture in our homes . . . The child must be able to use everything he comes across in the house and he must be able to do the ordinary tasks of everyday life—sweep, vacuum the rugs, wash and dress himself. The objects surrounding the child should look solid and attractive to him, and the "house of the child" should be lovely and pleasant in all its particulars; for beauty in the school invites activity and work . . .[3]

Maria Montessori constantly encouraged teachers to give children freedom of opportunity to choose their own activities and objects as well as the time to concentrate on whatever fascinates them. How else is discovery possible? She believed that

The environment itself will teach the child . . . Little by little, it will seem to the child that he hears the silent language of objects advising his actions: "Pay attention, look! I am a newly varnished end table; don't scratch me or make me dirty!"

Through constant active involvement with the environment, children learn responsibility and appreciation in addition to the countless intellectual, motor skills that are part of the simplest activity.

"The house of the child," our school rooms, must be places where the children can touch, move, manipulate, change, build, invent and rearrange![4]

Judy Tough, director of the North Broadway Children's Center in Columbus, Ohio, emphasizes another aspect of shelter that must be remembered as teachers design their space.

Young children are very territorial. We have to allow them to stake their claims. Remember, many children don't have their own rooms or space of their own at home. At school, they need a special group of chairs, rugs, or mats—special places—respected as quiet spaces within areas of activity to rest, think, wonder, and observe. If it's not built into equipment, then you have to set it aside, designate it. Those places are best if they're behind some low barrier (a form of protection), a corner, a place against a wall, a special little circle.

Judy's classrooms usually have about eight rugs available for children who want to take them to a private place for a "break." She finds that children have a feeling of security and reassurance just to know that those "safety zones" are available. When these areas are explained at the beginning of the year, children learn to use them when they want to and learn respectfulness and thoughtfulness toward others.

Teachers like Felicity Boxerbaum, Mindy Davis, Connie Swain, and Pam Recko make their own classroom furniture out of tri-wall cardboard sheets. They have constructed simple and sturdy furniture, shelves, rooms, dollhouses, playhouses, and slides. "It's one-third the cost of plywood," Felicity explains. "Paint it. Use it. Enjoy it." Felicity's workshop, "Cardboard Carpentry," is one of the most popular at the Community Learning Exchange in Columbus, Ohio. If you are interested in enhancing your shelter by constructing your own furniture and accessories out of tri-wall cardboard sheets, write for information and directions from: Workshop for Learning, 5 Bridge Street, Watertown, MA 02172.

Scrounging is the most popular way creative teachers find materials and items for their classrooms. They send notes to families, rummage through basements, visit garage and lawn sales, and nudge neigh-

bors to find such excellent shelter items as umbrellas (open them, throw a sheet or blanket over them); folding wooden clothes-dryers (the top is like a roof; they make excellent little houses); floor pillows; mats and rugs; cardboard boxes of all sizes (safety is the first item of business with any box or compartment in which children enjoy playing or hiding; always be sure there are openings, and discuss safety); coffee tables and end tables; odd sheets; clotheslines (hang two clotheslines near each other and turn a corner of the room into a tent by draping a sheet over the lines); blocks, Leggos, Tinkertoys, any building materials; old Monopoly games (save the houses and hotels); miniature cars, farms, animals, and trees of cardboard and plastic; tongue depressors and toothpicks; and scraps (carpet, wool, rugs, contact paper). Children have fantastic imaginations and do not need exact replicas to be able to play.

Simplicity and accessibility are important criteria in the classroom. And, as Maria Montessori affirmed, "The aesthetics, too, both of things and of the environment itself, encourage attentiveness in the active child; for this reason, everything ought to be multi-colored, brushed brightly colored . . . Attractive objects invite the child to touch them and then to learn to use them . . ."[5]

It is no accident that Maria Montessori, Mattie James, Lisa, and the Head Start children talk about aesthetics. Nearly two thousand years ago, the Roman architect Vitruvius described three goals of architecture that have been adopted by architects throughout the world: use, strength, and beauty. Shelter has been discussed above as useful for protection and safety. Obviously, such a practical structure must be strong. Whether built of sod, sand, stone, straw, or stained glass, our houses must withstand wolves and winds. Beauty, unfortunately, is often considered an extravagance rather than a basic goal. Yet, every civilization has decorated its structures, within and without.

Children need not read Vitruvius or study architecture to embrace beauty as one of their primary interests in exploring shelter. Recall that the very first thing Pam Slayter's Head Start children did with their "house" was paint it, decorate it. I had an interesting talk with my friend Ruthie, who is three years old. She told me why she likes to visit people in their houses: "All houses are different. Some are blue, some are white . . . I like to see people's pretty fish tanks, plants, and books with nice pictures . . . I paint pretty pictures for Mommy and Daddy to hang up in our house."

As you read the following sections of this guide, keep beauty and its creation in mind as an important aspect of shelter. You will not have to introduce the idea to your children. They already know: "We are the people/Living together/All of us together."[6]

DISCOVERY TIMES

- All people live in some kind of shelter.
- People build houses out of the materials they have.
- Houses protect people from cold, heat, snow, and rain.
- Sometimes many people live in one house; sometimes only one person or two people live in a house or an apartment.
- No matter what kind of shelter people live in, it is home and is very important to them.
- A neighborhood or community is made up of houses near each other, with stores, shops, streets, and services that help people live better lives.
- Most communities have shelters, such as a school, YWCA, recreation center, and community center, where people are welcome.
- Everyone in the house should be responsible for taking care of the house and everything in it.
- School is like a home away from home, and everyone should care for the people and things in the school.
- When people show respect for each other and cooperate with each other in keeping their houses in order, family life and community life are enriched. Everyone benefits.

SUGGESTED VOCABULARY

house	floors	shower	fireplace
home	windows	garden	clothes washer
apartment	doors	lawn	clothesline
tent	pipes	steps	clothespins
hut	wires	stairs	magazines
cabin	closets	stoop	mailbox
mobile home	key	elevator	mail
farmhouse	lock	fire escape	outside
tenement	bedroom	shades	inside
igloo	kitchen	curtains	warm
tepee	living room	table	games
nest	paint	chair	parties
hutch	make	bed	visitors
den	build	couch	share
ant colony	wood	pictures	decorate
beehive	stone	fish tank	village

doghouse	brick	refrigerator	street
Habitrail	glass	freezer	block
watch TV	straw	stove	neighbor
sleep	cement	oven	friend
eat	mud, clay	TV	vacuum
play	painter	stereo	fix
read	carpenter	lights	clean
study	electrician	lamps	dust
homework	plumber	books	sweep
food	porch	toys	pick up
family	yard	dishwasher	put away
room	basement	sink	telephone
ceiling	attic	toilet	address
roof	laundry	shelves	colors
walls	bath	chimney	work

As with food and clothing, young children's knowledge of words associated with their homes and neighborhoods is extensive and cannot be contained in a short vocabulary list. In addition, children have special vocabularies based on their housing arrangements. If they live in trailer parks or on houseboats, they will probably have somewhat different vocabularies from children who live on farms. Likewise, city children will have their own set of words that contrast with those of children who live in rural areas.

You will learn from your children as they introduce you to words and ideas from their own lives that describe and clarify their concepts of shelter. Your word list will evolve each day as you and your students share, learn, and grow together.

SOME BEGINNING ACTIVITIES

Start with a bird nest. These fascinating objects compel the attention of children and adults. How is a bird nest made? What is it made of? Why do birds make nests? Compare the composition and size of different types of bird nests.

Start with a fish tank. Like a bird nest, a fish tank stimulates discussion about shelter. What do the fish do in the tank? How do they eat? Where do they sleep? Do they have toys?

Start with photos or pictures of animals and their "houses." These are excellent starters for discussion and activities about shelter. Give the children time to observe, react, and make connections.

Start with a large box. If you have not already discovered firsthand how eagerly children turn boxes into houses or have not

been inspired by Alexander and the Head Start children, bring in a box and see for yourself.

Start with a problem. Raggedy Ann and Raggedy Andy dolls started a group of first graders on a study of shelter. The teacher asked the children: "Where can Raggedy Ann and Raggedy Andy live?" The children built them a small house out of blocks, in a protected part of the room, and even gave the house an address. The project was an excellent way to stimulate the children's thinking about shelter and what it means in our lives.

Start with a song. You need not be a musician or singer or even know the melody or all the words to enjoy singing with your children. I love Graham Nash's lovely song "Our House," and even though I do not know all the lyrics or even the correct tune, that did not stop me from sharing parts of the song with a group of kindergartners as a way of introducing the topic of shelter!

When the song was over, I asked the children: "Do you have two cats in your yard? Do you have flowers in a vase? What do you have in your house, your very very very fine house?" Here are just a few of the answers that were written on the board as the children spoke. Note how many important points were introduced by the children's responses:

> We have no cats and two babies.
> We have gerbils in the basement.
> No pets. My dad's allergic. Just rooms and people.
> Just make-believe pets like my teddy and new TV.
> My own room with my brother to share. All our toys.

Start with a walk around the neighborhood. Look, listen, talk, and compare as you walk. A second-grade class saw an apartment house with lots of windows, an "old pointy house" with a drugstore below and an apartment above it, two men painting a house white, and a wooden house with a hex sign on the outside.

Start with pictures of different kinds of houses. Igloos, tepees, grass huts, castles, skyscrapers—all are captivating images to young children. Such books as *Simple Shelters* (Lee Pennock Huntington, Coward, McCann and Geoghegan, 1970), *Have You Seen Houses?* (Joanne Oppenheim, Addison-Wesley, 1973), *What Kind of House Is That?* (Harry Devlin, Parents Magazine Press, 1969), and *The True Book of Houses* (Katherine Carter, Childrens Press, 1957) contain illustrations of a variety of houses and are perfect for looking, thinking, and talking.

Spend some time in the library looking at back issues of such magazines as *National Geographic*, *Smithsonian*, and *Arizona Highways* for excellent photos of shelters around the world. "How would you like to live in this house on stilts? What do you think it would be like to live in this tent?"

TALK TIMES

Because young children believe they are at the center of the world, extensions of their world, such as their clothes, food, friends, toys, and homes, are major topics of conversation. Children always have something to say about shelter, unless their shelter is not a safe and secure place. In that case, children should be encouraged to talk about home because they will find in you a reassuring, caring, grown-up friend.

Questions. The list of questions to spur interesting and important discussions has no bounds. Here are a few ideas to start your own mind sparking.

What's in your house?
What is your house made of?
Do you have windows in your house? What else do you have in your house?
Why do we need houses?
Who built your house?
How did people learn to build houses?
Do all people live in the same kind of house? Can you think of different kinds of houses?
If you were a bird, where would you live?
If you were a bee, what kind of a house would you have?
What are the favorite places in your house?
What do you like to do best in your house?
Do you like to visit other people's houses? Why?
Who lives in your house? What do you do together in your house?
Do you have a house for your toys or dolls?
How do you help take care of your house?

If you eavesdrop on children, you will find that much of their conversation concerns their homes, what happens there, and a new toy or game they play with at home. Home is the center of children's lives, with school usually running a close second.

One night there was a severe thunderstorm. The next day, I talked about the storm with a group of children at the Jewish Center in Columbus, Ohio. "Did anything unusual happen last night?" I asked. Josh jumped with his astonishing news and announced dramatically, "I had a thunderstorm in *my* house last night!"

A group of prekindergartners talked about shelter. Their observations and comments included the following.

I help Mom. I have a little vacuum cleaner and I vacuum.
Well, we live in houses. We need to. We have mouths and need food so we need houses, too.
Houses are to keep us warm.
We need houses to watch TV in.
My favorite thing to do in my house is color.
Our house was already there. The storeman built it.
I don't have a dollhouse. I keep my dolls on my bookshelf.
That's where they live now.
I help 'cause I pick up my toys and put them away.
We need houses for our beds to stay so we can go to sleep.
If I'm in my house, I don't get wet when it rains.
My house gets all messy when my brother comes home.
Grandpa's painting our house yellow. It's a pretty color.
Doors are my favorite parts. I like to turn the doorknob and ring the bell.
I look out my window every day to see if Michelle is on her bike outside.

Questions, surveys, round-robin participation, and one-to-one conversations are important and exciting ways to help children practice their language and learn about the experiences of others. "Talk Times" also lead to activities involving art, music, creative writing and movement.

ART TIMES

Given a room rich with accessible and easy-to-use materials, young children create images and designs from their own lives. Because shelter is a primary theme, chances are they will already be embarked on many projects that express their feelings about homes and communities. The following suggestions will enhance their understanding and introduce them to new concepts.

Construction sites. Set aside a building area in your room and stock it with blocks, boxes, Tinkertoys, Leggos, and Erector Sets. Children who like to construct houses, cities, and worlds will work with great concentration and energy. If there is a lull in the activities, suggest that some children build a house for the puppets, dolls, and stuffed animals, and that those who want to sit quietly by themselves for a little while also make important contributions to the class.

Sandbox structures. It is hoped that your room or playground has a sandbox available, because children truly enjoy building castles, tunnels, bridges, walls, cities, and houses of sand. Wet sand holds shapes. Powdered tempera dusted on the sand adds life and color. Enhance the sand community with clay sculptures, shells, pebbles, leaves, toy cars, plastic people, and pinecones.

Milk carton houses. Save small house-shaped milk cartons. The children rinse them out and cover them with Magic Markers, colorful construction paper, and paste-on designs. Use a tabletop or set aside floor space to arrange the houses into neighborhoods, with streets and toy cars, animals, and people.

Shoe box housing projects. Shoe boxes are the right size for a variety of housing projects. Alexandra Stoddard, in her lively book *A Child's Place*, shares experiences with a group of six- to eight-year-old children who were given boxes and challenged to create an environment inside the box. The children asked such questions as "Am I allowed to make mine a garden?" "Does mine have to be my own bedroom?" "Am I allowed to divide it into more than one room?" Stoddard reassured them: "You may do anything you wish."[7]

The children used materials such as wallpaper, rugs, Magic Markers, fabric swatches, scissors, glue, tape, and excellent scrounge materials. Empty spools of thread were made into end tables. Wooden coffee stirrers became posts on a canopy bed. The top of a can of shaving cream was used as a lamp shade. A lace doily was colored and decorated to be used as a hook rug on a kitchen floor. Paper cups were cut in such a way that they became modern chairs. The

children were asked to bring in treasures from home that could be adapted to the project and to cut out pictures from magazines of things they liked.

As Stoddard explained, "The imagination and creative input was inspirational. . . . I realized that these children didn't want it to end with an eighteen inch cardboard box, they wanted to create their own rooms . . ."8

Shoe box houses. Each child received a shoe box to turn into a house or apartment with different rooms or spaces, walls, and windows. These houses frequently become regular play articles to which the children added characters, plots, and movement.

I visited a class of kindergartners and spent a long time investigating their shoe box houses. I was about to tell one young architect that he had a wonderful house when he "ssssshed" me. "Don't talk loud," he admonished, "the babies are napping." On closer, second look, I saw two tiny toy bunnies tucked under a little red blanket in the bedroom of his house.

Shoe box apartment houses. An excellent way to convey the idea of apartment houses is to clear a place against the wall, and when the children have finished creating their own shoe box houses or apartments, pile the boxes on top of and next to each other to create the idea of an apartment house.

Shoe box communities and streets. Many children enjoy making their own houses, while others are enthusiastic about creating larger living areas like streets or communities. Their shoe boxes become the landscape for miniature cities or farm areas. Wooden blocks, toothpicks, small boxes or box covers of all sizes, pinecones, dried flowers, and clay shapes are all excellent scrounge materials to use in addition to crayons, paint, Magic Markers, and glue or paste.

Cardboard cities. Large milk cartons (rinsed, painted, and decorated) and paper towel rolls make excellent high-rise buildings. The children design their own buildings, paint or draw windows and wall designs, and put the rolls and cartons together for a fine cityscape.

Lean-tos. The lean-to is a very old form of housing that is still used in many parts of the world. Children enjoy building small lean-tos for their toy animals and people, and larger lean-tos for themselves.

Small lean-tos. Gather twigs, lollipop and Popsicle sticks, strong leaf stems, cut-off match sticks, and similar materials. The children lean a group of the sticks against the side of a box, shelf, or wall to create miniature lean-to communities.

Large lean-tos. Scrounge long wooden sticks or poles. Place the bottoms in pots of clay or plaster of Paris; lean the tops against a wall. Drape a sheet or blanket over the sticks, and you have a perfect lean-to for children to play in.

Tents. Here are just a few examples of easy and successful tents.

Tiny tents. Use lean-to materials of sticks and twigs. The children create their tents in boxes or on sheets of cardboard. They tape, glue, or paste the tops of the sticks together. Some teachers use rubber bands or tie them with wool or thread. The children cut scraps of colorful material or paper to paste or tape to the outside of the sticks. Surround the tents with animals and articles to complete their Indian village.

Annelyn's tepee. Annelyn Baron and her kindergartners at the Jewish Center in Columbus, Ohio, created a marvelous Indian tepee to enrich their study of Indians. They tied the tops of a few broomsticks together and steadied the other ends on the floor with cement blocks (the kind many people use to support shelves for bookcases). They spread a large sheet on the floor and painted it with Indian symbols for moon, snake, tree, and water. They draped the sheet over the poles and pinned back a front flap. Four children could fit in the tepee at a time. They surrounded their tepee with a village, large cardboard pictures of trees, a make-believe red-crepe-paper fire, and a picture of a river.

The tepee and the meeting circle around the "fire" became the center of the children's play for many days. Stories, songs, original plays, and other art projects developed.

Quiet-time tent. At a conference in Michigan, a first-grade teacher told about her students who noticed that there was no place in their room where someone could be alone and quietly relax for a little while. So they created one. They decorated a sheet in lovely, relaxing colors and images—"quiet ideas," one shy boy explained. They draped their sheet over a bridge table (donated by one of the parents) in a special corner of the

room. Over their tent was the sign "Quiet-Time Tent."

Class tent. A parachute was hung from the ceiling and walls of a classroom by hooks, tacks, masking tape, and clothespins to create an all-encompassing tent. Everything in the room was inside the tent. This excited the children and stimulated stories, drama, and games. "Let's pretend we're in a forest . . ." "Let's be long ago . . ."

Cornstarch igloos. Hilary Talis and her young children at the Jewish Center in Columbus, Ohio, are excellent builders of challenging structures. They crushed newspapers into balls and formed a large round shape. Then they made a paste of cornstarch, salt, and water (see cornstarch box for recipe) and smeared and patted the mixture over the round structure. When it dried they had a marvelous white igloo. With Magic Markers, they drew lines for ice blocks. The igloo was large enough for one child at a time.

Egg-cup igloos. Egg cartons are among the best scrounge materials. Save white egg cartons, many of which are styrofoam, and cut out each cup. The children can make individual scenes of an Eskimo village using a box or a sheet or shirt cardboard as a base, or contribute to a large class project based on a table or a special area of the floor. Cotton puffs surrounding the egg-cup igloos make wonderful snow. Cut colored construction paper for water, trees, and animals.

Scrounge village. Nancy Rosen likes to take her young students in Columbus, Ohio, for a walk to gather materials to create villages. Leaves, pebbles, twigs, bark, Popsicle sticks, pinecones, and wood scraps are among the most popular resources. These are added to the scrounge collection, which usually includes small boxes of all varieties and sizes, styrofoam packing materials, fabric scraps, bits of jewelry, Christmas tree ornaments, discarded parts of model railroad villages, and charms from cereal boxes. The children create buildings out of tongue depressors, Popsicle sticks, twigs and bark, glued and pasted together. Some children make houses in the oldest way by piling up little stones and pebbles to build structures. Toilet-paper rolls painted the colors of tree trunks and covered with real or paper leaves make excellent trees.

Clay furniture and housewares. Like a

sandbox, a supply of clay is essential in the classroom. Young children enjoy working with clay and creating furniture for shoe box, sandbox or large box houses and rooms; jugs, mugs, pots, pans, plates, and bowls for play box kitchens; and people and animals to live in newly furnished homes. Clay is excellent material for holding down trees, street lamps, bridge supports, and other vertical structures.

What's-inside-a-house collage. Use a bulletin board, a chart, or a large sheet of poster paper in the shape of a house. Follow a "Talk Time" about the things found inside houses with naming, cutting pictures out of magazines and shopping catalogues, drawing original pictures, and filling the board or paper with the images. Label as many of the items as possible.

House portraits. The children enjoy drawing or painting pictures of their houses. Themes include:

The Outside of My House (apartment, mobile home, and so on)
The Inside of My House
The Shape of My House
My Room (or Where I Sleep)
The People in My House
The Colors of My House
The Feelings of My House
The Sounds of My House
What I Like Best in My House
My Favorite Places in My House
Things I Do in My House
My House in the Morning
Holidays in My House

Encourage the children to tell you about the pictures. Their real or imagined stories and experiences are valuable. Be a good, sensitive listener, not a critic. As often as possible, write and tape the stories to the pictures. Display them all.

Housing arrangements. Cut out pictures of different kinds of houses or the shapes of different kinds of houses. Cut out pictures and construction paper shapes of other buildings, trees, cars, and children. Children arrange their own housing scenes by choosing pictures to paste on a sheet of white or colored paper. Be sure there is an ample supply of interesting house shapes from which to choose.

Our sheltering tree. Pam Slayter of the Head Start Program in Columbus, Ohio, tells of another memorable Head Start project that started as a talk and walk time.

The children discussed shelter and decided that trees were associated closely with houses. They provided shade, protection for birds and animals, and enjoyment for people.

On a walk, the children found a tree that had been cut down. They took one of the large limbs, carried it back to their room, set it in a bucket of plaster of Paris and called it "Mr. Tree." Mr. Tree was part of the room for the whole school year. The children celebrated holidays by decorating Mr. Tree with colorful designs. They put signs on Mr. Tree to welcome people to their room. They sat under Mr. Tree and read, sang, and told stories. They changed the colors of Mr. Tree's leaves for different seasons.

What is a house without a tree?

Who's looking out the window? One of Annelyn Baron's favorite projects follows a discussion of windows, which are, as one child described, "The eyes of a house." All the children receive construction paper cut in the shapes of houses with large window areas. The children color and design them in original patterns. Now the question "Who's looking out the window?" is discussed and is turned into pictures of: "Daddy"; "My cat"; "My fish in their tank"; and "Me." The pictures are pasted to the windows of the house. It is amazing how much life one little face looking out a window adds to a scene.

Picture these unusual houses. Children are intrigued by such challenging questions as

Can you draw, paint, or build:
a clown's house?   a good witch's house?
an elf's house?   a zoo keeper's house?
a giant's house?   Cinderella's house?
a space-person's house?   the Three Bears' house?
a king or queen's house?   the President's house?
a wicked witch's house?   a snail's house?

What color is it?
What's in it?
What kind of rooms, furniture, and paintings does
   it have?
Is there a yard?
What's in the closets?

Encourage the children to tell you about their drawings. Write their comments and titles on or near their pictures.

Develop your own community. On a large bulletin board or sheet of paper tacked to the wall, encourage the children to draw, paint, or paste on images describing the season and the landscape. Enjoy looking at it and talking about it for a few days. When it becomes part of the room, introduce the idea of adding animals to the picture. Enjoy that enrichment for a while as children look at and talk about squirrels, deer, rabbits, dogs, and birds scattered throughout their seasonal scene. Now it is time to develop the area by adding houses. The children draw and cut out their own houses (with your help, if needed). When the children's names are called, they place their house in the scene.

Before your eyes, this pastoral scene is dotted with communities. Houses mean people and people add a special dimension. Make house and street signs. Title the houses with the children's names.

Window frame scenes. Encourage the children to paint on sheets of paper what they see from their window. Suggest they really turn on their bright lights so they do not miss colors, shapes, objects, and special signs of the weather. When they finish their pictures, give them narrow strips of paper to paste across their pictures as window frames.

Names, addresses, and phone numbers. When you think of houses, you think of addresses and telephone numbers. Young children usually learn their addresses and phone numbers quickly because they are drilled on that information by cautious family members who have vivid images of lost children.

A large, colorful chart with the children's names, addresses, and telephone numbers is an excellent focal point of discussion and comparison, as well as a popular room decoration. Write in the addresses and telephone numbers for children who do not know their own.

Decorative house symbols. If you drive through Pennsylvania Dutch Country, you will see hex signs on the barns and houses. Many people believe that hex signs are intended to ward off evil spirits, but students of the Pennsylvania Dutch culture, such as Alfred Shoemaker, who wrote *Pennsylvania Dutch Hex Signs* (Photo Arts Press, 1970), believe that the signs celebrate those things which play important roles in the life of the people and are "chust for nice."

Show and talk about the diverse and colorful Pennsylvania Dutch signs with your children. They will notice symbols that include birds, hearts, flowers, stars, petals, and geometric shapes in bold colors. Discuss the things that are important in the children's lives and encourage them to create their own symbols and designs on construction paper circles. Display all the signs before sending them home as family gifts to be taped or tacked to doors or windows—not for superstition, "chust for nice."

Going home. This extended experience follows stimulating "Talk Times" and stories about different kinds of shelters. The children draw or paint and cut out such animal shelters as bird nests, fish tanks, squirrel holes in trees, beehives, turtle shells, and spider webs, as well as people shelters. Pictures of animals and people are also drawn or colored and cut out. When all the images are ready, display various animal and people shelters on a special bulletin board or wall. The children take turns matching the animals and people with their shelters. This is an excellent activity for a felt board.

If you are really ambitious, help children construct models of bird nests out of straw, string, grass, and glue, and spider webs out of thread. Instead of pictures of various animal houses, many children enjoy making models. These visual images can also be used to make up original class stories about animals, people, and their shelters.

MUSIC TIMES

Songs of welcome and hospitality. What is a house without guests? What better way to say "Come in, make yourself at home!" than with a song? Even the grumpiest people cannot resist being cheered by children singing them a welcome.

The old, familiar camp song "We Welcome You to _____" can easily be turned into a welcome song for your class.

> We welcome you to our room
> We're mighty glad you're here.
> We'll set the air reverberating
> With a mighty cheer.
> We'll sing you in.
> We'll sing you out.
> For you we'll raise a mighty shout!
> Hail! Hail! The gang's all here and
> You're welcome to our room!

The melody of "Happy Birthday to You" was adapted for a welcome song sung by first graders to all their visitors.

Come into our room.
Come into our room.
Come into our room.
We're glad you're here.

Any familiar melody can be changed to a welcome song. Better yet, with your children, make up an original song of hospitality.

Looking out the window. "Windows are the neatest part of houses!" a first grader concluded after looking out the window. Stand at the window and see what you see. You can draw it, talk about it, pantomime it, or sing about it. Songs like "I See the Moon and the Moon Sees Me" are perfect for musical observations: "I see a car and the car sees me," or "I see the school bus and the school bus sees me." The children take turns making up a lyric about what they see out the window. Songs turn into drawings, stories, poems, games, and dances.

Taking inventory: counting songs. Children enjoy counting and singing about it. After you and your children have built a community of houses, take inventory with some counting songs. The popular children's song "My Hat It Has Three Corners" was delightfully changed to an inventory song about a kindergarten room. Here are two of the verses.

Our room it has four windows.
Four windows has our room.
And if it didn't have four windows.
It wouldn't be our room!

Our room it has six closets.
Six closets has our room.
And if it didn't have six closets.
It wouldn't be our room!

Chairs are fun to count. A group of first graders formed a line behind their teacher and sang a kind of chug-a-lug cheer as they counted chairs. Later she told me, "It was the simplest thing and so much fun! The children didn't want to stop!"

Sounds of houses. Houses are full of sound. Each sound is a challenging musical idea for exploration and experimentation. Talk with the children about sounds heard in houses, and write their ideas on a board or chart as a guide for many activities.

The following are some house sounds suggested by young children around the country. See how easily they turn into exciting musical experiences.

People knocking on doors. Some people knock once. Some have a special knock, a signal. The children enjoy using percussion instruments; tables, desks, and floors; and their bodies and voices to create knocks.

Wind chimes. I have heard young children imitate the delicate sounds of wind chimes with their voices as well as with tiny bells, pipes, and flutes. Encourage a variety of musical expressions.

Telephone ringing. Suggest that the children practice different voice pitches and rhythms to catch the steady, predictable "song" of the telephone. They enjoy finding instruments that express the urgency of the ringing as they work on creating sound patterns.

Teakettle whistling. The telephone rings, stops, rings. The teakettle keeps whistling till someone removes it from or turns off the heat. "The teakettle doesn't stop calling you till you get it," a first grader commented. Children enjoy practicing "teakettle songs" of long, steady notes with voices and instruments.

Clocks ticking. The tick-tock of clocks is so much a part of the music of houses that we hardly notice it. The song of the clock is like a pulse. Children try it many ways—tapping, snapping, clapping, clicking, and "tch-tch-tching" voice sounds. One little girl even clicked her teeth!

Now that you have the idea of using body sounds, voices, musical instruments, and furniture, imagine how much fun you and your students will have turning the following house sounds into songs.

water splashing	dishes scraping	birds chirping
alarm clocks ringing	door bells ringing	dogs barking
music boxes playing	people talking, laughing, whispering, yelling, snoring, singing	cats meowing
doors banging		people practicing piano, guitar, violin, drums
feet walking	TV, stereo, and radio playing	rain hitting the window

There is no formula for developing any of the above suggestions. Here are only a few possibilities for you to consider.

Explore one idea at a time with the whole class. After experimenting and practicing, the group as a whole demonstrates a house sound set to music.

Small groups concentrate on different ideas. One group of children may want to focus on door knocking while another works on teakettle sounds. The process may be cacophonic, but the results will amaze you.

Each child chooses a sound to practice and share. Some young children are independent and self-initiating. If your children like to work on their own, encourage them to pick their own house sound and improvise musical representations to share with the class.

Sequence of house sounds. After the children have practiced individually or in small groups, decide on a sequence of sounds. Add a dynamic dimension by agreeing on one sound to repeat throughout the composition.

Symphony of house sounds. What a fabulous experience for children to discover the interesting combinations of sounds. Experiment with different groups of house sounds and create your own symphony. Encourage the children to take turns as conductor.

Tape the house sounds. Children enjoy hearing recordings of their voices and music. They really listen!

Make up a story featuring the sounds of a house. Your musicians will be eager to supply the sound effects and music.

City sounds, country sounds. City children know the cacophony of horns, brakes, sirens, traffic, crowds, and airplanes. Country children hear the sounds of animals and farm equipment. Talk with the children about the sounds they hear around home, school, and neighborhoods. Use voices, bodies, and instruments to capture the flavor of environmental sounds.

"Talk Times" about the need to control noise are relevant. Although some sounds are impossible to minimize, most can be controlled. Many people object to the building of factories and airports near their communities because of the noise. Young children easily understand the need to regulate noise. Watch them hold their ears and close their eyes at loud sounds.

Horas, hambos, and polkas: ethnic sounds. Throughout this book, you have been encouraged to help children develop an appreciation of and respect for the rich diversity of our country. We are a nation of immigrants, and many of our communities reflect the music, language, clothing, and housing of different subcultures.

My aunt and uncle have lived in the same neighborhood in Manhattan for the last thirty-five years. When I am in New York City, I walk up Broadway for a few miles to visit them. The music I hear from open windows, doors, and stores along the way clearly defines the people who have settled there. On my last trip, I noted Vietnamese, Thai, and Cambodian music. Those sounds blended beautifully with the Cuban, Puerto Rican, and black music of older Broadway inhabitants.

Who lives in your neighborhood? What songs do they sing? What music do they play? What sounds are familiar to you and your children?

Whistle while you work: clean-up songs. Children are never too young to begin learning responsibility for the quality of their environment. When children learn to care about their immediate surroundings, it is only a short step away from caring about their larger environment. Because of the daily practice of straightening and cleaning their room, they become aware of litter in the streets and begin to assume responsibility for their behavior.

Clean-up time can be a special time when music enlivens the process. Woody Guthrie's song "Pretty and Shiny-O" (Folkways Music, 1954), for example, helps children smile and sing as they clean the room.

It is also easy to improvise simple little clean-up songs to old, familiar tunes. A group of first graders conscientiously completed their jobs as they sang (to the tune of "Pickin' Up Paws Paws, Put 'Em in Your Pocket"):

Pickin' up papers, put 'em in the basket.
Pickin' up papers, put 'em in the basket.
Pickin' up papers, put 'em in the basket.
Cleanin' up our room.

A delightful singing game was improvised to the tune of "A Tisket, a Tasket." After projects that left a mess all over the floor, the children picked up and disposed of the materials while they sang the following song.

A tisket, a tasket,
Throw litter in the basket.
If you miss, you don't get a kiss
Till you throw it in the basket!

Encourage the children to compose songs for other chores, such as dusting, putting away toys, sweeping, folding clothes, and storing art supplies.

Music and songs from children's homes. When children feel cared about and safe, they are eager to share records and songs played and sung at home. When children bring in records from home, be sure to play them sometime during that same day, even as background music. Encourage children to sing and teach a song learned at home. The link between home and school should always be strong and positive.

MOVEMENT AND PLAY TIMES

Young children's homes and schools are their primary shelters. Throughout this book, suggestions have been made to insure that school is a shelter for children—keeping them safe, protecting them from dangers, providing feelings of warmth and companionship. For too many young children, school is the only such shelter.

Home and school are places where children learn and grow through play. In the schoolroom, they create dynamic mini-environments: stores, gas stations, spaceships, boats, and—the most popular and basic—houses or shelters. Give them a room of blocks, boxes, sand, clay, scrounge toys and materials, and they will build as instinctively and eagerly as beavers. They build homes for puppets, pets, dolls, stuffed animals, and themselves.

Children want to be involved in the arrangement and architecture of their classroom. Encourage their participation in solving such familiar problems as how to arrange furniture, where to put toys, and how to display artwork. When young children feel they have contributed to the structure and activities of their school day, they feel important and responsible for the success of the program.

A small group of five-year-olds had created a neighborhood in an area of their room. One of the structures they were using for a house was a small stepladder. Its location was clumsy and two children not in the neighborhood game had already tripped on it. Joshua watched for a while from his racing cars across the room. He walked over quietly and in the most diplomatic voice suggested, "Can you guys move this building? Someone's gonna get hurt. I'll help you." Without a note of tension, the group rearranged their buildings. This kind of responsibility in play is not rare. Watch children in a room where their input is welcomed by responsive, encouraging teachers, and you will see them caring about each other and their environment.

Rearrange everything. Tune into your group of children. If they are flexible and open about new experiences, they will enjoy this once-a-year (perhaps halfway through the year) challenge to rearrange their room. Talk about it. Decide what should and should not be changed. Enlist the cooperation and effort of all the children as they see that out of disorganization can come a new order, one that they design.

Name the places in your room. Children enjoy giving special names to different areas of their room. After the names are chosen, you or the children (depending on their ability to print or write) make lively signs to tape or tack throughout the room. Here are a few examples from various rooms where young children live.

Book Nook	Circus Village	Picture Wall
Storytown	Costume Closet	Sticky Shelf
Block City	Paint Place	(glue and paste)
Sand Land	Art Gallery	Paper Drawer
Animal House	Artists at Work	Seed Center

"Turn yourself into . . ." walk. Using the places in the room as stops along the way, encourage the children to extend the idea of a special place. For example, at the Book Nook, turn yourself into a person reading a funny book, a sad book, a scary book, and so on; at the Paint Place, turn yourself into a great artist and pantomime the way you paint; and at the Paper Drawer, turn yourself into a large, flat sheet of paper, a crumbled paper, a blank piece of paper, a paper filled with colorful pictures, and so on.

Transportation trip around the room. Instead of walking, tour the room by different modes of transportation. Between the Book Nook and the Paint Place, turn the children into a train; from the Paint Place to the Paper Drawer, airplanes.

Hands tell it all. After talking about houses, sit comfortably in a circle and suggest that the children use just their hands to show such interesting actions as knocking on a door, ringing a doorbell, turning a doorknob, putting a key in a lock and turning it, opening and closing a door, sliding a door open and shut, picking up a telephone, turning water faucets on and off, flushing the toilet, and going upstairs and downstairs. Hands also make wonderful shapes for roofs, windows, peepholes, doors, window shades, and rooms.

Encourage children to experiment. Remember, there is no one way, or right way, to demonstrate these concepts. Let the children find their own ways. Make up little songs, poems, or finger and hand plays.

What goes on in our homes and school: pantomime riddles. Discuss the children's responses to the question "What are some things people do in their homes?" Then invite the children to choose an answer to pantomime. The rest of the group guesses.

Animal shelters: "What if . . .?" The following ideas related to animal shelters provide opportunities for children to explore imaginative movement experiences. "What if you were a turtle? Let's crawl. Feel your shell. Uh-oh, something scary! Quick! Hide in your shell! O.K. Safe to peek out."

"What if you were a bird? How would you build your nest? Let's fly around and pick up straw and tiny twigs with our beaks!" After this activity, you will be amazed at the awe you and the children feel about this bird behavior.

"What if you were a bear? Bears hibernate in caves or hollows. Let's lumber around, fill our tummies, and find a nice, warm cave to sleep in all winter. How's this? (Try several places.) Too small! How's this? Too low! How's this? Just right! Goodnight. See you in the spring."

Now that you have the idea of how simple these activities are, encourage the children to respond to the following. "What if you were a fish? Some fish make bubble nests! What if you were an ant? How would you build an ant colony? What if you were a bee? What would it be like to live in your hive? Buzz around and show us!"

All of these ideas correlate with songs, stories, and art projects.

People shelters: "Let's pretend . . ." After talking, reading, and looking at pictures together of various kinds of human shelter, children usually play "pretend" games by themselves. If they do not, encourage them by suggesting: "Let's pretend we're Indians and this is our village"; "Let's pretend we're Eskimos and these are our igloos"; and "Let's pretend we're Bedouins and these are our tents." Such follow-up challenges as "What are we doing? Where do we sleep? What shall we eat? Where shall we cook? What are we saying to each other?" help develop the game if the children have not caught the momentum themselves.

Use all the crafts projects and props possible to enhance the game. Always try to expand art activity into drama, play, and creative writing experiences. Imagination needs nourishment.

Walls, rooms, floors: group shapes. When children discover that shelters usually have common elements like walls, floors, windows, doors, rooms, and roofs, they are delighted to show that they understand these concepts in ways that go beyond pictures and building models. How? Through body movement.

Ask a group of children to use their fantastic bodies to show the idea of a floor. Without hesitation, most children will lie flat, arms and legs extended. When they lie near each other, they really convey the feeling of a floor. Many children will extend the simple initial shape to demonstrate designs on the floor: "Hey, if we all touch hands and feet, we can make tiles!" "Let's make squares like my aunt's linoleum!"

Walls are excellent movement challenges. Children line up side-by-side, touching, and, in a matter of minutes, show a solid wall of bodies.

Their wall can easily turn into a room if they form themselves into a square pattern. Now they have an inside and an outside.

Puppets are marvelous helpers in developing ideas with children.

Puppets can say something like: "Look at this room. Wonder who lives inside. What kind of a room is it? We can't see through the walls. Let's look around and maybe we'll find a window or a door." This stimulates the children to create a door and windows in their room. Then puppets can look inside.

Create a story, a plot, an adventure, a character, and so on for the room children build with their bodies. After the game, write the story and illustrate it.

Andy, age 8

Different houses for different folks. Kings and queens live in castles; Peter Pan and the Lost Boys live in an underground hiding place; giants live in gigantic houses; and munchkins live in tiny dwellings. Turn your room into a castle, a giant's house, an underground hiding place, a munchkin village. Turn your room into a gingerbread house, a house for each of the Seven Dwarfs (Grumpy's house certainly looks different from Happy's house).

Questions celebrating the five senses are relevant to this theme. "What do we see? Hear? Smell? Taste? Touch? What do we do? How do we feel? What's in this house? How do we sleep? Eat? Relax? Work? Care for this house?" Within each of these improvised environments, encourage the children to explore, through movement, drama, dialogue, art, and music, their specific features and qualities.

Let's build a community, city, or town. This is an unforgettable experience shared with a class of first and second graders in the Glendening School, Franklin County, Ohio. The children were studying houses, villages, and cities. Expanding their understanding into movement-drama was a highlight of the school year.

The scene was a room with a phonograph, chalkboard, children, and two teachers. We filled the board with the children's suggestions for building a village, and we gave their ideas a logical sequence. These were some of the ideas conveyed through movement improvisation.

Cleared the land
Chopped down trees
Cut trees into building logs
Worked together to build cabins
(Small groups of children formed the shape of houses with their bodies.)
Planted seeds
Built more houses
Built stores, firehouse, church, synagogue, school
Cleared paths for roads
Built bridges (Children have the most imaginative ways to show bridges.)
Houses getting older
More people coming
Cleared land for building higher houses so more people could live in them

At the end of our hour-long session, the almost empty room had magically turned into a bustling city of structures of all sizes and purposes, vehicles, air fields, train stations, and traffic jams—all demonstrated through imaginative body movement.

When the children who had formed a factory accompanied their "puffs of smoke" with explosive sounds, one of the boys held his nose and said, "Yuk! Pollution!" which led to a "Talk Time" about ways to preserve our air, water, and land.

When the original houses were built, the children celebrated with a traditional barn-raising circle dance, loosely choreographed to a record of Appalachian music.

The teachers reported that the art, music, and creative writing projects that followed this unusual movement session were the most vivid and original of the work that year.

Strange and mysterious shelters. Hans Christian Andersen's Thumbelina lived on a water lily floating on a pond before a friendly mole took her to his dark, cold, underground home. She finally married a tiny prince who lived in a flower. The Old Woman Who Lived in a Shoe had so many children, she didn't know what to do. For a little while, Jonah lived in the belly of a whale. Antoine de Saint Exupéry's Little Prince lived on his own little planet, scarcely larger than a mouse.

What if we lived on a leaf?
What if we lived in a house in a flower?
What if we lived in a shoe?
What if we lived in a pumpkin shell?
What if we lived in a whale?
What if we lived in a house on a star?
What if we lived in a house in the rainbow?
What if we lived in a house deep inside a birthday cake?
What if we lived in a house inside a carrot?

Draw or tape a door or window shape to a picture of any object, animal, plant, or place. This suggests that inside the original image is a house. Suppose you drew a little door on a picture of an apple. It is easy to imagine someone living inside the apple. "Let's pretend it's us! What do we see, hear, smell, taste, touch, say, do, feel? Where do we sleep, eat, work, play?" Pretend it. Play it. Move to it. Draw pictures of it. Make up poems about it. Create stories about it.

Stories and poems to improvise. The illustrations in a book or a scene from a story may be the focus of movement-drama improvisations. Perhaps only one part of a longer piece lends itself to the theme you are discussing. Do not hesitate to enrich that segment with movement and play. Enjoy the following examples of stories and poems that children have enthusiastically explored.

With young children of all ages, we have acted out parts of Ann Nolan Clark's book *In My Mother's House* as it is read.

The delicately illustrated, poetic story *Where Does the Butterfly Go When It Rains?* suggests excellent ideas for movement interpretation.

And the mole
and the bee
and the bird in the tree—
Where do they go when it rains?
A mole can stay in his hole.
A bee can fly back to her hive.
I've heard
that a bird
tucks its head under its wing.
But, where does the butterfly go
when it rains?[9]

Children easily dramatize moles, bees, and butterflies, as well as birds, cats, snakes, and grasshoppers. They definitely comprehend shelter as protection from the elements.

"Skyscrapers," by Rachel Field, is a good example of how poetry can provide ideas for movement and drama. The first stanza of the poem clearly points the way for bodies, hands, and arms reaching to the sky.

Do skyscrapers ever grow tired
Of holding themselves up high?
Do they ever shiver on frosty nights
With their tops against the sky?[10]

"Block City," Robert Louis Stevenson's poem, is excellent accompaniment for a pantomime of building a city of blocks. The children are encouraged to shape their own dream town: "What are you able to build with your blocks?/Castles and palaces, temples and docks."[11]

When the poem and the pantomime are finished, ask the children to describe their towns, draw pictures of them, and make songs about them.

"Oh, Joyous House" by Richard Janzen is an example of a child's poem that celebrates the warm recognition of our own house.

When I walk home from school,
I see many houses
Many houses down many streets.
They are warm, comfortable houses
But, other people's houses
I pass without much notice.
Then as I walk farther, farther
I see a house, the house.
It springs up with a jerk
That speeds my pace; I lurch forward.
Longing makes me happy, I bubble inside.
It's my house.[12]

We have "danced" this poem many ways. One of the simplest and most satisfying is to talk about how we feel about our own houses; read the poem to the children; then take a walk together, keeping a steady, casual rhythm, arms swinging, holding hands. "I see a house, the house" is the line that changes everything. We stop. We focus on an agreed-upon image or place in the room for "the house." We walk faster, faster, break into a run, and run all the way home.

Folk tales and nursery rhymes to improvise. Shelter is an important theme in many folk tales and nursery rhymes. Children often know them already and are imaginative in interpreting and expanding upon them.

"The Three Little Pigs" is an excellent story for movement-drama interpretation. The children form three small groups or one large group and demonstrate the three houses with their bodies. A house made of straw falls down fairly easily; a house made of sticks is a little harder to blow down; a house made of bricks withstands the strongest gusts.

The different kinds of houses challenge the children to differentiate body shapes and movements. A house of straw does not require nearly as much muscle and body control as does a house of bricks. After a movement session, a first grader explained why he liked the house of bricks best: "I used all my muscles!" One of his classmates preferred the house of straw: "Because I like feeling floppy!"

Many nursery rhymes lend themselves to challenging movement activities. After reciting what I remembered of "There Was a Crooked Man," a class of second graders and I "played" this rhyme many ways. One of my favorites was to ask the children who wanted to be the crooked house to form their "crooked house" shape together, and to ask the children who wanted to be the man, wife, cat, and mouse to walk their crooked mile to the crooked house. After our movement session, the children drew pictures of and wrote stories about the crooked house and its crooked inhabitants.

Original hand and finger plays are so easy to invent to accompany cumulative folk poems like "This Is the House That Jack Built." How many ways can you and your students interpret this poem? With one group of children, we encouraged individual interpretation, and the variety of finger and hand plays was astonishing. With another class, we decided as a group how we would show the many ideas.

Time and space limit the number of suggestions for movement and play activities celebrating shelter. You have no doubt already begun to develop ideas and resources from your own experiences. Be open to the possibilities in every song, game, story, shape, idea, or image you enjoy.

VISITORS AND FIELD TRIPS

Visitors

Maintenance person, plumber, carpenter, repair person, electrician. People who take care of your school building are honored to be invited to visit with your children and talk about their work. The children learn to appreciate the effort and competence needed to keep shelters clean, efficient, and safe.

Turn the experience around and create a "mini-field trip" by visiting these people in their work areas as they work.

The children's thank-you notes and pictures are always appreciated by the people who "keep a building going," as one school janitor explained.

Interior decorator, architect, designer. Ask these visitors to bring some of the materials and tools they use in their work of making shelters beautiful. Children like to look at illustrations and sketches.

If these people cannot come to the classroom, try to arrange for a trip to their studio or shop.

Gardener, groundskeeper, landscape architect. The land around houses is almost as important as the houses themselves. People mow, plant, cut, prune, and spend a lot of time caring for their lawns and gardens. Invite to your classroom people involved in beautifying and caring for the land. They will welcome the opportunity to share their work and feelings about land with young children. Correlate these visits with challenging art and writing projects.

Locksmith, quiltmaker, and others. Each community has its own special resources, but chances are yours has more people and places than you realize to enhance children's understanding of "where they live." Invite some of the following people to talk with your students (or visit them to watch work in progress): locksmith, quiltmaker, cabinet maker, furniture maker, furniture salesperson, furniture repair person, lumberyard worker, window washer, house cleaner, carpet cleaner, and antique dealer. You will not only help expand awareness of important aspects of shelter, but also introduce the children to different kinds of work and careers.

Pets in the classroom. Pets are very important long-term visitors because children can observe their habits, express feelings about and toward them, and learn to take responsibility for their well-being. The most popular classroom pets are turtles, fish, gerbils, birds, hamsters, guinea pigs, chicks, and rabbits. Whether your pets live in commercially manufactured Habitrails or improvised environments, each will have a special dwelling place and a special kind of care to go with that shelter.

Safety first and last. It is very important to give young children information about safety precautions, because many serious accidents occur at home. In many communities, police or fire officers visit classes and explain home safety to the children. In other communities, the Red Cross, Safety Council, and PTAs provide volunteers to visit with children and speak about safety in the home. Encourage these speakers to keep it simple (too many rules and warnings are confusing) and interesting, to demonstrate as well as talk, and to ask the children to participate.

Perhaps you have a well-informed, articulate, fun-loving parent or friend who will come to your classroom dressed as a favorite TV, fairy tale, animal, or original character and present the information in an entertaining way. Or turn yourself into a mysterious classroom visitor! Puppets, mimes, and clowns are also outstanding in presenting important points to young children.

After the visit, bring on your own classroom puppets, stuffed animals, and dolls for a repeat home safety lesson by the children. Repetition is a must, but make it fun.

Field Trips

House being built, painted, repaired, or renovated. City children have the advantage of nearby construction sites and are able to watch high-rise buildings emerge from the debris. If you live in a suburban or rural area, be alert to the housing activity in your vicinity. If a house is being built, painted, repaired, or renovated, take a field trip to the site. When children see how things happen, comprehension and appreciation are increased.

Homes of children in your class. During the school year, a group of prekindergartners in Michigan visited eight classmates' homes. At each home they had a guided tour and lunch or a snack. Of course, this kind of program is not possible with all groups of children (geography, economics, and parent cooperation are factors), but if you have families who are unusually involved in the school and are willing to host a field trip, try it.

Unusual homes or housing areas in your neighborhood. Do you live near an Indian reservation? Ask someone in that community if you and your children may visit and learn about the interesting kinds of shelters there. (Turn the experience around and invite someone from the Indian community to visit your class and tell about their homes, as well as other interesting aspects of their lives.) Do you live near a historically restored area like Old Town in San Diego, Old Town in Alexandria, Virginia, German Village in Columbus, Ohio, or Market Area in Philadelphia?

Do you live near a trailer court, a harbor with houseboats, a street of old brownstones, a proud Southern mansion, rambling farmhouses and red barns, wooden shacks near a swamp, or glass and steel condominiums? Look at them. Think about them. What stories do they tell? Talk to people who live there. What would it be like to live there? Talk, ask, wonder, share ideas and feelings. The secret ingredient is respect.

Climb a hill, look down and around. Florence, Italy, is known as much for its red clay rooftops as for its magnificent cathedrals. The white stone houses in Jerusalem blaze in the noonday sun. People call Jerusalem "The City of Gold" because of the way light shines on the white stone.

If there is a hill near your school, take the children for a ride and look down on your community. Children enjoy discovering the shapes, colors, patterns, and designs

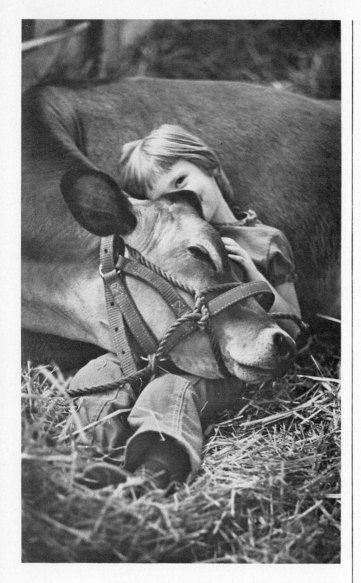

Yellow Pages. A visit to a beehive is a real event. Ask the beekeeper to explain some of the remarkable rituals of the bees.

Walk around the street. Walk around the neighborhood and look at different houses and buildings. As you walk, talk. What are the shapes? Do they all have the same kind of roofs? Do they have stairs? Are they on one level or more? Are the houses attached to each other? Is there cement or grass between them? Notice the doors and windows. Count the houses. When you return to the classroom, the children have a lot to write, draw, sing, move, and play about.

Construction site. City construction usually occurs right in the middle of a bustling street and is surrounded by high wooden walls. If you are able to walk to such a site, peep-holes and cracks in the walls make it possible for you to observe the action.

Young children are fascinated by the construction process. Look first, then return to the classroom and share observations and feelings. Turn them into stories, songs, games, dances, pictures, and puppet shows.

of buildings, rooftops, trees, bridges, streets, and parks. Take paper and crayons and sketch the scene. Use all your senses. Encourage the children to write their ideas and observations. Share the pictures and stories.

Birds and bees. If there is a state or national park nearby, the rangers will show the children bird nests, beaver dams, and squirrel holes. Many museums and wildlife centers have exhibits featuring animal shelters. The variety of bird nests is always intriguing. If you live near a zoo, visit the bird house to see tiny hummingbird nests and huge eagle nests. The insect house, with ant colonies and varieties of webs and cocoons, is amazing.

You may have a beekeeper in your community and not even know it. Check the

NOTES

1. Ann Nolan Clark, "Home," *In My Mother's House* (New York: Viking, 1972), p. 10.
2. A. A. Milne, "In Which a House Is Built at Pooh Corner for Eeyore," *The World of Pooh* (New York: Dutton, 1957), pp. 157–172.
3. Maria Montessori, *The Child in the Family* (New York: Avon, 1970), p. 96.
4. Montessori, pp. 66–67.
5. Montessori, p. 67.
6. Ann Nolan Clark, "The People," *In My Mother's House* (New York: Viking, 1972), p. 12.
7. Alexandra Stoddard, *A Child's Place* (New York: Doubleday, 1978), p. 67.
8. Stoddard, p. 68.
9. May Garelick, *Where Does the Butterfly Go When It Rains?* (New York: Scholastic, 1972), np.
10. Rachel Field, "Skyscrapers," *Arrow Book of Poetry*, ed. by Ann McGovern (New York: Scholastic, 1965), p. 65.
11. Robert Louis Stevenson, "Block City," *A Child's Garden of Verses* (La Jolla, Calif.: Green Tiger Press, 1975), p. 67.
12. Richard Janzen, "Oh, Joyous House," *Miracles*, ed. by Richard Lewis (New York: Bantam, 1977), p. 144.

SELECTED BIBLIOGRAPHY

A Houseful of Books for Children

Alain. *The Magic Stones*. New York: McGraw-Hill, 1957.

Allen, Thomas. *Where Children Live*. Englewood Cliffs, N.J.: Prentice-Hall, 1980.

Billout, Guy. *Stone and Steel: A Look at Engineering*. Englewood Cliffs, N.J.: Prentice-Hall, 1980.

Carter, Katherine. *The True Book of Houses*. Illustrated by George Rhoads. Chicago: Childrens Press, 1957.

Case, Bernard. *The Story of Houses*. New York: Sterling, 1957.

Cauley, Lorinda Bryan. *The New House*. New York: Harcourt Brace Jovanovich, 1981.

Devlin, Harry. *To Grandfather's House We Go*. New York: Parents Magazine Press, 1967.

———. *What Kind of House Is That?* New York: Parents Magazine Press, 1969.

Firmin, Peter. *Basil Brush Build a House*. Englewood Cliffs, N.J.: Prentice-Hall, 1981.

Hoberman, Mary Ann. *A House Is a House for Me*. Illustrated by Betty Fraser. New York: Viking, 1978.

Hughes, Shirley. *Moving Molly*. Englewood Cliffs, N.J.: Prentice-Hall, 1981.

Le Sieg, Theodore. *In a People House*. Illustrated by Roy McKie. New York: Random House, 1972.

Lionni, Leo. *The Biggest House in the World*. New York: Pantheon, 1968.

Mendoza, George. *Need a House? Call Ms. Mouse*. Illustrated by Doris Smith. New York: Grosset & Dunlap, 1980.

Oppenhein, Joanne. *Have You Seen Houses?* Reading, Mass.: Addison-Wesley, 1973.

Pinkwater, Daniel Manus. *The Big Orange Splot*. New York: Scholastic, 1977.

Rockwell, Anne. *The Awful Mess*. New York: Scholastic, Four Winds Press, 1980.

Rockwell, Anne, and Harlow Rockwell. *I Play in My Room*. New York: Macmillan, 1981.

Scarry, Richard. *Busy Houses*. New York: Random House, 1981.

Schaaf, Peter. *An Apartment House Close Up*. New York: Scholastic, Four Winds Press, 1980.

Spier, Peter. *Village Books*. New York: Doubleday, 1981. (Titles are: *Bill's Service Station*; *The Fire House*; *My School*; *The Pet Store*; and *The Toy Store*.)

Teacher Resources

Hungton, Lee Pennock. *America at Home: Four Hundred Years of Ameican Houses*. New York: Coward, McCann & Geoghegan, 1981.

King, Mary Louise. *A History of Western Architecture*. New York: Walck, 1967.

For teachers, but with good illustrations for children

Adkins, Jan. *How a House Happens*. New York: Walker, 1971.

Adler, Ruth, and Irving Adler. *Houses*. New York: Day, 1964.

Bergere, Thea, and Richard Bergere. *From Stones to Skyscrapers*. New York: Dodd, Mead, 1960.

Barton, Byron. *Building a House*. New York: Morrow, Greenwillow, 1980.

Foster, Joanna. *Homes: Shelter and Living Space*. Illustrated by Kathleen Heiden. New York: Parents Magazine Press, 1972.

Huntington, Lee Pennock. *Simple Shelters*. New York: Coward, McCann & Geoghegan, 1979.

Jupo, Frank. *A Place to Stay*. New York: Dodd, Mead, 1974.

Leacroft, Helen, and Richard Leacroft. *The Buildings of Ancient Man*. Reading, Mass. Addison-Wesley, 1973.

Stoddard, Alexandra. *How to Create a Room for Your Child—A Child's Place*. New York: Doubleday, Dolphin, 1978.

Thompson, David. *Easy Woodstuff for Kids*. Mt. Ranier, Md.: Gryphon, 1980.

Walker, Les. *Housebuilding for Children*. Woodstock, N.Y.: Overlook, 1977.

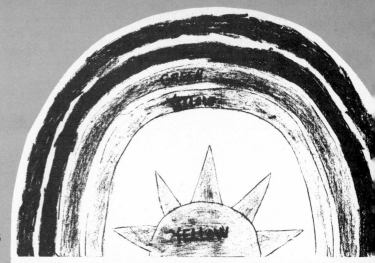

Joy, Nili, Alyssa, Becky, and Shanna, age 5

Wally, age 4

PART FOUR

Nikki, age 8

OUR
COLORFUL
WORLD

WE
DISCOVER
SHAPES

WE
LEARN
OUR LETTERS
AND WORDS

WE
ENCOUNTER
NUMBERS

10
OUR COLORFUL WORLD

These four ribbons hanging here on the stem are the four quarters of the universe. The black one is for the west where the thunder beings live to send us rain; the white one for the north, whence comes the great white cleansing wind; the red one for the east, whence springs the light and where the morning star lives to give men wisdom; the yellow for the south, whence come the summer and the power to grow . . .[1]

THE BASICS

Perhaps more than the other seasons, autumn offers spectacular colors: bright red berries of firebushes and firethorn; multicolored mums sharp and clear as the colors of saltwater fish; oaks, maples, and sycamores with their leaves of fiery gold, rust, and burgundy; ripening yellow, green, and red apples; and gourds, pumpkins, and squashes of every size, shape, and color.

Colors are often a way of talking about life. In sharing their feelings about colors, Neela, six years, and Tali and Tirza, both seven years, made some profound observations.

> We'd be dead if we had no colors—our skin color, our hair color, our eyes, our lips. We'd be dead.
> Everything in the whole world has colors—trees, houses, all of life.
> Things got their colors from God.
> God's color is clear!

Colors affect our lives in many ways. They describe and define the physical world, and they influence behavior and emotions. We go at the green light; our bank balance is in the red; she is green with envy; he turned white with fear; I've got the blues.

Colors symbolize country, school, class, caste, clan, and cause: red, white, and blue of the American flag; scarlet and gray of Ohio State University; purple of royalty; red and white tartan of the Menzies clan; and redcoats of the British. Colors are also associated with holidays: red and green for Christmas; green for St. Patrick's Day; red for Valentine's Day; and orange and black for Halloween.

Colors affect the way we feel and react. Anna Grace, a gifted young singer, touched on some of these dimensions.

> Some colors make me feel peaceful. I love light lavender. When I wear light lavender, I feel good about myself. Colors like reds, yellows, and certain greens wake you up! They're energetic. Colors take on qualities. Say, if it's a bad day and you see a color pleasing to you, you're drawn to it. It lifts your spirits.
> I have a friend who's an artist. He also loves music. You can see movement and rhythm in his colors. Almost like seeing sound. The colors run in and out of each other. You can see music in the colors.
> I see colors in music, too. Jazz is always vibrant, full of life. Reds and purples. When I sing the "blues," I don't think of blues, more like grays and blacks—doldrums! Calypso and reggae are yellows and oranges—earth tones.

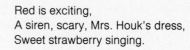

WHAT IS RED?

Red is a fall leaf,
Spaghetti, pizza, tomato, hot pepper,
And my favorite color.

Red is barbecued potato chips,
Bright cherry pie, ketchup, guitar,
A circus parade of balloons marching.

Red is exciting,
A siren, scary, Mrs. Houk's dress,
Sweet strawberry singing.

Red is little hands freezing,
Cherry happy popsicle, rose ringing,
And a big hen clucking.

Red is a jumping apple,
A slow sunset sinking,
And an adventuresome balloon bursting.

Thelma Barrett's
second grade class

Our earliest ancestors celebrated colors. They discovered that natural pigments existed in minerals and plants. The stone lapis produced the color blue. Crushed animal teeth and bones, when roasted, became rich black "paint." Irises and elderberries also yielded blue. Madder roots and the inner bark of birch trees produced red. Clay, coal, iron, fish, and insect shells were all found to produce colors.

An experience similar to one that our cave-dwelling relatives probably enjoyed thousands of years ago was repeated by a group of children at the "7 Days of Creation" summer camp in Ohio. The children and their counselors spent the morning sloshing barefooted through the cool waters of a creek. They waded, splashed, and searched for treasures on the sandy, stony creek bed. An excited shout rang out as one of the children found that a stone he had lifted out of the creek "wrote blue" when he scratched it on a large flat rock. The adventure continued through the afternoon as the children found stones that produced blues, reds, yellows, grays, blacks, and greens on rock, paper, and themselves.

Look around your neighborhood, street, city, and countryside. What colors do you see? The palette of the Southwest contrasts sharply with that of the New England coast, and the colors of New York City clearly differ from those of the Nebraska plains. Consider how these colors change at different times of the day and the year. Too often we are an unappreciative audience of this fantastic light and color show.

Ed Jacomo, one of the nation's most colorful teachers, a consultant in art education, and the chairperson for creative and performing arts at the University Liggett School in Grosse Pointe Woods, Michigan, speaks passionately about colors and young children. Teachers, Ed suggests, do not teach children color, because the children already know it. "Teachers," he says, "facilitate learning, help kids affirm what they already know, and help heighten perception."

Ed sends letters to his students' families that encourage them to participate in celebrating colors. Here is one of his letters.

Dear Parents,
Throughout the school year, we will be adding color words to our vocabularies so that we can describe the things we see. You can help your children add new color words and use those they already know. Here are some suggestions:

1. As you help your children select clothes for school, talk about the blue dress, green slacks, and red socks rather than just the dress, slacks, and socks. This is a good time to show children how some colors go together better than others.

2. As you take a walk or ride with your children, play guessing games with color. You can say, "I spy something yellow" (or red or blue or orange), and let the children continue guessing until they name the object. When they guess it, let them choose something and give its color. Then you guess what it is.

3. Look at color photographs or magazine pictures and pretend that you and your children are walking into the pictures together. As you walk along, what colors do you see? Take turns describing the colors of things in the pictures.

4. Look for books in the library that tell about colors. One of the following may be in your library: _Is It Blue As a Butterfly?_, by Rebecca Kalusky; _The Color Kittens_, by Margaret Wise Brown; and _What Color Is Love?_, by Joan Walsh Anglund.

5. Look at things through pieces of brightly colored cellophane or colored glass.

Sincerely,

Ed Jacomo

Ed's letters usually include a poem that is rich with color images to further encourage and inspire children and their families.

The most imaginative teachers have trouble separating color activities from other activities. They think color all the time!

When our eyes, minds, and hearts are open, we are able to appreciate seeing and even go beyond it. We can hear colors in music, in voices, in bird songs. We can perceive colors with all our senses, not just our eyes. Young children, sensitive adults, and most artists experience such synesthesia.

This phenomenon occurred when I gave each child in a kindergarten class a seed and asked the children to close their eyes and feel the seeds in their hands. Then we smelled the seeds and finally, opened our eyes to look at the seeds. I asked: "What does the seed smell like?" "Can you see the flower in your seed?" "What color will it be?" My aim was to encourage the feeling of wonder for seeds and all growing things.

The children quickly responded: "My seed smells like oranges"; "My seed has a red flower in it"; "My seed smells like pine trees"; and "My seed is full of a yellow dandelion!" The stimulus of a seed evoked responses from several senses.

Think about people who have never seen colors, people who have been blind since birth. To blind people, colors are words and concepts that they must shape in their minds on the basis of cues from other senses. Through their imaginations, such people give life to colors.

What is the impact of color on people who, spontaneously or through surgery, regain or gain their sight after years of blindness? In _Pilgrim at Tinker Creek_, Annie Dillard relates the findings of Marius von Senden, who studied such individuals.

In general, the newly sighted see the world as a dazzle of color patches. They are pleased by the sensation of color and learn quickly to name the colors, but the rest of seeing is tormentingly difficult. Soon after his operation, a patient generally bumps into one of those colour-patches and observes them to be substantial, since they resist him as tactual objects do. In walking about, it also strikes him . . . that he is continually passing in between the colours he sees . . .

A twenty-two year old girl was so dazzled by the world's brightness, she kept her eyes shut for two weeks. When, at the end of that time, she opened her eyes again, she did not recognize any objects, but the more she now directed her gaze upon everything about her, the more it could be seen how an expression of gratification and astonishment overspread her features; she repeatedly exclaimed: "Oh God! How beautiful!" [2]

Those who take the miracle of sight for granted do a disservice to their students. How can we help young children learn to appreciate the wonders of life if we fail to see, observe, and feel?

The late singer-composer Harry Chapin wrote a poignant song called "Flowers Are Red" (Electra/Asylum Records). It is about a little boy who wants to use all the colors in his crayons to draw flowers. His teacher, a narrow-minded person, corrects him and tells him the "right way" to look at colors. She sings:

> Flowers are red, young man.
> And green leaves are green.
> There's no need to see flowers any other way
> Than the way they always have been seen.

The little boy responds:

> There are so many colors in the rainbow.
> So many colors in the morning sun.
> So many colors in the flowers,
> And I see everyone.

The teacher considers the little boy a troublemaker, and he is kept inside to work on the color lesson until he gets it right. All his classmates are playing outside and he wants to join them, so he agrees to the lesson of the day.

After some time, the child moves to another place and goes to another school. In that school,

> The teacher there is smiling.
> She said, "Painting should be fun.
> There are so many colors in the flowers,
> So let's use every one."

But it is too late. The little boy has learned his lesson well. No, he tells the new teacher,

> Flowers are red.
> And green leaves are green.
> There's no need to see flowers any other way
> Than the way they always have been seen.

In our fast-paced, mechanized, computerized society, children learn at young ages to "turn off," be cool, and keep a low profile. Astonishment, excitement, and joy are diminished, even extinguished. This book is dedicated to preserving spirit and imagination by encouraging young children to use and enjoy their minds, appreciate their senses, and express curiosity and wonder.

DISCOVERY TIMES

- We live in a world of colors.
- Colors make the world a beautiful and more interesting place.
- Sometimes colors give us messages, like red lights and green lights.
- We recognize things by their colors: white milk, orange juice, lilacs, goldfish, redbirds, and evergreens.
- Colors can be symbolic: the red cross; the white dove of peace; and the colors of weather flags for ships at sea.
- We need light to see colors.
- All of the colors we see have names.
- Black absorbs sunlight and white reflects it, so we often wear light-colored clothes in summer and darker clothes in winter.
- Red, yellow, and blue are called primary colors. All other colors result from mixing two of the primary colors: red and yellow make orange; yellow and blue make green; blue and red make purple.
- When black is added to a color, it darkens the color; when white is added to a color, it lightens the color.
- When black and white are mixed, gray results.
- Some colors are bright and clear, others are dull.
- It is fun to mix and use colors in our pictures.
- All over the world, throughout history, people have found ways to mix colors and paint pictures.
- Painting pictures is special to the "people family."

Only people know how to use colors in different kinds of arrangements and designs, always making up new patterns and combinations.

- The human family is colorful—we have many different colors of eyes, hair, and skin. The colors of other people are beautiful and should be respected and appreciated.
- Blind people use their imaginations to picture colors.
- People with eyesight should use all of their powers to see and appreciate the many colors in the world.

SUGGESTED VOCABULARY

colors	palette	sky	party hats
rainbow	easel	grass	birthday
eyes	paintbrush	flowers	candles
see	crayons	flags	fruits
sun	chalk	stamps	candy
sunset	picture	wallpaper	cake
sunrise	painting	carpets	sunglasses
red	artist	rugs	cellophane
yellow	mix	books	tissue paper
blue	add	picture books	wrapping
primary colors	clothing	Christmas	paper
orange	skin	St. Patrick's	greeting cards
green	eyes	Day	scarves
purple	hair	Valentine's Day	curtains
violet	balloons	Thanksgiving	beach towels
gray	spectrum	opaque	spring
black	reflection	translucent	autumn
white	circus	light	winter
lavender	vegetables	dark	summer
pink	bubbles	bright	fish
navy blue	kaleidoscope	dull	birds
light green	prism	clear	ocean
dark red	magic	muddy	forest
turquoise	dye	colorful	ice-cream
	stained-glass	transparent	flavors
	windows		

Many words in the above list were contributed by children during conversations about "colorful things." Words like circus, ice-cream flavors, balloons, flowers, birds, and fish convey colorful images known and loved by young children.

Some of the words on the list may seem technical or too advanced for your students. But most children will surprise you with how easily they learn new vocabulary. Do not hesitate to use such words with young children.

As you talk about or become involved with your surroundings through activities, specify objects by their colors as often as possible. Ed Jacomo's letter directed families to refer to clothing by colors. Expand that kind of awareness to everything around you. Label and describe the colors in your room so that children continue to relate colors to objects and places. Because you are helping the children to see colors in everything around them, they will learn to appreciate and enjoy this amazing world.

SOME BEGINNING ACTIVITIES

Start with a display table. Barbara Kienzle's favorite way to launch a focus on color with her kindergartners and first and second graders at Indianola Alternative School in Columbus, Ohio, is to fascinate children with such hard-to-resist items as prisms, kaleidoscopes, sunglasses, magnifying glasses, plastic "stained-glass" strips, colored tissue paper, and cellophane. She encourages the children to see, touch, experiment with, and talk about light and color.

Start with a rainbow. A real rainbow is preferable, but if nature does not cooperate, a book about rainbows, such as Don Freeman's *A Rainbow of My Own* or *Rainbow Rider*, or a beautiful photograph or painting of a rainbow, is irresistible.

Start with a color walk. Walk and talk around the room, school, schoolyard, street, or neighborhood. As you walk, stop and look. "What colors do we see? How many colors can we name? Which colors do we like the best?"

Start with a color day. Fun-loving, dynamic teachers across the country experiment with variations of this idea. Celebrate one color. Have a Red Letter Day, or a Blueness Day, or a Green for a Day Day.

The children celebrate the color many ways: they wear a ribbon or patch, or a construction-paper hat, headband, armband, bow, or bowtie in the color; make up songs and poems about the color; name things defined by the color; draw, paint, and color pictures and designs in the color; connect the color to feelings and ideas ("This color makes me feel . . ."); play music that expresses the color; make up puppet shows about the color; make up games and riddles about the color ("I'm thinking of something way above our heads, high above us, very wide and high that often shows our special color." Answer: The blue sky!); correlate the special color with letters, numbers, and shapes; make tissue-paper flowers of different shades of the color; and read books and find pictures that feature the color of the day.

There are more ideas of this kind later in the guide.

Start with a color buddy search. Guide 5 features "buddy" ideas guaranteed to succeed in your room. Here is an example of a buddy activity that starts a focus on colors. Give each child a design or card of a distinct color. Ask children to hold up their cards and walk slowly around the room to find friends who have cards of the same color. When they find their "color buddies," they form a small group.

This project can be easily expanded. For example, each color group has a special activity for the day, which is written or pictured on a large colored card. The children match their colors to the activity cards.

Each group can also lead an exercise. The yellow group, for example, decides to do jumping jacks; when the yellow card is held up, everyone does jumping jacks.

Start with a famous painting. Nothing is more dramatic for children than discovering that artists begin with blank canvas and, by adding colors, shapes, and lines, create images and scenes that satisfy senses and emotions. Children are dazzled by the colors of Van Gogh's *Sunflowers* and *Starry Night*, Monet's *Gardens at Giverny* and *Waterlilies*, Gauguin's South Seas landscapes and villages, Homer's seascapes, Cassatt's *The Boating Party* and *Children at the Seashore*, Degas' dancers and horses, Renoir's children and parks, and Chagall's circuses and villages. Browse through the art catalogues and prints in your local library and borrow the paintings you enjoy, and introduce your students to them.

Start with darkness. Turn off the lights and pull down the shades. Ask the children to close their eyes and hide their faces behind their hands (like peek-a-boo). "What do you see in a dark room with your eyes closed and your face hidden?" Nothing! Ask the children to take their hands from their faces and open their eyes. "What do we see?" Shapes and colors in the dim room. Lift the shades, turn on the lights, and ask the children to really look at the room. "Now what do we see? Are the colors brighter, the shapes clearer?" This is an effective way to begin thinking about colors and light.

Start with eyes and hair. Children are fascinated by the colors of their eyes and hair and those of others. Look in mirrors.

Look at each other. Say each child's hair and eye colors. Marvel at the diversity. Start the children thinking about how boring it would be if everyone had exactly the same eye and hair colors.

Go from eyes and hair to the mind-boggling varieties of flowers, sunsets, animals, fish, birds, sea shells, vegetables, leaves, and stones. These are nature's marvelous colors. Also consider the variety of colors that people choose for their homes, rooms, clothes, cars, and toys.

Start with a challenge. Young children usually respond to challenges with enthusiasm, for example: "Let's see if we can find ten blue things in our room"; "Let's look out the window and see if we can count five different colors"; or "How many things can you find in our room that match the color of this red book?" Invite the children to turn on their bright lights and press their alertness buttons.

Start with the children's clothing. Celebrate a special item of clothing described by its color for each child in your class. You can say it or sing it, but be sure to include everyone. When, for example, you start the morning by taking attendance with

clothing colors, you cannot help noticing colors for the rest of the day.

Feel free to use suggestions from later sections of this guide and from other guides as beginning activities for colors. Puppets, songs, stories, and art projects are all excellent starters.

TALK TIMES

Ed Jacomo says, "Colors lasts all the year. Colors is all the time." Children never tire of talking about colors. Remember, they are in the process of learning colors, and the spectacle of daily life is a constant source of discovery, amazement, and joy of recognition. Always be ready to add to any topic of conversation with the question "What color is it?" For example: "What color is your dog? Cat? Hamster? Fish?"; "What color is your new doll's hair?"; and "What color is your car?" Adding color to the conversation adds awareness, vocabulary, relationships, and appreciation.

Carol Price's colorful "Talk Times" with her kindergartners in Worthington Estates, Ohio, encompass such topics as the colors of football, baseball, and cheerleader uniforms; the colors of traffic lights and what they mean; how some animals, like snowhair rabbits, wolves, and salamanders, change colors to protect themselves; the colors of seasons; how dull our lives would be without colors; how colors change in different kinds of light; how some colors make us sleepy and others make us bouncy; and why certain colors are our favorite ones.

I visited Caroline Botchie's second-grade class at Indian Run School in Dublin, Ohio. It was Todd's eighth birthday. We talked about doing something special for a person on his or her birthday. Here is Todd's classmates' gift to him on his eighth birthday.

I flew up to the sky. The stars flickered their lights around me. I turned invisible. It rained and I washed out into the rainbow. I ran around the colors. It smelled like strawberries. I heard the song of the rainbow:

The Song of the Rainbow
Happy birthday to you,
You live in a rainbow.
I give you blue.
I give you orange.
I give you pink.
I give you red.
I give you purple.
I give you yellow.
I give you green.
I give you brown.
I give you autumn leaves.
I give you a closet of rainbow clothes.
I give you a forest of wildflowers.
I give you a school full of colorful kids.
Happy Rainbow to You!

Leading questions spur children on. Todd's rainbow story was developed and enriched when, during pauses in the children's suggestions, questions were asked, such as: "What happened when you flew into the sky?"; "What did you do in the rainbow?"; and "What did you smell? What did you hear?"

Steven Conkle, a poet working with the Ohio Poets in the Schools program, turned a "Talk Time" into a collaboration on a poem with a group of second graders at St. Bernadette Elementary School in Lancaster, Ohio. They shared ideas about wishes and colors, and Steve encouraged the children to suggest a color in every wish. Here is part of their collaboration.

I wish I had a blue fish in my home
brown puppy in my backyard
red and white rabbit in a fish tank
polka-dotted monkey in my mouth
black and blue cat in my bed
blue and white bird in my desk . . .[3]

Jean Williams, kindergarten teacher at the Douglas Alternative School in Columbus, Ohio, says:

Everything starts with talking. We have a special week, a Color Week. Each day we talk about a different color, and we wear something in that color. We talk about how that color makes us feel and where in the room we can find that color. We talk about how much fun it is to feature that color in pictures and collages; then we do it. We read books about a different color each day and talk about the books.

Another favorite color-related topic is based on the wonderful colors of people. We use Peter Spier's book *People* (Doubleday, 1979) to start us off. We look at his wonderful pictures and talk about how every person is special and has unique combinations of colors. We talk about our own colors and those of our classmates. We talk about how lucky we are to live in such an interesting world of so many colors and shapes.

Talking about the diversity of peoples' colors leads us to the range of colors in flowers. Once again, through talking and looking, we reinforce appreciation for the exciting world we live in.

Every activity in this book is accompanied or inspired by "Talk Times." So keep talking.

ART TIMES

In rooms where color is an everyday topic, children enjoy a variety of art experiences, constantly building on what they did before and combining new ideas. Ed Jacomo raids automobile dealers for their bright posters. "They always use wonderful colors so people will see the posters and be drawn to them," Ed explains. He cuts up the posters and uses the pieces for classroom activities.

Teachers like Ed scrounge color chips, color swatches, purple and green dividers from apple crates, crepe paper, waxed paper, newspaper, old plastic squirt bottles, shoe-polish applicators, sponges, food coloring, ribbons and bows, medicine droppers, tongue depressors, swabs, crayons, finger paints, colored chalk, charcoal, buttons, tempera, watercolors, stones that produce colors, catalogues, magazines, greeting cards, and clay.

Enjoy the activities suggested below and be ready to adapt them to you and your children. Think color.

Color charts. Children like to see their names connected with concepts they understand. Brighten your room with color charts celebrating eye colors, hair colors, favorite colors, favorite flower colors, and favorite vegetable colors.

One color at a time. Correlate this activity with a Color Day or enjoy it for its own sake.

Theresa Gelonese, who works with young children at Immaculate Conception School in Columbus, Ohio, likes to start out with the color white. The children look at pictures of white; color, chalk, and paint with white; and talk about ideas and feelings evoked by the color white. Words and pictures are combined. Then Theresa adds, one by one, the primary colors red, blue, and yellow. The children paint with each color so they get specific feelings from the color. Later, the three primary colors are offered at the same time. Theresa encourages the children to experiment and make their own discoveries when they mix the primary colors.

More activities for Color Days. Lynn Salem, first-grade teacher at Immaculate Conception School, Columbus, Ohio, Carol Price, and Ed Jacomo pooled some of their favorite art activities for Color Days.

On *Brown Day*, Carol's kindergartners make chocolate-pudding fingerpaint. After they paint their pictures, share them, and display them, they eat them!

On *Green Day*, Carol's students make paperbag Kermit the Frog puppets, painted green and with long strips of green paper for legs. The children improvise puppet shows and sing "It's Not Easy to be Green" from "Sesame Street."

On *Red Day*, Lynn's first graders make red Jell-O; wear red designs taped to their clothing; read about Johnny Appleseed and his apples; create a still life of red objects, such as a basket of shiny red apples, a red heart, and a Red Cross; and paint still lifes of red objects.

On *Blue Day*, Ed asks the children to "gather blue." "I brought blue to school today," he tells the children. "Had it in my freezer and forgot to take it out. It's not really defrosted yet!" The children delight in the combination of imagination and reality

as they imagine blue defrosting and as they find blue in items and objects.

Ed fills a big fishbowl with clear water. He plays "magical music" and pours blue dye into the fishbowl. The children watch it swirl to the music. "Where is it lightest? Where is it darkest?" They make important observations as they celebrate this Color Day!

On *Orange Day*, Lynn's first graders fill the room with orange paintings. They write their names and all their words in orange. Each child receives an orange to smell, touch, look at, and make observations about. All the oranges are placed together. The children paint or color the pattern. Then the challenge is: can they find their own orange again? You would be surprised at how many children succeed.

My favorite colors picture. Ask the children to choose their favorite color or colors to celebrate in a picture. Encourage the children to title their pictures. If they want to tell stories about their pictures, write the

stories for them if they cannot write their own, and display them with their pictures.

Color trays. Ask the children's families to save the styrofoam packing trays from the market. When you have enough, give one to each child. The children choose their favorite colors of Magic Marker and fill their trays with bright, beautiful colors. The trays are easily attached to the wall with masking tape, and they make a fine display of color.

Scratch a color. This activity takes muscles. The children fill a sheet of paper with crayon blobs of their favorite colors. Be sure they press as hard as they can so the colors are solid and pure. When their paper is filled with a design of different colors, suggest that they color their papers with black crayon and that they press hard so that the colors underneath are hidden.

Now you are ready for the magic. With hairpins or toothpicks, the children scratch out shapes (for example, circles, rectangles) or drawings on their papers. Wherever they scratch, the black crayon is cut away and the bright colors underneath show beautifully.

Class flags. Talk about flags and their special colors. Decide together what colors the children would like for their class flag. When the colors have been chosen, give the children sheets of paper to color their flag. The flags can be displayed on a wall or taped to sticks for a parade. Wave them high!

"Glorious trash" color pictures. One of Ed Jacomo's favorite art activities begins with gathering things the children like that have especially attractive shapes and colors.

We arrange the things on a big piece of paper and spend time just looking at them and enjoying the different colors and textures. Maybe we'll have a yellow pencil, a brown flowerpot with a red flower in it, a white napkin, a pink mitten, a white baseball. Then we remove one of the items and paint or crayon its shape and color in the empty spot. One by one, we replace the objects with their colors and shapes on the paper. Finally, all the "glorious trash" is gone, but the color patterns on the paper are reminders of it. We hang our unusual art on the wall and admire it for a long time.

Follow the colors of famous artists. Artists use color in amazingly diverse ways. Their techniques offer examples to young children, who are known for their openness and willingness to experiment.

Choose one famous painting at a time to celebrate. Encourage the children to really look at the way the artist used color. Is the color pure or mixed with other colors? Is it confined to a shape or does it blend with other colors? Did the artist make little dots of color or large, thick strokes?

Children especially enjoy studying such artists as Rembrandt and Vermeer. Their exquisite paintings show how light clarifies objects and people. The contrasts of darkness and light in the paintings of this school show colors in dramatic ways.

The paintings of the late nineteenth and early twentieth century Impressionists dazzle children with the power of light and sunshine on water, fields, flowers, hair, faces, and streets. Artists like Seurat captured light and color with precise, tiny dots. His painting *A Sunday Afternoon on the Island of La Grande Jatte* is a dramatic example of his distinctive technique. Van Gogh's swirls of blended colors in *Starry Night* are easily discerned and imitated by children. Chagall's dream-like colors immediately touch the imagination. Children enjoy finding Chagall's favorite images, present in most of his paintings—sometimes hidden, sometimes obvious. A group of kindergartners had a marvelous time painting Chagall-type pictures with their own hidden images and dreamy colors.

Children need to learn that there is no right way to paint or to use colors. When they practice many different ways, they learn coordination and confidence, as well as openness and appreciation.

Tree of many colors. Real or cardboard trees are popular in classrooms. Lynn Salem considers her cardboard tree a regular feature of her first grade. It stays up all year.

But we keep changing its colors. We always think of something new to go in the tree. We always connect the ideas with seasons, holidays, special themes. One of our favorite, most colorful tree colors was autumn leaves. Here's how we made them. We cut sponges into small pieces and used them to cover sheets of paper with different colors of tempera. We gathered leaves from outside and traced their outlines on the brightly colored paper. We cut out the leaf shapes and taped them to our tree.

Classroom trees are splashed with such colorful ideas as snowflakes, valentine hearts and notes, birds and buds, balloons, and color poems.

Words and colors. Every color creates its own vocabulary. Colors evoke vivid images and children enthusiastically respond to the

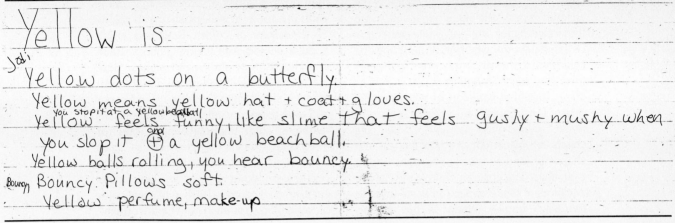

Yellow is

Jodi

Yellow dots on a butterfly.
Yellow means yellow hat + coat + gloves.
Yellow feels funny, like slime that feels gushy + mushy when
You stop it at a yellow beach ball
you slop it ⊕ a yellow beachball.
and
Yellow balls rolling, you hear bouncy.
Bouncy Bouncy Pillows soft.
Yellow perfume, make-up

Jodi, age 7

challenge of thinking of words inspired by specific colors. There are many ways to celebrate the fusion of words and colors. Here are a few samples.

Color frames. On sheets of white paper, paint, crayon, or paste strips of colors around the borders. In the center of the paper, words are written in the same colors as the borders.

Color-word explosion. On a large sheet of white paper, the name of a color is written or printed in large letters. Ask the children to embellish the name with paint, crayon, or chalk so that it really stands out. Fill the rest of the paper with words and pictures that are suggested by the color word. The final pictures explode like color-word fireworks.

Color-word posters. The children celebrate their favorite colors with a composition of pictures and words expressing their feelings about that color.

Color-word picture montage. Children enjoy working on these projects individually or in small groups. Using magazines, catalogues, and greeting cards, children cut out pictures of objects in the color they are featuring. The pictures are pasted on a large sheet of paper. Many teachers write the name of the color in large, wide poster letters. All the pictures are then pasted inside the outlines of the letters of the word.

Word-color balloons. Draw large circles on a sheet of paper or one circle on a smaller sheet. Ask the children to press hard on their crayons to present the color as strongly as possible. If they are using paints, ask them not to dilute the paints with water; the colors should be as pure as possible. When the balloons of colors are finished and dried, fill the balloons with words triggered by the colors. A blue balloon in a kindergarten class carried the words "sky," "water," and "my eyes."

Pass the color. This exciting activity is based on Michaelangelo's theory of art. Michaelangelo believed that the shape was hidden in the marble and his job was to release or free the shape. Share this fascinating idea with the children and suggest that every color has inside it special words and images it wants to express. Give each child a different color crayon or Magic Marker and a large sheet of paper. Ask the children to write words and draw images that their colors want to express.

After a few minutes, stop the activity. Ask the children to pass their color to another person; they, in turn, will receive another color from a neighbor. With a new color, repeat the activity, this time expressing the words or designs the new color wants to say. Repeat the activity so that the children have a chance to concentrate on at least three or four different colors. Celebrate all the works.

Construction-paper mosaics. Children can spend hours cutting, pasting, and arranging colorful shapes. Cut sheets of brightly colored paper into small squares, circles, triangles, rectangles, and other shapes. The children cover sheets of paper with glue and affix the shapes. Unless you are working on a specific assignment combining counting, colors, and shapes, encourage the children to create their own patterns with the small, colorful shapes.

Tissue- and waxed-paper stained-glass windows. Cut out brightly colored shapes of tissue paper. Smear sheets of waxed paper with glue or paste. Encourage the children to paste the tissue-paper shapes on the waxed paper. Press the different colors of tissue paper down firmly. When they dry, tape them to the windows and enjoy the way the light shines through each color.

A delightful variation of this activity is one of Lynn Salem's most popular ways to make stained-glass windows. She cuts sheets of black construction paper into shapes of window frames and gives one to each child. The children choose their favorite colors of tissue paper and paste them to the black frames. When all the window frames are hung in the classroom windows, the result is spectacular.

Coffee-can-lid stained-glass windows. Ed Jacomo likes to make stained-glass windows by scrounging the plastic lids from coffee cans. He gives one to each child. The children brush one side with liquid laundry starch and lay colored tissue paper on the starch. They are encouraged to overlap colors and shapes. When the lids are dry, they punch holes in them and hang them on the window.

Chalk it up. Teachers like Jean Williams experiment with ways to make colors. She encourages her kindergartners to discover the variations in color when they use different parts of crayons or chalk. "We color with the point, the side, and the blunt end," Jean explains. "We.paint every day; painting is part of everything we do. We use tempera, watercolor, crayons, and chalk." Her children like to fill manila or construction paper with colored chalk designs. They try wet chalk on dry paper, dry chalk on wet paper, white chalk on black paper, and every possible combination. What better way to practice creativity?

Note: Gently spray chalk pictures with one push-button of hair spray to set the colors and keep them from smearing.

Weather pictures. "Let's paint a sunny day!" "Let's paint a rainy day!" "Let's paint a cloudy day!" Weather and colors are inseparable. Children enjoy turning daily weather reports into weather pictures, with colors carefully chosen to express the elements.

Rainbows, circuses, and other colorful celebrations. Certain ideas are packed with colors. The children's suggestions on the vocabulary list include many of these Technicolor celebrations. Talk first, share ideas, then begin a series of activities that culminates in a room or wall splashed with colors.

Rainbows of colors. Rainbows are a popular subject with young children. Rainbows come in all sizes and varieties. Here are just a few. Draw them on T-shirts with Magic Marker; paint them on waxed paper and tape them to windows for stained-glass rainbows; color rainbow badges, one for every child; create a huge rainbow, as big as a wall, to which every child makes a colorful contribution; paint or write rainbow books cut in an arc shape and with a different color of the rainbow for each page; and combine with words for each color of the rainbow.

Circus of colors. Talk about clowns, elephants, balloons, jugglers, horses, acrobats, costumes, lions, tigers, tightropes, parades, monkeys, dogs, dancers, three rings, seals, and crowds of people. Turn your room into a circus tent. Each day work on one circus idea. For example, one day everyone colors a beautiful balloon. Tape the balloons to the walls or hang them on mobiles. The next day, work on clowns. Encourage the children to use the brightest, most delightful colors for clowns' hats, faces, and costumes. Add the clowns to the scene. By the end of a week, your room will be a circus of colors.

Other colorful celebrations. The following are examples of gathering colorful images around a central idea. Most of these projects continued for more than a week and covered most of the room. They included a garden of colors (flowers, grass, birds, vegetables, butterflies); seasons of colors (different colors for each season); and an ocean of colors (shades of blue and green, fish of every shape and color, ocean plants, snails, sand, stones, shells). Lynn Salem's first graders did a colorful series of murals, mobiles, and pictures of birds in the sky, in the jungle, on the farm, in the city, and in Antarctica.

Art activities are part of all activities. A word, a song, or a game flows into and from an art experience. Every book of colorful pictures or vivid ideas inspires art activities that further enrich the story and strengthen imagination. Lynn Salem said it beautifully: "Reading can't be just reading! We're drawing, cutting, pasting, coloring—making new books from the original stories!"

Ezra Jack Keats's *The Snowy Day* challenges children to paint their own ideas of a snowy day. Arnold Lobel's *The Great Blueness and Other Predicaments* stimulates delightful variations such as "the Great Greenness," paint everything green; "the Great Redness," paint the town red. Mary O'Neill's marvelous collection of color poems, *Hailstones and Halibut Bones*, spurs individual and class books of answers in words and pictures to "what is yellow?" "what is orange?" and so on through the color wheel.

As you read and enjoy these guides, correlate ideas, discovering how they overlap and cannot be separated. Think color. Splash colors on everything. Add a little color to your daze!

MUSIC TIMES

Learning names of colors and becoming more aware of colors are ideas worth singing about. Encourage the children to make up songs and hums about colors, and, as often as possible, learn them as a group and sing along. Many of the songs described in these pages were composed by young children and their spirited teachers.

Improvised songs that celebrate the children's colors. Clothing, eyes, hair, and names are favorite topics in early childhood classes. Here is a brief excerpt from a long series of color verses, improvised for each child, sung to the tune of "Mary Had a Little Lamb."

Bob is wearing a yellow shirt,
A yellow shirt,
A yellow shirt.
Bob is wearing a yellow shirt
On this Wednesday morning.

Laura's wearing a red and blue skirt,
Red and blue skirt,
Red and blue skirt.
Laura's wearing a red and blue skirt,
On this Wednesday morning.

Each child was featured in a stanza. Afterward the children colored pictures of their special clothes.

If your children know their colors and are ready for lots of ideas at once, expand the "Mary Had a Little Lamb" tune to include more observations such as:

Seth has such blue blue eyes,
Brown curly hair,
Tan cowboy boots.
Brett has on his green cowboy shirt
On this Wednesday morning!

What a way to start the day with eyes open and minds sharp.

Original songs, cheers, and chants about colors. A group of prekindergartners celebrated a Yellow Day at the Jewish Center in Columbus, Ohio. They wore something yellow, painted yellow pictures, tied yellow ribbons and strings on their arms, and made up a song about yellow to the tune "For He's a Jolly Good Fellow."

For it's a jolly good yellow
For it's a jolly good yellow
For it's a jolly good yellow
That nobody can deny!

Here is a rhythmical cheer celebrating the color blue, created by a class of second graders.

Blue for the sky (clap/clap/clap)
Blue for our jeans (clap/clap/clap)
Blue for blue eyes (clap/clap/clap)
Blue for blueberries (jump/jump/jump)

Colors of musical moods. Give the children opportunities to listen to a variety of music and ask them to respond in challenging ways, such as: "Listen to the music. What pictures do you see? What colors does this music make you imagine?" Pass out papers, crayons, paints, chalk, and Magic Markers. Ask the children to listen to the music and, as they listen, to cover their papers with the colors and designs that the music evokes. Remember, all interpretations should be accepted and respected.

Scrounge your own, your neighbors', and the libraries' record collections for examples of music that express different moods. Through the years, I have shared a wide range of musical selections with young children. Their artistic interpretations and expressions are always highly original. Lynn Salem's first graders thoroughly enjoy this activity and especially respond to ballet music, marching band music, lullabies, and jazz.

Colors of musical instruments. Listening

with sharp, sensitive ears to the sounds of specific instruments is a valuable and enjoyable experience for young children. Correlate such listening with art and ask the children to imagine the colors and designs each instrument or family of instruments evokes. Children of all ages have listened to and painted the colors of such diverse instruments as Pete Seeger's banjo, Ravi Shankar's sitar, Carlos Montoya's flamenco guitar, Clarence Clemon's saxophone, and Orff's percussion instruments, bells, and flutes.

Label the pictures with titles and stories the children suggest. A six-year-old added these feelings to his bright red picture of the sound of gypsy violins: "These violins are red because the sky turns red at night when you hear their music."

Musical sky colors. Many musical selections suggest images of skies and weather. Grofé's *Grand Canyon* Suite inspires sensitive pictures of sunrises and of sudden rains; Debussy's *La Mer* is all clear sky and ocean; Mussorgsky's *A Night on Bald Mountain* helps children paint the dramatic colors of thunderstorms; and Brahms's *Lullaby* is a perfect palette of sunset colors.

Color-cued rhythm bands. Designate a different color for each group of instruments in your class rhythm band. Make a color chart of the instruments and their color cues. Paint or color large cue cards; use any design or outline of instruments. Now the children are ready to take their musical cues from the cards.

A delightful variation of this activity is to use dark and light shades for each instrument. For example, when light blue is held up, the drums are played softly; when dark blue is the cue, the drums are played with gusto.

Ed Jacomo carried this idea a step further. He correlated shades of colors with numbers of instruments played. "When yellow is very very pure, all eight tambourines play," he instructed his youngsters. The children had to look carefully at the cards to distinguish the degree of brightness and respond with the brightest sounds.

Musical rainbows. Expand on the above activities. Assign different families of instruments to colors of the rainbow. For example, the triangles are purple. All the children playing triangles wear purple ribbons, string, or scarves; or purple paper taped to their shirts; or purple hats. They stand to form an arc. Behind them, in another arc, stand children with another color and another group of instruments. Continue this pattern to form a rainbow. Now all the colors of the spectrum are celebrated by their own musical sounds played by a rainbow of children. Have a rainbow parade.

Musical backgrounds to colorful stories. Children's picture books are often brilliantly illustrated by outstanding artists. Choose books that offer colorful illustrations and ask the children to decide what kind of music or sounds could accompany specific pictures.

Arnold Lobel's *The Great Blueness and Other Predicaments* (Harper & Row, 1968) is a good book to set to music. As the Wizard paints everything one color and the world turns into that color, children enjoy creating the sounds of the world turned blue, turned yellow ("the Great Yellowness"), and turned red ("the Great Redness"), until a symphony of instruments expresses the fabulous finale when all the colors are celebrated in a world that is "too beautiful ever to be changed again."

A wonderful picture book like Brian Wildsmith's *The Circus* (Oxford University Press, 1980) inspires bouncy, cheerful circus music that children enjoy creating and moving to as each of Wildsmith's circus images spurs a new musical interpretation.

A group of six- and seven-year-olds in Columbus, Ohio, had an exciting time deciding which instruments and rhythms to use with Wildsmith's images. When we talked about music for the two seals balancing colorful balls on their noses, Timmy suggested, "We better not play anything too rough or they'll drop the balls!"

Gerald McDermott's Caldecott-Prize-winning book, *Arrow to the Sun* (Viking, 1974), based on a Pueblo Indian story, is enjoyed for its unusual dramatic colors, inventive illustrations in which all the characters are different shapes, and music of the language. Children play drums, bells, and tom-toms in Indian rhythms to accompany each illustration.

Red light, green light. The children play their favorite instruments to familiar or improvised music. Hold up a bright red circle to signal "stop the music." Hold up a bright green circle to signal "start the music." The children learn those important signals as they discover something about silence and sound—the dramatic pause.

Expand this activity with other color symbols and by signalling faster, slower, louder, and softer responses.

National flags and ethnic music. The children learn that countries have their own flags with special color combinations. Correlate flags with music. Teach the children countries and their flags, one at a time. Begin with the American flag. The children color flags on sheets of paper or white scrounged material. As the flags are displayed or waved, play music representative of the country.

Songs with color words. Many colorful songs are waiting in your knapsack to be shared with your children. Start a list of songs about colors and you will be surprised at how many you know. At a recent workshop, teachers made lists that included "Blue Skies," "Around Her Neck She Wore a Yellow Ribbon," "Scarlet Ribbons," "White Christmas," "Black Is the Color of My True Love's Hair," "Red River Valley," "Red Sails in the Sunset," "Follow the Yellow Brick Road," "The Rainbow Connection," "Yellow Submarine," "I Can Sing a Rainbow," "Greensleeves," "Five Foot Two, Eyes of Blue," "The Green Leaves of Summer," "Mary Was a Redbird," "Mary Wore a Red Dress," and "White Coral Bells."

Improvised songs about colors. Teachers like Carol Price enjoy making up their own songs, as well as teaching children songs composed by others. Carol's kindergartners in Worthington Estates, Ohio, enjoy her original song "Traveling Rainbow," which has a melody similar to "Hi Lili, Hi Lili, Hi Lo," from the film *Lili*.

Traveling Rainbow

I found me a traveling rainbow
On a happy and warm summer day.
I found me a traveling rainbow
With colors so bright and so gay.

I touched it and it felt like sunshine
With wings soft as cobwebs and lace.
I touched it and it felt like sunshine
With sprinkles of dust on its face.

But, I can't keep this traveling rainbow
It's part of the blue summer sky.
I can't keep this traveling rainbow—
For it's really a butterfly.

Add music to colorful celebrations. A list of suggestions for colorful celebrations was presented in "Art Times." Add music to those themes. Music adds another dimension to any experience. As the children paint, color, or sculpt circus ideas, play circus music; as they paint bright colors on their jungle birds, play African folk music.

A variation of this idea is to encourage the children to create original music and sound effects for their celebration. Tape their music and play it to accompany the various activities of their celebration.

Colorful birthdays and other special parties. What is your Birthday Child's favorite song? What music does your Child of the Week want to play or sing? Listen to, play, or sing the child's favorite music during the party. Make flags of the child's favorite colors and wave them as you sing or play music.

Music for the colors of outer space. Children are familiar with the adventures of space journeys, the blast-off of rockets, and the strange rhythms of space exploration. What color is outer space? The children paint and draw pictures and murals and make mobiles of planets, stars, suns, and comets. What are the sounds of outer space? The children create their own space music with instruments, objects, bodies, and voices, or choose music like that of *Star Wars* to be played as they improvise space trips.

Sounds for colors. Here is an opportunity to encourage imagination and experimentation. Show and discuss one color at a time. Ask the children to imagine the sounds of that color. The children usually begin with words like "loud," "soft," "scary," "fast," "bouncy," "tinkly," "lazy," and "peaceful." Write down all their words, but keep going.

Then ask the children to try making the sounds of the color with their voices, bodies, instruments, and anything else in the room that makes sounds. Children discover that they can make musical sounds by tapping two pencils together, shaking a jar of paper clips, clinking spoons against each other or a tabletop, and waving paper. An imaginative second grade decided that blue had the sound of wind—"blowy" and "airy." They worked out an extraordinary symphony of sounds and melodies to express music of blue.

Here is a chance to make another musical rainbow as groups of children work on the sounds of different colors of the rainbow. Give each group a chance to share their color's sounds by themselves; then go around once more, adding each color's sounds to the others as all the colors of the rainbow are played together.

MOVEMENT AND PLAY TIMES

Carol Price organizes every day with colors. Her children sit at tables identified by different colors. The mugs on the tables that hold scissors, pencils, crayons, and other supplies are the same color. The children's cubbyholes are painted different colors, and Carol refers to the colors when she instructs the children about daily business. For example: "The children who have blue cubbyholes may put their toys away."

Activities are printed on colored cards, held together by colored clothespins or stored in colored envelopes. The children's jobs are written in special colors and so are their names. Carol moves the children among color groups so that they work and play with new combinations of friends and do different kinds of things. *Colors are never used competitively*, such as "Color Wars," which is done in so many summer camps. Rather, they are used as identification, reference, and aid in instruction. Children are never on "teams" where they become winners or losers; they are totally involved in work and play and are constantly reminded of the colors of their belongings, surroundings, games, and routines. Color is part of everything they do.

As you read and enjoy the following suggested activities, find ideas that fit your interests, personality, and group of children.

Color magicians. Doug Henning, an outstanding magician, believes that the real magic is everyday life and the best tricks are the ordinary events we take for granted. Because we have all become so "cool" and contained, we need magicians to jolt us into the feelings of astonishment that we forget we have. Henning believes that once these feelings of astonishment and wonder have been revived, we will be able to use them in appreciating the miracle of our daily lives.

Fortunately, young children have not yet lost the gifts of wonder and amazement.

Perhaps we can help them (and ourselves) preserve that spirit a little longer. For that reason, many imaginative teachers add a touch of magic when they demonstrate the mixing of colors.

Change children into magicians. Young children are easily turned into magicians with a few words of wonder from you, a little story, a magic wand, or a spray of magic dust. Once the children are turned into magicians, they demonstrate the following "tricks" with authority, excitement, and pride.

Soufflé cups and crepe paper. This is one of Ed Jacomo's most magical ways to show the mixing of primary colors. Each of his "color scientists" receives three soufflé cups. The soufflé cups are filled with water. Each child receives pieces of yellow, blue, and red crepe paper. When the children dip the yellow crepe paper into one of the soufflé cups, it turns yellow. Shazzam! Then they dip, into the same cup, a piece of blue crepe paper. Abracadabra, the yellow turns green. What a fabulous trick! The children continue with the other two cups to discover other mixtures.

Food coloring and jars of water. Probably the simplest and most popular way to show what happens when two primary colors are mixed together is to fill three large clear plastic soda bottles with water. Be sure to remove the labels. As the "color magicians" look at the three bottles, encourage them to turn on their magical powers.

Release a single drop of red, yellow, or blue food coloring into one of the bottles. Observe what happens to the water. Give the children turns to drop more of that color into the bottle. "Is everyone ready for the magical happening?" Make it dramatic. Into the bottle of red water, with your magicians' help, add drops of yellow (to make orange) or blue (to make purple).

Finger paints and Formica tables. Marilyn Cohen and her kindergartners at the Shraga Arian Hebrew Academy of the Capital District in Albany, New York, first make their finger paints out of liquid starch, Ivory Snow flakes, tempera, and water. They start with blue or yellow. First they finger-paint one color on a Formica table. They press pieces of paper on the table and make prints of their designs. Then they mix the second color with the first on the table. Presto! The blue and yellow finger paints turn green.

They press more paper and print green designs.

Napkin batiks. Another of Marilyn's most effective tricks for her color magicians is to give each child a white napkin. The napkins are opened all the way. The children fold them any way they want to and fasten the folding with a pin or a paper clip. They dab drops of red, blue, and yellow food coloring on the napkin, and the colors flow through. When they open their napkins, beautiful batiklike designs appear. The children mount their napkins on wallpaper for place mats or on construction paper for wall hangings.

Colorful clay. Suzanne Raymo, who has been nicknamed Ms. Rainbow by her students at the University Liggett School in Grosse Pointe, Michigan, uses clay and paint to help children see the drama of primary colors mixing together. The children make interesting clay shapes. They paint their shapes with a primary color in tempera or thick watercolor. They choose another primary color to paint over the first one. Before their eyes, the clay turns color.

However you choose to show children how primary colors mix to form secondary colors, do it with pizzazz. Mix it with wonder.

Rose-colored and other colored glasses. Color magicians have many wonderful ways to look at the world, including rose-colored glasses. Scrounge eyeglass frames or make frames out of the round plastic holders used for six-packs of beer or soda by cutting out two holders and fastening them around the children's heads with string or strands of wool. Tape different colors of cellophane to the frames.

When the children wear the glasses, everything looks different to them. Make up a game like, "Color Magicians, what do you see through your magical colored glasses?" The children make lively observations, such as: "I see yellow paper towels, yellow water in the fish tank, yellow windows!" or "Through my magic red glasses, I see red cookies! I see red milk! Marcie's face turned red!" Art projects and creative writing readily follow from this activity.

Magic color wands. Marilyn Cohen's color magicians have marvelous color wands. They are made by cutting cardboard paddles with a hole in the middle and covering each paddle (wand) with a layer of cellophane in one of the primary colors.

When the children look through their magical wands, the world changes color. Put two different-colored wands together and look through them. Zingo! The world turns a new color. Play mysterious music as the children perform this color wand feat. Use the color wands in stories, songs, puppet shows, and improvisations.

How are they alike? Jean Williams, kindergarten teacher at Douglas Alternative School in Columbus, Ohio, enjoys making up new games. Here is one of her favorites. She calls children to the front of the room and asks the rest of the group to look at them carefully. "How are they alike?" she asks. She makes groupings, such as three children with blue eyes, six children wearing blue jeans, four children wearing the color white, and two children with green name tags.

Her classes quickly learn that they must go beyond obvious answers, such as "They all have hair on their heads," or "They all have noses!" When children offer these responses, Jean smiles and replies, "How else are they alike? Keep looking!" Invariably, the children guess correctly.

Try the same game with objects, plants, and pictures.

Colorful movement and mime for special days. This is a variation of "Turn Yourself Into . . ." that celebrates ideas inspired by colors. Correlate these activities with Color Day celebrations or simply use it throughout the year.

Talk first, then move. "Let's talk about the color red. What are some red objects that we think of immediately?" "Fire engines." "Fires." "Robin red breast."

Start off by asking the children to turn themselves into a bright red fire engine, zooming around the room (everyone moving in the same direction, of course!). Stop. Shake out the fire engine. Ask the children to turn themselves into a red fire, flaming and smoking. Half the class can be the fire; the other half can be the fire engine. Whoosh. The fire hoses successfully put out the fire. Children show the fire going out. You will probably have to do this twice and give children a chance to be both fire and fire engine.

Shake out those two red ideas and try the third suggestion, robin red breast. The last time we did this activity, the children tapped their chests and said, "Mmmmm. Beautiful red!" Some of them wanted to tape red construction paper to their shirts. We fluttered and pecked and slept with our heads under our wings.

Expand this activity into color books, murals, poems, charts, and collages with red pictures of fire engines, fires, robin red breasts, and other red ideas the children may have.

Color dances. First look at and talk about a color. Then share ideas about what that color makes you think, how it makes you feel. From these suggestions, select one or two images to experiment with in movement.

Here is an example from a recent session with first graders.

CHILD: Blue, I think of the sky.
CHILD: I think of blue, blue water.
TEACHER: Maybe we can think of movement to express sky and water.
CHILD: Sky is high. We can stretch way up.
CHILD: It's all over above us—we can wave our hands over our heads to show how big it is.
TEACHER: Let's try that. First stretch as high as you can stretch. Now wave hands and arms over our heads, above us. That looks beautiful! Shall we keep that and remember it for our blue movement?
CHILDREN: Yes!

Continue with other colors. For each color, think of ideas. From the ideas, develop one or two movements. The children learn and perform them when the color is mentioned or shown.

All kinds of music can be used for accompaniment. Color cards or posters can be used to direct the sequence of dances. Give the children opportunities to rearrange them.

After a group of kindergartners learned four color movements the children planned to take turns deciding the order. One girl placed the color cards in the pattern blue, red, white, and black. When the children finished performing the colors in that order, another child had a turn to rearrange the cards. He decided to keep the same order. "Don't you want to try changing it around?" I asked. "No. It's perfect this way!" he announced. And that was the way the class decided to keep it.

Color exercises. Ask the children to name their favorite exercises. Write them on the board. Then ask the children to name the same number of colors. Write them on the board. Decide, with the children, which exercises match which colors. Make a chart on which each exercise is printed in a special color, or make exercise cards, each one a different color. Add stick figures to the cards or chart. Each day, assign different children to select exercises to lead. After a while, they will be able to announce the exercises by their colors alone.

"Old MacDonald Had a Farm" of colors. Add colors to the beloved children's singing game "Old MacDonald." Give each child a picture of a fruit or vegetable. When the fruits and vegetables are called into the game, describe them by color, for example, "And on his farm he grew *green* cucumbers."

Tribe of colored feathers. Playing, dancing, improvising, and singing about Indians are activities that young children especially enjoy. Cut feathers out of construction paper, each one a different color. Glue or tape them to cardboard or scrounge headbands. Now you have a tribe of young Indians with names such as "Melissa Blue Feather," "Neal Green Feather," and "Caryn Yellow Feather." Improvise Indian dances (rain, planting seeds, growing crops; eagle, horse, rabbit, and other dances in honor of animals) and call the individual dancers by their colorful feather names to join in so that the dance builds from one or two dances to the whole group.

Colorful clowns. As part of your circus celebration, make cardboard clown hats (from triangles and circles); or scrounge colorful pompons, ribbons, bows, crepe paper, and yarn. Let the children choose their favorite colors for hats or pompons. Now they are part of the World Famous Color Clowns, known far and wide for their sensational tricks and dances.

Call the children by their color names and give each one a chance to show special routines. "Ladies and Gentlemen. Here are two of our fabulous Color Clowns to do their circus trick for you! Todd Red Clown and Tia Purple Clown! Here they go!" The "acts" will probably take about 20 seconds and will range from hopping on one foot to doing somersaults. Applaud all the children, even the color clown who does a standing-still, sucking-his-thumb act.

When the clowns form a circus parade to bouncy music, encourage them to move in a variety of ways according to colors. "Wow! The Blue Clowns are playing drums in the parade! The Yellow Clowns are twirling batons! The Red Clowns are riding horses!" Keep changing ideas as the parade continues so the children have many opportunities to follow new directions and enjoy new movements.

Rainbow machines. Lynn Salem's first graders are rainbow-crazy. They read about, write about, paint, color, and dance rainbows. One of her most enjoyable experiments is to challenge the children to invent a rainbow-making machine. They can draw it, make it out of scrounge materials, or show it with their bodies.

Machines are excellent movement ideas, because all the parts must work together for it to succeed. There is no right way or wrong way to make a rainbow machine; encourage the children to try as many body combinations as possible before they decide how they want their rainbow-making machine to work.

Color dress-up time. Spread out the clothes in your clothing collection so they are easily seen. The "game" is to ask a child at a time to put on one of the items that you describe by its color. "Dominique, will you put on the black hat?" "Priscilla, will you put on the brown shoes?" Encourage the children to move and play in the clothes for a few minutes, look in the mirror, and exchange clothes (if time and spirit permit).

Stories, folk tales, nursery rhymes, poems, and songs to improvise. Here are just a few suggestions to start you thinking about possibilities in story and song. Even when a story is not about color, it usually contains enough references to color to be useful.

Stories and folk tales. Don Freeman's *A Rainbow of My Own* (Viking, 1966) is the story of a little boy who sees a rainbow so beautiful that he wants to catch it for his very own. Since that is impossible, he imagines having his very own rainbow that follows him and plays with him. He has a delightful time with his beautiful rainbow, and when he goes home, he finds that the sun shining through the water in his fishbowl beams a rainbow on his wall.

This is such a lovely story to improvise, especially if you give the children strips of brightly colored crepe paper stapled together at one end to hold and let trail behind them as they run. In this way the children really have rainbows of their own that follow them, swirl around them, and become rainbow capes, rainbow tails, and rainbow wind.

Marilyn Cohen puts a mirror in a dish of water. When the sun shines on the mirror, a rainbow is reflected on the ceiling of the room—a perfect ending to the children's adaptation of *A Rainbow of My Own*.

An Oriental legend is adapted and illustrated by Marilyn Hirsh in her book *How the World Got Its Color* (Crown, 1972). Once the world had no colors except for a set of paints given to an artist by the gods. The artist's young daughter, Miki, watched her father paint every day with the beautiful colors. One day, when her father went away, Miki took his paints outside and painted everything she saw. When her father returned, he scolded her fiercely, but the gods who had made the world were pleased and liked the colors. They smiled, and everything that Miki had not already painted was filled with color. We have had colors ever since.

One of many ways to expand this story is to tell it with puppets. The children have so many ideas for dialogue as their puppets decide what to paint: "I think I'll paint those flowers purple and red!" "Let's paint the snow white!" "Oooh, we need to paint these cars!" Puppets love to lose their tempers. What a wonderful opportunity for the puppets playing Miki's father to have magnificent tantrums.

Nursery rhymes and poems. Colorful nursery rhymes can be moved to, mimed, improvised, turned into puppet shows, or transformed into games. A simple nursery rhyme like "Baa, Baa, Black Sheep" can become a delightful movement game by changing the color word; for example, "Baa, Baa, Green Sheep."

A familiar rhyme like "Little Boy Blue" easily becomes a new game. Give children turns to be Little Boy or Girl Blue by taping blue badges to their clothes, tying blue crepe paper strips around their waists, or making blue paper hats. The rest of the children turn into sheep and cows, munching grass in the meadow. Little Boy or Girl Blue finds a nice cozy spot and falls asleep.

It is fun to embellish the poem by interspersing lines such as: "Now where can

that Little Boy/Girl Blue be? Sheep, have you seen him/her? Cows?" Nothing is more exciting for young children than to be found. When sleeping Blue boys and girls are awakened, what do they do? Blow their horns (pretend or real).

Three or four children can wear blue and be sleepy shepherds at the same time. Be sure to give a turn to all the children who want one.

Poems like Rachel Field's "Taxis" are packed with colors. Here are a few lines from this vivid poem.

> Ho, for taxis green or blue
> Hi, for taxis red,
> They roll along the Avenue
> Like spools of colored thread!
> Jack-o-Lantern yellow,
> Orange as the moon,
> Greener than the greenest grass
> Ever grew in June.[4]

The children can play this poem many ways. Here are just two ideas. Each child can roll one of the toy cars from the class garage along the avenue. Correlate the traffic with red and green traffic lights. When all the cars are moving together, the children enjoy reciting these lines from the poem: "Don't you think that taxis/Make a very pleasant sight?"

Even more than rolling toy cars, children enjoy pretending to be cars themselves. Ask the children to listen to the poem and take a sheet of construction paper that is one of the colors mentioned. Tape the colors to the children. They become taxis and create traffic. Control the flow of traffic with red and green lights.

The Trees Stand Shining, edited by Hettie Jones with paintings by Robert Andrew Parker, is a beautiful collection of poems by North American Indians. Many of these simple yet powerful poems have color images and ideas that children enjoy listening and moving to. The following Papago poem is a perfect example of how naturally a poem can turn into a dance, with children wearing something yellow.

> A little yellow cricket
> At the roots of the corn
> Is hopping about and singing.[5]

Keep improvising the poem by changing the color and asking the children to tape or tie the appropriate color symbol to their clothes.

The following Nootka poem is inspiring for young children. They dance it like a prayer, with gentle movements that seem to touch everything.

You, whose day it is,
Make it beautiful.
Get out your rainbow colors,
So it will be beautiful.[6]

After the children hear the poem, they easily imagine their power to make the world beautiful, to cover it with rainbow colors. Ask them to show with their arms, legs, and heads how they would paint the world with rainbow colors. Play Indian chants or songs to accompany the dance.

Remember, there is no one way to interpret the poem. Accept and encourage the children's own movement patterns.

Navajo songs, chants. An effective way to keep children alert to colors around them is to adapt the perspective of many Navajo prayers and songs. These repetitive chants express traditional Indian feelings of harmony with the universe:

With beauty may I walk.
With beauty before me, may I walk.
With beauty behind me, may I walk.
With beauty above me, may I walk.
With beauty below me, may I walk.
With beauty all around me, may I walk.[7]

Ask the children: "What are the colors before you? Look behind you, what do you see? Look above you, what colors do you see? Look below you, what do you see? Look all around you, what colors do you see?" Here is a segment from some first graders' explorations on a lovely spring day.

Above us, white clouds.
Below us, brown dirt.
Before us, yellow school bus.
Behind us, green trees.
All around us, yellow dandelions.

These ideas are easily interpreted in movement as children experiment with ways of showing the concepts of above, below, before, behind, and all around.

Songs. Children enjoy moving to songs, especially soft, soothing songs in living color, such as "I Can Sing a Rainbow"

(Ginni Clemmens, *"Sing a Rainbow"* and *Other Children's Songs*, Folkways Records). I like to call our dance to this song a "color dream." Imagine how easy it is to invite the children to "float" around the room and brush colors with their fingertips. Add verses about other colors you see.

Color songs that help children care about each other and the environment. Young children have no trouble understanding that when chemicals, oil, and sewage enter clean water, when cigarette smoke and industrial smoke mix with clean air, and when litter is thrown on streets and fields, our earth, as one six-year-old put it, "gets junked up!" What happens to the beautiful colors of the earth when we fail to take care of the earth?

Tom Paxton's "Whose Garden Is This?" is a powerful song with an important message. (John Denver's album *Whose Garden Was This* [RCA] features the Paxton song, and it is sung with great feeling and power.) Even if young children comprehend only part of it, the song has value for them as they begin what we hope is a lifetime of concern. With a group of first and second graders, we made up a story about how people neglected the air, water, and land. The air was full of chemicals and dark smoke; the rivers were full of garbage; and the land was full of litter. We pretended we were walking through this sad scene, and Tom Paxton's song helped the children respond to each element. (In many places this activity could be a real, not an imaginary field trip.)

Pete Seeger's song "My Rainbow Race" (*The World of Pete Seeger*, Columbia Records) gives the children a chance to bring all their colors together, join hands, walk in a circle, and feel part of a group. After all, the children are a special family—"the rainbow race," a family of beautiful colors.

VISITORS AND FIELD TRIPS

Visitors

Make-up artist. Leslie Zak, who teaches creative dramatics in the Junior Theater of the Arts in Columbus, Ohio, is a popular classroom visitor. One of her specialties is body and face paint. She paints the children's faces in their favorite colors and designs. Be sure to have mirrors available to help the children remember their "rainbow faces."

Magician. Every community has at least one magician willing to dazzle young audiences with brightly colored scarves, flowers, hats, and juggling balls—the tricks of the trade.

High school or college cheerleaders, athletes, band members. Teenagers like to visit young children and show their school colors. Uniforms, pompons, flags, and caps, combined with cheers, music, and warm-up exercises, make an enjoyable classroom visit.

Friends from different ethnic backgrounds. In most guides you have been encouraged to invite people from different cultural backgrounds to visit your children. Be sure to ask these friends to wear the colorful clothing of their culture and, if possible, to bring examples of their colorful arts and crafts.

Clowns. Clowns wear cheerful, colorful costumes. Their make-up and wigs are wonderful to behold.

Color characters. Parents, colleagues, friends, family members, and neighbors can be imaginative classroom visitors, such as Mrs. Rainbow, Mr. Green, Ms. Blue, and Mr. Purple. It is fun to dress up and enjoy demonstrating colors in delightful and original ways. Wonder what Mr. Purple has in his purple pockets?

Yourself as a color character. Carol Price surprises her kindergartners by dressing from head to toe in whatever color is being celebrated. She becomes, for example, the Red Lady or the Green Lady. "After we've celebrated a lot of different color days, I come in wearing my clothes of many colors with my rainbow wig and introduce myself to the children as the Rainbow Magic Lady!"

Field Trips

Seasonal walks. The colors of the seasons always beckon. On a clear day, walk with your children through autumn leaves, softly falling snow, blankets of spring grass, or budding flowers. Stop. Look. Look again. When you return to the classroom, celebrate with song, art, movement, and story.

Poems like Arnold Adoff's "A Song" enrich the meaning of a color walk.

A Song

I am of the earth   and the earth is of me.
I am all the colors of the corn field,
          and the corn field
     is all the colors of me.
I am all the colors of the plowed-up garden,
          and the plowed-up garden
     is all the colors of me.
I am of the earth   and the earth is of me.
We are together   under the blue sky.
We are together   under the yellow sun.
We are together   under the gray clouds.
We are together.[8]

Sky walks. Each day, the sky offers a show of color changes. Take a walk. Find a comfortable place to stand or sit as you focus on the colors of the sky. Talk and look. When you return to the room, paint sky pictures and make up sky stories, poems, dances, and songs.

One-color walks. Focus on one color. See how many places and in what shapes or things that color exists. Share observations and ideas. Add a touch of fun by giving each child a balloon in the special color to carry on the walk.

Vegetable store, fruit stand, or supermarket. Fruits and vegetables are beautifully shaped and colored. Manufacturers know the importance of packaging their goods in bright, attractive colors. Children enjoy walking through the aisles of stores to see the variety of colors and designs.

Clothing or department store. A wealth of textures, materials, designs, and colors are featured in this kind of store. Look at scarves, shirts, dresses, suits, socks, hats, shoes. What are the most popular colors seen? What color combinations are the children's favorites?

When you return from a field trip such as this one, send thank-you notes to the proprietors and expand upon the experience with classroom activities.

Florist, greenhouse, or conservatory. Pictures and talks about flowers are valuable but do not match the experience of seeing and smelling the amazing array of plants and flowers of every possible color combination.

Designer or interior decorator's studio. Here people work with color charts, carpet samples, and swatches of fabric and wallpaper. Children appreciate the study and arrangement of colors.

Stained-glass windows of churches and synagogues. Many places of worship have beautifully designed and crafted stained-glass windows. Following the field trip, make stained-glass designs to brighten your room.

Art gallery or museum. Children respond with enthusiasm to a walk through a gallery or museum to see how artists colored canvas with people, landscapes, weather, and abstract designs.

Artist's studio or art class. Check your community resources to learn about artists who welcome visits from young children. If there are artists working in glass, your class will be fascinated by the pure, glowing colors of glassworks. A visit to an art class at a high school, college, or recreation center is an opportunity for your young artists to discover new ways that people work with colors.

Throughout this book are excellent ideas for field trips mixed with color. Add color to trips to pet stores, zoos, fire departments, restaurants, factories, houses, farms, libraries, apple orchards, and pumpkin patches. Always remember to look for colors.

NOTES

1. John G. Neihardt, *Black Elk Speaks* (New York: Simon & Shuster, 1972), p. 2.
2. Annie Dillard, *Pilgrim at Tinker Creek* (New York: Bantam, 1975), pp. 28–29, 30–31.
3. "I Wish," *Good Old Poems/I Love Them* (Columbus: Ohio Foundation on the Arts, 1979), p. 49.
4. Rachel Field, "Taxis," *Anthology of Children's Literature*, 3rd ed., ed. by Edna Johnson, Evelyn R. Sickels, and Frances Clarke Sayers (Boston: Houghton Mifflin, 1959), p. 1043.
5. Hettie Jones, ed., *The Trees Stand Shining* (New York: Dial, 1971), np.
6. Jones, np.
7. George W. Cronyn, ed., *American Indian Poetry: An Anthology of Songs and Chants* (New York: Ballantine, 1962), p. 93.
8. Arnold Adoff, "A Song," *All the Colors of the Race*, illustrated by John Steptoe (New York: Lothrop, Lee & Shepard, 1982), p. 44.

SELECTED BIBLIOGRAPHY

Celebrating Colors

Carle, Eric. *Let's Paint a Rainbow*. New York: Putnam, 1982.
Crews, Donald. *Carousel*. New York: Morrow, Greenwillow, 1982.

Duvoisin, Roger. *The House of Four Seasons*. New York: Lothrop, Lee & Sehpard, 1956.
Emberly, Ed. *Green Says Go*. Boston: Little, Brown, 1968.
Freeman, Don. *A Rainbow of My Own*. New York: Viking, 1966.
Freschet, Berniece. *The Web in the Grass*. Illustrated by Roger Duvoisin. New York: Scribners, 1973.
Friskey, Margaret. *What Is the Color of the Wide, Wide World?* Chicago: Childrens Press, 1973.
Grossman, Barney. *Black Means . . .* Illustrated by Charles Bible. New York: Hill & Wang, 1970.
Hirsh, Marilyn. *How the World Got Its Color*. New York: Crown, 1972.
Kalan, Robert. *Rain*. New York: Morrow, Greenwillow, 1978.
Knight, Vick. *The Night the Crayons Talked*. Alhambra, Calif.: Borden, 1974.
Krasilovsy, Phyllis. *First Tulips in Holland*. Illustrated by S. D. Schindler. New York: Doubleday, 1982.
Lionni, Leo. *A Color of His Own*. New York: Random House, 1975.
———. *Frederick*. New York: Pantheon, Pinwheel, 1973.
Lobel, Arnold. *The Great Blueness and Other Predicaments*. New York: Harper & Row, 1968.
Luenn, Nancy. *The Dragon Kite*. Illustrated by Michael Hague. New York: Harcourt Brace Jovanovich, 1982.
O'Nell, Mary. *Hailstones and Halibut Bones: Adventures in Color*. New York: Doubleday, 1961.
Ross, Tony. *Hugo and the Man Who Stole Colors*. Chicago: Follett, 1977.
Seuss, Dr. [Theodor S. Geisel]. *Green Eggs and Ham*. New York: Random House, 1960.
Simin, Heidi. *The Magic of Color*. Illustrated by the author. New York: Lothrop, Lee & Shepard, 1981.
Tidon, Annette, and Taylor Tallus. *The Adventure of Three Colors*. New York: World, 1971.

Identifying and Enjoying Colors

Bond, Jean Carly. *Brown Is a Beautiful Color*. Illustrated by Barbara Zuber. New York: Watts, 1969.
Brown, Margaret Wise. *The Color Kittens*. Illustrated by Alice and Martin Provensen. Racine, Wisc.: Western, Golden Books, 1977.
Charles, Donald. *Calico Cat's Rainbow*. Chicago: Childrens Press, 1975.
Curry, Nancy. *An Apple is Red*. Photos by Harvey Mandlin. Los Angeles: Bowmar/Noble, 1967.
Ginsburg, Mirra. *Three Kittens*. Illustrated by Giulio Maestro. New York: Crown, 1973.
Hawkinson, John. *Paint a Rainbow*. Chicago: Whitman, 1970.
Hoban, Tana. *Is It Red? Is It Yellow? Is It Blue?* New York: Morrow, Greenwillow, 1978.
Ipcar, Dahlov. *Black and White*. New York: Knopf, 1963.
Kellog, Steven. *The Mystery of the Missing Red Mitten*. New York: Dial, 1974.
———. *The Mystery of the Stolen Blue Paint*. New York: Dial, 1982.
Krauss, Ruth. *I Want to Paint My Bathroom Blue*. New York: Harper, 1956.
Moncure, Jane Belk. *Magic Monsters Look for Colors*.

Illustrated by Diane Magnuson. Elgin, Ill.: Childs World, 1979.

Provensen, Alice and Martin. *What Is a Color?* Racine, Wisc.: Western, Golden Books, 1967.

Reiss, John J. *Colors*. New York: Bradbury, 1969.

Scarry, Richard. *Richard Scarry's Color Book*. New York: Random House, 1976.

Steiner, Charlotte. *My Slippers Are Red*. New York: Knopf, 1957.

Tripp, Paul. *The Little Red Flower*. New York: Doubleday, 1968.

Wildsmith, Brian. *Fishes*. New York: Watts, 1968.

———. *Puzzles*. New York: Watts, 1970.

Teacher Resources

Adler, Irving. *Color in Your Life*. New York: Day, 1962.

Arnheim, Rudolph. *Art and Visual Perception*, rev. ed. Berkeley: University of California Press, 1974.

———. *Toward a Psychology of Art*. Berkeley: University of California Press, 1966.

Babbitt, Edwin S. *The Principles of Light and Color*. Secaucus, N.J.: Citadel, 1967.

Birren, Faber. *Color Psychology and Color Therapy*, rev. ed. Secaucus, N.J.: Citadel, 1961.

Forte, Imogene, Mary Ann Pangle, and Robbin Tupa. *Concerning Creative Writing*. Nashville, Tenn.: Incentive Publications, 1974 (chapter on color splash).

Healey, Frederick. *Light and Color*. New York: Day, 1962.

King, Joyce, and Carol Katzman. *Imagine That!* Pacific Palisades, Calif.: Goodyear, 1976 (chapter on color talk).

Paschel, Herbert P. *The First Book of Color*. New York: Watts, 1959.

Sargent, Walter. *The Enjoyment and Use of Color*. New York: Dover, 1964.

Sharpe, Deborah T. *The Psychology of Color and Design*. Totowa, N.J.: Littlefield, Adams, 1979.

Wayman, Joe. *The Colors of My Rainbow*. Carthage, Ill.: Good Apple, 1978.

A lifetime exercise that begins immediately after we are born is to bring order out of chaos, to begin to organize the kaleidoscope of impressions that dazzle our senses. We start collecting information about our new world. We see, touch, smell, hear, and taste. What are the objects of our attention? And how do we comprehend them?

We move from the unfamiliar to the familiar, from vague generalizations to specifics. Slowly, in bits and pieces, our world takes shape. That warm, soft, gentle blob becomes "Mother"; that noisy, furry, bouncy shape is "dog"; that delicious, warm, white liquid is "milk"; and that round, bright sphere is "ball."

As we learn these and thousands of other objects, we discover that they are not interchangeable. We begin to differentiate, compare, and organize. We want to give things names and fit them into our expanding framework. This process of sorting, categorizing, labeling, and filing is part of the thought process.

E. H. Gombrich, in his brilliant book *Art and Illusion* (Princeton University Press, Bollingen Paperback Edition, 1972), offers a fascinating study of the psychology of perception. He compares the progression of learning to the game of "Twenty Questions." An object is explored through a series of categories until, through the process of exclusion and inclusion, we find the correct answer. We ask such questions as: "Is it big? Is it small? Is it alive? Is it dead? Is it an animal? Is it a person?" Once we know and name the object, it is ours.

An important and exciting category for organizing and learning about our world is shapes. If you limit your concept of shapes, your focus will no doubt be dull. As a young teacher reported at a recent workshop: "We do our basic circles, squares, and triangles, usually in the first month of school. We get it over with fast!" When you and your students give time and attention to noticing the many and varied shapes all around you, you will be as fascinated as you were by the study of colors.

When we study the shapes of peoples' features, we can never say that all people of a certain race or color look alike. When we study bird nests, we see the similarities and differences between, for example, a wren's nest and a robin's nest. When we look for

11
WE DISCOVER SHAPES

We made these little gray houses of logs that you see, and they are square. It is a bad way to live, for there can be no power in a square.

You have noticed that everything an Indian does is in a circle, and that is because the Power of the World always works in circles, and everything tries to be round. . . . The wind, in its greatest power, whirls. Birds make their nests in circles, for theirs is the same religion as ours. . . . Our tepees were round like the nests of birds, and these were always set in a circle, the nation's hoop, a nest of many nests, where the Great Spirit meant for us to hatch our children.[1]

circles, we can find at least a hundred of them in no time at all. When we follow a cause, we recognize it by the shape of its symbol—an eagle, a cross, a star, a hammer and sickle, a statue of liberty. When we care about friends and family, we read the shapes of their bodies for clues to their feelings. When we go beyond simple observation and identification, we find meaning in specific shapes and may even attribute special qualities to them, as did Black Elk, holy man of the Oglala Sioux, when he spoke of the power of a circle. With all this in mind, how can we "get it over with fast"?

Good teachers know that learning is a process of integrating new information with what is already known. Susan Hendrickson, who teaches four-year-olds at the First Community Church Early Childhood Program in Columbus, Ohio, always relates and integrates ideas: "Everything reinforces! We talk about shapes in relation to seasons, numbers, letters, clothes—everything."

Shirley Davis, who works with young children at the Jewish Center Child Care Program in West Bloomfield, Michigan, echoes Susan's approach.

We try to include all the concepts we are learning in everything we do so that they are related to each other. Here's an example. We painted a carton and decorated it as a robot. We talked while we worked about its shape; the shapes, colors and numbers of things we were using for decorating; the letters R-O-B-O-T, what else starts with R, and so on. You would be surprised at how many different ideas young children are able to play with at the same time and how excited they are when they can use familiar concepts in new situations.

Shirley and her lucky students also make shapes part of their everyday conversation: "May I have the rectangular box of chalk?" "Let's sit on our carpet squares." "How about playing with that round, red ball?"

While Shirley and Susan are helping their young students recognize and name the basic shapes in their lives, teachers like Moira Logan and Ken Valimaki are fascinated by the concepts of the shapes themselves. Moira Logan, assistant professor of dance education at Ohio State University, works with children of all ages and explores ways of experiencing the implications of shapes through imaginative movement activities.

We have many clever teaching tools that *show* children how to recognize circles. That recognition is intellectual. We also need to learn things with our *minds and bodies*. Through movement, we go beyond seeing and recognizing a circle. What is the movement of a circle? How do we express the kind of movement a circle defines? We build on the children's knowledge of the shape. They are able to respond to the idea of a circle because of their experiences in recognition and identification. Movement helps us perceive more deeply. Circles stimulate different movement responses than squares or rectangles.

Ken Valimaki, a gifted art teacher in the Columbus Public Schools, never relies on a single learning experience to teach a concept as full of rich possibilities as shapes.

I present alternatives. When we talk about, say, circles, we don't look at just one circle but at circles of different sizes and colors. We talk and look at many examples. We compare. We explore the room, the school, the neighborhood. We ask a lot of questions and make observations. We try to see relationships, see how other ideas fit with this new one. We use nature a lot. We're open to discovery. *I want to do things that excite the kids. That's crucial!*

Let's get into shape for this guide! Let's study the shapes of everything we see, notice details, make connections and comparisons, share observations, and express feelings. The activities in this guide will get you started. You'll like the shape of these suggestions!

DISCOVERY TIMES

- We live in a world of shapes.
- Basic shapes include circles, squares, rectangles, ovals, and triangles.
- Circles are round.
- Squares have four equal sides and four corners.
- Rectangles have opposite sides of the same length and four corners.
- Ovals are egg-shaped.
- Triangles have three sides and three corners and are pointy.
- Some shapes are flat, have length and width, and are two-dimensional.
- Some shapes are solid and take up more room in space. They have length, width, and height or depth; they are three-dimensional.
- Objects usually keep their shapes. That is how we identify them.
- Sometimes shapes change, as when a piece of ice melts, a leaf hardens and shrivels, and a bud opens into a flower.

- Some things change shape dramatically, as when tadpoles become frogs and caterpillars turn into butterflies.
- We put similarly shaped things in the same category, such as animals, houses, cars, people, and books.
- Shapes are often associated with special occasions or holidays, such as hearts for Valentine's Day, four-leaf clovers for St. Patrick's Day, wreaths and angels for Christmas, cats and witches for Halloween.
- Bodies have shapes.
- We can usually tell how people feel or think by their posture and facial expressions.
- It is fun to make and rearrange shapes with crayons, paint, clay, and building materials.
- When we use our imaginations, we can see shapes in clouds, stars, stones, and clay.
- Artists train themselves to notice many things about shapes that most people miss because they do not look carefully.

SUGGESTED VOCABULARY

shape	small	animal	touch
form	straight	flower	feel
outline	crooked	person	grow
shadow	zigzag	bird	change
silhouette	dim	fish	freeze
size	hard	toy	slouch
circle	soft	heavy	droop
square	wobbly	light	crumble
triangle	narrow	strong	whirl
rectangle	wide	weak	melt
corners	curly	scary	shrink
space	sharp	funny	paint
angles	pointy	silly	carve
sides	thick	happy	sculpt
oval	thin	sad	build
sphere	open	friendly	compare
things	closed	unfriendly	statue
objects	round	sick	sculptor
posture	curved	healthy	architect
facial	flat	different	artist
expressions	smooth	same	designer
still	rough	clear	choreographer
moving	leaf	look	pattern
big	tree	see	design

As in all the lists of suggested words, different categories emerge. Here are words that describe and qualify shapes, words that enrich vocabulary as well as observations. Each adjective provides another ticket to looking and helps us notice qualities we may have otherwise missed.

Feelings words are included in this list because we respond to shapes emotionally.

We are affected by the contours and patterns of the world around us.

Think of the words as resources for activities, as a starting point for new experiences.

SOME BEGINNING ACTIVITIES

Start with visual stimuli. Ken Valimaki likes to launch a study by exciting children with interesting and varied stimuli. Ordinary items such as doughnuts, bagels, wedding bands, or paper plates immediately start students thinking about circles. Try shoe and cereal boxes and doors and windows to demonstrate squares and rectangles. A hard-boiled egg is an excellent example of an oval shape.

Start with a search-and-find game. The simplest games are the most enjoyable. Wonderful games begin with questions like: "How many circles can you find in the room?" "Let's see if we can find ten square shapes in this room!" and "I see five triangle shapes in our room. Can you find them?"

Start by wearing a shape badge. Children cut out construction paper in the shapes of circles, squares, triangles, or rectangles and pin or tape them to their shirts. The badge reminds the group to focus on a shape and find objects of that shape during the day.

Start with "What if . . . ?" Young children enjoy jokes, riddles, and challenges. "What if wheels were square? What if ladders were round? What if we blew triangular bubbles? What if hens laid square eggs? What if oranges were shaped like bananas? What if we had pointy heads?"

Note: Children's sense of humor changes as they develop. If the children do not respond enthusiastically, either they do not comprehend or they are not quite ready for this kind of play. In addition, each group of children has its own dynamics. Experiment. There are no formulas.

In order for children to understand and enjoy the craziness of "What if wheels were square?" they must understand that wheels are round and that only circles can roll smoothly. As Theodore Roethke observed, "The nuttier the assignment, the better the result!"[2] Enjoy and experiment.

Start with a close-up study of a painting. Such artists as Henri Matisse, Alexander Calder, Paul Klee, and Pablo Picasso painted works characterized by basic shapes.

Browse through art books and catalogues and find this kind of painting for the children to observe and discuss.

Start with a book of hidden pictures. Intriguing books like Tomi Ungerer's *Snail, Where Are You?* (Harper, 1962) help children learn to pay attention to details as they try to find the snail shape in a series of entertaining and challenging scenes and characters.

Start with "bugs on a log" and other shapely snacks. Susan Hendrickson says that "bugs on a log" are excellent snacks for introducing shapes. She and her prekindergartners stuff celery with peanut butter and add raisins. Before they eat this snack, they look at the lines in the celery, the cylindrical shape of the celery, and the wrinkled and oval raisins.

Cookie cutters are of many sizes and shapes. Bake cookies with your children in the shape of circles, squares, stars, and so on. Before the children eat the cookies, ask them to name the shapes.

Start with mail. Think about a letter or greeting card. The envelope is usually square or rectangular, as is the stamp. The postmark is usually round.

Start with marking the floor. With masking tape or chalk, make a large circle, square, and triangle on the floor. The children will be surprised and fascinated the moment they come into the room. See "Movement and Play Times" for activities to fit these shapes.

Start by sitting in a circle and a square. Sit in a circle of children, without leaders, without beginning or end. Then change the circle to a square. How does sitting in a square feel compared with sitting in a circle? Talk about it with the children.

Start by sitting on a circle and a square. Most classes have carpet remnants, sometimes called "sit-upons." Cut sit-upons for each child in the shapes of squares and circles. Now you can play such games as: "Maria, will you pick out a red square sit-upon?" and "Chana, can you find a green circle sit-upon?"

A variation of this idea is to mix and match shapes. Form a circle and sit on circles or squares; form a square and sit on squares or circles.

Start with a silhouette game. Cut dark-colored felt or construction paper in different shapes like a rabbit, a horse, a house, a tree, and a person. Ask the children to identify each one. Go one step further and ask, "How do you know?" You are on your way to talking about the idea of shapes.

Start with fingers. Finger plays are popular activities. Try making circles, squares, and triangles with fingers. Make up poems to accompany finger works.

Here is an excerpt from a finger-play poem improvised by a group of five-year-olds.

First we make a circle.
Then we make two.
Turn them into glasses
And look right through!

Start with shadows. What is more dramatic for young children than their own shadows following or leading them along the ground? Children are intrigued to discover that their shadows imitate their bodies as they change shapes.

For an enjoyable variation, try a shadow-play with a white sheet for a screen and a light behind it, or with a clear section of the wall that is bright with light and catches the silhouette of a shape held in front of it. Children use their hands and bodies or hold up dolls, toys, cars, puppets, or cutouts to tell a story that introduces the idea of shapes.

Start with a Shape Day. For every day of school, you can have a special celebration. The last guide suggested ways to celebrate colors, and many of those suggestions can be easily adapted to shapes.

On shapes days, Shirley Davis and her children label the room by taping construction paper shapes to objects that correspond to the shape of the day. Susan Hendrickson launches a shape day by cutting easel paper in a circle, square, or triangle and placing it on the easel. As soon as the children arrive, they know something is in store for them. All day, art, music, movement, games, snacks, stories, and songs reinforce the concept.

TALK TIMES

Because conversations about shapes can be all-inclusive, they are difficult to end. Conversations about shapes inevitably involve comparisons and contrasts, careful observations, and telling details. Conversations about shapes are also an important means of expressing emotions.

Dawn Heyman and her student teacher, Tracy Skistimas, at McGuffy School in Columbus, Ohio, were amazed at their third graders' spirited responses to the topic of shapes. Here is just a portion of their discussion.

TRACY: What are some of your favorite shapes?

SHAWN: Car bodies. Also, ovals, because ovals make me think of moving spaceships.

TURHAAN: Twinkling stars, because they change shape.

TRACY: Some shapes have the idea of feelings. What do you think are happy shapes? Sad shapes?

JOHN: A happy shape is a running horse.

KENITA: Love is a heart shape, but sadness is a torn heart shape.

FRANKIE: This is the saddest shape. (He drew a paddle for spanking.)

JEFF: A mountain struck by lightning—that's the saddest shape.

TRACY: A sad shape is a teardrop.

SAUNJIA: A sad shape is a dying, drooping flower.

JOHN: A sad shape? A circle cut in half and turned upside down—that's a sad shape.

SHAWN: A shaking wire is a nervous shape.

DOUG: A nervous shape is a red square pierced by a black triangle.

DAVID: A tire is a happy shape.

DOUG: You know what a proud shape is? Many gold and yellow circles.

CARMEN: A sad and scary shape is a rundown picket fence. The shape of a person's mind is wisdom.

Note how easily children expand their thinking when they are familiar with basic information. Doug's image of a red square pierced by a black triangle as a "nervous shape" shows the development of imagination and symbolism that proceeds from an understanding of the concepts.

When the children's activities are based on their own feelings and suggestions freely expressed during "Talk Times," the experiences become more meaningful and relevant. Imagine, for example, a class collage featuring twinkling star, running horse, mountain struck by lightning, teardrop, drooping flower, and gold and yellow circles. A stimulating exercise for the children is to paint a picture of the shape of a person's mind. "How can we show wisdom?"

Patti Link's five-year-olds at First Community Church Early Childhood School in Columbus, Ohio, are as fascinated by shapes as the older third graders. Enjoy this excerpt from their talk session:

LAURA: Books are rectangles, but there are some round books, too.

ERIC: If you had a round book for colors, it would be a rainbow.

PATTI: Does everything have a shape?

BEN: No, air doesn't.

ERIC: Hair doesn't.

PATTI: What shape is hair?

CHILDREN: Lines . . . lines are shapes.

BEN: Soap doesn't have a shape.

CHILDREN: Yes, it does!

BEN: No, liquid soap doesn't have a shape!

PATTI: Faces have different shapes. Look around.

CHILDREN: Ovals, triangles, squares.

PATTI: What's a sad shape?

BILL: An upside-down smile.

ERIC: An upside-down rainbow.

LAURA: A banana shape. An arc.

STEVE: A flat tire is a sad shape.

JILL: A shoelace is a happy shape.

ERIC: So is a clown.

LAURA: My finger is a rectangle with a little circle (nail) at the end of it.

The younger children are still working with the technical aspects of shapes. They are very specific and insist on using basic terminology, as demonstrated by Laura, described the shape of a banana as an arc. Here again, we see that children enjoy going beyond simple observations to more imaginative levels. All they need is a little encouragement.

A wonderful way to develop excellent listening habits is to suggest to the children as you begin a "Talk Time" that something special is going to happen at the end of the discussion, so they need to pay careful attention. Try playing a guessing game by asking such questions as: "Who said a tire is a happy shape?" "David!" "Who said a teardrop is a sad shape?" "Tracy!" Or you can ask the children to draw a picture of a shape they remember talking about. When the pictures are finished and shared, encourage the children to remember who suggested them.

Ken Valimaki and his students spice every art session with talk about the shapes of traffic signs; natural objects such as rocks, leaves, trees, and mountains; houses; animals; and machines. They explore aspects of the shapes before they begin to draw, paint, or sculpt.

In Shirley Davis's room, the children talk before they start an activity; they talk quietly as they work; and they gather together afterward to talk about what they did.

"How can you learn without talking?" Shirley asks in disbelief when we wonder how young children can be taught in silence.

Shape up for good conversations filled with questions, answers, observations, experiences, and wisdom.

ART TIMES

Shapes, like colors, is a constant theme. Children learn through repetition and reinforcement. You can never have enough books, stories, and activities about shapes. Children celebrate the familiar and feel good when they can use new knowledge. Their experiences are cumulative.

While there is a great variety of excellent commercial materials that help children learn about shapes, there are also many resources at hand that are equally successful in accomplishing this goal. The following ideas are just a fraction of what is possible. Read them to trigger your own variations and rearrangements.

Big shapes, little shapes. Ken Valimaki shares one of his most popular activities: "I like to start kids off thinking about shapes with big shapes and little shapes. We talk, demonstrate, look around the room, and look at books to gather ideas. Then we go to our easels and paint or color big and little shapes. We put them in rows, overlap them, put them in circles, combine them with special colors, and make collages."

Tear a shape. This activity is popular with Ken's young students, who need lots of opportunities to cut, tear, paste, and make patterns. Ken and his students work with great satisfaction in creating irregular, rough-edged shapes; tearing frees them from the more concise expectations of cutting. They talk about what they see in their shapes. Walking and talking, they find irregular shapes in nature. They gather twigs, leaves, wood clumps, and stones and bring them back to the classroom to study and compare with their own torn shapes.

Tree full of shapes. Shirley Davis and her three- and four-year-olds grow shapes instead of leaves on their construction paper or real tree. Shirley often designates different shapes for different branches and asks the children to fill the tree with a branch of circles, of squares, and of triangles, usually correlated with special colors and numbers so the lesson is multifaceted. For example, Shirley suggests: "Let's put five green circles on this branch."

Books for squares, circles, and other shapes. As part of your focus on a shape, cut paper in that shape. Staple pages together so that each child has a book of circles, squares, or other shapes. Now the children are ready to fill their circle books, for example, with circle pictures, designs, poems, and stories.

Going-around-in-circles mobiles. Children color and decorate different-sized circles and attach them on strings to a simple wood or hanger mobile. When the room is dotted with circles, enjoy talking about how that design makes everyone feel.

Do not limit your mobiles to circles. After you have studied all the shapes, fill the room with combinations of interesting mobiles.

Weather shapes. With your class, design special shapes for particular weather conditions, such as rain, fog, sun, snow, wind, and storm. Be sure to make them on heavy construction paper; laminate them if possible. Use them every day as "weather helpers" to show and tell the weather report.

Funny people shapes. Another of Shirley Davis's most popular activities is to have the children cut pictures of people from magazines and put heads on one paper plate, arms on another, and legs on yet another. The children use body trunks of construction paper and glue on different heads, arms, and legs to make funny-looking people. Shirley's classes also enjoy arranging circles, triangles, squares, and rectangles to make people.

What you can make from shapes. Cut out an ample supply of basic shapes from brightly colored paper. Encourage the children to discover what surprises lie in store as they make patterns and experiment with the shapes. When they find combinations they like, they glue or paste the shapes to their papers.

This is a marvelous way for children to find out (without the aid of ditto sheets or workbooks) that a circle and a triangle make an ice-cream cone, a clown with a party hat, a bird's head, and a little sailboat; a square or rectangle and a triangle make a house, a building, a rocket ship, and a pencil; a face with eyes, nose, and mouth can be easily composed of circles and triangles; and trains, trucks, and cars are fun to make from circles and squares or rectangles.

Ovals and self-portraits. Talk is an important part of understanding. Talk about what makes up a face and its expressions. Start with ovals and ask the children to add features to make self-portraits. Mirrors are helpful in this activity.

Ken Valimaki adds an idea to this activity. Before the children use mirrors in creating self-portraits, he asks them to draw themselves as they think they look. The children make stimulating observations about the two self-portraits.

Still life of different shapes. Young children practice the art of careful looking as they study a group of different shapes and try to represent their special qualities. Encourage the children to experiment with thick, thin, dark, and light lines as they work. Some children especially like to work with large crayons. Susan Hendrickson offers her students an array of materials: "Some kids like Magic Markers. Others prefer crayons or paints. Still others like to build the idea with blocks. Then there are the kids who favor using felt and other textures."

Clay shapes. What better way to learn about shapes than sculpting clay? Watch spheres, cylinders, boxes, and bottles emerge before your eyes.

For variety, spray shaving cream on the children's work spaces and encourage them to shape the cream.

Robots. Space-age children need no prodding to see how shapes combine to form fabulous robots. Give the children an assortment of shapes to use on their own papers, or spread a large piece of paper (for a mural) on the floor and encourage the children to fill it with robots. To the basic shapes of rectangles and squares, add circles and triangles for knobs and eyes.

After the children name their robots, suggest that they make up stories about them. Attach the stories to the mural or to their individual pictures.

Scrounge shapes for collages, montages, and sculptures. Scrounge buttons of all sizes and colors; Popsicle sticks; twigs; magazine pictures; parts of toy cars, trucks, and planes; greeting cards; playing cards; bubble wrap; styrofoam; confetti; pieces of jewelry; pie tins; paper cups; spools;

and baby food jars. Encourage the children to experiment with these materials and see what new patterns they create.

Make something stand. Ken Valimaki introduces young students to three-dimensional shapes by handing out construction paper and paste or glue and instructing them to "Try to find a way to make the paper stand by itself." The children twist, fold, roll, tear, and pinch their papers until—presto—they have standing forms. Their paper sculptures can be looked at from every side, and they learn the difference between two- and three-dimensional shapes.

Shapes and feelings. Children have no trouble relating feelings to shapes and, going a step further, creating images that give shape to feelings. With whatever materials they choose, children respond enthusiastically to the suggestion that they paint, color, draw, or sculpt a happy shape, a sad shape, an angry shape, a silly shape, a shy shape, a proud shape, a friendly shape, a strange shape, and a new shape. As often as possible, ask the children to tell you something about the shapes they create.

One kindergartner showed me a flattened-out strip of clay and explained, "When I'm sad, I just lie down and wait till it's over. That's the lying-down part of sad."

Shapes for the Seven Dwarfs. Snow White's friends, the Seven Dwarfs, correlate marvelously with feelings and shapes. Talk about the dwarfs, their names, and their special qualities. Enrich the discussion with movement activities (see movement section). The children may choose to celebrate one dwarf with a special design, picture, or shape, or they may choose several, even all seven.

Divide the walls into seven sections, one for each dwarf's pictures, and label the sections. Turn the shapes into badges that the children can wear to express their feelings. Write stories and songs about the dwarfs.

This activity provides an excellent opportunity to discuss shapes and facial expressions and how one little change of a line or curve can turn a happy face into a grumpy face. One group of children created all seven dwarfs using only circles, squares, rectangles, ovals, and triangles.

Favorite shapes. After you and your class

have studied and talked about shapes for a while, it is time to select the shapes that are most pleasing.

Gather ideas, write or diagram them on the board, and ask the children to choose a favorite shape. Now they are ready to concentrate on how to celebrate their favorite shapes in patterns.

Some children fill a sheet of construction or drawing paper with their shape in different sizes and colors; other children experiment with their shapes overlapping or exploding from a central point. One child chose birds as her favorite shape and used Magic Marker to draw a flock of migrating birds. Ariela designed a pattern of hearts, beginning in one corner of the paper with a tiny red heart and ending in the opposite corner with a large red heart.

This activity can be an effective way for children to learn about perspective. They look at their papers and see that some of the shapes appear far away, while others seem near. Discuss their discoveries.

Collectible shapes. With your students, scrounge large cardboard boxes from your local supermarket and designate a different shape to be collected for each box. One group of first graders lined seven boxes along the wall, each labeled and decorated. The children, over a period of weeks, collected boxes of circles, squares, triangles, rectangles, leaves, animal shapes, and people shapes. The boxes were filled with such items as magazine pictures, cutouts, coloring book pages, bits and pieces of games and toys, snaps and knobs and buttons, plastic tops of cans, geometric patterns, and paper dolls.

This assignment had the children on their toes in seven ways for weeks, because they were on the alert for samples of the seven types of objects they had decided to gather. As they played with the contents, they marveled at how their boxes filled.

As a follow-up activity, the children were asked to choose one or more of the items gathered and make an arrangement or sculpture. Interestingly, a few children chose only one or two kinds of shapes and worked intently. Only two or three children chose to work with all seven ideas. Their works had titles such as "Jason's Study of Triangles," "Leaves and Squirrels," and "Cheryl's Study of People, Circles, Leaves,

and Cats." The exhibit of all the art was enthusiastically received by the children, other classes, and parents.

Turn yourself into a shape. The children design shapes that represent them. Record their shapes on a chart next to their names. After a while, the children learn their classmates' shapes. Play such games as: "When I draw your shape on the board, please stand," or "Guess whose shape I'm coloring." Use their shape symbols as often as possible for helper assignments, game positions, activities designations, buddies, and play groups.

Your name is a shape. Probably the first word children learn to recognize and spell is their own name. Print or have the children print their names in their favorite colors on a sheet of paper. Encourage them to make a design or shape out of their names by outlining the letters, coloring them, and creating patterns around them. Use these pictures alone or combined with the children's photographs, symbols (see above), or self-portraits.

Dinosaur shapes. Annelyn Baron and Lori Salczer had a lively discussion about "interesting shapes" with their prekindergartners at the Jewish Center in Columbus, Ohio. Many shapes were mentioned, but the one that took the day was dinosaurs. This led to a full week of activities about dinosaurs.

The children studied the names and shapes of the different dinosaurs. They noted the triangular bony plates along the back of Stegosaurus and the long curvy neck and tail of Brontosaurus. In a short time they could recognize and name each dinosaur by shape alone.

Lori and Annelyn drew the different shapes on manila paper. To create "prehistoric" textures on the animals, the children colored coarse salt with food dye and sprinkled it on the glued surfaces of the shapes. Details were drawn with Magic Markers. The name of each dinosaur and a sentence about it was printed below the picture.

Another popular event of the week was the creation of "Little Dinosaur Village" in a large cardboard box with sawdust on the bottom. The children made and scrounged trees, plants, rocks, and toy dinosaurs and spent a lot of time arranging and rearranging their village. Lori and Annelyn found an excellent record, "Our Dinosaur Friends" (American Teaching Aids Inc., P.O. Box 1652, Corrina, California 91722), that not only taught the children about dinosaurs but also provided delightful music to move and play to.

Picture books and shapes. There are so many outstanding picture books that contain interesting shapes. Only a few are discussed here.

Maurice Sendak's *Where the Wild Things Are* (Harper & Row, 1963; Scholastic Book Services, 1974) is one of young children's most beloved books. The hero Max is a study of shapes, with triangles for ears and crown, circles for buttons, and semicircles—right side up and upside down—for mouths. The shapes of the monsters are even more fascinating.

After the children read or hear about the variety of monster shapes, they wel-

come the opportunity to create their own monsters. Correlate this art activity with original stories and movement.

Swimmy by Leo Lionni (Pantheon, 1963; Pinwheel edition, 1973) celebrates the shapes of fish and other sea creatures in a most brilliant style. Children like the patterns and designs that Swimmy and his friends make. The dramatic climax is an unusual study in shapes that causes readers of all ages to pay special attention. *Swimmy* makes children want to swim over to paints, crayons, and Magic Markers to create their own shapes for ocean creatures.

Sesame Street's Random House Pictureback (Children's Television Workshop, 1974) *Grover and the Everything in the Whole Wide World Museum* is a wild and wacky story that tries to divide everything in the whole world into categories such as tall things, small things, underwater things, very light things, and very heavy things. The story inspires children to create their own categories of things to express in pictures and stories.

There is probably a wide choice of excellent books in your room this very minute that lend themselves to activities celebrating shapes. Some of Ken Valimaki's favorites are: "Dr. Seuss stories for their unusual and distinguished illustrations and Bill Peet's books, *Wing Ding Dilly* and *Wump World*. Mercer Mayer's books are also excellent for stimulating awareness of shapes. Actually, we surround the children with so many wonderful books that they *must* get the message!"

The shape of things we see. Ask the children to look around the room for shapes that catch their attention. Focus on them. Draw, paint, and sculpt them.

On a clear day, go for a walk outside. Take paper and crayons, markers, and pencils. Find a scene filled with interesting contours, buildings, trees, and sky. Pay close attention to the details as you talk about what you see and catch the shapes, lines, and colors on paper.

This activity provides a good opportunity to notice the shapes of mountains, hills, bridges, factories, rivers, clouds, sun, trees—whatever is special about your territory. These pictures are excellent pen-pal gifts.

Enrich this activity with creative writing about the experience.

Kyia, age 6

Animal shapes. Young children have a strong love for animals. Encourage the children to notice the roundness of turtles, the long, curvy lines of snakes, the ovals and circles of rabbits. "An alligator is like a triangle," five-year-old Caryn observed.

Encourage the children to draw, sculpt, and paint animals using their new knowledge about shapes.

Food and shapes. In her most interesting book, *The Seeing Eye* (Macmillan, 1960), Freda Lingstrom hopes to help readers train their eyes so that they think about everything they see. She hopes that everything will take on a new and enchanting meaning (p. 8). The art activities in this book are based on the same philosophy.

Nowhere is this ability to see the extraordinary in ordinary everyday objects as dramatic as when we look at food. Fruits and vegetables come in wonderfully diverse shapes. They are popular subjects of still lifes by the world's greatest artists. Children appreciate not only the wonderful colors of fresh produce but also their beautiful shapes as they study apples, oranges, pears, grapes, cherries, bananas, carrots, squash, peppers, and other fruits and vegetables.

But do not limit yourself to observing the outside. Look inside! Susan Hendrickson's young students enjoy such experiences as coring apples and cutting them into six equal segments. The segments are like arcs; the center is like a circle. When Susan cuts apples horizontally, the children discover the star-shaped formation of the seeds.

Trying to end this section of the guide is like reading Sesame Street's *Grover and the Everything in the Whole Wide World Museum.* Activities left unmentioned include shapes on charm bracelets, belts, necklaces, and T-shirts; clotheslines of shapes; puppet shapes (Ms. Circle, Andrew Square, Priscilla Triangle); shape-up salad, circle sandwiches, and melon balls; shapes for seasons and holidays; shapes of constellations (connect the dots); hand shapes, sign language, and gestures; and geometric shapes of American Indian designs. Every guide is packed with shape-related art activities. So skim through the book with pencils ready.

I warn you, you will not have room in your notebook for all the possibilities waiting right before your round or oval eyes and under your triangular nose. Freely combine art with other areas of learning.

MUSIC TIMES

Shapes of musical instruments. Susan Hendrickson describes one of her most enjoyable ways to combine musical instruments and shapes. "When I teach the children about Indians, I get out the drum and announce that I'm the Chief. I beat the children's names rhythmically and call them to form a circle. We talk about the drum having a circle shape and about our circle of friends around the drum."

Each instrument has a shape and design that children find fascinating to study. They learn to recognize and name instruments by their shapes. When your students listen to different kinds of music, show them the instruments, or pictures of the instruments, that are making the music.

Begin this year-long activity with instruments the children already know from home and school. Move from the familiar to the new.

Follow the shape of the instrument. One way to conduct your rhythm band is to show a picture or drawing of the instrument to be played. Some teachers make a chart showing all the instruments, and the leader points to the desired instrument.

The shape of music. Just as the children enjoy translating the music they hear into colors, so they relish the challenge of listening to different kinds of music and imagining the shapes they hear. Give the children the opportunity to use the art materials they prefer as they listen to a variety of short musical selections and fill their papers with shapes.

A first grader explained the dark triangles on his jazzy paper: "That music kept popping up like rockets, with pointy notes." A kindergartner clarified his picture of circles tumbling across the paper as his response to a cowboy song: "The music is full of wheels rolling along." And a second grader drew lively stick figures to music by the Ohio State University Marching Band. "This music makes you do gymnastics," she explained.

Parade of musical shapes. After the children have studied the shapes of musical instruments, organize a parade according to families of shapes. Instruments that are circular and spherical cluster together. Here come the tambourines, bells, drums, and maracas! Next are rectangular and cylindrical instruments such as flutes, horns, and pipes. Don't forget the triangles!

You may want to organize the parade of musical instruments into categories like big instruments (guitars and banjos) and small instruments (bells, triangles, or whistles). Another idea is to ask the drum majors or cheerleaders to hold up pictures of each instrument in the parade followed by the children playing those instruments.

Compose cheers and rhythms for each instrument or group of instruments.

The shape of musical notes. You need not be so technical about musical notes that young children lose interest, which is often the case. Children have no trouble learning that music has its own language and that the language helps us to sing and play songs. The shape of the language is very interesting and easily recognizable.

The staff has five parallel lines; the treble clef "is all swirly," as five-year-old Jackie observed; and the bass clef looks like "a question mark with two little dots," Monica told her first grade friends. "To me, it looks like a fish's face. See his eye. And the two dots are two little bubbles!" Andrew added. "The notes are little ovals with thin lines connected to them," Jeffrey showed his kindergarten colleagues. "When the notes go up the lines in the staff, you sing higher and higher," Scott explained. "Like climbing a ladder. The notes tell you that. You have to watch them," Kira piped in.

As you can see from these fragments of children's discussions about the language and shape of music, imagination, sharing ideas, and enjoying discovery are more important than a short-answer quiz in notation.

Try turning musical notes into happy faces when simple, happy songs are sung, such as "Good Morning to You" and "Pop Goes the Weasel." A few curves and lines give musical notes sleepy faces when lullabies are sung. This activity also provides the opportunity to review the power of shapes in conveying facial expressions and feelings.

Animal sounds and shapes. Children are knowledgeable about animal shapes. Even city children, whose firsthand experiences with animals may be limited to squirrels, pigeons, dogs, and cats, can recognize and name many different animals by looking at their pictures or outlines.

Every animal has its own sound. Give children the chance to identify an animal from a picture or an outline, then demonstrate its sound. This idea can flow in many directions. Here are just a few suggestions.

Divide the children into animal groups. When their animal's shape is held up, they make that animal's sounds. Give the group time to practice the sounds so they can work them into patterns and rhythms.

What happens when two different pictures are held up at the same time? Which two animals make the "best music" together? Listen to all the combinations and decide which sound the best. Use the animal pictures to set the sequences and arrangements.

Encourage the children to use their imaginations to create sounds for such animals as fish, caterpillars, butterflies, ants, ladybugs, giraffes, and lizards.

Move from verbal and body sounds to musical instruments. "What instruments and rhythms shall we use to produce bird songs? What instruments shall we choose to make the croaking song of frogs?" Develop a symphony of animal shapes and sounds. Correlate this activity with movement and drama.

"What is the shape of a cat's meow?" Michael Rosen likes to challenge his young students. After looking at animal shapes, identifying them, and listening to and talking about their sounds. Michael asks the children to draw, paint, and color the "shape of their sounds." The results are remarkable. Be sure to label pictures with the children's own titles. Four-and-a-half-year-old Jennifer proudly showed her paper covered with tiny, colorful dots. The title of her picture was "A Baby Bird Cheeping."

Music for basic shapes. In Rhoda Linder and Wendy Wohlstein's class of three-and-a-half-year-olds at the Jewish Center Early Childhood Program in Columbus, Ohio, a day was devoted to celebrating squares. Wendy decorated herself in colorful squares pinned and taped to her clothing. She wrote a sing-song poem that she sang to and later taught the children.

I'm Sarah Square
And I don't care
If the shapes on my skin
Tickle my chin, pinch my nose
Or scratch my cheek.
No—I don't care—this is Shapes Week.

I've got green ones, orange ones, red ones and blue.
I know what the shape is today, do *you*?
It's not a rectangle, no, not at all.
Not a circle, not shaped like a ball.
Not a triangle, in case you care,
The shape of my body is a
  SQUARE!

When Susan Hendrickson and her students dedicated a day to round shapes, Susan composed a poem-song for the celebration:

Round is a doughnut,
A penny, a hug.
Round is a cookie,
A kiss and a bug.
Round is whatever you feel outside
When your inside smiles up
And sings to the sky.

A group of kindergartners who spent the day celebrating squares talked about the kind of music that fits the shape of squares. After experimenting with different kinds of music, the children chose marching music. Why? "Because we march in straight lines and turn sharp corners!" "And we're real even, like squares are even all around."

In trying to decide what kind of music reflects the special qualities of circles, a class of first graders listened to about five offerings and voted for "The Children's March" from Rogers and Hammerstein's *The King and I.* They did so "Because it sounds like somersaults and somersaults are circles rolling."

On Triangles Day a group of four-and-a-half-year-olds thought the 1–2–3 Latin-American rhythm of a conga fit the three angles and three lines of a triangle. If you were a triangle, wouldn't you want to listen to and do the conga? No question about it!

Shape up your rhythm band. Why should your young musicians sit or march randomly when they can form a circle, square, triangle, or rectangle and play their music? "Ladies and gentlemen, we present a square of fine musicians!"

If the group decides to become a marching band, a circle of musicians will march in a circle, a square of musicians will march in a square, and so on.

Combine this activity with the children's interpretation of special music for their special formation. Have fun exploring this challenge.

Shape up your conducting. Orchestras and music makers need conductors. When conductors' minds are filled with basic shapes, they are able to use those shapes as they conduct.

Give the children chances to take turns conducting records and live classroom music. Encourage them to lead with the body language of shapes. Their skillful hands and arms draw imaginary shapes in the air as they direct the music. Take a turn yourself.

Next time you watch great conductors at work, notice how many circles, squares, triangles, and spirals they draw in the air with their hands.

Travel the world through shape and sound. Brilliantly colored travel posters can motivate you to begin saving for a vacation. Just looking at a poster of the blue ocean and white sand beaches of Jamaica conjures up the smell of coconut suntan oil, the taste of cool lime drinks, and the captivating sounds of calypso music.

Young children enjoy combining shapes and sounds. They quickly learn to look at travel posters (scrounged or homemade) and associate a large, flowing sombrero with Mexican music; a lovely flower lei with Hawaiian ukeleles; a bucking bronco with Western cowboy songs; a lush, African jungle with African drums and the lullaby "Kum Ba Yah"; snow-topped Alps with yodeling; a Scot in plaid kilt with bagpipe music; and an Indian Chief in feather headdress with tom-toms and Indian chants.

Blend travel posters with music. Children need every opportunity to learn to love the music of the people of the world.

Shapes and songs. As often as possible, inspire the learning and singing of a favorite song with an appropriate shape. Check resources at your fingertips, such as books, magazines, and record covers, to help children make connections. Create your own images out of felt or construction paper.

Inventive teachers across the country find railroad trains to roll along with railroad songs, rivers to flow with songs about rivers, sun to warm the vocal cords for songs about sunshine, ships to sail along with songs about ships, and rabbits to hop along with songs about rabbits.

Skinny songs, fat songs. A group of first graders talked about the thin and thick qualities of lines and shapes. About a half hour after the discussion, the children had a singing session. They took turns singing lines alone, and the whole class joined in for the chorus. One of the girls observed that "When one person sings, it's a skinny sound; and when everyone sings, it's fat!" Children teach us to apply new knowledge and make unexpected and often captivating connections.

MOVEMENT AND PLAY TIMES

Shirley Davis's students are constantly reminded about shapes. Labels like "rectangular shelves" and "circular tables" are taped to their corresponding objects. At snack times, napkins are folded into square, triangular, and rectangular shapes. The children talk about round plates and records, square record covers, rectangular books, round doorknobs, and square windows. Awareness is in the air in Shirley's rectangular classroom!

Singing games change shapes. Familiar children's games take on special meaning when they become part of a focus on shapes. In "Ring Around the Rosy," children sing two words, "ring" and "around," that reinforce their understanding of circles. Shirley Davis turns "Punchinella" into a shapes game by having the circle of children sing to the child in the middle:

What shape can you make, Punchinella, little fella?
What shape can you make, Punchinella, little dear?
We'll make your shape, Punchinella, little fella.
We'll make your shape, Punchinella, little dear.

When the children circle around for "Have You Ever Seen a Lassie," encourage the child in the center to make interesting body shapes "this way and that way." Good old "Old MacDonald" has a farm of shapes. Pin or tape shape badges to the children; combine with colors. Now Old MacDonald boasts:

On his farm he had some circles . . .
On his farm he had some blue squares . . .
On his farm he had some triangles . . .

"Let's give those kids a round of applause!" Spark your demonstrations of appreciation (which I hope are frequent) by clapping for yourselves. It's good for circulation and celebration. Instead of the usual hand clapping, try clapping in a circle shape—a round of applause. Clap in a square pattern: "Let's give ourselves a square of applause!" Clap in a triangular pattern: "Let's give these kids a triangle of applause!" In all of our classes, this has become a way of rejoicing with each other.

Show-me games. These games are modified by innovative teachers to fit whatever theme they are highlighting. "Douglas, show me something in the room that's square." "I'm thinking about something in the room that's a red circle. Can you point to it, Danny?" "I see three green squares of different sizes. Can you find them, Jeanie?"

The children enjoy being the "instructor" in this kind of game and directing challenges to their classmates. Nothing is more satisfying to young children than to be able to relate different areas of learning as they demonstrate their cumulative knowledge by identifying objects by number, color, and shape!

Floor shapes. So many discoveries about shapes are made through mind and body working together. Here are some of the challenges given to young children as they looked at the floor clearly marked with a large circle, square, and triangle. "Can you find a shape that has no straight lines and step inside it?" "See if you can find a shape that has corners and walk around it."

One of the children began walking around the circle shape. A few of his classmates shouted corrections to him. One of them explained, "There are no corners in a circle!"

"Find a shape with three sides, hop around it, and call its name!" "Find a shape with four corners, shout its name, and march along its sides."

After the children have had lots of time to experiment with the floor shapes, expand their new understanding to art, poems, stories, and songs.

Going around in circles. This activity involves a series of developmental activities.

Can you make a circle with your fingers? With your hands? Show me!

Are there circle shapes on your bodies?

Are you wearing circles on your clothes?

Look around the room. Where do you see circles?

Can you shape circles in the air with your arms and hands—above you, below you, around you?

What kind of body shapes and movements tell something about circles?

Let's draw circles on the floor with our feet. Circles in the air with our elbows, our heads, our hips.

After this exercise with circles, the children are ready to expand their thinking. "What are some bigger things you see or can do that remind you of circles?" Children have enthusiastically suggested ferris wheels, three-ring circuses, juggling balls, pizza pies, and carousels.

My memories of these experiences are bright, but one incident stands out. With a group of preschoolers (four-and-a-half-year-olds), we concluded our study of circles by enacting a merry-go-round. The children were horses, poles, riders, and ticket-takers. They placed themselves inside a large imaginary circle designated as the merry-go-round. Everyone had a part in the merry-go-round (self-determined, of course), everyone except Normie, who simply watched.

My always-ready, bouncy music was waiting on the phonograph.

"Gosh, we need someone to turn on the merry-go-round," I said. "Normie, will you start us off?" Normie just looked up, open-mouthed, hardly moving. "Thanks!" I gushed and turned on the music.

The horses bobbed up and down, the poles stood straight and still, the riders swayed up and down and back and forth, and the whole group slowly moved within the circle. Normie was ecstatic! Did he *really* turn on a merry-go-round? Another example of Edwin Markham's poem came to life:

He drew a circle that shut me out
Heretic, rebel, a thing to flout.
But Love and I had the wit to win
We drew a circle that took him in.[3]

The pictures, sculptures, songs, stories, and poems that flow from these movement experiences are characterized by unusually rich images and feelings.

Bounce a ball, throw a snowball. The idea of circles and spheres becomes clearer when you bounce, throw, and catch balls. On snowy days, make snowballs, igloos, and snow people. Remember to make square forts and snow triangles as well. When the shapes melt, you can talk about why and how shapes change.

Mystery box of shapes to show and guess. Kay Callander, elementary and drama teacher at Shady Lane School in Columbus, Ohio, likes to fill a large sack or box (a mystery box) with clearly defined pictures of objects or the objects themselves. The children take turns reaching into the "mystery box," looking at the picture or object, and demonstrating it through pantomime and improvised body movement for their classmates to guess.

A variation of this activity is to fill the "mystery box" with objects only, and ask the children to take turns identifying them by touch alone.

Body shapes. There are so many excellent ways for children to develop understanding and appreciation of shapes through body movement. Only a few ideas are presented here.

Challenge shapes. Moira Logan asks her young students to respond with their bodies to "movement questions" such as the following:

Let's change our bodies into tired, silly, strong, weak, straight, crooked, lumpy, heavy, light, smooth, and curvy shapes. (One at a time, of course.)

Let's make shapes with our bodies that have windows, spaces, or holes.

Let's close our shapes . . . open them.

Let's make zigzag shapes, round shapes, angular shapes.

Moira reminds the children that they are in one shape or another all the time.

Change shapes, hold shapes. Children really feel their powers with this exercise. Ask them to hold their shapes—freeze! Give them a drumbeat, tambourine shake, or hand clap to change their bodies to another shape.

Hold! Freeze! Change again . . .

Grow shapes. Begin with low-to-the-ground, closed-up bodies. Slowly expand and develop body shapes, one at a time. When the children have grown to their tal-

lest, widest, and strongest, ask them to hold that shape for ten counts. Then shake out or do the following movement.

Shrink shapes. Slowly, almost imperceptibly, the children begin to shrink their body shapes. The exercise ends with bodies as small and formless as when they began the growing process described above. Charge imaginations by talking together about things that grow and shrink.

Group shapes. Groups of children combine body shapes to form a circle, square, triangle, and rectangle; a sad shape, happy shape, flat shape, zigzag shape, wide shape, and narrow shape; an animal shape, a machine shape, and a shape from nature; and a closed shape, an open shape, a moving shape, and a still shape.

Body shapes for stories, songs, and poems. Discover how easily children learn shapes through movement interpretations of their favorite stories and songs.

Stories. The Seven Dwarfs have distinct shapes and movement patterns determined by their names. Encourage the children to

develop special walks, dances, and games for each dwarf.

The Tin Man, Scarecrow, Cowardly Lion, Dorothy, Toto, Munchkins, Flying Monkeys, Good and Bad Witches, and Wizard inspire children to explore body shapes that express the qualities of these characters from *The Wizard of Oz.* Children also learn important aspects of shape, such as loose, tight, crooked, and straight.

A. A. Milne's beloved characters are recognized by their shapes and personalities. Kanga, Tigger, Eeyore, Rabbit, Owl, Winnie the Pooh, Christopher Robin, and Baby Roo stimulate imaginative demonstrations introducing characters by their shapes and movements.

The Gingerbread Boy features not only the Gingerbread Boy and the Old Man and Old Woman, but all the animals and people who chase the Gingerbread Boy. Children and teachers also enjoy improvising the story.

Nursery rhymes like "Humpty Dumpty" provide rich material for children to interpret. Humpty Dumpty is a stout, oval-shaped character; how do bodies feel demonstrating that kind of shape? Humpty Dumpty falls off the wall; falling down is usually the children's favorite part. Here come the king's horses and men, clippity-clop. Bodies change to this shape and movement. Oh, no. They can't put Humpty together again! Some children keep their broken shapes, while others try to fix Humpty's splattered form.

Picture books like *Try Squiggles and Squirms and Wiggly Worms* (by Imogene Forte and Joy MacKenzie, Incentive Publications, 1978) feature ideas for changing shapes. From animals to airplanes, from machines to trees, from body poems to movement words like "spread," "stoop," "bend," and "sway," children are encouraged to create body shapes that demonstrate their comprehension of concepts.

A poetic, sensitive book, *Sometimes I Dance Mountains* (by Byrd Baylor, Scribners, 1973) contains images, such as rain, wind, thunder, and mountains, that help children express feelings and moods through body shapes.

Songs. Just about every song can be moved to. Pretend (in some cases you will not have to pretend) that there are children in your class who do not speak English. Use movement translations as often as possible. This is not only fun but also valuable in helping children communicate the meaning of words.

Some songs that evoke original movement responses are "The Bear Went over the Mountain," "Take Me Out to the Ball Game," "Down in the Valley," and "On Top of Old Smoky." After a while, you will find it impossible to sing without thinking of body movements.

Poems. Many poems are about shapes, but all poems can be shaped up for extra enjoyment and appreciation. Shel Silverstein's poem is an example of a poem about shapes.

Shapes

A square was sitting quietly
Outside his rectangular shack
When a triangle came down—kerplunk!—
And struck him in the back.
"I must go to the hospital,"
Cried the wounded square,
So a passing rolling circle
Picked him up and took him there.[4]

Children can enrich this poem with "tell and show," puppets, and improvised music, song, dance, and games.

A. A. Milne's "The Four Friends" presents four animals of different sizes and personalities. Children listen to the words and decide which animal they want to show with their bodies. The first stanza gives an idea how the children must understand the concepts in order to interpret the poem through body movement.

> Ernest was an elephant, a great big fellow,
> Leonard was a lion with a six-foot tail,
> George was a goat, and his beard was yellow,
> And James was a very small snail.[5]

Through the rest of the poem, each animal has a distinctive description and action in every stanza.

Square dances and round dances. On a day of celebrating squares, enjoy a simple square dance. If you do not know one, experiment with one such as the following.

Help the children form a square. Those on opposite sides (two sides at a time) skip toward each other, bow, and skip back. Opposite sides move toward each other, clap hands, and move back. Again, the sides move toward each other and rub noses, touch elbows, do jumping jacks, stamp feet, or shake fingers and move back. Each pattern is done twice so that all sides have the chance to enjoy it.

Choose traditional square-dance music or any music with a steady, lively rhythm.

On a day of celebrating circles, enjoy a simple circle or round dance. All join hands and circle around. Skip, slide, run, gallop, jump, or walk around the circle. Change directions to make it more interesting.

Reminder: If you run out of circular ideas, replenish your resources by returning to Guide 5 and reading "twenty ways to love a circle."

Shape of time. Each time has its own shape, its own angle. Children look at the wall clock, hear the time announced, and copy the position of the hands of the clock with their arms and legs. Six o'clock is a great stretch, and at six-thirty you touch your toes!

Because our daily lives are full of shapes, movement and play ideas that extend shapes concepts can be gathered readily. Consider the following possibilities.

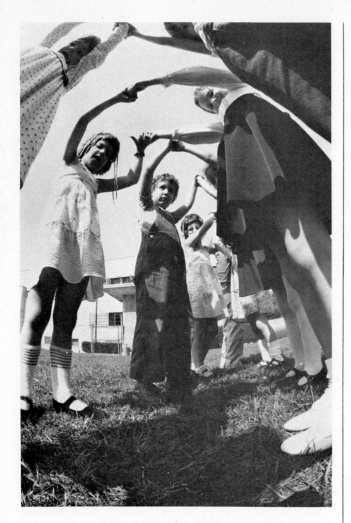

Shapes for all seasons. Show a winter shape with your bodies. How does a leaf change its shape from summer to autumn?

Shapes for holidays and special occasions. Turn your bodies into Halloween statues—a George Washington cutting down the cherry tree, or an Indian or Pilgrim shape.

Shapes for places and objects. How can you show the shape of a bridge with your bodies? A city with tall buildings? A rambling farmhouse? A river? A desert? A town?

Shapes for toys. Turn your bodies into the shape and movement of bouncing balls, wind-up toys, Raggedy Ann and Andy dolls, robots, toy airplanes, and stuffed animals.

Shapes that change. Explore the way bodies change to convey ocean water, water in a teakettle boiling, steam, and ice.

Shapes that meet. One day a group of circles meet a group of squares. How do they look? How do they greet each other? How do they speak? What do they do together? How do they say goodbye?

VISITORS AND FIELD TRIPS

Visitors

Mime. One of the amazing feats a mime accomplishes is carving shapes in space with body movements. Objects, people, animals, and elements of nature appear before your eyes. You perceive heights, widths, depths, circles, squares, triangles. Mimes are like magicians. Encourage your guest to share exercises with the children. Their participation is very important.

Artisans. Invite persons such as woodcarvers, basketweavers, glass blowers, ceramicists, potters, jewelers, toy makers, furniture makers, quilt makers, and rug weavers to visit you and talk about the kinds of shapes and designs that are most appealing to them. Ask them to bring samples or to give demonstrations. Encourage the children to ask questions.

Actors and actresses. Invite a group of community theater members, older students, or university thespians to do improvisations about shapes and shadow plays using silhouettes behind a white sheet; to recite poems about shapes; and to create plays and stories about shapes. Again, the involvement of your students will guarantee success and enjoyment.

Make-up artist. In the last guide, make-up artists like Leslie Zak were suggested as excellent visitors. Children's understanding of the effects of shapes on feelings and experiences is reinforced as they watch a face turn from sad to glad with the stroke of a make-up crayon. Be sure that all the children who want to, have their faces made up.

Field Trips

Your own room. If your room is full of colorful displays of children's work, photographs, paintings, murals, and sculptures, it merits special attention. You may even want to sell tickets (in the shape of circles, squares, or rectangles). Guide the children around the room so they look at familiar surroundings in new ways. Ask them to find objects and images that are circles, squares, rectangles, triangles, spheres, cylinders, and other shapes. Combine with counting. Extend this in-house trip to other rooms.

Cloud "trips." Ask your students to walk to the windows and look up at the sky, or if the weather is warm enough, walk outside on a day when marvelous, puffy clouds are

floating by. With your children, talk about the shapes they see in the clouds.

As often as possible, allow time for follow-up with an art activity in which children create cloud shapes of cotton or white paint or chalk on sky-colored paper. Charles G. Shaw's book, *It Looked Like Spilt Milk* (Harper & Row, 1947) is an excellent book to enjoy after the children have seen interesting shapes in the clouds.

Expand the activity to writing and sharing original poems, songs, and stories about cloud shapes.

Shapes walk. As you walk, correlate shapes with other topics. In autumn, for example, children in the Midwest and the Northeast pick up round brown buckeyes and red berries. Most children will note the special shapes of traffic and street signs, the round street lamps, triangular rooftops, rectangular buildings, square and rectangular doors and windows, and round wheels of cars, buses, and trucks. When you return to the room, translate the shapes you gathered into pictures, poems, sculptures, songs, and games.

Food stores and supermarkets. Be sure to include observations and discussions of the shapes of products and produce during your trips to stores. Note with your children that cans are round, boxes are square or rectangular, peas are round, and potatoes are lumpy and bumpy. These descriptive words become part of the way children look at things.

Sculptor's studio. Because children are natural sculptors, always forming shapes out of whatever material is at hand, they are fascinated by the art and intensely interested in the sculptor's ideas, feelings, and experiences. Ask the sculptor to talk about and, if possible, demonstrate such concepts as positive and negative space (open and closed forms), the wide range of materials used for sculpting, some of the tools needed, where ideas come from, and how a shape emerges from the material.

Follow the session with a sculpting so

that the children can immediately apply their new knowledge and understanding.

You may want to invite the sculptor to visit your class, rather than going to the studio.

Florist, nursery, and park. These kinds of trips help children to appreciate the diverse shapes of nature. If possible, take crayons and paper and encourage the children to write and draw their impressions. Otherwise, follow up in school as soon as possible with enriching art activities.

Sporting goods store. What better place to see round, oval, spherical, and cylindrical shapes, such as basketball hoops, balls of every size, racquets, paddles, and cans of balls?

Five-and-dime or sewing store. Children notice the wonderful shapes and colors of buttons, bangles, snaps, and beads, always so attractively displayed.

Bakery. Cakes, doughnuts, bagels, pies, and certain breads are circular and spherical. Cookies come in many different shapes. How many shapes of delicious-smelling baked goods can your children identify?

Wallpaper and floor covering store. The designs and colors of wallpaper, rugs, and tiles are fabulous. Children easily spot basic shapes and marvel at how cleverly they are combined with other shapes and with colors. Design your own rugs, wallpaper, and tile when you return to the classroom.

Art gallery or art museum. Focus on shapes as part of your students' experience at an art museum, gallery, or studio. Here they may also discover the phenomenon of optical illusion. "Are those circles moving?" "Is that square bigger or smaller than the others?" "Are those lines waving?"

Responses to paintings and sculpture can be readily combined with movement activities, art, drama, song, and creative writing. Here are a few examples of how easy it is to ask children to connect ideas and express themselves. "Use your super eyesight. In this room are three paintings that feature circles. Draw an imaginary circle with your hands in front of each of those paintings." Again, "Look around the room. When you see a painting of a large, rectangular purple house with a green triangular roof, stand in front of it and show the roof's shape."

The town square and other shapes of interest. Most towns and cities have a central place identified by its distinct shape. A. A. Milne's Christopher Robin "takes his penny to the market square." Ohio State University students meet at the Oval, the center of campus. New Yorkers double their shapes by going to a play at the Circle in the Square Theater. A baseball field is diamond-shaped; a tennis court is rectangles; and a circus has three rings. Check your area and find places that are clearly defined, perhaps even named by their shapes.

Throughout this book you will find many ways to include shapes in visits and field trips. People, places, things, animals, indeed everything in the whole wide world, helps us make comparisons, discern patterns, discover relationships, categorize, name, and identify. As five-year-old Davie, whose class was studying shapes, noted wearily, "It's getting so I can't go a step without noticing everything's shape. I even dream about it!" My dreams are in circles. How do yours shape up?

NOTES

1. John G. Neihardt, _Black Elk Speaks_ (New York: Simon & Shuster, 1972), pp. 164–166.
2. Theodore Roethke, _Straw for the Fire_ (New York: Doubleday, 1974), p. 234.
3. Edwin Markham, "Outwitted," _Modern American Poetry, Modern British Poetry_, Combined Mid-Century Edition, ed. by Louis Untermeyer (New York: Harcourt Brace Jovanovich, 1950), p. 106.
4. Shel Silverstein, "Shapes," _A Light in the Attic_ (New York: Harper & Row, 1981), p. 77.
5. A. A. Milne, "The Four Friends," _The World of Christopher Robin_ (New York: Dutton, 1958), pp. 16–18.

SELECTED BIBLIOGRAPHY

Shapes Are All Around

Anno, Mitsumasa. _Anno's Journey._ New York: Putnam, 1978.

Bendick, Jeanne. _Shapes—Science Experiences._ New York: Franklin Watts, 1968.

Borten, Helen. _Do You See What I See?_ New York: Abelard-Schuman, 1959.

Brown, Marcia. _Listen to a Shape._ Photos by Marcia Brown. New York: Franklin Watts, 1979.

Budney, Blossom. _A Kiss Is Round._ Illustrated by Vladimir Babri. New York: Lothrop, Lee & Shepard, 1969.

Campbell, Ann. *Start to Draw*. Illustrated by Ann Campbell. New York: Franklin Watts, 1968.

Children's Television Workshop. *Sesame Street Book of Shapes*. Boston: Little, Brown, 1970.

Crews, Donald. *Truck*. New York: Morrow, Greenwillow, 1980.

Emberly, Ed. *Ed Emberley's Drawing Book: Make a World*. Boston: Little, Brown, 1972.

————. *Ed Emberley's Great Thumbprint Drawing Book*. Boston: Little, Brown, 1977.

————. *The Wing on a Flea*. Boston: Little, Brown, 1969.

Hoban, Tana. *Circles, Triangles & Squares*. New York: Macmillan, 1974.

————. *Shapes and Things*. New York: Macmillan, 1970.

Kessler, Ethel, and Leonard Kessler. *Are You Square?* New York: Doubleday, 1966.

Matthiesen, Thomas. *Things to See (A Child's World of Familiar Objects)*. Photos by Thomas Matthiesen. New York: Platt & Munk, 1966.

Pienkowski, Jan. *Shapes*. New York: Harvey House, 1975.

Poulet, Virginia. *Blue Bug's Treasure*. Illustrated by Mary Maloney and Stan Fleming. Chicago: Childrens Press, 1976.

Reiss, John J. *Shapes*. New York: Bradbury, 1976.

Seuss, Dr. [Theodor S. Geisel]. *The Shape of Me and Other Stuff*. New York: Random House, 1973.

Tester, Sylvia Root. *The Parade of Shapes*. Illustrated by Rose-Mary Fudala. Elgin, Ill.: Childs World, 1976.

Thoburn, Tina. *Discovering Shapes*. Illustrated by James Caraway. Indianapolis, Ind.: Bobbs-Merrill, 1970.

Wolff, Janet. *Let's Imagine Thinking of Things*. Illustrated by Bernard Owett. New York: Dutton, 1961.

Teacher Resources

Bates, Kenneth F. *Basic Design*. New York: Harper & Row, 1979.

Berger, John. *About Looking*. New York: Pantheon, 1980.

————. *Ways of Seeing*. London: Penguin, 1972.

Dewey, John. *Art as Experience*. New York: Putnam, 1980.

Edwards, Betty. *Drawing on the Right Side of the Brain*. Los Angeles: Tarcher, 1979.

Gregory, R. L. *The Intelligent Eye*. New York: McGraw-Hill, 1970.

Lingstrom, Freda. *The Seeing Eye*. New York: Macmillan, 1960.

Springer, Sally P., and Georg Deutsch. *Left Brain, Right Brain*. San Francisco: Freeman, 1981.

Steele, Fritz. *The Sense of Place*. Boston: CBI, 1981.

Stevens, John O. *Awareness: Exploring, Experimenting, Experiencing*. Moab, Utah: Real People Press, 1971.

Taylor, John F. *Design and Expression in the Visual Arts*. New York: Dover, 1964.

Williams, Christopher. *Origins of Form*. New York: Architectural Books, 1981.

12

WE LEARN OUR LETTERS AND WORDS

In Praise of ABC
In the beginning were the letters
wooden, awkward, and everywhere.
Before the Word as the slow scrabble of fire and
  water.

God bless my son and his wooden letters
who has gone to bed with A in his right hand and Z in
  his left,
who has walked all day with C in his shoe and said
  nothing,
who has eaten of his napkin the word Birthday,
and who has filled my house with the broken speech
  of wizards.

To him the grass makes its gentle sign.
For him the worm letters her gospel truth.
To him the pretzel says, I am the occult
descendant of the first blessed bread
and the lost cuneiform of a grain of wheat.

Kneading bread, I found in my kitchen half an O.
Now I wait for someone to come from far off
holding the other half, saying,
What is broken shall be made whole.
Match half for half; now do you know me again?

Thanks be to God for my house seeded with dark
  sayings
and my rooms rumpled and badly lit
but richly lettered with the secret raisins of truth.[1]

246

THE BASICS

In A. A. Milne's delightful story "Rabbit's Busy Day," Piglet comes upon grumpy Eeyore, who is looking at three sticks on the ground. Two of the sticks touch at one end but not the other, and the third stick lies across them.

Eeyore asks Piglet if he knows what the sticks are. Piglet, flustered, does not know. Eeyore explains, "It's an A." "Oh," said Piglet. "Not O, A," says Eeyore severely, then adds, "Christopher Robin said it was an A, and an A it is—until somebody treads on me."

Then Eeyore asks, "Do you know what an A means, Little Piglet?" Of course, Piglet does not. "It means Learning, it means Education, it means all the things that you and Pooh haven't got. That's what A means...to the Educated, not meaning Poohs and Piglets, it's a great and glorious A. Not just something that anybody can come and breathe on!"[2]

Eeyore is not a linguist, but he has the right idea about equating the meaning of that "great and glorious A" with learning and education. If we had the time to trace the origins of A, we would follow the long, complicated, fascinating history of the evolution of human intelligence and communication.

We would have to go way, way back to prehistoric time, about 50,000 years ago, when our ancestors painted pictures on the walls of their caves and on nearby stones and rocks. Their pictures marked events, told stories, had magical powers. If they painted a picture of animals with hunters' spears in their bodies, that picture was like a prayer for a successful hunt.

Through the ages, people expressed themselves not only in paintings but also through language and movement—speech, song, and dance. Unwritten stories, myths, chants, prayers, and ballads were passed from generation to generation.

Ancient peoples like the Chinese, South American Indians, and Egyptians painted images that represented objects. They painted a fish to mean "fish," a bird to mean "bird," and a mountain to mean "mountain." This kind of writing is known as a "pictograph" or "hieroglyph." But there were feelings and qualities that could not be expressed by simple pictures, such as the passage of time, the peacefulness of a sleeping baby, and the sweetness of a grape.

To meet this need, "ideographs" evolved. The Chinese, for example, combined the symbols of sun and moon to say "bright." A lion became the Egyptian symbol for power. Images changed from simple representations to more abstract designs that conveyed meanings understood by all members of the community.

In the middle East, one of the world's most culturally fertile regions, soft clay tablets were marked on. The tool used was a stylus, and it produced wedge-shaped marks—a form of writing that became known as "cuneiform." When the tablets were covered with symbols, they were baked and preserved. The people who excelled at this technique were the Sumerians, who are generally credited with introducing written language, because their cuneiform tablets—filled with legends about the Great Flood, Creation, and the epic adventures of King Gilgamesh—are considered the oldest evidence of such writing and date back approximately 5,500 years.

As sailing, trading, bartering, conquering, and governing—the stuff of cultural exchange—accelerated, people borrowed ideas from one another and adapted them to their own needs. Writing systems were evolving with specific symbols for images, sounds, and syllables. Many of the word-symbols for picture ideas were shared by diverse groups. For example, both the Phoenicians and the Hebrews had a symbol and a word for "ox." Their word was "aleph." Another symbol they shared was for "house." Their word for "house" was "beth."

These two symbols and words, aleph and beth, traveled with Phoenician sailors to Greece. The Greeks adopted the shapes of the letters and changed their original Phoenician and Hebrew names just a little. Aleph and beth were called "alpha" and "beta," which became the first two letters of the Greek alphabet. Say alpha and beta together and you say alphabet. In French, the word for illiterate is "analphabete," or "without alphabet."

These and other letters of the Greek alphabet were adopted by Roman conquerers, but not before the Romans adopted their written symbols as well as some of their ideas in art and sculpture. Handed down from Phoenicians, Hebrews, Greeks, and Romans, alpha and beta became the letters A and B in the English alphabet.

The impact of written language upon the peoples of the world was immeasurable. They could write letters to each other, keep journals, publish books and newspapers, post announcements, carry proclamations to distant places, scrawl graffitti on the walls of buildings, and share poems and stories with people living in different times and places. They could keep records of their transactions, write inscriptions on tombstones, advertise products and services, make shopping lists, and write prayers. Written language was considered so great a gift to human civilization that most ancient cultures believed it came from the gods.

Eeyore is right. Our "great and glorious A" is not "just something that anybody can come and breathe on!" Its story is part of the history of written language. You can learn more about this history by reading Franklin Folsom's *The Language Book* (Grosset & Dunlap, 1963) or Fred West's *The Way of Language* (Harcourt Brace Jovanovich, 1975).

Henry Wadsworth Longfellow's Hiawatha learned not from books but from his grandmother, Nokomis, who sang, showed, and told him how to recognize the signs of his world. He learned to "read" many things, such as the pictures of stars, the meaning of comets and rainbows, the whispering secret of pine trees, the dance of the firefly, the message of wild flowers, deer prints, and the rustle of wind. From Nokomis he learned the names of birds, trees, plants, and animals; the paths in the woods; and the directions of stars to lead him home.

Modern-day Hiawathas do not rely on grandmothers and legends alone to help them read the world. Rather, they go to bed with A in their right hand and Z in their left hand, so beautifully described by Nancy Willard in her poem "In Praise of ABC." The letters of the alphabet are as integral a part of their world as were animal tracks and the marks on trees in Hiawatha's world.

Today children pretend to read and write at very young ages. I watched a ten-month-old "read" his book with great concentration, then "write," with his pencil grasped firmly in his little hand. Through play, children practice reading and writing.

Children know many words even before they are one year old. They understand words even if they do not yet speak them. By the time most children start kindergarten, they comprehend thousands of words, even though they may use only a fraction of them. Considering their wordless beginnings, young children acquire language at an astonishingly fast rate.

I recently visited two first grades where we talked together about many things, especially words. "Boys and girls," I said, "You know so many words. Look around the room. You know words for everything you see, right?" They agreed: window, door, closet, books, crayons, coats, and so on. "You know a word for every person in this room and for everything on each person, right?" Again, they agreed: hair, noses, teeth, eyes, glasses, earrings, shoes, and so on. We continued adding words for everything the children saw outside and in their houses, for animals and toys, and for food and clothing. The children were proud and excited about how many words they knew.

HAMBURGER

With this rich background of resource material, we talked about favorite words. "Of all the thousands of words you know, some of them are your favorite words, words you really like to hear and say. Which are your very favorite words?" In less than five minutes, writing frantically, I filled the board with words the children eagerly suggested—words such as mother, father, baby, house, grandma, grandpa, friend, dog, candy, flower, and birthday.

I asked the children to pick one of the words and write anything they wanted about it for one minute. Spelling did not count. After we discussed their feelings about the words, I gave them this challenge: "I bet each of you can think of a hundred words you like very much." The children gasped and shook their heads. Impossible. "Ask your families, teachers, and older friends to write down the words, as you think of them, on a piece of paper. When all of you have a hundred words each, call me and we'll have a big party!"

About two weeks later, their teachers called me. "Every child has an envelope full of at least a hundred words. Some children have more. They can't stop!" "We're ready for the party," they announced. Now it was my turn to gasp.

I gathered my son, who was then a magician, and friends who played guitars, and off we went to the party. When we entered the large double room that the two first grades shared, we could not believe our eyes. From floor to ceiling, on every wall, were hundreds and hundreds of words. The children were so proud of their accomplishment. They took me by the hand to show me: "That's my 'aunt' and there's my 'tulip' and up there's my 'orange' and my 'tricycle'!" That was a party to remember!

In Guide 10, the exercise "Pass the Colors" was described. With older children, words are encouraged instead of pictures or designs. Different-colored crayons or Magic Markers, together with large sheets of drawing paper, are distributed to the children, who are asked to imagine what words a particular color wants to write and to write them as fast as they can. Then the children pass their colors to others and repeat the activity with a new color.

One day, while I was sharing this enjoyable experience with a class of fourth graders, the four-year-old sister of one of the students came to visit the class and participated in the activities. The four-year-old listened intently as the instructions were given to the above exercise. When she was given the first color, she quickly marked her paper. When she received the next color, she was intent on her work. When the third color came around, she stopped. She was stuck. The teacher saw the problem and went to her.

"What's wrong?" she asked the little girl. "I can't think of any words brown wants to write," the child answered sadly. "Well, what about 'tree,' 'dirt,' or 'mud'?" the teacher suggested. "Great! Thanks!" the four-year-old answered as she jumped into action.

Only at the end of the day, after the children had handed in their papers as they left, did the teacher remember: "Oh my! I forgot! She's only four! She can't write yet!" Yes and no. The child's paper was covered with "writing"—the beginnings of words. In the child's mind, she was writing.

Becky Moore has extensive experience in teaching people of all ages how to read. After ten years of teaching reading in the public schools in Columbus, Ohio, she joined the faculty of Columbus Technical Institute and works with adults and foreign students. She reminds teachers that most children begin to learn letters at a very early age. Our society encourages that learning, from families, television, books, and signs.

Becky's experiences echo the findings of many researchers in the field, especially those of Marie Clay of New Zealand. In New Zealand, all children enter kindergarten on the Monday of the week they turn five years old. Classroom teachers have to meet the challenge of children entering school at different times of the year. One of their major goals is to involve children in reading as soon as possible. For some five-year-olds, reading comes easily; for others it is a difficult process. Why?

Marie Clay tried to find out. Here is what she discovered. Children who learned to read quickly and easily were those who had been read to and had a sense of story; were able to recognize a word on the page; knew that one reads from left to right; knew

that at the end of a right-hand page, one turns the page and starts reading on the left-hand page; knew that the print on a page is letters and that letters make up words and words carry the message.

Becky's work with young children reinforces Clay's findings. Becky advocates a multidimensional approach. She urges parents and teachers to surround children with books and to encourage the children to handle books, to read and reread them. Even children who cannot read but pretend to do so are learning about the process.

Becky emphasizes that nothing is more important than reading to and with children. Show them with your fingers as you read how the print progresses on the page. Stop and look at pictures. Talk about the story. Read in small groups. Read one-to-one. Read with the whole class. Read with a child on your lap. Ask children to retell the story, to "read" it back to you, to "read" it to dolls, puppets, pets, and friends.

Becky reminds teachers not to be afraid to use books with expanded vocabu-

lary. Young children understand many words, even complicated ones. Although most children begin with their ABC's, learning individual letters first, some teach themselves to read without even knowing the names of letters. The words that mean the most to children are the words they want to learn how to read and write.

Because children know the names of letters does not necessarily mean that they will learn how to read. They need a concept of print and story. Children learn best when teachers and families are accepting of early attempts, when stories are stressed, and when children are encouraged to use their own language to talk about the stories. Becky responds insightfully to the controversy over "why Johnny can't read." She observes:

Isn't it interesting that children learn how to walk and talk in a loving, accepting atmosphere, but when it comes to learning to read, the environment too often gets hostile? Parents become tense and anxious. They demand programs that lock children in patterns. (We know children don't learn that way!) In too many environments, the tension over reading creates emotional problems that block learning.

We have to take the tension and worry out of beginning reading. We want children to start out loving books and to enjoy reading for the rest of their lives.

Taking the tension and worry out of reading is a major goal of Dr. Merle Ivers, associate professor in the education department at Capital University, Bexley, Ohio. As coordinator of a widely acclaimed reading conference each summer and as director of the Reading Center at Capital University, Dr. Ivers works with children from first to twelfth grade. Walk into the Center and you will not know that it is a reading laboratory. The walls are bright with children's pictures and stories; the atmosphere is informal and friendly.

Dr. Ivers emphasizes the importance of giving children a variety of choices. It is important that children choose their own books and their own topics. The Capital University students who serve as reading tutors are encouraged to use various methods. "We're eclectic," Dr. Ivers explains. She continues:

The philosophy underlying all our methods is respect for and encouragement of children. We want children to enjoy reading. Out of the hour that children spend with their individual tutors, about forty minutes is spent talking about the story and personal experiences, play-acting, and improvising. That concentration on oral language, on eye contact and closeness is so important. We don't ever teach skills in isolation, but rather in the context of words and sentences in our book or our conversations. The relationship between children and teachers is the key ingredient.

Our society is just about saturated with books about letters and words. Programs in reading abound. But children do not always fit into learning schemes. Some children save you the trouble and teach themselves to read at the age of four; other children defy every approach and program.

Reading and writing go hand in hand. Remember that our children play at writing

Janet comes in to the Doctors office and slips, I help her up into a chair. Then I look at her foot and put it on a chair and open the chest, I get out the needle and give her a shot. Then I wrap her leg up. I help her up and ask her for the money she says she hasent any and I set her down take her bandage of and kick her out.

long before they learn their first letter. Children should be encouraged to write *every day*—their names, titles for pictures, stories, poems, songs, directions, and labels. As often as possible, display their writing and make books, anthologies, newspapers, and letters to families.

Do not belabor spelling skills with young children. Never allow anxiety about correct spelling to block children's desire to write. Spelling skills will develop each day as you talk about, read, and display words. The freedom of spirit necessary to enjoy writing is fragile and can be easily broken by too heavy concentration on perfecting spelling and handwriting.

The more children write, the easier and more satisfying writing becomes. When writing is part of their everyday activities, it ceases to be a foreign and formidable exercise that arouses tension and fear. Johnny and Joanie *can* read and write. The key words are *eclectic, flexible, encourage, share,* and *read and write together.* As one first grader advised, "The way to teach us to read and write is to love us kids."

DISCOVERY TIMES

- A way of understanding each other is called language. While our primary language is English, many people in our country speak more than one language.
- Many languages are spoken throughout the world.
- Some people in our class may speak more than one language.
- Words are the most important part of language.
- Words can be spoken, written, read, illustrated, and dramatized.
- Words have meanings that people agree on.
- Every word has its own special sound. We hear it and understand its meaning.
- Every word looks different. We read it and understand its meaning.
- All words are made up of letters.
- There are twenty-six letters in the English alphabet.
- All the words in our language are composed of combinations of those twenty-six letters.
- Every letter has its own sound and shape.
- When you know how to read, you can enjoy stories, poems, and information that other people have written, even people who lived long ago and far away.
- When you learn how to write, other people can read your words.

SUGGESTED VOCABULARY

sounds	read	plays	posters
words	talk	puppet shows	signs
letters	speak	nursery	author
alphabet	tell	rhymes	writer
ABC's	listen	fairy tales	playwright
names	recite	folk tales	journalist
questions	page	legends	poet
answers	print	movies	editor
people	books	TV shows	question mark
places	newspapers	journals	comma
things	magazines	diaries	sentence
feelings	posters	calendars	capital
ideas	mail	lists	letter
imagination	postcards	notebooks	small letter
information	telephone	chalkboard	handwriting
news	book	chalk	exclamation
reports	dictionary	paper	point
meanings	stories	pencil	notes
understand	poems	pen	message
write	riddles	crayon	communication
	songs	typewriter	character

In his book *Straw for the Fire* (Doubleday, 1974) the late poet Theodore Roethke shares wit and wisdom about language. He writes: "In this first assignment, just care about words. Dwell on them lovingly."[3]

Words have power. They affect the way we see and react to things. They are the stuff of our ideas and imagination. They enrich our experiences and help us to know one another.

SOME BEGINNING ACTIVITIES

Start with names. What more wonderful group of letters than those in our names? On the first day, the children receive colorful, clearly printed name tags. Linda Goldsmith, who teaches at the Jewish Center in Columbus, Ohio, includes a special symbol on the children's name tags. Even if children do not yet know the letters of their names, they recognize their symbols, which Linda also uses on charts, pictures, and papers.

Start with delivering a letter. A delightful way to begin your year-long study of letters and words is to give each child a letter of the alphabet cut from cardboard, construction paper, or felt. Add excitement by asking the children to close their eyes while you give them their special-delivery letter.

Start with admiring a letter. Wendy Sample teaches art in elementary schools in Dearborn, Michigan. Many of her students are from Arabic backgrounds and English is their second language. Wendy and her students look at the letters of the alphabet as if they were works of art. "We talk about which directions the shapes are going, how they are connected, and whether they have curved or straight lines."

Start with the word of the day. Tape it to your clothes; tack it to the bulletin boards; tape it to the children's backs. Border the room with the words you celebrate, adding a new word each day.

Start with a red-letter day. Adapt the above idea to introducing a new letter instead of a word. Cover yourselves and your room with that letter. Combine it with a color. Imagine the children's delighted response to walking into a room covered by red, yellow, or blue S's.

Start with an alphabet puppet. Assign one of your puppets or stuffed animals the job of introducing new letters and words. On the day of a new letter or word, your alphabet puppet is dressed head to toe in the design of that letter or word. Sometimes the puppet can be the questioner. "What's this?" the puppet can ask, pointing to a special letter.

This activity lends itself to variations. Here are just two: a different puppet for each letter of the alphabet, such as Albert for A and Bobby for B; and animal letter puppets, such as a cat puppet for C and a dog puppet for D.

Start with a letter search. Children enjoy seek-and-find games. Give them opportunities to look for letters in books and magazines and around the room. See how many occurrences of a letter the children can find in just a short time.

Start with name-tagging everything in the room. At the beginning of the school year, after the children have received their name tags and are accustomed to wearing them, encourage the children to help you tape name tags to areas and objects in your room. After a while, the children will learn to read all the names. How will you know? Mix them up and see what happens! Or make new tags, remove the old ones, and ask the children to tape the new ones in the right places.

Start with a missing letter. Make alphabet cards and show them to the children, beginning with A. "Uh-oh! A letter is missing! Darn! Which one is missing? What does it look like? Where could it be?" Be sure it

is hidden in an interesting place. "Could the Alphabet Puppet be sitting on it? Hmmmmmm. It might be hidden on an object that begins with that letter." You never can tell where missing letters are hiding!

Start with a letter or word in your pocket. Pockets are popular with young children. Designate or sew on a special pocket that is full of surprises all year long. Sometimes the surprises are letters or words to celebrate all day.

Start with a favorite-words chart. Clearly print your children's names on a large chart and leave space after each name. Talk about favorite words. Ask the children, one at a time, to tell you their favorite words. Next to each of their names, print one or more of their favorite words. Talk about them, draw them, act them out, make games and riddles out of them. Children like to see their names in print and easily learn to recognize words associated with their names.

TALK TIMES

How else can children learn a language than by talking? Young children have many ideas and memories about learning their language. They feel grown-up when they share recollections of how they learned letters and words.

Four-year-old Pammy, who came to visit with her Aunt Patti, wrote her name easily and talked about learning her letters: "My Aunt Patti helped me learn my ABCD's. She sang the alphabet song to me. We look at lots of books and I play with my magnetic letters. I like letters with lines the best. My favorite letters are E and F and X."

Her Aunt Patti began "playing" letters with Pammy when she was almost two years old: "We'd write letters and draw pictures. Everything evolved out of playing together. We started with shapes—circles and lines. 'Pammy' came out of the shapes. P came out of a circle and a line! We often talk about letters. Wherever we go, we point out the letters we see, as part of everything."

One winter day when the temperature was below zero, few children made it to the Early Childhood Program at the Jewish Center in Columbus, Ohio. This day provided a rare opportunity for me to visit with a cross-section of children in a less structured

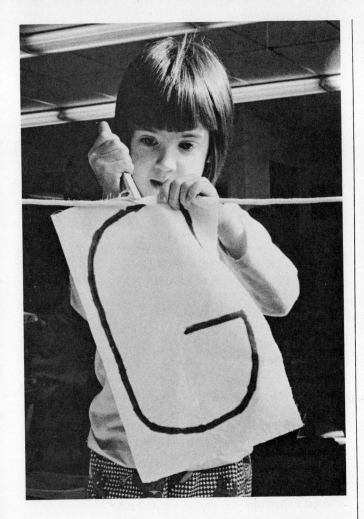

Babette and Heidi, among the youngest children, three years old, hung back. Finally they shyly entered the discussion.

> BABETTE: I don't know my letters yet. I just know I have to start with a B.
> HEIDI: My H has two ones and a line across (shows with her fingers).

After all the comments, I looked wonderingly at the children and remarked, "Isn't it amazing that when you were little babies you couldn't say even one word, and now you can say so many words and you know your letters and how to write your names. How do you account for that?" Three-and-a-half-year-old Jonathan folded his arms across his chest and explained, "We're smart!"

Just as ancient peoples imagined mysterious and magical ways written language came to people, so young children express remarkable responses to the question "How did we get letters and words?" Cheryl Harbold asked her kindergartners at Hilliard Elementary School in Hilliard, Ohio, to use their imaginations as they thought of some answers. Here are some of their ideas.

> TANYA: When you say the ABC's, you sound them out and get letters and words.
> ERIC: They made words using your imagination.
> MICHELLE: We have words so we can read and talk.
> STACY: If we didn't have words, we'd have signs. With our fingers. People who are deaf use sign language.
> CHERYL: Where did we get the idea of sign language?
> MICHAEL: God made up sign language.
> CHERYL: What if we didn't have words or sign language? What would we do to communicate?
> TJ: We could draw a picture of it.
> ERIC: If we didn't have words, we could just move our mouth.

Annelyn Baron and Lori Selczer's prekindergartners at the Jewish Center in Columbus, Ohio, also considered the origins of letters and words.

> People made them out of plastic.
> We get them from the letter store.
> We got them from God.
> They fell down from the sky.
> We put letters together and that makes words.
> We get letters and words from our house.
> Words come from pencils.

setting. They gave themselves totally to our discussion about letters and words. They had many important memories and ideas to share. Here is a brief sampling from that talk-filled hour.

> JESSI: Well, I have a letter box at home. I teach letters
> (5 years) to my dolls, my Mom, my Aunt and Uncle, and my Grandma and Grandpa. I'm the teacher. I can write Y-E-S. Do you know what that spells? It spells YES!
> NILI: I have a chalkboard. I can write "hi." I can
> (5 years) write "love." It's spelled L-O-V-E (demonstrates on paper).
> JONATHAN: I learned from *Sesame Street* and *The Electric*
> (3 1/2 years) *Company*, and that's about all. I can spell my name. Well, I can spell Julie's name from her basket, J-U-L-I-E. I learned how to spell "January" from the calendar in our room.
> ANDY: You know how I learned my letters? My Dad
> (4 years) helped me with the newspaper. He flipped it over. He kept finding my letters—A, N, D, Y—all over the paper, on all the pages!
> RACHEL: My Moms and Dads showed me. They read
> (3 1/2 years) stories to me and showed me the words in the books.

Talking about and comparing alphabets is a fascinating topic of conversation for young children. Betsy Distelhorst recalls that when her son, Roy, was in prekindergarten at Indianola Alternative School in Columbus, Ohio, a Greek alphabet chart was brought into the class.

The children were fascinated by the unusual symbols and were interested in comparing them to letters of the English alphabet. They talked about alphabets in general, their own alphabet, and that people around the world speak different languages. In their class were a few children from homes where Spanish, Portuguese, or French was spoken. One of the most amazing discussions centered on the fact that the Spanish, Portuguese, and French use letters of the English alphabet to make other languages.

Talking about the different alphabets and exploring the differences helped the children to understand the English alphabet clearly. One little guy was way behind the others in language development. In a short time he was able to differentiate among letters of the English alphabet.

Talking about words leads to writing and reading words. Combine "Talk Times" with art, music, creative writing, movement, and drama, and note improved comprehension and greater appreciation.

ART TIMES

Finger-paint letters. Combine letter writing with favorite colors. Ask the children to use their favorite color of finger paint to write their letters and names. Dry and display all works.

Snowy letters and words. If you live in a wintery place, bundle up and go outside on a sunny, snowy day so that the children can write in the snow with sticks, shovels, hands, feet, and elbows. If the weather stays cold, their letters will remain frozen and you will be able to see them every day.

Sand script. Sandboxes and beaches are excellent places to write letters and words. Linda Goldsmith, Jo Ann Bell, and their kindergartners at the Jewish Center in Columbus, Ohio, fill large cake tins with wet sand and make letter cakes.

What's in a word? Popsicle sticks, tongue depressors, toothpicks, pipe cleaners, twigs, pebbles, buttons, cutout shapes, and Tinkertoys are a few examples of scrounge materials that can be glued, pasted, taped, and pinned together to form letters and words. Display the children's creations.

Playdough, clay, and mud letters. Roll, pound, squeeze, and pinch letters out of Playdough, clay, and mud. Linda Goldsmith and Jo Ann Bell's kindergartners roll out Playdough letters and bake them in the oven. When the letters are dry, the children paint them with tempera.

Mosaic letters. Cut colored construction paper into small pieces; collect tiny pebbles; and save scraps of gold, silver, and glitter from greeting cards. Outline the children's names, letters, or favorite words on heavy construction paper or shirt cardboard. Cover the letters with glue or paste. The children fill in the letters with mosaic material.

One of Shirley Davis's favorite ways to help her children in West Bloomfield, Michigan, learn the letters of their names is to paint their names on construction paper. The children go over each letter with a finger of glue. They attach twigs, cut straws, sand, glitter, and stars to their names.

Name and word collages. Print the children's names or favorite words in block letters on large sheets of construction paper. Ask the children to think about the meaning of their name or word and how they can show it by cutting out, designing, and pasting pictures and textures on the block letters. Five-year-old Jake filled in the letters of his name with pictures of football players.

Connect the dots. Dot letters, names, and words on paper. When the children connect the dots, they discover their initials, names, and favorite words. They enjoy going over the dotted letters with different colors, which not only gives them practice in writing, but also results in a room of bright and lively words.

"Alphabelts." When five-year-old Katherine explained language, she told about the "alphabelt": "That's your ABC's. You start at A and try to get to Z!" How do you do that? Katherine went on, "You rememberize. That's how you get from A to Z."

Katherine's word for alphabet is a delightful project. Cut out strips of heavy paper or an old white cotton sheet, long enough to fit around the children's waists. With crayon, Magic Marker, or fabric marker, the children print all their letters, names, or favorite words on the length of

Amanda, age 7

the strip. Two paper clips hold the belt in place.

Rock letters. On one of your walks, gather small rocks of different shapes and sizes. As a change from painting designs and faces on the rocks, suggest that the children paint letters and words on them.

Greeting cards for all occasions. You cannot have enough reasons for writing letters and words. One very good reason is to make greeting cards that have not only beautiful decorations and pictures but also important messages. Be sure the cards are mailed or delivered personally. Children also enjoy making cards for classmates as part of friendship projects.

Make room for letters. Michael Rosen of Columbus, Ohio, likes to divide the room into letters the children are learning. In those areas, the children draw, cut out, paste up, hang mobiles, and make collages showing words and things that begin with those letters.

Charts full of words we know. Spread magazines, catalogues, greeting cards, and newspapers in a central place in the room. Ask the children to cut out words they know how to read. Scrounge poster-size paper and fill the posters with the children's words. Encourage the children, if they can, to paint or color their names under the words they contribute.

Go a step further by using the words for art activities, songs, movement improvisations, riddles, and games.

Catch the letter and spirit of words. Talk about the meaning of different words. The word "bird," for example, evokes images of colors, wings, sky, clouds, song, flight, and freedom. Clearly print words the children suggest on sheets of poster, tag, or construction paper, one word to a sheet. Ask the children to go over the printing of the word a few times with crayon or Magic Marker so the letters are clear and can be read from a distance. Encourage the children to illustrate their words in the most imaginative and liveliest ways possible.

A second grader put wheels on the bottom of each letter of his word, "car," and a third grader colored her paper blue-green and filled it with fish swimming around her word, "fish."

Cover a wall with the exciting display of words.

Special projects for special letters. Marilyn Cohen and her kindergartners in Albany, New York, celebrate every letter with a special activity. For the letter B, for example, they sewed beautiful buttons and beads on a burlap letter B. The wall hangings made a fine display. For the letter Z, they scrounged zippers of all sizes and colors, and zipped and unzipped zealously.

Around the country, I have seen children make elephants for E day, puppets for P day, robots for R day, and snow people for S day.

Edible alphabet. Marilyn believes that one way to children's minds is through their stomachs. She goes through the alphabet, from A to Z, making food that celebrates each letter: for example, cookies for C; and doughnuts for D. Her favorite is homemade pretzels shaped into special letters.

Name those T-shirts. Ask families to send in old T-shirts and scrounge extras. The children decide what words they want to

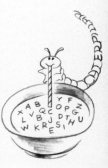

```
                              i lev ju   Dedi  ztrf ggbb dnmmykizukkrmdgf
bbb snnb vbgg fgdff     a    Anjauu izkkk kk kkkkkkklw  ms h  jjjjj 7t kira7.sz

p1pp  k uhh h76123456789hks,,y ,y.l ooizuööööööööö-;Joorkkhlbm  vbfgdhhiii kjn
  r 32 6zz8uiiiimv1234567 91omoon n   mfuzj.,mmm n tmjjj hguiz  MWUHJFKLÖS KJ M?

EDGC NB        NV LD ,mnhgjJjitrzfhn cbvj  nbhgfvcvcvcvcvcv vcvccwvvvvcvf
  fcbb b      b v   gf  hjjzh kjhntnb bv    j   bnhghghghghghghgh h h hghghg
AnnaAnna    AGbvc vc fxy ,m,jhnb nbnbnnbjdh !?jjjghrfh gghcnxm  w b h m nb
```

Kira, age 6

write on their T-shirts. Do not be surprised if the choices range from initials to names to whole sentences. One first grader wrote on his shirt, "I'm a Good Kid." The easiest method is to write with fabric or felt pen. Be sure that you make one, too.

Original alphabet books. Many outstanding alphabet books, on a wide variety of themes, are available at libraries and bookstores. Be careful when you choose alphabet books, because some of them, though brilliantly illustrated, are confusing to young readers. They combine a picture of a noun with the letter of a verb, or they have so many unrelated pictures on a page that the meaning is unclear.

Surround your children with effective word and alphabet books to read and enjoy. After the children have become familiar with alphabet books and have started to study letters and words, they are ready to write their own alphabet books. Every page is devoted to a different letter and shows something that begins with that letter.

Alphabet books need not be complicated projects, but if you enjoy creating unusual books, as does Greg Siegler, teacher and director of Miami Elementary Tutorial School, Miami, Florida, you and your students can make books the following way. On heavy cardboard covers, press squares of cotton or polyester batting. Cover the batting with pieces of scrounged material. Secure the thick, soft, material-filled covers with clear contact paper. Use colorful contact paper for the inside covers. Drill three holes in the covers to fit loose-leaf paper, and paste grommets around the holes for added strength.

Greg and his students use dividers with plastic tabs to make a combination alphabet book-address book. Every section has drawings, words, and pictures starting with the same letter, plus names and addresses of classmates whose last name begins with that letter. By the end of the school year, the children's books are filled with important ideas about each letter as well as important information about their classmates.

Michael Rosen encourages children to create alphabet books of favorite themes. His students work together to write and illustrate alphabet books of birds, food, zoos, flowers, names, places, nursery rhyme characters, and exercises. Each letter is written in the style of the book's theme, for example, exercise figures make up the letters in exercise books.

John Hancock exercises. Their own names are probably the first words that children learn how to write. As they become proficient in writing their names and practicing other letters and words, try some silly exercises that give them a chance to practice small muscle coordination, show their handwriting abilities, and use their imaginations.

Seven Dwarfs' handwriting. Ask the children to pretend to be the Seven Dwarfs and write their dwarf names in the style of their personalities. Grumpy's handwriting will be surly; Sleepy's handwriting will be sooo tired; Dopey's handwriting may be a little hard to read; and Doc's handwriting will reflect his know-it-all mind. Do you think Bashful writes big or small? Uh-oh, what if Sneezy *sneezed* while writing his or her name? Well, Happy Happy Happy—how would you write?

Worst handwriting, best handwriting. If you want to see your students puff up with pride and confidence, give them the opportunity to do a series of names or words, from their very sloppiest to their very best handwriting. Display all the papers. They make fascinating reading.

Sign here. As often as possible, ask the children to sign their names to agreements, directions, and projects. This activity will teach them the importance of a person's signature, as well as give them practice writing letters and names. Use chalkboard, wall charts, bulletin boards, and doors.

One first-grade classroom featured a sign that read: "We want to go outside on the first warm day." Twenty-two children's names were signed below, in addition to one teacher's and one student-teacher's name.

Combine such exercises with colors: "Sign your name in red if you want to hear a story"; "Sign your name in blue if you want to sing a song."

We are tops, from A to Z. Tape two or three large sheets of paper together to make a huge alphabet chart. Each letter begins an adjective describing how wonderful the children are. Make room for all the children's signatures first, followed by:

We are:

Adorable	Natural
Beautiful	Original
Cute	Playful
Daring	Questioning
Educated	Responsible
Friendly	Silly
Great	Terrific
Happy	Unreal
Interesting	Valuable
Jumpy	Wonderful
Kissy	Exciting (children's suggestion)
Loving	Young
Musical	Zippy

Add bright, lively illustrations and self-portraits to the chart.

Create A–Z charts for animals, ice-cream flavors, story and TV characters, and fruits and vegetables.

Words and pictures. Constantly encourage the children to write stories, poems, journals, reports, and letters. If they cannot write for themselves, volunteer family members and older children to take their dictation, or do it yourself. Read their works to classmates. Ask the authors and poets to illustrate their writing. Display it. Collect their pieces into individual books of writing or a class book.

MUSIC TIMES

Alphabet songs. As three-and-a-half-year-old Jonathan explained, no one taught him the alphabet song, he simply "learned it in his bed." If your children have not learned this song in their beds, be sure to teach it to them. They never tire of singing it.

Make up your own alphabet songs as well, or songs for every letter of the alphabet. Sing them while you practice writing letters and words. Here is a song that a class of prekindergartners composed with their teacher after they studied the letters S and T. Try your own melody to the words.

S S S.
S is very curly.
T T T.
T is very straight.

Some of you may remember the popular song, "A, you're adorable/B, you're so beautiful/C, you're a cutie full of charm . . ." Sing it to your children and watch their faces brighten.

Spelling songs. Can you spell M-I-S-S-I-S-S-I-P-P-I without singing it? Michael Rosen learned how to spell "encyclopedia" through the Mickey Mouse Club's Jiminy Cricket's spelling song. Michael admits that occasionally he still sings the spelling in his mind as he writes the word.

Turn the children's names into spelling songs, or use the spelling of their favorite words as lyrics to original spelling songs.

Spelling cheers. Each word should have its own cheer.

Gimme an F.   F!
Gimme a U.   U!
Gimme an N.   N!
What does it spell?
FUN!   Hip Hip Hooray!

Experiment with different rhythms and movements. Point to or show the letters as they are called.

Syllable songs. How many songs do you sing with the lyrics "la la la"? It is amazing how these lyrics fit so many melodies.

Winnie the Pooh constantly composes "hums" with such choruses as "Tra-la-la, tra-la-la" or "Tiddely pom, tiddely pom."

Many cultures have songs with syllable sounds. The music of Native American tribes, for example, is full of words like: "Hi Yo Wa. Hi Yo Wa. Ya Ah Ah. Ya Ah Ah. Hey Oh Hey. Hey Oh Hey. Oh Yah. Oh Yah. Hey Hey Doney Ho. Hey Hey Doney Ho. Yo Hey Ah. Yo Hey Ah. Hey Yah. Hey Yah. Hey Yah."

Hassidic Jews, who trace their cultural roots to eighteenth-century Eastern Europe, composed thousands of "Niguns," or songs without words. They believed that God, who knows everything, does not require the words to all songs. God knows the words they sing in their heart. Nigun chants include: "Ya Ya Ya. Ya Ya Ya. Ah Ah Ah. Ah Ah Ah. Ya Ya Yay. Ya Ya Yay. Bim Bom. Rum Ta Da Du. Bim Bom. Rum Ta Da Bum." These kinds of chants are easy for young children to learn as well as recognize in print.

Ella Jenkins's cheerful song, "It's a Holiday" (*Jambo and Other Call-and-Response Songs and Chants*, Folkways Records) is filled with easy-to-sing and easy-to-read syllables. The basic verse is "It's a holiday," and the long, rhythmical chorus is: "La La La La La/la la la la la/La La La La La/la la la la la." Repetition makes these songs easy to learn.

Imagine how easily children sing and learn to recognize the chorus of "Old MacDonald"—"E-I-E-I-O," or the syllabic refrain of the Christmas song "Deck the Halls with Boughs of Holly"—"Fa la la la la/la la la."

Alan Lomax and Elizabeth Austin's well-known camp and school song, "Hey Lolley Lolley Lo," also helps children learn their L's, hear rhymes, and enjoy the play of language. Print the refrain "Hey lolley lolley lolley, Hey lolley lolley lo" in a bright color, and point to it as you and your children sing.

Song cards. As each new song is learned, print the name of the song on a special card. The children enjoy decorating or illustrating the card. Keep the cards in a designated place. Children select songs they want to sing by choosing the cards and holding them up for the others to see.

Correlate this activity with daily helpers' and song leaders' duties. After a while, your children will be able to identify the song cards and sing at the sight of the names.

Songbooks. Collect the songs your class sings into a large songbook complete with clearly printed words and the children's illustrations. This book will be one of the most popular books in your class.

I watched a kindergartner hum and sing his way through a large book of class songs. His teacher explained that "Every day, during freeplay, at least one child chooses to read the songbook!"

Alphabet instruments. Print name cards for every instrument in your room. Combine with shapes and colors. After the children are familiar with the name cards, deal them. The children receive their cards, find the corresponding instruments, and experiment with different sounds.

Sheet music. Scrounge a white sheet. With Magic Markers or fabric markers, print the words to songs the children know, until the sheet is filled. Drape the sheet across a wall or hang it on a clothesline. The song leaders of the day point to the songs they want to lead.

Alphabet music. As you introduce individual letters for study, include music and song as part of the festivities. Sing a song that begins with that letter or ask the children what kind of music they want to play on their rhythm instruments that especially fits the letter of the day.

Singing telegrams. For special occasions, singing telegrams are a popular form of communication. In this activity, the children do the singing when the message is read to them. The singing telegrams contain simple, cheerful songs—"good morning" songs, "happy birthday" songs, and holiday songs.

Better letter lyrics. When the children know and recognize their letters, give each child a card with a letter printed on it. Ask them to make up a song about the letter on their card.

Here are the words to five-year-old Tanya's song about the letter M.

> Mmmmmmmm Mmmmmmmm M M M.
> Mmmmmmmm Mmmmmmmm M & M's.

Tanya associated her letter with one of her favorite kinds of candy and created a little song that became part of the class repertoire.

Musical notes and alphabet letters. Musical notes are named after letters. The children cannot help but notice the relationship as they look through music books in the classroom. Even children who are not interested in the more technical aspect of music are fascinated by the idea that when musicians play and sing music, they read notes. Your youngest students will proudly recite the notes printed on a page of guitar or piano music.

Call-and-response songs. An excellent way for children to learn is a form of singing known as call-and-response. The leader sings a word or phrase and the group echoes it. "Oh, You Can't Get to Heaven" is an example of this style.

Children respond enthusiastically to these songs, which are easy to make up as you work, talk together, greet each other, and walk along. Improvise spelling and alphabet songs in this style. For example, go down the alphabet and use a little melody:

> TEACHER: A B
> CHILDREN: A B
> TEACHER: C D
> CHILDREN: C D
> TEACHER: E F
> CHILDREN: E F
> All the way to Z!

The children's names make excellent lyrics for call-and-response songs. Take attendance this way. As the children's names are sung, the class points to their names on a name chart.

Alphabetical parade. After the children have learned to recognize the first letters and perhaps the words for the musical instruments in the room, organize the instruments for a parade according to their letters. For example, all the T instruments are grouped together; here come the triangles, tambourines, and tom-toms. There are even instruments for U (ukelele) and X (xylophone).

The children add to the theme by wearing alphabet letter cards around their necks or taped to their backs. They wave paper or cloth flags featuring letters of the alphabet.

Sing-along nursery rhymes. Nursery rhymes are an excellent way to introduce children to the idea of rhyming words. Make up melodies to favorite nursery rhymes. As you sing together, listen to the rhymes. These are stepping stones to greater language awareness.

Sing-along limericks. Children enjoy the repetition and silliness of most limericks. A group of second graders made up limericks for most letters of the alphabet. They sang them with twinkly eyes and mischievous grins.

There once was a letter A.
We found it in the hay.
It fell over B
And couldn't C
And hid behind the D.

The music of language. Language itself is musical, rhythmical, melodic. Every word can be played on an instrument, hummed as a melody, and used as a lyric in a song.

A group of first graders composed a lively musical interpretation based on days of the week. Monday through Friday and Sunday are two beats each, and the first syllable is stressed. Saturday is three beats, and the first syllable is stressed. The children experimented many ways before they decided on their favorite musical patterns. Here is the way they started.

Monday—CLAP clap
Tuesday—CLAP clap
Wednesday—CLAP clap
Thursday—CLAP clap
Friday—CLAP clap
Saturday—CLAP clap clap
Sunday—CLAP clap

Eric, age 9

The days of the week were printed on the board so that the children remembered the order. In a short time, the children recognized the words by sight.

The children improvised basic clapping rhythms by interspersing softer, tapping sounds between each day.

Monday—CLAP clap (tap tap tap)
Tuesday—CLAP clap (tap tap tap)

They played with variations of loud, soft, fast, and slow.

Use the children's names, characters from books, and everyday vocabulary words as material for making music.

The sounds of the earth and other onomatopoeias. Many words represent sounds, for example, hiss, buzz, drizzle, swish, bobwhite, brush, pop, snap, and flop. Challenge your children's imaginations and increase their awareness of sounds and letters by asking such questions as: "What are the sounds of snow falling? Of ice thawing? Of gentle, misty rain? Of a thunderstorm? Of boots walking on snow? Of sand blowing? What are the sounds of seeds growing? Of buds blossoming? Of leaves falling? Of wind blowing? What are the sounds of trees rustling in the breeze? Of water splashing? Of mud forming after the rain?" Then ask the children to suggest the letters needed to make the sounds into words. Write all their suggestions on the board.

Change "the sounds of the earth" into musical patterns played by classroom musicians using rhythm instruments and improvised sounds. In this way, a second grade composed a "Symphony of Four Seasons." One section developed a theme, from the almost imperceptible hush of seeds growing, to buds opening, to drizzle, to rainfall, to a thunderstorm.

MOVEMENT AND PLAY TIMES

Show-me games. Children and teachers consider these games among their favorites. Children eagerly respond to such challenges as: "Show me the letter X"; "Find your name"; and "Point to the word 'Hi.'"

These games can be played a variety of ways. Call the children's names individually to point to a letter, picture, or word. Suggest that when they point to the object, they do something about it. For example: "Look for the letter A. When you find it, clap your hands."

"Call me by my initial." One day Jon, Josh, and Jason were full of energy. Their kindergarten teacher could not get their attention. "Jon! Josh! Jason!" their teacher scolded. They kept running. "Boys! Come here this minute!" They did not respond.

After a few more attempts, the teacher had an idea. "Will all those people whose names begin with the letter J come right to this circle!" In one great leap, the three boys joined the circle and listened intently to their teacher as she explained the upcoming activity.

Many teachers enjoy playing initial games with their students. "Will all those children whose names begin with the letter D start putting on their coats." "Today, the children whose names begin with the letter G will lead the singing." "Where are our children whose names begin with the letter T? Can you do your favorite tricks?"

Initials and exercises. A variation of the above activity is to go through the alphabet from A to Z, stop at each letter that begins the first names of children in your class, and give those children a chance to lead an exercise. In one group, the initials were A, B, L, J, and M. The A's led jumping jacks; the B's led sit-ups; the L's led push-ups; the J's led touch-toes; and the M's led twists. If possible, show the letters as you call them.

Alphabet activities. Gather ideas for a different activity for each letter of the alphabet. Here is an example of a few alphabet activities suggested for a second-grade class.

A	Act out an animal, ask a question, arrange the farm
B	Build a sculpture, blow up a balloon
C	Cut an interesting paper shape, color a weather report
D	Draw a design, dress a puppet
E	Eyes to the window (What do you see?), ears to the room (What do you hear?)
F	Feed the fish, fill the texture box
G	Gather interesting shapes, give a gift
H	Houses and horses are fun to draw. How about it?
I	Ice-cream cones are interesting shapes. How many flavors can you draw?
J	Jog in place, jump like a jack-in-the-box

Always encourage and include your students' suggestions.

Alphabet treasure hunt. Alphabet letters are popular clues to a treasure. Correlate letters with colors, pictures, words, or arrows. When the children reach Z, they should find some kind of treasure, such as balloons, cookies, lollipops, apples, or a special storybook.

Pin the word on the object. As part of labeling or name-tagging your room, adapt the popular game "Pin the Tail on the Donkey." Print word cards for all the objects in your room. The children pick a card, one at a time. Read it to them if they cannot read. They find the object the card describes and pin or tape the card to the object.

The game should be played in an atmosphere of fun and helpfulness, not competition or tension. When the game is over, your room is full of words that the children will soon recognize.

Alphabet trains. Children enjoy making a train with their bodies. They form a single line, one person behind the other, with hands on the shoulders in front of them. Give the children (or have them pick out of a grab bag) a letter card to tape to their shirts or sleeves.

Duke Ellington called his great jazz piece "Take the 'A' Train," and what better way to start your train? "All aboard. We need our A car!" The child with the letter A hangs on behind you or starts the train. Go through all the letters until every child is attached. Now the train is ready to roll!

After a few runs, the train is ready to leave various cars. "Z car getting off!" or "A car getting off!" Continue until all the cars are scattered around the room.

Post office. Mark special boxes, hanging pockets, or cubbyholes with letters of the alphabet. Encourage children to write notes, cards, and letters to their classmates. Many teachers suggest exchanging letters on "Buddy Day."

The children print or write the buddies' names on an envelope or on the outside of the note or picture. They put their greeting in the box whose letter of the alphabet corresponds to the first initial of their friends' names.

The "game" is played many ways. Here are just two variations. The children take turns finding their mail by looking for the box with their initial and thumbing through the letters until they find their own. Or the children take turns being the postal clerk who finds their mail and gives it to them.

Alphabet fingers. Ask the children to show you a letter of the alphabet with their fingers. See how many letters the children can make. Name and celebrate each letter.

Alphabet bodies. If fingers can do it, why not whole bodies? Can you "turn your bodies into a letter of the alphabet?" The children squirm, stretch, bend, and twist to form the letters, most of which are easily recognizable. Do as many as possible standing up; then try the whole alphabet lying down.

Encourage children to work together to form, for example, M, K, and A. The children are excited by this challenge, and before you know it, they are ready for the next activity.

A delightful spinoff is to turn the children into a can of alphabet soup, with each child a different letter. What happens to that letter when the soup is cooked? Let's see!

Body words. Working in pairs, children can form the words TO, IT, IF, and IS. Working in pairs or groups of three or four, children can shape their bodies into HI, LOVE, CAT, DOG, PAL, and FUN. In no time, the floor is covered with energy-filled words that are easy to read and recognize.

An enjoyable variation is to ask small groups of children to form the same word, but with different qualities. Groups of four first and second graders filled the floor of a gym with the word CATS. Each group was unique. There were fat CATS, skinny CATS, mean CATS, shy CATS, silly CATS, snobby CATS, and scary CATS.

Alphabet exercises and T parties. While the children are shaping their bodies into letters, offer them this opportunity. Using the letter T, for example: "If you were the letter T, what exercises could you do without losing your basic Tshape?" The children try different ideas. Keeping their T shapes, they jump (legs held tightly together), twist, turn, tremble, tickle twirl, tiptoe, and tighten. It is amazing how many of these T tricks begin with the letter T!

Now "The letter T is going to a party." What kind? A T party! Play rhythmical music that helps the children move energetically. After a few minutes, stop the music and ask the T's to take a T bow and curtsy.

Follow this activity with art projects creating unusual letter and word posters and pictures.

Dance through the alphabet. Choose an exciting word that begins with A and turn it into a dance. Continue through the alphabet.

Here are some of the A–Z dances enjoyed by Patti Polster and Betty Griffith's students at the Jewish Center in Columbus, Ohio. For A they danced alligators; B, birds; C, clowns; and D, dogs. Their favorite letter dance was R; they danced robots.

Use music, tambourine shakes, drumbeats, and hand claps. Follow with pictures, stories, poems, and songs based on the children's suggestions.

A story for every letter. As part of his class's celebration of a letter of the alphabet, Greg Siegler reads a story that fits the letter. "If we study the letter K, I'll read a story about a king. Then we'll draw K's and knigs in our alphabet books and, finally, pretend we're kings."

Greg's students enjoyed their P word, "planets," so much that they started a space project that developed for weeks and included creating a planetarium and designing and building a space city.

Alphabet trees. Linda Goldsmith and Jo Ann Bell's kindergartners arrived at school one day to find their classroom tree covered with construction-paper upper- and lower-case letters, all mixed up. Linda chal-lenged them to "find the little b and place it near the big B; find the little c and place it near the big C."

Shirley Davis tapes different letters to different branches. The children find a branch of A's, a branch of D's, a branch of Y's, and so on. They play games in which the children are asked to remove letters, one at a time, to spell a word or name.

Playwriting. Children are fascinated by written words, even more so when the words are their own. As children improvise puppet shows and skits, write their dialogues on charts or chalkboard. After reading her scene a few times, a first grader observed, "Every time I read it, it says the same thing!"

Live alphabet books. Like the most successful alphabet books, you and your students can combine letters with a theme. How about an alphabet circus?

The ringleader announces each circus act in alphabetical order. Children hold up the letter card and the card announcing each act: A for acrobats, B for bears, C for clowns, D for dancing dogs, and so on.

Experiment with such themes as alphabet zoo, alphabet pet shop, alphabet ice-cream flavors (the children play ice-cream store), and alphabet restaurant. Afterward, make alphabet books on the same theme.

Letter charade. Fill a shoe box or shopping bag with word and picture cards. The children pick cards and pantomime their cards. The only "hint" they give the others is the beginning letter.

Clap for the special letter. This is one of Shirley Davis's favorite games. She shows the children a letter, talks about words that begin with that letter, and explains that she is going to say words. Some of the words will begin with the special letter; others will not. When the children bear a word beginning with the special letter, they clap their hands.

If clapping hands becomes tedious, try snapping fingers, stamping feet, touching toes, blinking eyes, wiggling noses, or patting heads.

Picture books, poems, and nursery rhymes. Move to or mime every alphabet book in your room. Go through each book and ask the children to take the shape of every picture (or at least the ones you like best).Be sure to introduce the picture by its letter and sounds.

If everyone is feeling silly, interpret *Dr. Seuss's ABC*. The children have hilarious times showing the Q page: "The quick Queen of Quincy and her quacking quacker-oo."

Gyo Fujikawa's *A to Z Picture Book* (Grosset & Dunlap, 1974) features ample selections of pictures for each letter so that every child finds ideas to move to. Remember, there are no correct or incorrect interpretations. Encourage all responses to the ideas.

Shel Silverstein's delightful poem "Love" is fun to do by itself and to use as a basis of improvisation.

LOVE

Richy was "L," but he's home with the flu,
Lizzie, our "O," had some homework to do,
Mitchell, "E," probably got lost on the way,
So I'm all of love that could make it today.[4]

With this poem is a picture of a little girl holding up a V all by herself.

We play this poem many ways. The most popular one is a row of four children holding up the letters L, O, V, and E. As the poem is recited, each letter leaves the line. Only the V is left.

Try your own variations. Here is one of our favorites. Four children held up letters forming PLAY.

PLAY

Peter held the P but he dropped it.
Julie held the L but she lost it.
Jennifer held the A but it fell.
Y doesn't spell PLAY very well!

Because of their repetition and rhythm, nursery rhymes are excellent subjects for moving and playing while children learn letters, sounds, and words. "Jack and Jill" and "Jack Be Nimble" help children learn J's as they recite while tumbling down hills and jumping over candlesticks. If your students are having trouble with their P's, help them along with "Peter, Peter, Pumpkin Eater," to be chanted while they chase the wife they couldn't keep. "Diddle Diddle Dumpling, My Son, John" definitely clarifies the D sound. Children are delighted to show how they walk with one shoe off and one shoe on.

Cue cards. In our visually oriented society, children are accustomed to printed messages. Make cue cards for various activities, directions, and announcements. Say the words as you show the cards, and in a short time the children will respond to the cards alone.

Try variations. Have classroom puppets hold cue cards, or ask children assigned to special jobs to use the "Clean-Up Time" card or the "Get Ready for Snack" card.

Expand the idea of cue cards. If you and your children interpret Tchaikovsky's *Nutcracker* Suite in movement, help the children remember the different ideas by showing them cards such as "Sugar Plum Fairy," "Russian Dance," and "Arabian Dance." A class of second graders were cued into their original movement patterns for Prokofiev's *Peter and the Wolf* with cards lettered: "Peter," "Grandfather," "Duck," and so on.

Name-movement card game. This game evolved from a series of experiments with young children who were excellent at movement but who had reading problems. I tried many ways to use their natural talents in movement to strengthen their reading skills. The following activity was one of the most successful results.

The one word that children always recognize is their own name. On one side of a large index card, print a child's name. Make a card for every student in your class. On the other side of the card, print a simple movement instruction, such as run, jump, clap, slide, step, and kick. Spread the cards, name-side up, in the center of a playing space.

With your students, form a large circle around the cards. The children become excited when they see their names. What can this game be? One by one, call the children and ask them to go into the circle, pick up their card, but not look at it yet, and return to their place. To add fun, suggest that they not go to pick up their cards "in the same old boring way," but that they "do something different—do your favorite trick!" Children who wish to do so will cartwheel, somersault, roll, bounce, and tap dance into the circle for their cards.

Although the children can read or recognize their own names, many of them will be unable to read the word on back of their cards. Before they shrink in disappointment and frustration, say something like this: "Boys and girls, on the back of your card is a special word. Don't let anyone see it. It's a surprise! I'm coming to every one of you to have a secret little visit. Then we'll be ready to play this game." Move as quickly as you can to every child. Whisper, "Do you know the word?" If the child can read it and whisper it to you, go on to the next child. If the child whispers "No," immediately tell the child the word. This is not the time for a skills test! Now all the children know the special words written on the backs of their cards.

"Boys and girls, when I call you, show us with your body what your word says. We'll follow you. You'll be the leader. Then we'll try to guess the word." One by one, the children glow as they run, jump, stretch, stamp, clap, and so on. Classmates have no trouble guessing the special word. Every child is applauded after leading a movement.

If you want evidence that children learn the movement words, turn all the cards name-side down and ask the children to pick up their own card again. I was astonished at the immediate success.

In shaping an experience like this with children, be sure their feelings are the highest priority. The reason our sessions were so exciting and successful is because no child was ever humiliated or corrected. The game was *not* to catch the children who missed their words. The game was to give every child a chance to be a successful leader and, secondarily, to add words to their sight vocabulary.

Say "Aaaaah." There is no end to this silly vowel-pronunciation activity. Ask children to "Open your mouth and say 'Aaaaah,' 'eh,' 'ih,' 'oh,' and 'oooh.'"

Because vowel sounds are breath sounds, body movement is easily added to express the different vowels. Ask the children to take a breath and, as they exhale, to say a vowel sound and let that vowel shape their bodies. "How does 'oh' feel in your arms and legs? How does 'eh' make your neck, back, and head want to move?" Try them all and surprise yourself with discoveries.

VISITORS AND FIELD TRIPS

Your visitors have names, hobbies, talents, and careers. What are they? Write them on the board or on posters.

Invitations and thank-you notes show good manners and also help children learn how to write letters.

Questions and ideas about the guest or trip are important aspects of planning, doing, and evaluating. Write the children's suggestions on charts or boards. Their words have shapes that they will soon learn to recognize and read. This list of questions was printed on a first-grade wall chart in preparation for a trip to the airport.

1. Where do the planes come from?
2. Where are the planes going?
3. How do you get a ticket?
4. How do you know where to go to get on the plane?
5. Who flies the plane?
6. Where do you put your suitcase?
7. What if the plane is late?
8. Where do you go to meet people who are visiting from other places?
9. How can you get a job working on an airplane?

A guest or trip is more enjoyable if you brainstorm feelings, questions, and ideas before, during, and after the experience.

Visitors

Visitors from other cultures. Always be on the lookout for members of the community who can help children learn about people from different backgrounds. Ask your guests, if possible, to show the children examples of words written in their language. The beautiful brush strokes of Chinese letters, the right-to-left order of Hebrew, and the flowing, beautiful curves of Arabic are fascinating to children who are just beginning to discover their own language.

Storyteller. There are storytellers in every community waiting to be invited to share their art with young listeners. Encourage your guest to involve the children in the stories as much as possible by teaching them repetitive lines or choruses from the stories. Write down the lines to enjoy after the guest has left. Your students enjoy being storytellers. Give them every opportunity.

Folk singer. Most folk songs and ballads have choruses that children easily learn and sing. Children need to experience the richness of oral literature through stories and songs. Follow the visit with improvised lyrics for favorite songs, and with art, movement, and creative writing activities.

Writer or poet. Children need to know that just as woodcarvers work with wood, potters with clay, and builders with stone and wood, writers and poets work with words. Words are their raw material. Follow the visit with creative writing sessions.

Calligrapher. Writing letters of the alphabet beautifully is an art called "calligraphy." Calligraphers are excellent classroom visitors because they can demonstrate their skills. After such a visit, children are inspired to practice handwriting.

Puppeteer. Check your community resources for puppeteers. Ask your guests if they can improvise a skit in which letters and words are part of the plot. Encourage the guests to involve the children as much as possible. Follow the session with your own puppet shows.

Actor and actress. Be sure they bring their scripts along to show the children. It is important for young children to know that, except for some improvisational theater, actors and actresses begin with a script that they read and memorize. Ask your guests to read aloud from their scripts. Because their reading has feeling and power, your children will be inspired to read stories, poems, and plays with such expression.

Alphabet people. Unusual and funny guests (you, your colleagues, family members, and good-sport neighbors) reinforce learning in an entertaining way. The alphabet person is dressed from head to toe in a letter of the alphabet, which is taped, pinned, or written on clothing, hands, face, and head. Some alphabet people are covered with words beginning with a particular letter, and some alphabet people speak only in words that begin with their letter.

Field Trips

Letter and word walk. Take a walk and focus on the letters and words children see while they walk. If the children are old enough to write, take notebooks along and copy words as they are spotted. Walk. Stop. Write. If the children are not old enough to write, you keep the record as they point to the letters and words. Skywriting counts!

When you return to the classroom, write all the words on the board. Use them as a resource for art, drama, songs, and creative writing progects.

Arlene Alda's superb photographs in *Arlene Alda's ABC* (Celestial Arts, 1981) adds another dimension to your walk. Alda's photographs show letter shapes found in nature and the environment.

When children are looking for letters and words on their walk, encourage them to look beyond the obvious. They will see such fabulous sights as a tree in the shape of a Y, a stone that looks like a Q, a window frame with an E-shape, and a doughnut like the letter O.

Library, bookmobile, and bookstore. Where can children find a greater celebration of written language? Be sure the children have the opportunity to experience the range of subjects and materials available. Give them time to browse and wonder. Try

to coordinate your visit to the library with a story-telling program, often a feature of the children's room.

Newspaper. The daily newspaper is part of most children's experience. But where do all those words come from? Who writes them? How do they get into the paper every day? When you return from the newsroom and the printer, you may want to publish your own class newspaper.

Outdoor advertising company. These people are responsible for filling billboards with words and pictures. Find out if they have samples of advertisements and public announcements. The size of these items always amazes young children. The company may even give you some scrounge billboard-sized poster paper to use for your own giant letter-writing.

Graphic design studio or advertising agency. The goal of these businesses is to catch your eye by the way they design words and pictures. Children will see how these people use letters in artistic, humorous, and unusual ways.

Computer graphics agency or word processing office. Children are interested in modern technologies. They are curious about how a word processor arranges and changes words as fast as they can say them. They want to know how words seem to come out of smoke, out of animals' mouths, and out of mountaintops.

Sign painter's studio. "Sign painters have so much fun," a first grader observed after a visit to a sign painter's shop. "They get to write: 'Beware of Dangerous Dog,' and 'All the Pizza You Can Eat.'" After your visit, do not be surprised if your students spend the next few days painting their own signs.

Greeting card shop or stationery store. When children see so many ways of printing "Happy Birthday," "Get Well," and "Congratulations," the words will become familiar to them. Stationery stores also feature paper products with monograms and personal names. When you return to the classroom, the children will want to design their own cards and writing paper.

Airport, railroad station, or bus terminal. These are exciting places for young children to visit. Schedules, cities, and codes flash on screens and display boards. Travel posters, ads for rental cars, and instructions for travelers' aid and luggage abound. The practical value of reading is conveyed in dramatic ways.

NOTES

1. Nancy Willard, "In Praise of ABC," *Carpenter of the Sun* (New York: Liveright, 1974), p. 15.
2. A. A. Milne, *The World of Pooh* (New York: Dutton, 1957), pp. 231–232.
3. Theodore Roethke, *Straw for the Fire* (New York: Doubleday, 1974), p. 207.
4. Shel Silverstein, "Love," *Where the Sidewalk Ends* (New York: Harper & Row, 1974), p. 95.

SELECTED BIBLIOGRAPHY

Books for Beginning ABCers

Anno, Mitsumasa. *Anno's Alphabet*. New York: Crowell, 1974.

Azarian, Mary. *A Farmer's Alphabet*. Boston: Godine, 1981.

Beisner, Monika. *A Folding Alphabet Book*. New York: Farrar, Straus & Giroux, 1981.

Berger, Terry. *Ben's ABC Day*. Photos by Alice Kandell. New York: Lothrop, Lee & Shepard, 1982.

Brown, Marcia. *All Butterflies*. New York: Scribners, 1974.

Burningham, John. *John Burningham's ABC*. Indianolis, Ind.: Bobbs-Merrill, 1967.

Charles, Donald. *Letters from the Calico Cat*. Chicago: Childrens Press, 1974.

Crowther, Robert. *The Most Amazing Hide-and-Seek Alphabet Book*. New York: Viking, 1977.

Duvoisin, Roger. *A for the Ark*. New York: Lothrop, Lee & Shepard, 1964.

Eichenberg, Fritz. *Ape in a Cape*. New York: Harcourt Brace Jovanovich, 1952.

Farber, Norma. *As I Was Crossing Boston Common*. Illustrated by Arnold Lobel. New York: Dutton, 1975.

Feelings, Muriel. *Jhamba Means Hello: A Swahili Alphabet Book*. Illustrated by Tom Feelings. New York: Dial, 1974.

Fujikawa, Gyo. *A to Z Picture Book*. New York: Grosset & Dunlap, 1974.

Hoban, Tana. *A, B, See!* New York: Morrow, Greenwillow, 1982.

Lobel, Arnold. *On Market Street*. Illustrated by Anita Lobel. New York: Morrow, Greenwillow, 1982.

Matthiesen, Thomas. *ABC: An Alphabet Book*. New York: Platt & Munk, 1966.

Mendoza, George. *The Marcel Marceau Alphabet Book*. Photos by Milton H. Greene. New York: Doubleday, 1970.

Merriam, Eve. *Good Night to Annie*. Illustrated by John Wallner. New York: Four Winds, 1980.

Munari, Bruno. *Munari's ABC*. New York: World, 1960.

Musgrove, Margaret. *Ashanti to Zulu*. Illustrated by Leo and Diane Dillon. New York: Dial, 1976.

Oxenbury, Helen. *Helen Oxenbury's ABC of Things*. New York: Watts, 1972.

Pepp, Rodney. *The Alphabet Book*. New York: Four Winds, 1968.

Provensen, Alice, and Martin Provensen. *A Peaceable Kingdom: The Abecedarius*. New York: Viking, 1978.

Tudor, Tasha. *A is for Annabelle*. New York: Walck, 1954.

Walters, Marguerite. *The City-Country ABC: My Alphabet Ride in the City and My Alphabet Ride in the Country*. Illustrated by Ib Ohlsson. New York: Doubleday, 1966.

Wildsmith, Brian. *Wildsmith's ABC*. New York: Watts, 1963.

Letters Turn into Words

Alda, Arlene. *Arlene Alda's ABC: A New Way of Seeing*. Millbrae, Calif.: Celestial Arts, 1981.

Baskin, Leonard. *Hosie's Alphabet*. New York: Viking, 1972.

Charlip, Remy. *Handtalk: An ABC of Finger Spelling and Sign Language*. New York: Four Winds, 1974.

Eastman, P. D. *The Alphabet Book*. New York: Random House, 1974.

Elting, Mary. *Q Is for Duck: An Alphabet Guessing Game*. Boston: Houghton Mifflin, 1980.

Gackenbach, Dick. *Arabella and Mr. Crook*. New York: Macmillan, 1982.

Graham, Bill. *The First Words Picture Book*. Photos by Bill Gillham. New York: Putnam, 1982.

Gretz, Susanna. *Teddybear's ABC*. Chicago: Follett, 1975.

Gwynne, Fred. *Chocolate Moose for Dinner*. New York: Dutton, Windmill, 1976.

———. *The King Who Rained*. New York: Dutton, Windmill, 1970.

———. *The Sixteen Hand Horse*. New York: Dutton, Windmill, 1980.

Hefter, Richard, and Martin Stephen Moskof. *The Great Big Alphabet Picture Book with Lots of Words*. Illustrated by Richard Hefter. New York: Grosset & Dunlap, 1972.

Heide, Parry Florence. *Alphabet Zoop*. Illustrated by Sally Matthews. New York: McCall, 1970.

Hoban, Lillian. *Harry's Song*. New York: Morrow, Greenwillow, 1980.

Hoban, Tana. *Push-Pull, Empty-Full: A Book of Opposites*. New York: Macmillan, 1972.

Lionni, Leo. *The Alphabet Tree*. New York: Pantheon, 1968.

———. *Frederick*. New York: Pantheon, 1973.

McMillan, Ruth, and Brett McMillan. *Puniddles*. Boston: Houghton Mifflin, 1982.

Mendoza, George, with Zero Mostel. *Sesame Street Book of Opposites*. Photos by Secunda Sheldon. New York: Platt & Munk, 1974.

Miller, Jane. *Farm Alphabet Book*. New York: Scholastic, 1981.

O'Neill, Mary. *Words, Words, Words*. New York: Doubleday, 1966.

Pienkowski, Jan. *ABC*. New York: Simon & Schuster, 1974.

Pomerantz, Charlotte. *The Piggy in the Puddle*. Illustrated by James Marshall. New York: Macmillan, 1974.

Seuss, Dr. [Theodor S. Geisel]. *Oh, Say Can You Say?* New York: Random House, 1979.

Staats, Sara Rader. *Big City ABC*. Illustrated by Robert Keys. Chicago: Follett, 1968.

Testa, Fulvio, and Anthony Burgess. *The Land Where the Ice Cream Grows*. Illustrated by Fulvio Testa. New York: Doubleday, 1979.

Waters, Frank. *The First ABC*. Illustrated by Charles Mozley. New York: Watts, 1970.

Watson, Clyde. *Applebet: An ABC*. Illustrated by Wendy Watson. New York: Farrar, Straus & Giroux, 1982.

Watson, Nancy Dingman. *What Does A Begin With?* Illustrated by Aldren A. Watson. New York: Knopf, 1956.

Weil, Lisl. *Owl and Other Scrambles*. New York: Dutton, Unicorn, 1980.

Teacher Resources

Adelson, Leone. *Dandelions Don't Bite: The Story of Words*. Illustrated by Lou Myers. New York: Pantheon, 1972.

Adler, Bill. *World's Worst Riddles and Jokes*. Illustrated by Ed. Malsberg. New York: Grosset & Dunlap, 1976.

Alexander, Arthur. *The Magic of Words*. Englewood Cliffs, N.J.: Prentice-Hall, 1962.

Arnstein, Flora J. *Children Write Poetry*. New York: Dover, 1967.

Basil, Cynthia. *How Ships Play Cards: A Beginning Book of Homonyms*. New York: Morrow, 1980.

———. *Nailheads and Potato Eyes: A Beginning Word Book*. New York: Morrow, 1976.

Chenfeld, Mimi Brodsky. *Teaching Language Arts Creatively*. New York: Harcourt Brace Jovanovich, 1978.

Clay, Marie M. *The Early Detection of Reading Difficulties*, 2nd ed. Exeter, N.H.: Heinman, 1979.

Clay, Marie M., and Dorothy Butler. *Reading Begins at Home*. Exeter, N.H.: Heinman, 1979.

Dugan, William. *How Our Alphabet Grew: The History of the Alphabet*. New York: Golden Press, 1972.

Durkin, Dolores. *Teaching Young Children to Read*. Boston: Allyn & Bacon, 1972.

Espy, Willard R. *Grandpa's Almanac of Words at Play for Children*. New York: Crown, 1982.

Folsom, Franklin. *The Language Book*. New York: Grosset & Dunlap, 1963.

Gray Wolf [Hofsinde, Robert]. *Indian Picture Writing*. New York: Morrow, 1959.

Greenfeld, Howard. *Sumer Is Icumen In: Our Ever-Changing Language*. New York: Crown, 1980.

Koch, Kenneth. *Wishes, Lies and Dreams*. New York: Random House, Vintage, 1970.

Kohl, Herbert. *Reading, How To*. New York: Dutton, 1973.

Lillard, Paula Polk. *Montessori—A Modern Approach*. New York: Schocken, 1972.

Pflaum-Connor, Susanna. *The Development of Language and Reading in Young Children*, 2nd ed. Columbus, Ohio: Merrill, 1978.

Pulaski, Mary Ann Spencer. *Understanding Piaget*, rev. ed. New York: Harper & Row, 1980.

Rogers, Frances. *Painted Rock to Printed Page*. Philadelphia: Lippincott, 1960.

Russell, Sloveig Paulson. *A is for Apple and Why: The Story of Our Alphabet*. New York: Abingdon, 1959.

Spache, Evelyn B. *Reading Activities for Child Involvement*. Boston: Allyn & Bacon, 1972.

Van Allen, Roach, and Claryce Allen. *Language Experience Activities*, 2nd ed. Boston: Houghton Mifflin, 1982.

West, Fred. *The Way of Language*. New York: Harcourt Brace Jovanovich, 1975.

13

WE ENCOUNTER NUMBERS

Arithmetic

Arithmetic is where numbers fly like pigeons in and out of your head.

Arithmetic tells you how many you lose or win if you know how many you had before you lost or won.

Arithmetic is seven eleven all good children go to heaven—or five six bundle of sticks.

Arithmetic is numbers you squeeze from your head to your hand to your pencil to your paper till you get the answer.

Arithmetic is where the answer is right and everything is nice and you can look out of the window and see the blue sky—or the answer is wrong and you have to start all over and try again and see how it comes out this time.

If you take a number and double it and double it again and then double it a few more times, the number gets bigger and bigger and goes higher and higher and only arithmetic can tell you what the number is when you decide to quit doubling.

If you have two animal crackers, one good and one bad, and you eat one and a striped zebra with streaks all over him eats the other, how many animal crackers will you have if somebody offers you five, six, seven, and you say No no no and you say Nay nay nay and you say Nix nix nix?

If you ask your mother for one fried egg for breakfast and she gives you two fried eggs and you eat both of them, who is better in arithmetic, you or your mother?[1]

THE BASICS

Alexander just turned twenty-six months old. He is now able to name all his body parts, dolls, games, TV and story characters, food, names of family members and friends, household rooms and objects, pets, and neighbors. If you ask him his name, he will probably tell you straight, "Alexander Steele Boxerbaum." But sometimes he gets a mischievous twinkle in his eyes and answers you with a joke, "Jack Benny."

Alexander counts to thirteen. He just started taking a block at a time and reciting numbers as he piles the blocks in a group. Ask Alexander how old he is and he responds the way every toddler does, by holding up tiny fingers to show his age. Alexander shows two little fingers. Someday Alexander will learn his address, phone number, credit card numbers, medical insurance numbers, and student identification numbers. His life will be full of dates, times, temperatures, salaries, taxes, schedules, sales slips, scores, and prices. Welcome to the world of numbers, Alexander!

"Heck, how did we get numbers anyway?" a wide-eyed kindergartner asked, hands on hips. The story of how we got numbers is as fascinating and complicated as the story of language. In fact, it is really a part of that story.

Alexander and his toddler friends are on the right track when they tell you "how many" by showing you the correct number of fingers. Counting fingers and toes was the universal way of figuring numbers in ancient days. In addition to counting fingers and toes, people counted pebbles (a pebble represented, for example, a lamb, a cow, or a horse), cut notches on sticks, carved marks on rocks and tree trunks, tied knots on leather thongs, and made little dots.

These methods evolved into symbols. For example, early people used the word for "wings" to describe two objects and the word for "hand" to mean five objects. Some cultures like the Hebrews and Greeks used letters to represent numbers; A meant one, B two, and so on. This system led to complicated situations, because every word also had a numerical value.

Superstition, magic, and mystery became part of the language of numbers. Numerologists read meanings and divine messages hidden in numbers and words. Even today, Jews wear the symbol *chai*, two letters of the Hebrew alphabet which spell "life" and which also add up to the number eighteen. In many Jewish families, eighteen is therefore a lucky number.

Numbers that could not be divided by another number were considered magical or divine by ancient peoples. Numbers like three and seven were full of mystery. If you think people have abandoned superstitions, just visit the casinos of Las Vegas or Atlantic City.

Numbers and ways to mark and count them became part of the language of ancient cultures. Because fingers were the first way people counted, the mark for *one* looked like a finger. The Latin word for finger is "digit." When you think of the word "digits," do you think of numbers or fingers? Some cultures used ten as a base number (ten fingers?), while others used five (one hand?). The Mayans used twenty (two hands and two feet?).

When people started to write symbols for numbers, they had a lot of writing to do. If they wanted to write one hundred, they had to mark one hundred 1's. Because this took so long, people figured out an easier way to count, one that is still used today: groups of four vertical lines cut by a fifth line. Eventually, all the ancient cultures created their own symbols for numbers. Some were pictures, others were designs, and still others were like letters of the alphabet.

Because Romans occupied a large part of the ancient world, their number system was widely adopted. Roman numerals were based on letters of the alphabet. In the early years of the Roman system, the numerals were written in any order. If people wanted to know what they stood for, they just added them all together. In time the Romans worked out a way to write the same number with fewer numerals. They agreed that when the first of two symbols stood for a higher number than the second, the first would be added to the second. Therefore, XI = 11. When the first of two symbols represented a smaller number, the first would be subtracted from the second. Therefore, IX = 9.

Meanwhile, in another part of the world, the Hindus in India had created their own system of numbers, very different from that of the Romans. Many scientists and philosophers believe that the Hindu system was the most brilliant of all. Sometimes it is called the Hindu-Arabic system and even

our numbers are referred to as Arabic numerals, but the Arabs adapted the Hindu system and used it for hundreds of years before Muhammed Al-Khwarizmi, a ninth-century Arab mathematician, wrote an important book describing and giving instructions for using the Hindu system. Al-Khwarizmi's book found its way into Europe and began affecting the way scholarly mathematicians looked at numbers. Because the book was written in Arabic, the Europeans called that number system Arabic.

What distinguishes the Hindu-Arabic number system is the importance accorded the position of each number. The system is based on 10, and each number has its own symbol. Any number can be represented by these numerals, just as all of the words of our language can be formed from the same twenty-six letters. From 1 to 9, one-digit numerals are used; from 10 to 99, two-digit numerals; from 100 to 999, three-digit numerals; and so on.

When a number is written, the numerals are not interchangeable. For example, 142 cannot be written 421 or 241, as was the case with early Roman numerals. In the Hindu-Arabic system, the place or position of a number indicates its value. In two-digit numbers, the digit on the right-hand side stands for numbers of ones, and the digit on the left-hand side stands for numbers of tens. The number 25 means there are five ones and two tens (twenty). In a three-digit number, the value of hundreds is added. That is, 425 means there are five ones, two tens, and four hundreds.

This system of "place value" greatly simplified notation, counting, and calculations. Consider, for example, the simplicity of "1983" compared with MDCCCCLXXXIII and MCMLXXXIII.

The Hindus are also credited with one of the most profound and practical mathematical inventions—zero. Their basic number system was in use for thousands of years before they created a symbol for the concept of "none." Until this time, they left spaces between numbers (5 4 meant five hundred and four), then used dots (5.4). The zero, which means *nothing*, changed just about *everything*.

It took a very long time before people who lived under Roman rule changed to the Hindu-Arabic system. Most of the Roman Empire ended about 1,500 years ago, but the use of Roman numerals continued for about 700 years, until the introduction of the printing press helped spread the Hindu-Arabic system.

We cannot think about numbers without attending to one of their most important functions, measurement. We have come a long way from the days of measuring the passage of time by painting suns on animal skin or tree bark, or measuring distance with hands or forearms. Today our wafer-thin wrist watches provide time, date, temperature, jogging time, and times in other places of the world. Some watches have alarms or play music, some even talk. We now have instruments of measurement from A to Z, from altimeters to zymoscopes, but most of the questions people ask are the same now as they were in earlier times: how long, how high, how wide, how fast, how far, how dark, how wet, how hot? How to make sense of this world?

How quickly children develop a recognition and understanding of numbers, like their general development, is highly individual. Their rate of development is influenced by many factors, including the quality of their environment; interaction with siblings and older children; socioeconomic factors affecting family life; the games they play and the TV programs they watch; the degree of verbal and nonverbal communication; and the diversity of learning experiences. It is important to recognize that although Alexander can recite his numbers, he may not understand what it means to count to thirteen. Because he holds up two little fingers does not necessarily imply that he knows what it means to be two years old.

Extensive studies have been carried out to discover just what prekindergartners know and understand about arithmetic. Alfred Williams described one such study in which California children entering kindergarten were tested in eight categories: numbers and operations; geometry; measurement; functions and graphs; mathematical sentences; logic sets; and applications and problem solving. Many children were able to recognize circles, squares, and triangles; read the number 4; make three marks; locate the first object in a series; and find the shortest object among several presented.

The most difficult items, that is, those to which fewer than 25 percent of the subjects responded successfully, included reading the numeral 23; writing the numerals 4 and 8; locating the fifth element in a series; finding one more or one less of the objects in a series; knowing the sum of the numbers 2 and 3, and 2 and 1, and the remainder for 5 and 2; realizing the number of pennies in a nickel, number of nickels in a dime; showing the number of corners in a square and triangle; perceiving the likenesses and differences among similar objects; deducing the number relationships between line segments and dots, and functions of numbers shown in pictograph form; matching elements of subsets, and making sets not equivalent, or equal in number; solving number stories involving a missing addend or remainder, and deducing the missing elements needed to make two geometric constructions equivalent.[2]

The researchers found that the children who scored well on this test were those who showed rote counting ability; had older playmates or siblings who could count and who knew their age, telephone number, and house number; and played games that involved counting, dialing, and scoring.

In his conclusion Williams suggested a curriculum that is endorsed on every page of this book.

The kindergarten program could well include activities designed to help children develop adequate concepts, skills and abilities concerning a) age b) number c) telephone number d) telephone dialing e) television channels f) songs involving numbers and g) counting games involving spinners, dice and cards.

The program of instruction should include a wide variety of activities that include the use of "number."[3]

Children need words and explanations, but more important, they need many opportunities to discover ideas for themselves by counting, playing, building, spinning, cutting, pouring, digging, and touching. They need concrete experiences to help them find meaningful information, to help them understand.

DISCOVERY TIMES

- Numbers are part of our everyday life.
- Numbers help us count things.
- Numbers have their own words and symbols.
- Numbers are called numerals. Numerals are one, two, three, four, five six, seven, eight, and so on. They are also called cardinal numbers.
- Sometimes we talk about things in order: first, second, third, fourth. These are called ordinal numbers.
- Numbers tell us our age, height, and weight.
- Numbers tell us our telephone code, our house code, and our zip code.
- Numbers tell us the temperature and humidity.
- Numbers tell us how much things cost.
- Numbers tell us about money: pennies, nickels, dimes, quarters, half dollars, and dollars.
- Numbers tell us something about sharing so that everyone gets an equal amount.
- We can count so many things: people, animals, books, toys, houses, years, weeks, days, hours, and minutes.
- Sometimes stories have numbers in them, for example, "The Three Bears" and "The Seven Dwarfs."
- It is fun to play number games.
- When we cook or bake, we use numbers to measure ingredients.
- When we join numbers (or similar things) together and count them, we count a higher number than the original separate numbers. This process is known as addition.
- When we have a number (or similar things) and we take some away, we count a lower number than when we started. This process is called subtraction.
- Zero means nothing.
- There is no end to numbers. If you try to think of the highest possible number, you can always add another number to it. Thus numbers are infinite, without end.
- Learning numbers is like learning letters of the alphabet.
- It is fun to learn to read and write numbers.

SUGGESTED VOCABULARY

low	fifteen	whole	nickel
high	sixteen	half	dime
large	seventeen	all	quarter
small	eighteen	none	half dollar
full	nineteen	some	share
empty	twenty	zero	count
numbers	thirty	ruler	add
time	forty	yardstick	subtract
temperature	fifty	measuring	multiply
clock	sixty	tape	divide
watch	seventy	scale	take away
calendar	eighty	thermometer	measure
dollar	ninety	pounds	bunch
coins	one hundred	inches	group
recipe	one thousand	feet	herd
score	one million	date	flock
team	infinity	year	crowd
one	many	minute	stack
two	few	hour	pile
three	more	second	abacus
four	less	telephone	speed
five	a lot	number	speedometer
six	a little	address	circle
seven	same	age	square
eight	different	how old?	triangle
nine	equal	how tall?	rectangle
ten	single	how heavy?	dots
eleven	double	money	lines
twelve	triple	change	shapes
thirteen	over	price	nothing
fourteen	under	penny	everything
	high		

As you glance over these suggested vocabulary words, you probably realize how many of them you use every day. Words about numbers and number concepts are an integral part of our lives. How many people are we expecting? What's the temperature today? What time shall we have our snack? How many people will line up for a drink of water? What shall we do first? How many children are buying hot lunch today?

Because your room is full of conversation and nonverbal communication, your children will hear these words often and will be encouraged to understand and use them. When you say, "The *first* thing we will do today is sing our Rabbit Song," and follow that announcement with your song, the children begin to grasp the concept of order, or ordinal numbers. Say and do!

The activities in this guide are packed with vocabulary. Don't be the strong silent type! Children learn their language by using it and hearing it.

SOME BEGINNING ACTIVITIES

Start with the date. Even if your children are not yet reading or writing or counting, they will soon recognize the special words and numbers on the board or on a chart that signify the date. "Boys and girls, today is September 12, 1983." Each day is a new day with a new number, but the year stays the same for awhile.

Start with counting heads. The first day of school is a fine time to find out just how many children are in your class. Children are fascinated by the counting process, especially if you gently touch each head as you count (every person is so important in this process). Announce the grand total of children in your class. Write the number on a chart or on the board.

Start with treasure boxes. At the beginning of the school year, Carol Price sends letters to her kindergartners' families in Worthington Estates, Ohio, asking for a variety of scrounge materials for "treasure box" collections. The children bring in such items as bread tags, small lids or caps, seashells, pebbles, marbles, corks, wooden spools, buttons, nuts and bolts, and keys.

"With these things," Carol explains, "I begin our math program! We cover cigar boxes with contact paper and label each box according to its special items. The children put the seashells in the seashell box, the pebbles in the pebbles box, until all of our treasure boxes are full. We use them to learn counting, sorting, and comparing. They really are treasures!"

Start with ages. Children's ages are important numbers in their scheme of things. Write all the children's names on a chart; next to their names, clearly write their ages as they tell you.

Start with heights and weights. Measuring the children's heights and weights is one of the first things many teachers do at the beginning of the school year. Even the youngest children know the meaning of a mark, number, or color next to their names.

"That's how high I am," a four-year-old explained as he showed his statistics on a bright yellow chart.

When this delightful activity occurs early in the school year and is repeated every few months, the children learn a lot about their own development, and about measurements, numbers, and addition.

At the end of the year, Lynn Salem of Immaculate Conception Elementary School in Columbus, Ohio, cuts height markings from the measurement chart and gives the children their own colorful strips showing how they grew.

Enjoy experimenting with ways to measure. More measurement suggestions are provided in this guide.

Start with a counting song. One of the children's favorite songs, "Ten Little Indians," is easy to sing and easy to count with. We have changed "Indians" to "desks," "tables," "noses," "smiles," and "gerbils," and we have counted much higher than ten.

Start with an imaginative number story book. Your room is no doubt filled with a variety of colorful, interesting books that are constantly in use. But children love extra challenges. Read, look at, and talk about books that motivate children to make careful observations and sharp conclusions.

Such a book is Maurice Sendak's *One Was Johnny* (Harper & Row, 1962). Beginning with "1 was Johnny who lived by himself," each page introduces another crazy character and drama until ten ideas have been counted. Then, one by one, the characters depart, leaving "1 was Johnny who lived by himself and LIKED IT LIKE THAT!"

As the children count up to and back from 10, they are laughing at the silliness of the plot. More importantly, they are thinking up their own silly stories that begin with an idea and proceed to further adventures.

Be sure to write the children's stories if they are not yet able to write themselves. Volunteers from the community or older children are eager to transcribe the young children's stories and poems. Illustrations are also important.

Anno's Counting Book by Mitsumasa Anno (Crowell, 1977) is another picture book that inspires children to use their powers of observation and perception. This is a counting book with no words, only numbers and pictures.

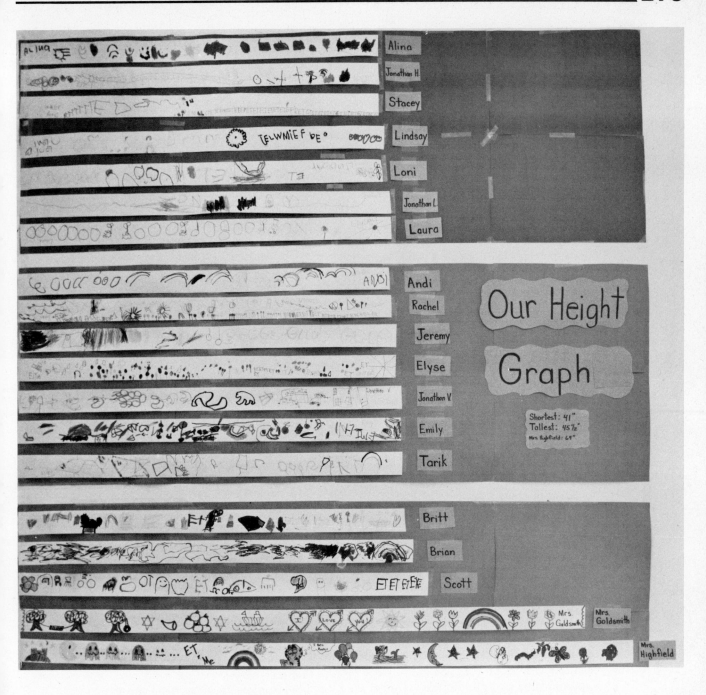

Children learn to recognize sets (like things) by finding the right number of cows or houses or trees as the scenes grow increasingly more complicated. You will find your students returning to this book again and again to see if they missed anything. **Start with absentmindedness.** Ina Mayer has discovered a most enjoyable way to start her first graders on a math spree at Olde Sawmill Elementary School in Dublin, Ohio. "I play dumb! I play absentminded. I deliberately count wrong or I write the wrong number on the board. The children gleefully correct the mistake. Oh my, sometimes we have so much to do, we just forget some things, don't we?" Ina twinkles.

Let me put in an extra word for a "making mistakes" game. When children know something, they need many ways of celebrating that knowledge. What more immediately satisfying and enjoyable way than to correct a mistake with humor and fun?

If you kid around and recite "One and

one are three" and get no response, that will tell you something about what your students do not know. So be human once in a while. Make some fun mistakes and watch how exuberantly your students set them right.

If you feel self-conscious playing "absentminded," then delegate that responsibility to a puppet, perhaps the same puppet or a relative of the puppet who sometimes fails to understand letters and words and other important ideas.

Start with first things first. Young children need experience with the concept of ordinal numbers like "first," "second," and "third." As often as possible, use the terms and follow or accompany them with actions that demonstrate the principle. For example, when you say "Kira will be the first person in line today," Kira stands to lead the line. Or "We have three important things to do this morning: first, to hear our story about the snow; second, to finish our pictures; and third, to go outside and play." Then do those things in order, with reminders along the way. At the end of the day, it is fun to summarize. Ask the children, "Do you remember what we did first today? What did we do second?"

Many teachers complain that their students have trouble understanding and following sequences. The kind of scheduling described above is helpful in clarifying the idea of sequences. Even more effective are movement activities suggested in "Movement and Play Times."

Start with the special number of the day. Colors, shapes, letters, words, children, holidays, animals—all are excellent causes for celebrations. So are numbers. Begin at the beginning with "good old number one," as Kenyatta introduced it to his fellow kindergartners. Talk about it. Write it. Count it. Draw pictures of the idea of it. Make up songs about it. Improvise puppet shows explaining it. Make mobiles of one item each. Cut out pictures and shapes demonstrating the idea of one unit of something. Correlate it with color. Dance it. Read books about it. Write poems and stories about it.

Here is a poem about the number one that was written by a class of kindergartners. I copied it from their colorful chart displayed on a wall filled with designs and illustrations.

Number One
Today is Number One's Day.
Here is Number One—1.
Number One is all alone.
One tree is number 1 and
One dog is number 1.
Today Number One is happy
Because it is Number One's day.

Start with a snack full of numbers. Peanuts, grapes, tiny pretzel sticks, and crackers are snack foods that are easy to distribute by numbers. "Today, everyone is going to have a special number of peanuts. Spread your napkins. Wait till all of us have our special number before we eat them. Let's count them first."

Add suspense and excitement by asking the children to close their eyes while the peanuts are distributed. Count them together. "Wow! We all have nine peanuts each! That's a lot."

With one group of prekindergartners, we really had fun asking them: "How will you eat your peanuts? One at a time? Two by two? Three by three? All at once? Hmmmmm?" Suggesting such possibilities was an important way to introduce number concepts. Be prepared for all the children to announce their choices. "I ate one at a time!" "I ate all mine at once!"

Start with a survey. Nancy Roberts and her first graders at Immaculate Conception Elementary School in Columbus, Ohio, often conduct surveys. They record their findings on charts and graphs and in number stories. Their questions include the following:

How many boys are in our class? How many girls?
How many six-year-olds are in our class? How many seven-year-olds? How many eight-year-olds?
How many people in this class have pets?
How many people live in apartments? In houses? In tents? On boats?
How many children have a tooth or teeth missing?
How many class members have dark hair? How many have light hair?
How many children like winter best? Summer best? Spring best? Autumn best?

All the activities in this guide are excellent starters. Once your imagination is in high gear, you will find possibilities in everything you see and do.

TALK TIMES

In the previous twelve guides, you have been reminded of how important talking and listening experiences are to the social and intellectual development of young children. The reason for the repetition of that reminder in this guide is a question asked by a young teacher of nursery school children when the topic of numbers and the importance of children's ease at communication was introduced.

"What's there to talk about?" she asked, without being sarcastic. "I mean, they have to learn their numbers and that's that."

Children have so many questions, observations, impressions, and feelings about *everything* in their lives, including numbers. When Ariela was six years old, she and I sat together quietly, visiting. Her head was bent over a paper filled with numbers. She broke her concentration to share her feelings and, with a dazzling smile, observed, "Aren't numbers beautiful?" When Ariela's sister, Adina, was seven, her class talked about the idea of infinity. Adina burst into the house that day and told her mother, "Do you know what my favorite number is? Infinity. Because it goes on forever!"

Ask Lynn Salem and Nancy Roberts "What's there to talk about?" Their first graders had so much to say about numbers that their teachers had trouble recording all their ideas. They talked about lucky numbers, the biggest numbers they could think of, how numbers came about, and what they wanted to learn about numbers. Enjoy the following excerpts of conversations from both classes. As you read, imagine the sounds of curiosity and excitement, the music of "Talk Times."

Let's talk about our lucky numbers.

BRIDGET: 32. My mom's age!

KEVIN: 17. I'm 7, and 17 is just about like 7.

PATRICK: 100. Well, one hundred dollars! What else?

TARRAINE: 6. Because when I play games, I always roll 6 with the dice.

JOHN: My lucky number is my birthday, 8.

NINA: 2 is my favorite. When you're playing and you have a friend, that's 2 and that's nice.

Let's talk about the highest number you can think of.

SEVERAL CHILDREN: Infinity.

VANESSA: 100. Because it takes a long time to count to 100.

MOLLY (I): If you can't write it, then that's the biggest number!

JANIE: 650 is the biggest. It's almost at the end of the numbers and that's how you know.

JIMMY: 99 zillion 999. Well, it's higher than 100 and less than 1,000!

How did you learn your numbers?

RACHEL: My Mom and Dad.

TERENCE: I tried to learn them myself.

JIM: I learned them by counting my fingers.

What's the best way to teach little children their numbers?

SHEAN: Show them your fingers.

MOLLY (II): Say the number first and they will say it after you.

KARA: Give them pencil and paper. Give yourself pencil and paper. Write the numbers and let the child copy them.

How do you think numbers started?

MICHAEL: God thought them up and put them in people's brains and they taught other people.

JAMIE: God sent Jesus down and he knew about numbers and he taught people about them.

JIM: One guy said, "There's one way or two ways to make numbers."

BRIDGET: Numbers got started when electricity started. If you didn't have electricity, you wouldn't have a clock. You wouldn't have numbers either. I think numbers really got started by George Washington and Abraham Lincoln because they're on the money.

JANE: One day someone went into the woods and there was a bear in a tree, two bears in another tree, three bears in another tree (all the way up to ten). They had to make up some numbers so they could count those bears!

MOLLY (II): Well, you know most people think that people like George Washington started numbers, but you're wrong. People started like gorillas. Well, one day, these gorillas started looking at their hands and they decided to do something with those fingers, so they counted them.

ADAM: God could have put it in Adam and Eve's brain and they told other people like Cain and Abel and they spread it around.

MARK: Numbers came from shapes.

BEN: Just people think them up.

JIM: Maybe they had little dots and they started to count them.

KRISTEN: They would put people in a line and start counting them.

ASPEN: If you didn't have letters, you wouldn't have numbers 'cause number words are made out of letters.

In a room filled with the dynamics of learning and sharing, numbers can turn out to be your number one topic of conversation. From the schedule of the day to directions for a new game, to how many cups of water are needed for a recipe, numbers are part of everything you do together. Do not miss opportunities to correlate numbers with all areas of interest. Be a number dropper.

ART TIMES

Preparations for art activities are excellent ways to reinforce the learning of numbers:

Each child gets three pieces of paper for this project.

Art helpers, please give everyone in the class two sponges and one cup of water.

When the paper helpers come around, boys and girls, please tell them if you want a large or small sheet of paper.

Boys and girls, in this project we have two important steps: The first step is to draw your design; the second step is to cut it out.

Art activities and numbers are so interrelated that we are often unaware of their connections. How many colors shall we use? How many flowers, trees, houses, people, and dogs shall we draw? How big? How small? Shall we cover our whole paper or concentrate on one area? Shall we make a picture of one idea or of many? How many buttons shall we glue to our collage? What if we cut our paper shapes in half?

As you grow more aware of the many ways numbers relate to art, you and your students will enjoy a diversity of experiences, deeper and more successful because different areas of understanding and imagination are combined. As often as possible, help your children discover relationships. When you do, you find not only the rainbow but also the pot of gold (and the gold pieces to be counted).

A word of caution. When you integrate ideas, do it smoothly. If you are heavy-handed and overly directed, you will turn every delightful art activity into a math lesson. A natural observation linking numbers to art might be: "Jason, I like the way you drew those two balloons in the sky." Easy does it.

Self-portraits. Before your children create self-portraits, take a count of body parts.

We need:

One head	One torso
Two eyebrows	Two arms
Two eyes	Two hands
One nose	Ten fingers
One mouth	Two legs
Two ears	Two feet
One neck	Ten toes

And we need "about a million hairs," suggested a kindergartner. Encourage the children to include as many body parts in their portraits as they can or want to.

Body parts chart. A large class chart or smaller individual charts showing different body parts by number and name are entertaining and informative. This activity gives children the chance to focus on specific body parts without worrying about making them proportional to the rest of their body design, which so often causes anxiety.

A kindergarten class celebrated different body parts in original pictures that were glued to a large chart. As he concentrated on his assignment, one serious five-year-old noted that "Ears look like snails."

House pictures. Lynn Salem enjoys asking her first graders to paint or draw pictures of their houses. Lynn prints the street address on the bottom of the paper and proudly displays all the houses.

Then Lynn (and the children when they are able to write numbers clearly) prints all the addresses on envelopes, and the children play games matching the envelopes to the houses. Sometimes the envelopes are filled with letters and surprises. The children learn their own address and also often learn many of their classmates' addresses.

My pets. Children like to draw or paint pictures of their actual or wished-for pets. Always encourage the imaginative alternative. The labels or titles on the picture include numbers, for example, "My Five (5) Goldfish" and "One (1) Puppy Named Tillie."

Pictures of ones, twos, threes. As you celebrate different numbers, you will find your students responding enthusiastically to the idea of painting or drawing a picture of a particular number of things. Beginning with the number one, children may suggest one flower, one tree, one sun, one moon, one person, one dog, one house, one bike, one circle, one triangle, and one dot.

Rachel, age 8

We did this with a group of six-year-olds and Missy proudly showed her bright green picture with a tiny brown speck on one side of the paper. "One seed," she explained.

Montage or collage of ones, twos, and threes. A variation of the above activity is to encourage the children to cut out pictures from magazines and catalogues that show the featured number. The children paste their pictures to a large piece of paper taped to a wall.

Pictures of ones and twos and threes. After children demonstrate their comprehension of numbers, they enjoy the following challenge: "Wouldn't it be fun to make a picture that has *one* thing in it and, if you have room, somewhere else in the picture draw *two* or *three* similar things?" Always take time to talk about ideas first so the children's minds are simmering with possibilities.

Give your students the opportunity to create their own progression pictures and choose their own sets of things. Vary the challenge by deciding as a class the numbers and sets and asking the children to make their own interpretations.

Nancy Roberts's first graders planned winter pictures featuring one tree, two Santas, three reindeer, and four snowflakes. Even though the pictures had these elements in common, every one was an original interpretation.

Find the lucky number in the pictures. "How many ways can you show your lucky number in your picture? We'll look at your picture and try to guess the number you have in mind! Write your number on back of the paper."

Among the drawings of a group of second graders, Jackie's clown had four balloons in his hand and four bright buttons on his costume. Around him, four little circus dogs performed tricks. In one corner of the paper, Jackie had drawn a poster for the circus that read: "Circus, May 4."

Colorful class calendars. Divide a large piece of paper into the number of days for the month. Print the numbers clearly and leave room in each space for a picture. Assign each child to one or more days. The children draw their own little pictures and tape or paste them to their box or draw directly on the box. Talk about the season, month, and any holidays or special events.

A variation of this idea is to give each child a sheet of paper with the number of a day on it. Collect the papers and make a flip calendar featuring one day at a time. That day belongs to all the children, but it especially belongs to the child who illustrated it. Be sure all the artists sign their works.

Count-up/count-down picture charts. Excellent commercial versions of this idea abound, but children's original works are just as colorful and interesting. With your children, make a large number chart and draw or paste the items they suggest on each number row. Combine with colors and stories. Children usually become more imaginative when asked to think about related ideas.

A memorable count-up chart hung on the wall of a first-grade class looked like this:

Nutritious Foods (Count Up)

1   one banana

2   two apples

3   three oranges

4   four eggs

5   five carrots

6   six grapes

7   seven peanuts

8   eight glasses of milk

9   nine chunks of cheese

10 ten strawberries

Encourage the children to create their own count-up/count-down charts on their own themes. A third grade created a Halloween count-down chart complete with lively illustrations of 10 (ten) ghosts, 9 (nine) black cats, 8 (eight) witches, 7 (seven) pumpkins, 6 (six) pieces of candy corn, 5 (five) trick or treat bags, 4 (four) stars, 3 (three) kids, 2 (two) trees, and 1 (one) moon.

You can imagine how much fun the children had making stories, poems, games, dances, and their own pictures from this source material.

Children's original books of numbers. The easiest way for children to make their own books of numbers is for them to do one number at a time, one page at a time, beginning with one. On page one, one thing is drawn; on page two, pairs of things or any two items are drawn; and so on to ten. When the children are finished, ask them to make a colorful cover for their book. Staple or tape the pages together, and you have a library of books about numbers.

Sequential picture stories. Most children are familiar with comic strips and the concept of following the action of a story from one space to the next. So many ideas can be expressed in sequence. Be sure to talk first and share ideas.

One group of first graders talked about chicks hatching, then depicted each step of the action in a series of boxes, comic strip style. They numbered the boxes as they went along:

(1) there is an egg; (2) inside, a little chick is growing; (3) the chick is growing bigger and bigger; (4) the chick wants to get out; (5) the egg cracks; (6) it cracks again; (7) the egg breaks; (8) here is the chick. Yaaaay.

First graders at University Ligget School in Grosse Pointe Woods, Michigan, talked at length about what they did from the time they woke up until the time they went to bed at night. They listed activities such as brush teeth, get washed, get dressed, read a book, play a game, eat, and walk. On rolls of adding-machine paper, they chronicled their day and drew each scene in a box, beginning with getting up in the morning.

Follow any reading or story-telling session with a sequential picture summary.

Ten-speed "I Can" pictures. Give the children large sheets of paper divided into ten spaces, and ask them to number the spaces from 1 to 10. In every space, draw a picture or paste on a cutout picture showing something they can do. Teachers can do ten things, too! Add words. Cover a wall with your pictures and watch your student's self-image and respect for others grow.

As this activity is shared, emphasize that all your students can do hundreds of things and that they are only selecting ten at a time. Encourage them to do as many sheets of "I can" ideas as they want to do, and remind them that they always have more to add.

Addition pictures. Devote a whole wall to these ever-growing pictures. The children take turns contributing to the story as the plot thickens. Ideas for this activity are numerous. Here are a few suggestions for starters.

A bird feeder with no birds. Each day a new bird arrives to eat at the feeder.
A clown with no balloons. Each day a balloon is added.
A beautiful ocean with no fish. Each day a different fish swims by.
A barren plot of land. Each day a new plant begins to grow or a flower blooms.
A zoo with no animals. Each day we see another animal.
An ice-cream store with no ice-cream cones. Each day another ice-cream cone is shown.

Talk about your picture each day. Observe and count together as ideas are added.

Find fun ways for the children to discover when it is their turn to add to the picture. An easy way is to print the child's name on the board with the symbol next to the name. A complicated way is to ask the children to pick a piece of paper from a box or grab bag. On one of those pieces of paper, the idea is drawn. The child who picks the marked paper contributes to the class picture that day.

Special-number scrounge sculptures. "How old are you? What's your favorite number? What's your lucky number?" Use questions such as these to prompt children to create a sculpture. "What can you make out of five (for your age) pieces of scrounge material?" Or "Your lucky number is seven. Pick seven things from the scrounge box and see what amazing shape you can make with them."

Remember, there are no rights or wrongs in this activity. Be accepting and encouraging of all products. It is the process that counts.

Measuring plus. Young children are fascinated by the process of measuring. Graphs, charts, surveys, and polls are excellent resources because they involve the children in material of special interest to them.

Teachers around the country experiment with many approaches to measurement. Here are just a few of their most successful approaches.

Carol Price and her kindergartners are excited about measuring.

We read Leo Lionni's book *Inch by Inch*, about inchworms, and we talk about measuring things by inchworms. We design, color, and cut out inchworms for everyone, then go around the room measuring things by inchworms. We ask, "How many inchworms is that shelf? How many inchworms is this book?"

Then we use a bigger measurement—a pickle! Everyone gets paper, crayon, and scissors to make pickles to measure things with. Sometimes we find that a pickle equals two inchworms! We have lots of fun and the children get the idea that as long as we are all measuring with the same unit, we can make comparisons and draw valid conclusions.

Carol, who enjoys making things out of felt, paper, wood, and scrounge materials, also recommends using French fries as measurements.

We make French fries out of yellow cardboard and fill scrounged fast-food cartons with ten fries each. We ask, "How many cartons can we fill?" The children count and find that we fill ten cartons with ten fries each and that's one hundred. We use our French fries to measure how long it is around the room. "How many French fries around the room?" We found that six French fries, end-to-end, equaled a 12-inch ruler.

Carol, who works with concrete experiences before proceeding to abstract theories, has imaginative ways to teach children about charts and graphs. On a large sheet of butcher paper spread on the floor, she draws a shoe with a buckle, a shoe with a shoelace tied, and a plain shoe, each in its own space with plenty of room below. Then she asks her students to look at the chart, look at their own shoes, and find the category that matches their shoes. "We each take off a shoe and put it in the appropriate column. We look at our 'graph' and talk about how many plain, how many tie, and how many buckle shoes we have, and which category has the most shoes. We make comparisons and draw conclusions. The children's observations are very sharp in this kind of experience."

Carol also graphs her students' responses to questions about their favorite eggs (scrambled, fried, poached, or boiled) and their favorite transportation (car, train, boat, or plane).

Measure success in the number of opportunities children have to experience ideas.

Mosaics, designs, and patterns. Numbers are as important as colors and shapes in the creation of mosaics, designs, and patterns. How many squares of yellow are needed?

David, age 8

How many squares of red? How does this combination look? In projects with repeating patterns, whether the materials are crayons, paint, beads, cutout shapes, or pasted-on designs, encourage the children to think about number combinations as they select colors and textures.

A second-grade class enjoyed a challenging art assignment. The magic number was ten, and combinations of numbers that added up to ten were encouraged. Some children strung bead necklaces, bracelets, and belts. One of them explained his pattern to me: "See, five and five are ten, so I'm stringing five white beads and five black beads for my necklace!" One of his classmates was pasting color squares on a mosaic design. He chose an interesting combination of nine green squares and one yellow square. "Doesn't it look springy?" he asked.

Whether children design T-shirts, pins, drapes, belts, wallpaper, writing paper, greeting cards, or calendars, numbers can be featured. Be open to surprises.

MUSIC TIMES

Music expresses time. It has rhythm. It ticks, it tocks. It can be measured and counted. Music helps children recognize patterns and number combinations and helps them understand the concepts of ordinal numbers.

Counting songs and chants. Children sing numbers as easily as they sing sounds and words. Each time they repeat or improvise lyrics to a familiar counting song, their knowledge of the numbers is reinforced.

After a workshop, a few teachers of young children pooled songs about numbers and counting that they had used successfully in their classrooms. Add to their list the counting songs that you have gathered from your own experiences.

This Old Man	Inchworm
Three Blind Mice	Two Ducks on a Pond
Ten Little Indians	My Hat It Has Three Corners
Five Hundred Miles	Hickory Dickory Dock
Twelve Days of Christmas	Sing a Song of Sixpence
Rock Around the Clock	Take Me Out to the Ballgame

Improvised numbers and counting songs. Improvise familiar songs to use with numbers. The popular fingerplay "The Eensy Weensy Spider" evolved into an exciting counting experience for a kindergarten class. Instead of fingers, the children used their whole bodies to show the spider climbing up the water spout. They sang the song like this:

One eensy weensy spider climbed up the waterspout
Down came the rain and washed the spider out.
Out came the sun and dried up all the rain
And the eensy weensy spider climbed up the spout again.

Two eensy weensy spiders . . .

Three eensy weensy spiders . . .

The song continued until every child-spider was added to the song.

"Hickory Dickory Dock" became an imaginative numbers song when the children added such lines as:

The clock struck two
The mouse ran through . . .

The clock struck three
The mouse ran free . . .

"Ten Little Indians" can be expanded to include noses, hands, figers, shoes, and smiles. And don't stop at ten!

"Three Blind Mice" is easily changed to "Four Blind Mice," "Five Blind Mice," and so on, until all your young mice show you how they run, sing, and count.

Second verse, same as the first. A fine and fun way to help children understand ordinal numbers is to reinforce the idea of stanzas or verses. If you have ever been to summer camp, you know how children enjoy repeating lyrics, and more loudly each time.

A silly chorus that fits many songs helps children to sing more loudly while saying their ordinal numbers. I have heard it sung in many different melodies and rhythms, so feel free to create your own "loony tune" with your students. This is the chorus:

Second verse, same as the first.
A little bit louder and a little bit worse.

This idea has been used with such simple songs as "Row, Row, Row, Your Boat." Begin very softly, singing almost in a whisper. After the first singing, the chorus is chanted, and "Row, Row" is repeated, a little more loudly. With a group of four-and-a-half-year-olds, we stopped (for snacks) at this point: "Seventh verse, same as the first . . ." By that time, the room was rocking with the volume of song.

Vary the activity by substituting the word "faster" for "louder," and begin your song very, very slowly. Try experimenting with the word "higher" for "faster"; begin in very low tones and move up the scale each time you repeat the song. Of course, as the children sing, they hold up the number of fingers that corresponds to the verse.

Count on musical signals. The Indians used drumbeats to send messages, and the ancient peoples of the Middle East blew notes on rams' horns.

With your children, decide on musical patterns for messages. A group of first graders chose five loud, slow drumbeats followed by five little running beats as their signal to get ready for recess. Their signal for cleanup time was three loud claps of the cymbals, three counts of silence, and three more loud claps.

Your students not only will work out interesting musical rhythms, but their listening habits will improve dramatically.

Concentration on numbers and counting lends itself to tense situations. Avoid these at all costs. Enjoyment of the activity and encouragement of full participation are the most important values.

Solos, duets, trios, and quartets. Children have no trouble understanding that solo means one, duet means two, trio means three, and quartet means four. Give the children many opportunities to be featured as soloists or in groups of twos, threes, and fours as they play rhythm instruments or sing songs. Keep the arrangements low-key, with the emphasis on experimenting, sharing, and celebrating rather than performing.

When children are familiar with the sounds of solos, duets, trios, and quartets, play records that feature these arrangements as background music in the classroom.

Add and subtract voices and instruments. Give the children number cards. When their number is indicated, they contribute the sound of their instrument or their voice.

A group of first graders sang and played "Twinkle, Twinkle, Little Star." They began in silence. Then, one by one, the children contributed the sweet sounds of rhythm instruments and singing voices until everyone in the room was participating.

Reverse the above suggestion. After all the instruments and voices blend, stop each sound one at a time until there is silence.

Use the words "add," "subtract," "none," "everybody," and "nobody" as you explain the activity. Children need different ways to experience the concepts of addition, subtraction, and zero.

Sets and sounds. One of the most important mathematical ideas for young children to learn is the relationship of like objects, or a set. Organizing your rhythm band according to like instruments is an imaginative way to convey the idea of sets. "How many drums in our drums group? How many sets of bells in our bells group? How many pairs of rhythm sticks in our rhythm sticks group?" Each group can be defined by number, shape, color, and code.

Experiment with combinations of sounds as you begin with the smallest set of instruments and sets, one by one. Sets can play the same rhythm or individual rhythms. Children enjoy varying the experience.

An excellent picture book that clearly illustrates this activity is *One Dancing Drum* by Gail Kredenser (pictures by Stanley Mack, Phillips, 1971). In this lively, unusually illustrated story, a wild and wonderful park band grows from "1 dancing drum" to "10 crashing cymbals." Young children like to read and listen to the story and need no extra encouragement to pantomime playing the instruments, march and dance like the funny musicians, make their own music as each set of instruments is added, draw their own illustrations, and make up their own story of a band forming, counting from one to ten. For a finale to the story and related activities, play a marching band record and invite the children to play and march along with their own rhythm instruments.

Johnny One Note. Encourage children to take turns leading rhythms featuring one note at a time, two notes, three notes, and so on. They clap, stamp, snap, tap, whistle, or sing the beat. The progression from ones to threes or fours is very exciting. Try it with drums, tambourines, triangles, or rhythm sticks.

Musical minutes. How many seconds in a minute? Sixty tick-tocks. How many seconds in a half minute? Thirty tick-tocks. Count and clap, tap, stamp, snap, or sing thirty steady beats. Count and clap, tap, stamp, snap, or sing sixty steady beats. Count thirty seconds of silence, thirty seconds of sounds. Try ten silent counts, ten claps, ten silent counts, ten snaps, ten silent counts, ten foot stamps. What an interesting minute of sound and silence.

How far can we walk in a minute, keeping the rhythm of our time? "Our room is a minute away from the office," one kindergartner exclaimed after such a measuring experience. "It's sixty claps away," a friend chimed in.

What if our musical conductors keep a minute of time while the class sings or plays instruments? At the end of sixty counts, the music stops. We have just heard one minute of music. Now, let's hear half of that, thirty seconds of music. Let's count thirty seconds of silence. Then begin the music again. This is another concrete way children discover concepts of whole and half.

Whole, half, and quarter notes. Teachers who play musical instruments have a ready resource, but you do not have to be a musician to introduce whole, half, and quarter notes to your young students. A whole note is held for four counts; a half note for two counts, and a quarter note for one count. Four bouncy quarter notes equal a whole note.

After the children have experimented with these notes in their own voices, they appreciate hearing well-known arias. Play excerpts and watch your students' amazement at the range and strength of the human voice. After one such experience, a class of second graders applauded Leontyne Price. "Gosh. She ran out of whole notes to hold," one of the children observed.

Correlate this activity with movement and art. A whole note is a long note; a quarter note is a short note. Show the duration of a whole note with bodies. Take a breath and expand arms, legs, chest, fingers, and head as far as a whole note carries you. How do short, choppy quarter notes make your body move? What if you combined whole notes, quarter notes, and half notes in body patterns?

How can you show the feeling of a whole note, half note, and quarter note on paper, in clay, and with paints? Six-year-old Andy was pleased with his colorful interpretation of the whole notes he listened to as he drew. "It's the feeling of a street that just goes on," he explained as he worked.

Symphony of sounds and numbers. Children develop an appreciation of music as they become more aware of sounds and rhythms. Here is an example of a story created by a class of kindergartners demonstrating their knowledge of numbers combined with a feeling for the drama of sounds. All of the sounds described in the story were made with voices and instruments.

Once upon a time it was a very quiet morning. Not a sound could be heard. Suddenly, one rooster crowed (a child crowed cock-a-doodle-doo). The rooster woke up three ducks who quacked (three children quacked). The ducks woke up four baby chicks who peeped (four children peeped). The chicks woke up two cows who mooed (two children mooed). Oh no! Ten birds in the tree started to sing (ten children "flapped their wings" and began to sing). Just then the cuckoo clock chimed seven times (everything fell silent as the cuckoo-children chimed). What a noisy morning (everyone at once)!

Experiment with variations of this activity.

Top ten favorites. Write the titles of the children's ten favorite songs, from 1 to 10, on a colorful chart. Throughout the week, select songs from the list, calling them by number and title. "Peter, you're our song leader today. Which song shall we sing? Oh, good. Our number four song, 'Comin' Round the Mountain.'"

Reinforce understanding of ordinal numbers by suggesting such ideas as: "Boys and girls, we have time for only two songs today. Which song from our Top Ten list shall we sing *first*? Which shall we sing *second*?" A real accomplishment is to sing all ten songs, but not in order. "OK, you folks want to sing our number five song, 'Down in the Valley,' first. Here we go. . . . What's next?"

Vary the experience by having the children pull a number card out of a grab bag or box and find the corresponding song on the Top Ten list. Or make a number wheel and spin a spinner to decide what songs to sing. Change your list of songs every few weeks.

As you flip through the pages of this book, you will find many activities that involve counting and numbers. When children clap out the rhythms of their names and cities, they are counting beats and listening to the pulse of language. When children sing about one rabbit, one turtle, or one bird, they are imagining the idea of one. When you follow "Happy Birthday to You" with the lines "How old are you? How old are you? How old is Danny? How old are you?" you and your children are celebrating the most important numbers of all. And when you teach with an openness and willingness to try familiar materials in new ways, you will discover musical activities too numerous to number.

MOVEMENT AND PLAY TIMES

Taking inventory. Imaginative teachers and their young students count everything in their rooms. What wonderful inventory charts their findings produce. One group of kindergartners took inventory of smiles. "Just how many smiles are there in this class today?" Nineteen children, nineteen smiles.

Nancy Roberts and her first graders experiment with inventory activities. Nancy challenges her children: "Count your crayons. Find someone in the room who has the same number of crayons you do." "How many buttons are on your clothes today? Count them. Let's find people who have the same number of buttons."

Nancy's children outline their feet on butcher paper and cut them out. After all the feet are accounted for, children find feet that come closest in size to their own. Then they border the room with their footprints. "How many footprints do we need to go around the whole room? Do we have enough? How many more do we need?"

Guessing games. Children never refuse challenges such as the following:

Guess how many shells are in this jar.
Guess how many pebbles are in this box.
Guess how many leaves are on our tree.
Guess how many pages are in this book.

Their guesses indicate their knowledge of and familiarity with numbers.

Nancy Roberts has a winter guessing game full of delicious treats. She fills a round jar with marshmallows and, with her children's help, tapes a strip of black construction paper around the jar for a scarf, pastes on eyes, nose, and mouth, and thus transforms the marshmallow-filled jar into a snowman. Then Nancy asks the children to guess how many marshmallows are in the jar. The children write their guesses on a piece of paper with their names. After all the guesses are in, the marshmallows are counted.

The last time Nancy played this game, the children counted 62 marshmallows. The closest guess was 58. "Well, we counted the marshmallows and we counted the kids," Nancy explains. "We had 62 marshmallows and 29 kids, plus 1 teacher. We talked about this and figured out that everyone could have 2 marshmallows. How many did we have left over? Two, of course, which we gave to two neighboring teachers." What a delicious division and subtraction problem.

Children set place value. Ina Mayer's first graders enjoy discovering how place value works by making sets of sticks, tongue depressors, toothpicks, blocks, and straws. But one of their favorite ways is to use themselves. Each child stands for one unit of ten. When ten children are grouped together, Ina ties a loose string around them.

How many groups of ten children are in your class? If there are 24 children, you have two groups of ten children and four individuals with no strings attached.

Addition and subtraction in action. Children need experiences that are more involving than workbooks and ditto sheets. Remember the word "action" in "subtraction."

Many children's games involve subtraction ("you're out") and can be unhappy experiences for the children who always seem to be eliminated first. Take the tension out of such games by improvising some with built-in safety belts.

If you start from nothing (zero) and add one idea at a time, every child is included without anyone choosing favorites. After all of the children have been included, the subtraction process begins with a tiny tap on the head as each child pulls back from the whole until no one is left.

Correlate this idea with animals, robots, airplanes, cars, clowns, rollerskaters, and fire fighters. Whatever your class is studying, whatever your children's interests, turn them into a game of addition and subtraction.

Body machines of moving parts. When you control all of your muscles and hold your bodies still, you are on zero. Now one part moves. Tap out a rhythm on a drum, tabletop, or tambourine. The children decide which part they want to move. Then two parts move. Each child has a different pattern. Then three parts move. Some children move two feet and one hand; Tarik moves two shoulders and one wiggly nose. Continue to five or six parts. Then turn on the body machines and move all the parts you can.

One at a time, each machine stops (gently touch each head) until no machine is moving.

See Guide One for more variations on body machines.

Our magic-trick fingers. Children are enthusiastic magicians. The best tricks need no props. Hide all fingers in fists. "Where are our fingers? Where did they go? They disappeared? How many fingers shall we make appear? Two!"

Do you think you can do this incredible trick, magicians? What are the magic words? Abracadabra, peanut butter and jelly. Watch two fingers appear or I'll tickle you in the belly! (This is our students' favorite incantation.) Ta Da! Pow! Two fingers? What a trick!" Then three fingers appear, then four. Oh no! Ten fingers pop up!

Remember, magicians and teachers perform the best trick of all—changing something ordinary into the extraordinary. What is more ordinary than showing the fingers on our hands? Change the experience into magic fingers.

Number questions. Louise Johnson's first graders in Hilliard, Ohio, are kept on their ten toes because Louise constantly challenges them with such questions as: "Look at this picture. *How many* things can you see in it? I'll write all your ideas on the board" or "It's time for a round-robin story. When it's your turn, be ready to *add one idea* to the story. Here we go" or "What's your favorite number? Don't tell us, show us by doing something a certain number of times. We'll try to guess."

Ina Mayer also reminds her first graders about numbers in almost everything they do. "When we turn to page 41 in

Ted And The Three Red Jets

Ted has three jets. He has fun playing with the jets. He likes his red jets. He went outside and played with the jets. He threw one to hard and it went up in a tree. He went and got a ladder and

our book, I'll nudge: 'Hmmmm. How many tens in 41? How many ones?' We don't relegate math to a specific period of the day. We are always reminded of the ways math is part of our lives.

Number your exercises and dances. Throughout the guides, improvised exercises and dances have been encouraged. As children design group and individual patterns, challenge them to decide such questions as: How many jumping jacks? How many sit-ups? What shall we do first? How many times shall we repeat this pattern? What if half the class does exercise A and the other half does exercise B?

When children are constantly working with number patterns as part of their activities, their comprehension is enriched and their feelings of success are multiplied.

Weird recipes. Numbers and recipes are inseparable. Nancy Roberts's first graders are familiar with recipes from easy cooking sessions to mixing science and crafts materials. She and her lively students enjoy playing with the idea of recipes.

How to Make a First Grader

1 cup giggles	1 cup fingernail polish
1/2 cup snakes	5 cups shoelaces
1/2 cup sugar	6 papers
1/2 cup worms	2 cups American flags
1/2 cup teeth	800 lunch boxes
1/2 cup butterflies	10 cups games
1 cup whales	5 cups chalk
3 cups songs	800 workbooks
1/2 cup hair	8,000 cups mud
2 books	800 pencils
1/2 cup shoe polish	

Mix well and enjoy!

"What the children really enjoyed in creating this recipe," Nancy explained, "was the chance to use big numbers like 8,000 and 800. Young children don't have many opportunities even to talk about those numbers."

Try working out recipes with your children for a goldfish tank, a toy box, a baby-sitter, a puppy, a zoo, a pet store, a birthday party, and a playground.

Birthday exercises. How old is the birthday child? Seven! Seven-year-olds need presents in sevens. What special things can we do seven times each for our birthday child? Here are some of the suggestions made by thousands of children over the years.

7 claps	7 turnarounds
7 stamps	7 jumping jacks
7 kisses (throw kisses)	7 hops
7 spanks (spank the floor)	7 finger dances
7 cheers	7 jumps
7 smiles	7 blinks
7 waves in the air	7 kicks (kick legs out)

All the children I work with know that we celebrate birthdays this way. On my last birthday, I told the preschoolers at the Jewish Center in Columbus that I was 47 years old. "Oh no!" they cried. "No way! We can't do everything 47 times!"

Another of the many variations of birthday celebrations and numbers is to ask the birthday child to choose the birthday number of exercises to be featured that day. Last Friday, Molly was five. These are the exercises she chose for her class to perform:

1. Run
2. Touch-toes
3. Tiptoes and stretch arms
4. Twists
5. Turns

We practiced the five exercises in order. Soon the children remembered them by number, so when we played lively music we simply called out: "Number one" and the children ran, "Number two" and the children touched their toes.

Add movement ideas to the birthday chart or card.

For Molly's Fifth (5th) Birthday We Gave Her:
5 hugs
5 cheers
5 claps
5 laughs
5 funny faces

These Were Molly's Birthday Exercises:
1. Run
2. Touch-toes
3. Tiptoes and stretch arms
4. Twists
5. Turns

Parades of numbers. Children are always ready for a parade. Mix parades with numbers. Organize a parade of ones. Each child marches separately, one behind the other. The children can play instruments (real or imaginary), carry flags, twirl (imaginary batons), or just swing their arms.

After the fun of ones, you are ready for twos. Organize the parade with the children marching, prancing, and dancing two-by-two. As they enjoy the rhythm and life of the parade, they realize that twos are different from ones. Continue with parades of threes, fours, and so on.

Mix numbers with animals, TV characters, and story characters.

A parade of animals (everyone turns into a favorite animal as ones are featured)
A parade of Noah's Ark animals (animals in twos)
A parade of robot trios
A parade of four superheroes or superheroines
A parade of number groups of colors
A parade of number groups of shapes

Dances of numbers. Encourage the children to dance by themselves, a company of soloists, each dancer experimenting with individual movement patterns in response to the music. Then quickly organize the

children into partners. "Ladies and Gentlemen, here is the world-famous company of dancers dancing by twos!"

Three is a fine number for small circle formations. "Ladies and Gentlemen, before your eyes you will see a dance of threes. Three people in a dancing circle!" Start the music and watch the variety of movements your children improvise.

Your only limits in choreography are safety precautions. As long as the children are paying attention, following directions, and moving in response to music and idea, their dances are excellent. Plan for success. Keep challenging the children with new combinations.

Countdown, blast off! Our space-age children know all about counting backwards from 10. Turn yourselves into rockets. Scrunch way down, close to the floor. Slowly, gradually, stretch up. 10-9-8-7-6-5-4-

3-2-1. Now you are on tip-top toes, arms to the sky. Blast off! Jump as high as you can.

Elevator going up, going down. Counting up and counting down are part of playing elevator. Start at the bottom, as low as your body will go. Move slowly upward, stopping on each floor. When you reach the top, bodies are stretched to their tallest.

U-oh, the elevator is going down—tenth floor, ninth, eighth . . . first floor, when bodies are once again as low as possible.

Ten-speed run. This is a terrific activity for outdoors or a room with a lot of space. Be sure to push back chairs, desks, and tables.

Talk about ten-speed bikes. Each gear enables the bicycle to go faster and faster. Discuss the idea that our bodies and minds are like a ten-speed bike. We can go very-very slowly (first gear), a little faster (second gear), and so on, until at the tenth gear we are full speed ahead.

While the children are walking slowly in first speed, ask them, "What comes after one?" When they say, "two," increase your pace a little. "What comes after two?" "Three" increases the rate. There is no competition, no one loses.

We have played "ten-speed run" with the tap of a tambourine, the shake of maracas, the bounce of lively music on the phonograph, and the sound of children's feet increasing in force and tempo as the numbers increase. Try it many ways and find the ones that are easiest and most enjoyable for you.

Sequence stories. A fine way to reinforce comprehension of ordinal numbers is to improvise stories and situations that feature a special order of events and characters. "Talk Times" are the best inspiration for such experiences. If the children are interested in and excited about a topic, character, situation, or event, their ideas are charged with vitality.

Here are two examples of sequence stories that came from lively group discussions. Each activity was expressed in movement and mime. The children practiced ways to demonstrate each idea.

Nancy Roberts and her first graders talked about winter ideas. They decided to show a winter day in five movement improvisations.

1. Brrrrrrr. (The children hug themselves and shiver.)
2. Penguins are birds that live in snowy places. (The children move like penguins.)
3. Rub hands together to make them warmer.
4. Make snowballs and throw them.
5. Lie down and make snow angels.

Joy Jacobs and Sandi Jacobsen and their prekindergartners at the Jewish Center in Columbus, Ohio, had a big project. They went to the pet store to buy a pet with money they had earned from their *real* restaurant. There were so many different pets in the pet store that they had a hard time deciding which pet to buy, but when they saw the little black rabbit, their hearts melted. They named her Bruce and she is their pride and joy.

The children made a movement story of their experience. All the children moved to all of the ideas.

1. The first animals we saw were the fish.
2. The second animals we saw were the puppies.
3. The third animals we saw were the snakes.
4. The fourth animals we saw were the turtles.
5. The fifth animals we saw were the birds.
6. The sixth animals we saw were the gerbils.
7. The seventh animals we saw were the rabbits.

The children enjoyed turning into each of the seven different animals and exploring their distinct movement patterns. These stories are easily expressed in pictures, posters, movement, and song.

Giant steps, baby steps. "How many giant steps does it take to get you from your chair to the front of the room? How many giant steps do you need to cross the hall? How many giant steps from here to the office? How many giant steps take you around our room?"

"How many *baby steps* do you need to get from your chair to the front of the room? How many baby steps do you need to cross the hall?" Experiment with half-giant steps. Correlate giant steps with whole notes and baby steps with quarter notes. This activity is a good way to help children discover interesting facts about numbers and fractions.

Nursery rhymes, poems, and stories with numbers. Rhymes for young children are filled with numbers, for example:

> One, two, buckle my shoe.
> Three, four, shut the door.
>
> A diller, a dollar,
> A ten o'clock scholar,
> What makes you come so soon?
> You used to come at ten o'clock
> And now you come at noon.
>
> Baaa, Baaa, Black Sheep,
> Have you any wool?
> Yes, sir, yes, sir,
> Three bags full
>
> Rub-a-dub-dub,
> Three men in a tub,
> And who do you think they be?
> The butcher, the baker;
> The candlestick maker;
> Turn 'em out, knaves all three!

Act out the rhymes; dance to them; make up plays and stories.

A. A. Milne's poem about being six is

one that children want to hear and say and move to over and over again.

When I was One,
I had just begun.
When I was Two,
I was nearly new.
When I was Three,
I was almost Me.
When I was Four,
I was not much more.
When I was Five,
I was just alive.
But now I am Six, I'm as clever as clever.
So, I think I'll be six now for ever and ever.[4]

We like to begin the poem crouched to the ground and grow a little each year, until by six we are jumping in the air and cheering.

A poem like David McCord's "Alphabet" (*Take Sky*, Dell, 1962, pp. 76–81) encourages children to count the letters of the alphabet as the poem is read. As each letter is featured, the children show it through body shapes or fingers.

Shel Silverstein's poem "Flag" stimulates children to count the stars in the American flag.

One star is for Alaska . . .
One star is for Nebraska . . .
One star is North Dakota . . .
One star is Minnesota . . .
There are lots of other stars,
But, I forget which ones they are.[5]

We follow the reading of the poem with the counting of the stars. Fifty! One for each state.

"Eighteen Flavors," Shel Silverstein's delicious poem about ice-cream flavors, is another example of how much fun it is to count as you pretend to lick.

Eighteen Flavors

Eighteen luscious, scrumptious flavors—
Chocolate, lime and cherry,
Coffee, pumpkin, fudge-banana,
Caramel cream and boysenberry,
Rocky road and toasted almond,
Butterscotch, vanilla dip,
Butter-brickle, apple ripple,
Coconut and mocha chip,
Brandy peach and lemon custard,
Each scoop lovely, smooth, and round,
Tallest ice-cream cone in town,
Lying there (sniff) on the ground.[6]

Ask the children to name their favorite flavors. "Shall we make up our own eighteen flavors? How about twenty? Let's pretend to taste each one."

Numbers play an important part in the most beloved folk and fairy tales. We do not say, "Goldilocks and a Few Bears," but "Goldilocks and the Three Bears"; not "Snow White and a Bunch of Dwarfs," but "Snow White and the Seven Dwarfs."

The bear facts. Here is an example of how numbers can be included in celebrations and special events. Lynn Salem's first graders are bear-crazy. They fell in love with Winnie the Pooh and soon were in love with all bears. The children decided to have a week-long celebration of bears. They collected poems, stories, and pictures about bears and learned all about different kinds of bears, including polar bears, koala bears, brown bears, and Pooh bears. They designed bear wallpaper, note cards, and story illustrations.

At the end of the week, the children had a bear party. To help them celebrate, they brought in toy bears from home. They counted all the bears in the room and all their books about bears. They made up songs about bears that included numbers.

One of the children, Katie, insisted on bringing *all* her bears to school that day. Her Mom tried to discourage her: "Katie, you need just *one* bear, not all of your bears." But Katie paid no attention. She was busy covering her five bears in a straw basket. Katie's mother tried again: "Katie, I don't think you need to take five bears to the party. One will do, dear." Katie looked up at her mother with narrow eyes, her hand firm on her hip. She hissed, "I am so glad these five bears are sleeping and didn't hear you ruin the surprise of the party for them!"

There are so many more activities that include numbers, only a few of which can be mentioned here. These are: playing restaurant, store, post office, and house; playing games with dice and wheels of numbers; playing measuring games, guessing games, comparing games, and adding games; playing card games, bingo, hide and seek, and scavenger hunts (with number clues); and playing count the pumpkin seeds, apple seeds, and orange seeds.

As we introduce our young children to the world of numbers, let us do it with a sense of wonder. Shel Silverstein reminds us of the numbers of number questions left to our imagination:

How Many, How Much?

How many slams in an old screen door?
    Depends how loud you shut it.
How many slices in a bread?
    Depends how thin you cut it.
How much good inside a day?
    Depends how good you live 'em.
How much love inside a friend?
    Depends how much you give 'em.[7]

We still haven't found ways to measure the things that mean the most to us.

As we teach our children the important rules of measuring with yardsticks and rulers, let's be sure they have the fun of using French fries and inchworms, too.

VISITORS AND FIELD TRIPS

Visitors

Folk singer. Your visitor can use numbers to introduce songs: "For my first song . . ." "Today, I'd like to sing ten songs with you." Suggest that your guest include songs that feature numbers.

Storyteller. Without being told, storytellers usually know that children are more attentive when they hear numbers as part of the tales. Ears perk up to hear about "the three promises," "the four challenges," and "the six brothers." Most stories have words or phrases that have magical powers when they are spoken or sung a number of times. Be sure the children join in the repeating of such chants.

Stamp collector or coin collector. Collectors usually organize their materials nicely. Children can easily see which countries are most often represented. They can count the stamps or coins and note the numbers on their faces.

Magician. Be sure to ask your local magician to perform tricks featuring numbers, especially card tricks. The sharpness of your students' observations and guesses will surprise you.

Artisans and craftspeople. When painters, potters, weavers, designers, sculptors, and woodcarvers visit your room, concepts of sequence are usually part of their discussion of methods and techniques. It is to be hoped that visitors give your students and you a chance to participate in the creative process. If a guest is unaware of communicating a sequence clearly, politely ask such questions as "What shall we do first?" and "After we place our colors on the table, what comes next?"

Plumbers, mechanics, accountants, bus drivers, doctors, nurses, social workers, bank tellers, cashiers, and clerks all work with numbers and, as visitors, can help improve children's knowledge about and interest in numbers. Do not hesitate to stop the letter carrier, cook, secretary, messenger, and custodian in the school and invite them into your room to share some of their practical experiences. Numbers are also important in their daily lives.

Field Trips

Trips to such places as restaurants, supermarkets, clothing stores, airports, train stations, post offices, design studios, toy stores, libraries, and greeting card shops provide opportunities for children to learn number concepts through prices, cash registers, menus, zip codes, scales and measurements, credit card numbers, transportation schedules, dates, times, aisle and shelf numbers, addresses, and the exchange of money.

Numbers and counting walk. Take a walk and count cars, houses, trees, colors, people, buses, bicycles, and dogs. What a sensational chart or graph you will have when you compile your counts! Take notes and write down numbers you see on your walk: numbers of houses, speed limit signs, license plates, posters, mailboxes, calendars, and so on.

Pet store. In addition to all the other pleasures of this experience, count the different kinds of pets you see. "Aren't the puppies cute? Let's count them. I wonder how many there are in that cage. What do you guess? Let's see, are there more hamsters than guinea pigs? Let's count them and find out."

The zoo. As you admire the variety of animals with your children, take notes on how many of each kind you see, for example, the number of brown bears, white bears, and black bears.

Office building. Most office buildings have directories in the lobby that are filled with floor, room, and telephone numbers. The children ride the elevator and watch the numbers change. Mail and messages are delivered daily. The switchboard operator fascinates young children with an array of lighted and flashing buttons.

Athletic team or cheerleaders in practice. Your local high school or college will be honored to have you and your students as guest observers while their teams practice. Football fields have yard lines, uniforms carry numbers, and scores are numbers. Many cheers also contain numbers.

Science laboratory. If there is no government or commercial science research lab in your area, the local high school or college offers this resource. Children are fascinated by the skill and concentration of labworkers because of the need for accurate observations and careful measuring and recording.

Dance group in rehearsal. Check the Yellow Pages for dance teachers and studios, or find out if a community dance group is rehearsing for a program. As the children watch the dancers mark time, movement, and place, they realize how important numbers are to the total effort.

A bank. What better place to see numbers in action than at a bank? Checks are deposited, bills counted, and adding machines punched. When they return to the classroom, children will want to make paper money and play bank.

Computer center. Our children live in a computerized society. Numbers, letters, and words flash instantly when buttons are pressed. Children are fascinated by the speed, complexity, and excitement of computers. They need to be reminded that computers are the creation of the inventive human mind, the most dazzling computer.

Wherever you go, encourage children to make careful, meaningful observations. Ask such questions as How many? How much? How big? What kind? Which is the smallest? and Who has the most?

NOTES

1. Carl Sandburg, "Arithmetic," *The Complete Poems of Carl Sandburg* (New York: Harcourt Brace Jovanovich, 1960), p. 39.

2. Alfred H. Williams, "Mathematical Concepts, Skills and Abilities of Kindergarten Entrants," *Basic Skills in Kindergarten: Foundations for Formal Learning*, ed. by Walter B. Barbe, Michael N. Milone, Virginia H. Lucas, and Jack W. Humphrey (Columbus, Ohio: Zaner-Bloser, 1980), p. 200.

3. Williams, p. 202.

4. A. A. Milne, "The End," *The World of Christopher Robin* (New York: Dutton, 1958), p. 234.

5. Shel Silverstein, "Flag," *Where the Sidewalk Ends* (New York: Harper & Row, 1974), p. 24.

6. Shel Silverstein, "Eighteen Flavors," *Where the Sidewalk Ends* (New York: Harper & Row, 1974), p. 116.

7. Shel Silverstein, "How Many, How Much?" *A Light in the Attic* (New York: Harper & Row, 1981), p. 8.

SELECTED BIBLIOGRAPHY

Books to Count On

Allan, Robert. *Numbers—A First Counting Book*. Photos by Mottke Weissman. New York: Platt & Munk, 1968.

Anno, Mitsumasa. *Anno's Counting Book*. New York: Crowell, 1977.

———. *Anno's Counting House*. New York: Putnam, 1982.

Bayley, Nicola. *One Old Oxford Ox*. New York: Atheneum, 1977.

Carle, Eric. *My Very First Book of Numbers*. New York: Crowell, 1974.

———. *1,2,3 to the Zoo*. New York: World, 1968.

Charles, Donald. *Count on Calico Cat*. Chicago: Childrens Press, 1974.

Feelings, Muriel. *Moja Means One: Swahili Counting Book*. Illustrated by Tom Feelings. New York: Dial, 1971.

Gretz, Susanna. *Teddy Bears 1 to 10*. New York: Scroll, 1971.

Hoban, Russell. *Ten What? A Mystery Counting Book*. Illustrated by Sylvie Selig. New York: Scribners, 1975.

Hoban, Tana. *Circles, Triangles & Squares*. New York: Macmillan, 1974.

———. *Count and See*. Photos by the author. New York: Macmillan, 1972.

———. *One Little Kitten*. New York: Morrow, Greenwillow, 1979.

———. *Over, Under and Through and Other Spatial Concepts*. New York: Macmillan, 1973.

Hobzek, Mildred. *We Come A Marching . . . 1,2,3*. Illustrated by William Pène du Bois. New York: Parents Magazine, 1978.

Hutchins, Pat. *1 Hunter!*. New York: Morrow, Greenwillow, 1982.

Kredenser, Gail, and Mack, Stanley. *1 Dancing Drum*. New York: Phillips, 1971.

LeSieg, Theo. *Ten Apples Up on Top*. Illustrated by Roy McKie. New York: Random House, 1961.

Moncure, Jane Belk. *Magic Monsters Count to Ten*. Illustrated by Marie Fudala. Elgin, Ill.: Child's World, 1979.

Moore, Lillian. *My Big Golden Counting Book*. Illustrated by Garth Williams. Racine, Wisc.: Golden, 1957.

Moritz, Kennell. *Animal Counting Book*. Racine, Wisc.: Golden, 1969.

Nedobeck, Don. *Nedobeck's Numbers Book*. Chicago: Childrens Press, 1981.

Peek, Merle. *Roll Over*. Boston: Houghton Mifflin, 1981.

Scarry, Richard. *Learn to Count*. Racine, Wisc.: Golden, 1976.

Sendak, Maurice. *One Was Johnny*. New York: Harper & Row, 1962.

Sugita, Yutaka. *Good Night, 1,2,3*. New York: Scroll, 1971.

Tudor, Tasha. *1 is One*. New York: Walck, 1956.

Wild, Robin, ND Jocelyn Wild. *The Bear's Counting Book*. New York: Lippincott, 1978.

Wyse, Anne, and Alex Wyse. *The One to Fifty Book*. Toronto: University of Toronto Press, 1973.

Ziner, Feenie, and Paul Galdone. *Counting Carnival*. New York: Coward-McCann, 1962.

Thirteen Storybooks

Cleveland, David. *The April Rabbits*. Illustrated by Nurit Karlin. New York: Coward, 1977.

Eichenberg, Fritz. *Dancing in the Moon: Counting Rhymes*. New York: Harcourt Brace Jovanovich, 1955.

Elkin, Benjamin. *Six Foolish Fisherman*. Illustrated by Katherine Evans. Chicago: Childrens Press, 1957.

Froman, Robert. *The Greatest Guessing Game: A Book About Dividing*. Illustrated by Gloria Fiamminghi. New York: Crowell, 1978.

Gogan, Carol G. *Eighteen Cousins*. New York: Parents Magazine, 1968.

Keats, Ezra Jack. *Over in the Meadow*. New York: Four Winds, 1972.

Langstaff, John. *Over in the Meadow*. Illustrated by Feodor Rojankovsky. New York: Harcourt Brace Jovanovich, 1957.

Maestro, Giulio. *One More and One Less*. New York: Crown, 1974.

Mathews, Louise, and Jeni Bassett Picky. *Bunches and Bunches of Bunnies*. New York: Dodd, Mead, 1978.

Montgomerie, Norah, illustrator. *One Two Three—A Little Book of Counting Rhymes*. New York: Abelard-Shuman, 1967.

Seuss, Dr. [Theodor S. Geisel]. *The 500 Hats of Bartholomew Cubbins*. New York: Random House, 1938.

Sharmat, Marjorie Weinman. *The 329th Friend*. Illustrated by Cyndy Szekeres. New York: Four Winds, 1979.

Weiss, Malcolm. *Solomon Grundy, Born on Oneday: A Finite Arithmetic Book*. Illustrated by Tomie dePaola. New York: Crowell, 1977.

Teacher Resources

Andrews, F. Emerson. *Numbers Please*. Boston: Little, Brown, 1961.

Asimov, Isaac. *How Did We Find Out About Numbers?* Illustrated by Daniel Nevins. New York: Walker, 1973.

———. *Realm of Numbers*. Boston: Houghton Mifflin, 1969.

Burns, Marilyn. *The I Hate Mathematics Book*. Illustrated by Martha Hairston. Boston: Little, Brown, 1975.

Dendick, Jeanne, and Marcia Levin. *Take a Number*. New York: McGraw-Hill, 1961.

Ginsburg, Herbert. *Children's Arithmetic—The Learning Process*. New York: Van Nostrand, 1967.

Isaacs, Nathan. *A Brief Introduction to Piaget*. New York: Schocken, 1974.

Montessori, Maria. *Dr. Montessori's Own Handbook*. New York: Schocken, 1965.

Piaget, Jean. *The Child's Conception of Number*. London: Routledge and Kegan Paul, 1952.

Sigel, I. E. and F. H. Hooper, eds. *Logical Thinking in Children*. New York: Holt, Rinehart & Winston, 1968.

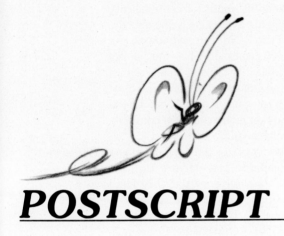

POSTSCRIPT

Writing about creative teaching is as difficult a challenge as writing about, say, swimming or bike riding. It is easier to do it than to describe or explain it.

Good teaching has aspects of the mysterious, magical, and mystical (the three M's). It continues to elude those who want to snare it and carve its definition on tablets of stone. Creative teachers know that once in a while, the most ordinary events become the most memorable; familiar, commonplace activities evolve into peak experiences. Most of the time, these transformations defy explanation.

Creative teachers know that although this book suggests hundreds of excellent activities clustered around thirteen major themes, none of the activities is guaranteed to succeed. Success depends on such variables as who, why, what, where, when, how, and which, mixed with luck and love.

As imaginative teachers read, they naturally mix and match, arrange and rearrange, and multiply their choices. They adapt ideas and activities they like to their own classroom situations and to their own special groups of children, who change

295

each year and may not express the same interests or qualities of their predecessors. Creative teachers know about change and are flexible and innovative in their responses.

This book is really addressed to your *freedom of spirit*, which enables you to soar over myriad possibilities and choose the ones that are most enjoyable and practical. I cannot tell you exactly how to discover that freedom, but when you find ways to teach that are most in harmony with your own spirit and that of your students, you will know it—as the old Shaker hymn describes, "The place just right . . . in the valley of love and delight." You will know because your students will insist on coming to school even when they are sick! They will write unassigned notes to their families like this one:

I am a person who needs metaphors to help clarify complicated relationships and phenomena.

Years ago a very dear friend and outstanding educator, Dr. Herb Sandberg from the University of Toledo, drove with me to a teachers' workshop one dark and rainy night. Herb told of how he had stayed up very late the night before, trying to find a way to explain what creative teaching was all about. What words to use? What examples to give? He agonized for hours, searching his books for quotations and definitions. Finally, when the first rays of light brightened the sky, it dawned on him. He thought of the Hans Christian Andersen story "The Nightingale."

In that story, you may remember, the nightingale is replaced in the emperor's palace and heart by a shiny, bejeweled artificial nightingale. The mechanical bird is of the brightest colors, its voice is almost as sweet as the banished nightingale, and the best thing is that whenever the emperor wants to hear its music, it automatically performs for him. Everything is fine until the emperor gets sick. Nothing and no one can cure him. He calls for his mechanical nightingale, but it is broken. Death sits on the bed of the emperor. Suddenly, the most beautiful, sweet, pure sound is heard—the music of the real nightingale, the common, everyday nightingale. The song is so powerful that even Death is moved and leaves the emperor. The emperor is cured.

Although we both knew the story, Herb zigzagged through city traffic, retelling it. When he finished, his voice lowered to almost a whisper. "Our children," he said, "have never heard the song of the *real* nightingale."

Creative teaching means helping our children and ourselves listen with heart and mind to the song of the real nightingale, which sings of the beauty of poetry, literature, dance, and music; which sings of the excitement of learning and discovery.

If we listen to the song of the real nightingale, we will help our children find poems and stories to cherish and remember. If we listen only to the mechanical bird, we will grade their poems and place more importance on writing the book report than on loving the book.

Another metaphor for creative teaching occurred to me in the midst of a teachers' conference as I was talking about "Teaching in the 'Key of Life.'" Every day, we wake up to find a voting booth in which only two candidates are listed: "Life" and "Death." We pull the lever. If we pull "Death," everything turns negative: the kids are noisy, dumb, unprepared, undisciplined; there is too much work to take a break; games and discussions are frills, laughter is for weekends; we are underpaid, unappreciated, burned out; we should have gone into real estate instead of education. If we vote for "Life," we vote for the positive: these children are amazingly clever, knowledgeable, curious, adventurous, humorous; these children have so many ideas, good questions, excellent suggestions; these children are fun to be with, they make me laugh, I can try out new ideas with them, we learn a lot together.

The best thing about this metaphor is that we get to vote whenever we want to. If at 7 a.m. we pull the lever for "Death" and start our downward spiral, we can return to the booth an hour later and vote for "Life," for teaching in the "key of life." The choice is ours.

This book would not be a legitimate educational experience without a handout, would it? A few years ago, I was scheduled to do workshops at a teachers' inservice day. "Do you have any handouts?" the coordinator called to ask. "Well, our workshop is about creative teaching and we'll be spending all of our time doing things together," I explained. He hesitated, then suggested that I find a handout to distribute; otherwise, people would not think our workshop was legitimate. Laughingly, I told him, "Creative education is as simple as ABC, so I guess I'll write a creative teaching alphabet."

Now I pass that handout to you.

TO: YOU, My Fellow Teacher
FROM: Mimi Brodsky Chenfeld, with a little help from her friends
WHAT: ABC's of Creative Teaching
WHERE: Everywhere
WHEN: Always
WHY: Silly Question

A Attitude, atmosphere, appreciation, awesome, acceptance, awareness, affirmation, answers (not always), adventure, arts, authentic, amazement, adaptability, animation, activities

B Brave, beliefs, borrow, beauty, bright

C Compassion, courage, (chutzpah), curiosity, commitment, climate, cheerful, competent, cooperation, care, celebration, crazy, curriculum, change, communicate, correlate, confidence

D Dignity, devotion, discovery, delight, dance, dreams, displays, dazzle, do

E Encourage, excite, enthusiasm, empathy, explore, exchange, experiment, expand, enjoy, experience, equality

F Friendly, fun, feelings, freedom, flexibility, forgive, faith, favorite (your favorite thing)

G Generous, growth, GOSH! (see awe and amazement), giving, goals

H Hope, helpful, humor, happy, hobbies, hang on!, healthy, humanistic

I Interrelate, integrate, inspire, influence, involvement, improvise, investigate, independence, intuition, imagination, initiate, ideas, ideals

J Justice, JOY, joke

K Kindness, KIDS

L Love, repeat LOVE, laughter, link (things together), learn, lively, life, life-affirming, learn, listen, loose (how to hang)

M Mutuality, mobility, motivate, meaningful, move, music, materials, magic, mess around, me

N NEVER: put down, humiliate, betray, reject, ignore, mark creative work with anything lower than an A or a GREAT-Terrific-Keep it up
NO: formulas, guarantees, blueprints, recipes
NOW (is the time)

O Openness, options, opportunities, originality

P Poetry, participation, persistence, philosophy, positive, probing, patience, pride, principles

Q Questions, qualities, quest

R Relevance, respect, responsiveness, responsibility, resources, resourceful, relate, rearrange, revise, reward, read
REDUCE: fear, tension, anxiety, caution, insecurity

S Safe place (your room), synthesize, serendipity, sensitivity, searching, success, strengths, sharing, skillful, shiny, spirit, sacred, scavenger, self-confidence, self-respect, self-worth, spunk, SURPRISE, soar, smile, swap (ideas)

T Trust, try, thankful, time, together, think, truth, touch, total, tolerance

U Unique, universal, useful, unusual, unity, us, understand

V Values, variety, visionary, vitality, vivacity, verve

W Wholehearted, wonder, warmth, write, wholeness, worth, wonderful, welcome, we

X Unknown factor

Y You, YES, young (your mind, your spirit)

Z Zany, zap, zealous
Add your own words
And you will see
It's as easy as ABC
To commit yourself
To CREATIVITY.

May you always vote for "Life."
May you and your children always hear the song of the real nightingale.

185 Regina Weilbacher; **187** © Michael Phillip Manheim; **198** © Jill Cannefax/ EKM-Nepenthe; **207** Martin B. Freedman; **209** Ellen Eisenman; **217** © Jill Cannefax/EKM-Nepenthe; **228** Carl Selinger; **230** © Elizabeth Crews; **240** and **242** © Larry Hamill; **243** © Elizabeth Crews; **249** Elizabeth Hamlin/Stock, Boston; **253** Chick Moorman; **262** and **263** © Larry Hamill; **266** Pam Hasagawa/Taurus Photos; **271** Chick Moorman; **275** © Larry Hamill; **286** Chick Moorman; **289** © Larry Hamill.

The author gives special thanks to the teachers and children whose projects and activities illustrate this book. She thanks, in particular: Doris Pichick and her third graders, Cindy Anderson and her second graders, and Kathy Schwarz and her first graders at the Berwick Alternative School, Columbus, Ohio; and Janice Roth, Betty Griffith, and their kindergartners at the Leo Yassenoff Jewish Center, Columbus, Ohio.

D
E
F   8
G   9
H   0
I   1
J   2